INTEGRATING MUSIC INTO THE ELEMENTARY CLASSROOM

THIRD EDITION

WILLIAM M. ANDERSON

JOY E. LAWRENCE

KENT STATE UNIVERSITY

Wadsworth Publishing Company

I(T)P™ An International Thomson Publishing Company

Belmont • Albany • Bonn • Boston • Cincinnati • Detroit • London • Madrid • Melbourne •
Mexico City • New York • Paris • San Francisco • Singapore • Tokyo • Toronto • Washington

Music Editor: Katherine Hartlove
Editorial Assistant: Janet Hansen
Production Service Coordinator: Debby Kramer
Production: Del Mar Associates
Print Buyer: Karen Hunt
Permissions Editor: Bob Kauser
Text and Cover Designer: John Odam
Copy Editor: Jackie Estrada
Autographer: Mansfield Music Graphics
Cover Photography: Mark Regan
Signing Representative: Arthur Minsberg
Digital Typography: John Odam Design Associates
Printer: Malloy Lithographing, Inc.

 This book is printed on acid-free recycled paper.

Printed in the United States of America
1 2 3 4 5 6 7 8 9 10—01 00 99 98 97 96 95

For more information, contact Wadsworth Publishing Company:

Wadsworth Publishing Company
10 Davis Drive
Belmont, California 94002, USA

International Thomson Publishing Europe
Berkshire House 168-173
High Holborn
London, WC1V 7AA, England

Thomas Nelson Australia
102 Dodds Street
South Melbourne 3205
Victoria, Australia

Nelson Canada
1120 Birchmount Road
Scarborough, Ontario
Canada M1K 5G4

International Thomson Editores
Campos Eliseos 385, Piso 7
Col. Polanco
11560 México D.F. México

International Thomson Publishing GmbH
Königswinterer Strasse 418
53227 Bonn, Germany

International Thomson Publishing Asia
221 Henderson Road
#05-10 Henderson Building
Singapore 0315

International Thomson Publishing Japan
Hirakawacho Kyowa Building, 3F
2-2-1 Hirakawacho
Chiyoda-ku, Tokyo 102, Japan

Library of Congress Cataloging-in-Publication Data

Anderson, William M.
     Integrating music into the elementary classroom/William
M. Anderson, Joy E. Lawrence.—3rd ed.
          p.   cm.
     Includes indexes.
     ISBN: 0-534-23736-3
     1. School music—Instruction and study. 2. Elementary school
teaching.   I. Lawrence, Joy E. II. Title.
MT1.A696 1994
372.87'044—dc20   94-29737

PREFACE

Most elementary schools in the United States require that students receive instruction in music. Although music specialists are found in large numbers of schools, much responsibility for teaching music falls to classroom teachers. Even in schools that have special music teachers, the amount of time they spend with students is quite small in comparison to the total time students spend with the classroom teacher.

Most classroom teachers realize their responsibility toward instruction in music (along with other subject areas) but often have a limited understanding about how music can be made to "fit" with the rest of the elementary program. Thus, we see a definite need for a practically oriented book of global design to show how music can be taught and integrated into other areas of the elementary classroom curriculum.

Integrating Music into the Elementary Classroom, Third Edition, emphasizes the importance of enriching children's lives by making music a central part of the elementary school curriculum. This book provides guidelines for elementary teachers with limited musical experience as well as for music specialists. The book is comprehensive, covering music fundamentals, materials, and methods for teaching music in the elementary classroom. It focuses on how children learn and presents popular, easy-to-use techniques for teaching singing, playing instruments, moving to music, creating music, and listening to music. Lesson plans are provided for kindergarten through grade six along with more than 160 songs selected from various historical periods and cultures. The book is unique in its focus on cultural diversity and in integrating music with the entire elementary curriculum. Finally, this third edition is carefully designed to meet the new National Standards for Music Education.

OVERVIEW OF SPECIAL FEATURES OF THE THIRD EDITION

- More activities for K–2
- Expanded chapter on singing
- More than 160 songs that cover a wide range of historical periods and cultures
- Singable English translations included for foreign language songs
- New CDs and videos
- Innovative sample lesson plans added, particularly for K–3
- More instrumental accompaniments provided
- More evaluation techniques included
- Review questions added at the end of each chapter

ACKNOWLEDGMENTS

The authors wish to acknowledge the assistance of the following people in the preparation of this manuscript: Virginia Hoge Mead, professor emeritus of music education, Kent State University, for her help with Dalcroze Eurhythmics; William Thomas, coordinator of vocal music, Cleveland Heights/University Heights Schools, for his help with interpretative movement; Kathryn Mihelick and Maria Foustalieraki for their help with folk dances; the Cleveland Orchestra and Joseph Karabinus and Associates, photographers, and Mary Ellen Ferrato for assistance with photographs.

We wish to thank the following reviewers for their comments: Elza Daugherty, University of Northern Colorado; Joyce Jordan, University of Miami; Catherine Mallett, Murray State University, Martha Riley, Purdue University; and Edwin Schatkowski, Kutztown University.

Our special thanks to Debby Kramer, production services coordinator; Robert Kauser, permissions editor; Nancy Sjoberg, production manager; Jackie Estrada, copy editor; John Odam, designer; and Katherine Hartlove, music editor, for their insight, encouragement, and patience through the production of this book.

And finally, to our families, a very special thanks for their support through the lengthy endeavor of preparing the third edition.

William M. Anderson
Joy E. Lawrence

CONTENTS

9 CREATIVE EXPERIENCES WITH MUSIC 369

10 INTEGRATING MUSIC WITH THE STUDY OF PEOPLES, PLACES, AND CULTURES 401

INDEX OF SONGS

INTRODUCTION

As a teacher, you are about to enter one of the most exciting domains of human experience—sharing what you know, cherish, and love with children, so that the quality of their relationships with others will be richer, their perception of the world around them deeper, and their own lives more rewarding and fulfilled. This book is for you, the classroom teacher in the elementary school. It is you who will have daily contact with children in grades K through 6 at least 5 hours a day, 25 hours a week, 900 hours a year. The formal education of a child rests in your hands. Your enthusiasm is contagious, your beliefs in life's wonders inspire, your understanding comforts, and your knowledge and skill motivate and mold the intellectual and emotional growth of the child in your classroom.

Classroom teachers have an awesome task, with responsibility in a great many subject areas, including language arts, mathematics, science, geography, history, physical education, art, and music. This book is based on the belief that *every* classroom teacher can accumulate knowledge and develop skills that will enable him or her to lead a child in meaningful experiences with music of all peoples in America's diverse society. Each of you has particular talents. Some of you sing well; others play instruments; still others may never have sung in a choir or played an instrument but enjoy listening and dancing to music. Some of you have traveled or read a great deal and would like to share music and arts of other countries and peoples with your students. Whatever your background, this book will help you build on your strengths to teach music and will expand your horizons so that you will be better equipped to integrate music experiences into the elementary school curriculum.

THE IMPORTANCE OF MUSIC AND OTHER ARTS IN THE ELEMENTARY SCHOOL

As you begin your study of music and develop materials for teaching, it will be helpful to ponder several questions that educators and parents often ask about the value of music and other arts in the general education of children: What is art? What is an arts experience? How does it differ from other experiences in life? Why is it important for children to have arts experiences?

At the outset it should be stated that there are many answers to the question "What is art?" When we talk about art, we are usually referring to music, painting, sculpture, dance, poetry, drama, and so on, rather than the sciences, such as physics, biology, and chemistry. An artwork expresses human feeling: excitement, relaxation, joy. As the artist manipulates and arranges the media unique to a particular art (sounds in music, color and design in painting, words in poetry), an expressive product emerges that we call a work of art (a musical composition, a painting, or a poem). The result is a projection of the personality and skill of the artist, a statement of the philosophy of the age in which it is produced, and an expression of a feeling or idea that transcends anything concerned with one individual or single period of time in history.

In studying works of art we need to focus our attention on some basic criteria. The first of these is *craftmanship*: How carefully has the artist used materials (sounds, words, paint, or movement)? A second criterion is *creativity* or *imagination*: What has the artist done to create something fresh and new? How is the work *expressive*—has the artist effectively captured a dimension of human feeling, and does this flow forth to the perceiver? As we select materials to be used in lessons for children, we will learn more about these criteria and how they can help us make decisions regarding our choice of artworks for use in the classroom.

The view taken in this book is that, in an arts experience, a person and a work of art are involved in intense interaction that creates a deeply satisfying sense of pleasure, heightened sensitivity to all dimensions of life, and a powerful feeling of self-worth and fulfillment. For instance, performances of Beethoven's *Symphony No. 5* consistently stir the hearts and minds of audiences. No matter how many times one hears this piece, it always reaches out with fresh and distinctly new meanings. This is the unique quality of a true work of art, and it is precisely here where the arts experience differs from other types of experiences. The uniqueness of an artwork is its embodiment of human feeling and the potential it has of sharing this feeling with you and me. Such arts experiences are essential in the general education of every child, for through the arts the child develops his or her own expression of feelings and grows in the ability to understand and appreciate how artists throughout the world have expressed these same feelings, thus enriching the quality and the meaning of life.

AN INTEGRATED APPROACH TO LEARNING AND TEACHING

It is important for elementary school teachers to help students integrate knowledge across subject areas. Specialization is evident in a number of areas of the elementary curriculum where there are teachers of music, art, physical education, and reading, and the daily schedule is organized around distinct segments such as mathematics and social studies. Although specialization has an important place, attention must also be directed toward fostering an integrated structure so that students develop some sense about how knowledge in one area relates to what is studied in another. If students are to learn to identify relationships among subject areas, they will need to learn from an interrelated perspective. We cannot assume that students will somehow assimilate information from various areas and then draw together the necessary integrated relationships on their own. In fact, students often do not see the most basic relationships among subject matter areas and thus must be shown how subjects are related. Teaching from such a perspective need not detract from the specialized study, but it does require teachers to go beyond current practices and to structure curricula based on the relationships within and among subject matter areas.

Integrating music into the child's daily classroom experiences has many advantages. Foremost is that children can be taught to perceive ideas that are related throughout their learning environment. They will discover that fundamental musical concepts—such as unity through repetition, contrast, and balance—are inherent in many subject areas. As students are asked to study music and the visual arts in relationship to history and social studies, they develop a clearer perspective of a particular period. For example, many students have studied the period of Washington, Jefferson, and Franklin without realizing that several of the world's greatest composers (Haydn, Mozart, and Beethoven) lived during the same time and that the minuet, the third movement in symphonies of the classical period, was also a popular dance of the American colonists. Further, through studying another area of the world, such as Japan, from an interrelated perspective, students often gain insights into a culture that would be difficult to acquire in any other way. Clearly, the primary focus of this book is to place music in an integrated learning environment, which we believe will contribute to meaningful and long-lasting educational experiences for students.

THE PLAN FOR THIS BOOK

It is important to design musical learning that focuses on multisensory experiences with music (learning through moving, seeing, and hearing music), as research has shown that children differ not only in the rate at which they learn but also in the way in which they learn best. Chapter 1 focuses on how children learn music, including those students with special needs. Chapter 2 suggests ways to design learning experiences appropriate to a variety of interests and levels of maturity. It also includes a segment on instructional technology.

Developing skill in understanding, performing, and interpreting music is possible for anyone willing to take the time to study, practice, and learn. Chapter 3 focuses on fundamentals of music. The classroom teacher requires knowledge and skill in the basic elements of music—melody, rhythm, texture, dynamics, tone color, and form—along with an understanding of how a composer uses these elements to express ideas, beliefs, and feelings. The chapter includes suggestions for activities that will develop skills emphasized throughout the text: singing, playing instruments, listening, moving, creating music, and relating music to peoples, places, and cultures from many world traditions and historical periods. Music is basic to life, and meaningful experiences with it can enrich the quality of our lives as teachers as well as the lives of students.

To be confident in teaching music a classroom teacher needs skill in teaching children to sing, play instruments, listen to music, express music through movement, and create music.

Chapters 4 through 9 are devoted to developing these skills and also provide Orff, Kodály, and Dalcroze techniques and materials for teaching and integrating these approaches into the basic curriculum.

In Chapter 10 the study of music as a world phenomenon leads to a greater understanding of countries, places, and peoples. Appropriate lessons are provided for both primary age children (ages 5, 6, 7, and 8) and upper elementary (ages 9, 10, and 11). These lessons are designed to provide experiences with music of a particular culture and through these experiences to enhance the understanding and appreciation of Western music.

Chapter 11 focuses on relating music and other areas of literary and visual arts, with the intent of helping students understand basic relationships between music and other art forms. The chapter includes suggestions for planning "integrative" programs suitable for open houses or similar events, as well as for creating "resource" units that make use of several arts.

The book concludes with an epilogue that features a plan for lifelong learning in music with suggestions for preparing children to attend live concerts of music, criteria for purchasing records, and possibilities for making music with friends outside of school. Appendixes provide fingerings for the recorder and guitar chord tablature.

This book can be used both as a methods text for students preparing to be elementary classroom teachers and as a teaching resource in the classroom. Teachers are encouraged to keep this text available for reference and to use the many materials and teaching suggestions as they begin their careers.

We hope that as you complete this book, you will have gained a new perspective on integrating music into daily learning experiences and that your students will grow in knowledge, sensitivity, and understanding of themselves and their world.

How Children Learn

As we begin to think about teaching music to children, we must consider (1) ways children learn, (2) what principles are involved in the learning process, and (3) how we apply these principles to musical learning. While many of the ideas presented in this chapter may apply to any subject area, our interest here is to relate them to the teaching of music and to integrated learning experiences with music.

BASIC TYPES OF LEARNING

Several basic types of learning should be considered when teaching music to children. The first of these may be categorized as *psychomotor learning*—that is, learning involving mental processes that control muscular activity. A second category of learning is *cognitive learning,* which deals with the acquisition of knowledge. A third category of learning is *affective learning,* which concerns itself with a feeling response to music.

PSYCHOMOTOR LEARNING

Students vary in their psychomotor learning abilities. Some children display considerable ability in singing, playing instruments, and moving to music, while others seem less responsive to such psychomotor learning activities. It is important for the teacher to nurture the musical potential of students regardless of their initial level of accomplishment.

Attention to developing psychomotor skills should begin early and continue as an integral part of the training children receive at more advanced levels. For example, an emphasis on movement to music is based on the premise that children should be able to physically feel and respond to musical stimuli before being asked to identify such stimuli on a cognitive level. Such an approach to musical study clearly parallels the pedagogical principle of "sound before sight."

Psychomotor learning is particularly important in training children to listen to music. Directed listening should be approached by having children physically respond to musical sounds; for example, students should learn to follow the beat and indicate changes in tempo through clapping, marching, and other body movements. They should learn to move in either twos or threes to demonstrate duple and triple meter, and to express high and low sounds with appropriate movements. Only after students have "internalized" sounds through movement and are able to respond accurately to musical stimuli should notation and other information about music be introduced.

An important aspect of psychomotor learning of music is the need for regular practice. Children seem to learn musical skills more effectively if they practice for short periods of time interspersed with intervals of rest. Thus, efforts should be concentrated on a specific task (such as singing, playing an instrument, or listening to music) for a short time each day rather than for a long time once or twice a week.

It is obvious that the classroom teacher is in a better position to help students with skill development, as a special music teacher may see students only once or twice a week. If children are to receive the frequency of training needed for optimum development of music skills, classroom teachers must allow time in the daily schedule for such skill development.

COGNITIVE LEARNING

In terms of music, we ask children to learn about such things as elements of music, composers, style periods, and instruments. One of the most important concerns in cognitive learning is for information about music to be closely linked with actual musical experiences. Children need to have many experiences with sounds to understand music information. For example, in teaching about 4/4 meter, the teacher may tell students that a quarter note receives one beat, a half note two beats, and a dotted half note three beats. Such information does not take on full meaning, however, until it is placed in an actual musical experience in which the students clap or march as they count the beats in various note values.

One of the practical problems teachers must deal with in cognitive learning is that information must be in language that children can easily understand. Teachers must be particularly aware of the level of language to be used when presenting information to students at various grade levels. An effective way of dealing with problems of music terminology is to use diagrams, symbols, or pictures. Often a child can more easily understand rondo form from a diagram, such as ○ □ ○ △ ○, than from several minutes of words spoken by the teacher.

AFFECTIVE LEARNING

If music is to be important in students' lives, the teacher needs to be aware of how music expresses human feeling. Students should experience music in such a way that they are increasingly aware of how composers have used sound to express deep inner feelings, which, like ideas, have transcended peoples, places, and cultures of many different eras. For example, as students learn to move to the long, flowing melody in Smetana's *The Moldau* and learn the folk song on which it is based, they should experience the power and feeling generated by the minor tonality of this melody. In affective learning students experience through an art form inseparable mixtures of feelings that words cannot begin to express. This education in the feeling expressed in musical artworks becomes a cornerstone on which all music teaching and learning are based.

ACTIVE VERSUS PASSIVE LEARNING

All learning needs to be "active." Students need to respond to music by moving, singing, playing instruments, and creating. Linking information about music with actual musical sound encourages students to be actively involved with musical learning. Through such involvement, students seem to assimilate and retain information more effectively and to exhibit greater interest and motivation to learn. For example, a teacher wishing to present rondo form to students must go beyond simply diagramming the form with letters (ABACA) on the chalkboard and telling students to listen for a recurring section of music (A) that alternates with contrasting sections of music (B, C). Students need to sing or play the melodies of various sections, engage in some type of movement (clapping, marching, etc.) to the rhythm, and perhaps place letters on a chalkboard to identify various sections of the form as they hear them.

TEACHER-CENTERED VERSUS CHILD-CENTERED LEARNING

In considering various approaches to learning music, you will want to explore both teacher-centered and child-centered methods. The teacher-centered approach features the teacher primarily as a lecturer who presents material to the class by *defining* and *explaining*. For example, the teacher who wishes students to learn about duple meter approaches the topic by *telling* students that duple means "two," that in duple meter there are, therefore, two beats in a measure, and that the first beat normally receives the greater accent. The teacher may use musical examples to illustrate the definition, but in this approach students assume a rather passive role.

In contrast, the child-centered approach to learning actively involves students in the learning process. In this approach the teacher presents students with a problem that needs to be solved. Under the teacher's guidance the students explore possible solutions through trial-and-error examination. The teacher guides students in their exploration, but the ultimate solution to the problem is largely student derived. For example, in presenting duple meter, the teacher first has the students sing a song in duple meter, then has them clap the beat or conduct as they sing the song again, asks them if they can feel which beat receives the greater emphasis (first), and finally asks how the beats seem to group themselves. The teacher guides the students toward their ultimate understanding that the beats are grouped in twos (duple meter).

As you work with students at various age or grade levels, you will undoubtedly use both teacher-centered and child-centered approaches. However, because students are more actively involved in the child-centered approach, teachers generally favor it, particularly in working with young children.

THE STRUCTURE OF MUSICAL LEARNING

In structuring musical learning for the classroom, you need to (1) make what you teach meaningful, (2) organize material sequentially, (3) experience music before labeling it, (4) use a conceptual approach to music, (5) design learning experiences with a spiral approach, (6) use a multisensory approach to learning, (7) use a multicultural approach to learning, (8) provide reinforcement, and (9) teach for transfer.

MAKE WHAT YOU TEACH MEANINGFUL

You should emphasize activities that closely relate to things children perceive as interesting and meaningful. Some possibilities include capitalizing on children's interest in trains by having them listen to Villa-Lobos's *Little Train of the Caipira* or the bluegrass composition "The Orange Blossom Special"; designing a unit of study on electronic music for those with special interests in electronics and machines; or studying nature through such pieces as Beethoven's "The Storm" (*Symphony No. 6*, fourth movement), or Smetana's *The Moldau*.

ORGANIZE MATERIAL SEQUENTIALLY

One of the most important aspects of structuring musical learning in the classroom is to develop a successful sequence of activities. In developing plans for teaching music, you need to arrange learning experiences into a logical continuum, carefully linking each step with preceding and succeeding steps. Sequence may vary from classroom to classroom; that is, one teacher may develop a sequence of steps that proves successful in teaching certain musical concepts, while a second teacher who is teaching other students the same material may develop a different but equally logical sequence.

Often teachers develop several alternative plans for presenting material. In a classroom of twenty-five students, there will usually be students with a variety of academic and musical abilities and backgrounds. Some students may have had considerable experience with rhythmic activities, for example, while others may have had none. In presenting a rhythmic learning experience to such a class, the teacher needs to consider several alternatives in the sequence of events undertaken by the students.

EXPERIENCE MUSIC BEFORE LABELING IT

A young child may have many experiences with an apple—such as eating it, feeling that it is round, and seeing that it is green or red—long before being asked to label it with the word *apple*. Music should follow this same pattern of learning—that is, the child should have many experiences with such concepts as high-low, fast-slow, and loud-soft before being asked to place a label on a sound. Because music is the most abstract of all the arts—that is, it passes through time and exists only in the memory—such experiences are essential if perception and understanding are to take place.

USE A CONCEPTUAL APPROACH TO LEARNING

Teachers have discovered that one of the most effective ways of helping students assimilate and retain information is through a conceptual approach to learning. Conceptual learning involves "students developing the ability to give a common name or response to a class of stimuli varying in appearance."* Teachers using a conceptual approach focus learning on

*Janice T. Gibson, *Psychology for the Classroom* (Englewood Cliffs, N.J.: Prentice-Hall, 1976), p. 243.

certain fundamental ideas considered basic to understanding music. These include concepts of melody, rhythm, texture, timbre, dynamics, and form. For example, melody as a fundamental concept in music involves a succession of pitches that are perceived as belonging together. Melodies may vary greatly with respect to their internal characteristics, such as differing number of pitches, various scales, movement principally by step or skip, variety of contour directions, and range. However different these internal characteristics may be, the central concept of melody is preserved as a meaningful succession of pitches.

Children develop a concept of melody through experiences with many types of melodies. In effect they learn the many guises a succession of pitches called a melody may have. It is, therefore, important that in the classroom students experience a wide array of melodies from various historical periods in Western music and from other major musical traditions of the world. They should explore characteristics of melodies through singing, playing instruments, and listening. If learning experiences are carefully organized over a period of time, students will indeed develop a concept of melody and the many characteristics it may have.

As lessons are organized around the musical concepts of melody, rhythm, texture, timbre, dynamics, and form, it will be helpful to refer to the characteristics of each of these as outlined in Chapter 3.

In addition to strictly musical concepts, analogous concepts are found in visual and literary arts. Among these are repetition and enlargement, contrast and variety, and balance (see Chapter 11). Each of these concepts operates in a similar fashion but through different means in various art forms. Experiencing a concept through several art forms encourages integrated learning.

DESIGN LEARNING EXPERIENCES WITH A SPIRAL APPROACH

A spiral approach to learning is closely linked with conceptual teaching. In the spiral approach, material is organized so that there is a systematic return to concepts at increasing levels of sophistication. The principal idea behind the spiral design is that the teacher seeks to help students develop concepts with increasing depth at successive grade levels (see Figure 1.1).

USE A MULTISENSORY APPROACH TO LEARNING

Students learn through a combination of their senses. Some learn more quickly through the visual sense, which is highly developed through watching television. A chart or musical picture provides these children with something tangible to relate music to. The visual image remains even though the sound may end. Others may learn more quickly by moving to the music. For example, a child might perceive triple rhythm more quickly by moving in some fashion, such as tapping his or her thighs or swaying with the beat. A third child might learn just as quickly through the aural sense—that is, by hearing a melody a second time. People have different aptitudes and talents; the skillful teacher recognizes these differences and creates lessons that involve as many of the senses as possible.

USE A MULTICULTURAL APPROACH TO LEARNING

Music and the arts from different cultures contribute to our understanding of both others and ourselves. As you create lessons that involve singing and playing instruments from many musical traditions, students are encouraged to experience, respect, and appreciate the

Figure 1.1. The spiral approach to music learning

Based on Ronald B. Thomas, *MMCP Synthesis* (Elnora, N.Y.: MEDIA, Inc., n.d.), p. 39.

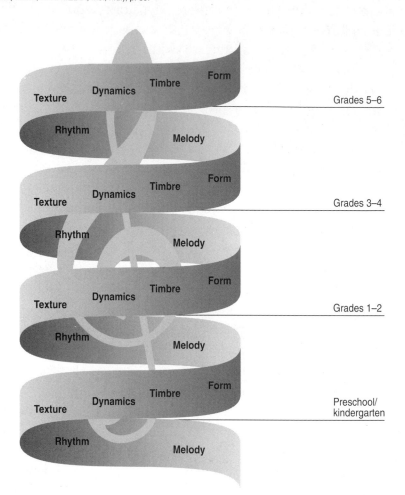

contributions of people, cultures, and eras different from their own. This may be true whether they are sharing music of the black gospel tradition or a Renaissance dance. In the United States one of the goals of education is to broaden and appreciate our heritage of diversity. Music and other arts provide valuable insights and opportunities for such growth and development.

PROVIDE REINFORCEMENT

One of the most important tasks in the learning process is to provide reinforcement for learning. Children seek to be successful at whatever they undertake, and teachers need to construct music lessons that include effective rewards.

The focus of any system of rewards should be on positive reinforcement. Positive reinforcement techniques should be applied consistently and in a variety of ways in every music learning experience. The proper use of praise, for example, is a powerful way of encouraging students to repeat something they have done well. Reinforcement can often be as simple as a smile. Teachers often reward by giving special privileges to students who successfully complete a task. These may be relatively simple, such as "Carlos, since you sang that part so well, you may now play the xylophone in this piece." Often the most effective types of reinforcement are those selected by the child. Children always have favorite things they like to do. Be sensitive and observant and use these things as rewards for accomplishments in the classroom.

Use reinforcement techniques during music lessons to reward both musical accomplishments and good behavior. Cooperative student behavior is essential if children are to accomplish musical tasks, so you should design reward techniques to encourage productive student behavior and optimize music learning.

One of the most important goals for music teaching is to have students learn for intrinsic as well as extrinsic rewards. The real excitement in learning about music occurs when students want to sing, play instruments, or listen to music because of the intrinsic rewards of the musical experience itself. While initially you may feel a need to use a variety of extrinsic rewards, you should encourage students to study music just because of the pleasure it gives them. Intrinsic rewards are especially important because they stay with students long after formal school experiences have been completed.

TEACH FOR TRANSFER

An essential goal in structuring musical experiences for children is *transfer*. You need to make a concerted attempt to encourage students to relate and use what they have previously learned to what they are currently studying. For example, if in a previous lesson students identified the balance of ABA form in the song "We Wish You a Merry Christmas," we hope that in a succeeding lesson they will be able to transfer the concept of balance through ABA form to another piece of music.

Children should also be encouraged to transfer ideas learned about music to other studies and to settings outside as well as inside the school. For example, they should be able to recognize concepts such as repetition and enlargement, variety and contrast, and balance in the visual and literary arts and in everyday examples at school and at home. They should also have some sense of how music and composers in a particular time period are related to history and social studies, geography, and other subject areas. For example, when students listen to a piece by Mozart, they should locate Austria on a map of Europe and learn about Salzburg and Vienna, where he lived and worked. As students identify the dates when Mozart lived (1756–1791), encourage them to associate these dates with famous Americans who lived at the same time (Washington, Jefferson, Franklin) and events that took place then (the signing of the Declaration of Independence and the American Revolution).

One of the principal advantages of teaching for transfer is that material will often take on a greater sense of meaning for children if they can see relationships with other learning experiences. Further, if children have learned material by using it in a variety of settings, they are more likely to remember the information.

MUSICAL EXPERIENCES FOR STUDENTS WITH SPECIAL NEEDS

Many times classroom teachers need to adapt techniques or materials to special needs of students, such as those who are visually impaired, hearing impaired, mentally retarded, or physically disabled or who have some form of learning disability or emotional disturbance. The philosophy of aesthetic education, which emphasizes music as an expression of feeling and active involvement in the learning process, applies to students with special needs as well as to the so-called normal student. Disabled persons who have capitalized on their musical skills are legion, but Itzak Perlman (polio victim) and Ray Charles (blind) are two of the most famous. This section of Chapter 1 focuses on guidelines for adapting techniques and materials for use with special students. It is important to remember that many students with special needs, whether in separate classes or "mainstreamed," are often very responsive to the arts. In fact many of them find some of their greatest joy and satisfaction in musical and other arts experiences.

When working with students who have some form of impairment or disability, it is vitally important that teachers focus on the individual's special capabilities and build on them, while at the same time attempting to alleviate or compensate for the individual's disability. The disabled student is an important human being with feelings, emotions, capabilities, and desires. It is our job as teachers to nurture and develop the positive aspects of a student's abilities, always focusing on what he or she *can* do rather than on what he or she *cannot* do. It is important to note that the appearance of handicapped students often does not indicate what their capabilities are.

Although special education has many divisions and a multitude of classifications, two general types are (1) normal intelligence but physically disabled, visually impaired, or hearing impaired, and (2) mentally retarded.

Generally, the same teaching materials or basic techniques can be used with special students as with "normal" students. Hands-on experiences with music are encouraged for all students at any level of development. Differences occur in adapting experiences so that students who have some form of impairment can function successfully. Here are some general guidelines for teachers of students with special needs:

1. Use positive reinforcement and frequent encouragement.
2. Do not let disabled students use their disability to get their own way.
3. Encourage and require a student to extend the range of his or her accomplishments. Avoid jumping in to "help" too soon.
4. Be patient, but make students aware of your expectations.
5. Structure lessons that recognize the "problems" of many such students (such as short attention span, difficulty with speech patterns, difficulty with motor coordination).

In addition, consider the following guidelines when structuring musical experiences for students with special needs.

NORMAL INTELLIGENCE

Physically Impaired: Confined to Wheelchair
1. Provide ample space.
2. Create alternative ways of responding to rhythm other than walking (moving hands or head, tapping fingers, playing classroom instruments).
3. Cover percussion handles with heavy carpet tape to make them bigger and easier to grasp.
4. Fasten instruments to wheelchairs with notebook binder rings so that students cannot drop them.
5. Place books, charts, instruments at level of wheelchair student.

6. Ask student for ideas for adapting activities (they are constantly adapting and often can suggest the best solution to problems).

Visually Impaired

1. Keep the physical setup of the classroom the same (instruments, piano, chairs, and so on in the same place).
2. Use tactile devices, such as rough and smooth surfaces, to aid in playing instruments.
3. Develop spatial consciousness (location of black and white keys on the piano, frets on the guitar, chord bars on the Autoharp or Omnichord).
4. Adapt movement activities by setting steps to number sequences (such as four steps right, two steps forward, three steps left). Blind students are highly sensitive to such directions and can often learn dance steps before their sighted peers.
5. Encourage blind students to lead in ear-training games. Their hearing sense is generally much more acute than that of sighted students.

(Many of the music series books are available in large print editions and Braille from the Library of Congress, Washington, D.C.)

Hearing Impaired

1. If possible, hold class in a room with a wooden floor, so that students can feel the vibrations of the music.
2. Have students feel the vibrations of a drumhead and create an inner feeling of beat by following a leader's motions.
3. Place such students in the front of the class where they can read your lips. Encourage them to "feel" the concept of high and low by placing their fingers on the throat of a companion student and having that student sing high and low pitches. Students with hearing impairment can gain a sense of pitch through this approach. They should be encouraged and allowed to sing in class, even though they may not always sing "in tune."
4. The use of earphones may enable students with hearing aids to hear the music, thus opening a world of sound to them.

MENTALLY RETARDED

General Characteristics

1. They learn at a slower pace than "normal" students.
2. They often have difficulty with motor coordination.
3. They may have speech problems.
4. They need constant and immediate reinforcement.
5. They have a short attention span.
6. They are often self-centered.
7. They require extraordinary patience and much love and understanding.
8. They are often very affectionate; they want to touch and be touched.

Guidelines for Musical Experiences

1. *Vocal range:* Limited, usually within an octave and lower range. Build confidence in the lower range, followed by developing the upper range. Use simple syllable patterns, such as:

sol mi sol la sol sol mi do do mi sol sol la sol mi

2. *Melody:* Choose songs with small intervals and avoid large skips. Melodies with repeated patterns are often the most successful.
3. *Rhythm:*
   a. Provide opportunities for experiences with rhythms on a variety of complexity levels. Allow extra time for student to play an instrument. Example: While the rest of the class plays on beats 1, 2, 3, 4, have the retarded child play only on beat 1 or at the beginning of a line or phrase.
   b. Allow the student to set the tempo of the rhythm and then follow the student. Example: Strum chords on the Autoharp, Omnichord, or synthesizer as student plays a drum.
   c. Use two students to play a two-beat pattern on a drum. The rest of the class claps with them.
   d. Encourage students to create patterns for others to follow.
4. *Harmony:* Limited use of chords on the Autoharp, Omnichord, or synthesizer. Identify chords with colors or use tactile materials (e.g., C chord = burlap, F chord = silk, G chord = velvet). Place chord names or symbols on charts and hang them around necks of students.
5. *Word meanings:* Give special attention to word meanings and pronunciation. Choose songs that are suitable for the intellectual age rather than the chronological age of the student.
6. *Movement:* Proceed from large to small motor movements. Design movement activities with emphasis on much repetition. Allow more time for the movement to occur (tempos may be somewhat slower).
7. Assign or ask for talented volunteers to help retarded students who may be mainstreamed. Be sure to change helpers often and have a student assistant assigned to one particular activity.

Do not talk down to students or use "baby" or "special" music; a Sousa march can draw the same strong rhythmic response from retarded students as any others. However, we as teachers may need to modify our expectations regarding a coordinated physical response to the beat. Classroom teachers must assess each student's special needs and then devise ways of bringing that student into the mainstream of activity. Musical experiences must involve *all* students, and the personal satisfaction is great for the teacher who sincerely tries to help a student overcome an impairment so that he or she can have success and pleasure with musical experiences.

INSTRUCTIONAL TECHNOLOGY FOR THE CLASSROOM

In this day of computers, with CD-ROMs capable of storing entire encyclopedias, classroom teachers need to use the emerging technologies to enhance the learning of music. Because computers are now common in most schools and many homes, students often come to the music classroom with considerable computer skills.

A number of music publishers are now creating software for use in the classroom. You will need to look in your local library or audiovisual center for the many catalogues, books, and magazine articles on the subject. Music programs can display musical notation and provide sounds of different pitches. With the addition of the MIDI (Musical Instrument Digital Interface), the computer can even become an instrument. Many schools have synthesizers that can produce different pitches, tone colors, rhythms, and textures. Classroom teachers, particularly those with a bent toward electronics, can use these instruments for music as well as math and science projects with children.*

Computers and synthesizers are especially helpful in providing individualized instruction. Many computer games can reinforce music teaching in the classroom. Some interesting applications of using computers to teach music are found in the publication *Music Fundamentals,* published by Silver Burdett Company (1985). Included are such games as the "Magic Balloon Game" in which brief fragments of music are played and the student decides whether the melody goes up or down or stays the same. To provide visual reinforcement, a balloon moves across the screen in the same direction as the musical fragment. As with many behavior-oriented computer games, if the student gives the correct answer, the next melodic fragment is played; if not, the first fragment is played again. Such exercises facilitate students' learning of melodic direction in music.

Following are some guidelines for choosing a software music program (you could also use these questions for evaluating any computer program):

1. What are the goals of the program? How are they addressed and what evaluation tools are included?
2. Is adequate documentation provided? Is there a clearly written sheet or booklet accompanying the program that describes prior learning required, information on loading disks, and procedures to follow in using the program?
3. Can the program be used with your equipment?
4. Does the program meet your curricular needs and objectives?
5. Is the program easy to use (is it user friendly)?
6. Does the program give adequate feedback to the student for right and wrong answers?
7. Is the subject matter presented accurately?
8. Is the music notation visually correct? (The notes and symbols should not be unusual sizes or shapes.)
9. Do the pitches sound in tune?

---

* For those wishing to explore further, please see Scott Wilkinson's "MIDI Basics, Part I" and "From the Top MIDI Basics, Part 2," *Electronic Musician,* vol. 9, no. 8 (August 1993), pp. 73–76; vol. 9, no. 9 (September 1993), pp. 70–73.

10. Does the music sound "electronic" or like real voices or instruments?
11. If the student hits a wrong key, does the program stop? (It shouldn't.)
12. Are there clear exit instructions? (Students should be able to get out of the program, go back to the main menu, or move to a new program with ease.)

A form for evaluating computer software is provided in Figure 1.2.

Figure 1.2. Music software computer evaluation form

Reviewer: _____   Computer program: _____
School: _____   Author: _____
Date: _____   Publisher: _____
Grade level: _____   Price: _____

Is this an update? _____ If yes, identify with appropriate number _____
Where did you hear about this software? _____
What do independent trade journals (such as *PC Computing*) say about this software? _____
_____

Hardware requirements: _____
Previous learning required: _____

Rate each of the following on a scale of 1 to 5

		(High)				(Low)
1.	Ease of use	1	2	3	4	5
2.	User friendly	1	2	3	4	5
3.	Appropriate feedback (when to move on)	1	2	3	4	5
4.	Presentation techniques	1	2	3	4	5
5.	Accuracy of subject matter	1	2	3	4	5
6.	Accurate music notation	1	2	3	4	5
7.	Accurate, in-tune pitches	1	2	3	4	5
8.	Program continues if student hits wrong key	1	2	3	4	5
9.	Clear exit instructions	1	2	3	4	5
10.	Clear documentation	1	2	3	4	5
11.	Adequate documentation	1	2	3	4	5

Program strengths: _____
Program weaknesses: _____
Other observations: _____

Source: Patricia Hackett and Carolyn A. Lindeman, *The Musical Classroom,* 2nd ed. (Englewood Cliffs, N.J.: Prentice-Hall, 1988), pp. 38–40.

QUESTIONS FOR REVIEW

1. What is psychomotor learning? Give a musical example.
2. What is cognitive learning? Give a musical example.
3. What is affective learning? Give a musical example.
4. What is the difference between *passive* and *active* learning?
5. What it the difference between *teacher-centered* learning and *child-centered* learning?
6. What does each of the following mean?
   a. Making what you teach meaningful
   b. Organizing material sequentially
   c. Experience before labeling
   d. Conceptual approach to learning
   e. Spiral learning
   f. Multisensory approach to learning
   g. Multicultural approach to learning
   h. Reinforcement
   i. Transfer
7. What are several "special" needs of students?
8. What are some ways you could adapt a music lesson (or any lesson) for students who have special needs?
9. What are three to four guidelines to follow in teaching music to students who have special needs?
10. Discuss several ways in which instructional technology can facilitate learning music.

DESIGNING INTEGRATED LEARNING EXPERIENCES WITH MUSIC

As you begin to think about teaching music in an elementary school classroom, there are a number of things you need to consider. These include (1) identifying long- and short-range goals; (2) deciding on musical concepts; (3) developing specific objectives that are related to learning abilities of various age levels; (4) choosing interesting and appropriate musical materials and activities that can be integrated with other classroom experiences; (5) involving students in logical and sequential activities that will enable them to learn easily and effectively; (6) deciding on length and frequency of lessons that focus on musical ideas or concepts; (7) relating music and activities to the life of the student; (8) involving students in multisensory activities that focus on seeing (visual), hearing (auditory), and moving (psychomotor); (9) developing multicultural experiences for students; (10) using audio-visual materials to enhance the lesson; (11) bringing review and closure to the learning experience; and (12) evaluating to ascertain if objectives have been met.

IDENTIFYING LONG- AND SHORT-TERM GOALS

The first task in teaching a music lesson is to formulate long- and short-term goals. Goals are generally concerned with what is desired in terms of musical interest and behavior over a period of time.

Long-Term Goals

"Students will develop an appreciation of jazz" might be a long-term goal. Other long-term goals might be (1) to foster perceptive listening so that the student will interact with the art of music with ever-increasing satisfaction and meaning, (2) to develop musical skills and understanding, and (3) to appreciate music of differing styles and cultures. Note that all these statements use verbs such as *develop, foster, appreciate, understand,* and *enjoy.* These statements represent the philosophy of the educator or the school system, and it is from these long-term goals that short-term goals and a variety of behavioral objectives are formulated.

Short-Term Goals

Short-term goals are related in language to long-term goals but are attained in a specified time. Short-term goals generally indicate what needs to be accomplished in a particular week or specific day. Examples of short-term goals include:

1. Using classroom instruments, students will create and perform a sound piece.
2. Using the solfège system of music reading, students will successfully sing songs appropriate to their age.

Teachers who take time to formulate long- and short-term goals tend to have a clear sense of direction about what students are to learn. Without goals, it is quite easy for both teachers and students to wander aimlessly and haphazardly through a series of musical activities without much learning taking place.

DECIDING ON MUSICAL CONCEPTS

One of the first decisions a teacher makes about a music lesson is what concept or concepts to cover. A *concept* has been defined by Woolfolk and Nicolich as "a collection of experiences or ideas that are grouped together based on some common properties."*

Principal musical concepts include melody, rhythm, texture, dynamics, tone color or timbre, and form. Within each of these large concepts are components or smaller concepts. Thus, duple meter is a component of rhythm, melodic direction is a component of melody, and ternary form (ABA) is a component of form. A more complete description of other musical concepts is found in Chapter 3.

Concepts may stand alone. In other words, you can teach students how repetition of a specific rhythm pattern gives unity to a composition or how perceiving the direction of a melody (up or down) can add pleasure to anticipation. But generally, teaching a concept occurs as part of a lesson and contributes toward increased perception and understanding of the music. If instruction focuses on perceiving such concepts as loud-soft, fast-slow, and upward-downward in isolation, students will not link them to the expressiveness of music. When this happens, music loses its meaning.

* Anita Woolfolk and Lorraine Nicolich, *Educational Psychology for Teachers* (Englewood Cliffs, N.J.: Prentice-Hall, 1980), p. 596.

DEVELOPING OBJECTIVES

As you plan specific lessons, state clear objectives as often as possible in terms of observable behavior (through seeing, hearing, moving, and so on). In other words, state your objectives so that you can observe students demonstrating what they have learned. For example, "Students will demonstrate an understanding of AB form by using sheets of colored paper to outline the formal design in the song 'Greensleeves.'" Other objectives might be "Students will use alphabet cards to identify the ABACA sections of Mozart's Horn Concerto in E flat (Third Movement Rondo)" or "Students will demonstrate their understanding of rests by clapping their hands on the appropriate rests in the song 'If You're Happy.'"

Following are some long-term goals that reflect expectations of various grade levels. You will need to develop short-term goals and specific objectives for individual classes.

Preschool/Kindergarten

Students will

1. Sing short songs in tune, with good breathing habits and tone quality.
2. Perform rhythms with a steady beat.
3. Perform music expressively.
   a. Loud-soft
   b. Fast-slow
   c. Legato-staccato
4. Respond to expressive qualities of music through movement.
   a. Duple meter and triple meter
   b. Strong accents and changing accents
   c. Steady beat
   d. Changing dynamics
5. Play simple rhythmic-melodic patterns on classroom instruments.
6. Sing, play, move, and create music expressive of individual imaginations.

Grades 1 and 2

Students will

1. Sing short songs in tune, with good breathing habits and tone quality.
2. Distinguish between high and low, fast and slow, and instrumental tonal colors.
3. Identify expressive use of repetition and contrast in simple songs and short listening examples.
4. Express through creative movement such musical concepts as
   a. Steady beat
   b. Accent
   c. Gradually getting louder or softer
   d. Staccato
   e. Legato
5. Engage in singing games.
6. Play simple rhythmic-melodic patterns on classroom instruments.
7. Read and create simple notation.

Grades 3 and 4

Students will

1. Sing short songs in tune, with good breathing habits and tone quality.
2. Sing simple rounds and descants in tune.
3. Sing songs expressive of text.
   a. Legato and staccato
   b. Dynamics
   c. Phrasing
4. Analyze music in terms of elements.
   a. Melodic phrases
   b. Tonal colors
   c. Formal structure
5. Read or create simple music notation.
6. Engage in singing games and dances.
7. Play simple melodies and rhythmic accompaniments on classroom instruments.

Grades 5 and 6

Students will

1. Sing songs in tune, with good breathing habits and tone quality.
2. Sing songs in two and three parts.
3. Demonstrate rhythmic sense through
   a. Identifying simple-to-complex rhythms (both verbally and aurally)
   b. Playing rhythms in 2/4, 3/4, 6/8, mixed meter
4. Play simple harmonic accompaniments on guitar, Autoharp, or Omnichord.
5. Play simple melodies and descants on melody bells or recorder.
6. Identify music from other parts of the world according to its use of melody, rhythm, texture, tone color, and formal structure.
7. Develop musical leadership by taking part in musical plays.
8. Read and write music notation.

CHOOSING APPROPRIATE MUSICAL MATERIALS AND ACTIVITIES

As you prepare lessons to teach to children, one important consideration will be to choose musical materials and design activities that (1) are within the capabilities of a particular class, (2) are interesting and fun, and (3) can be integrated into other classroom subjects and experiences. Always emphasize active involvement of students in musical experiences such as singing, playing instruments, and moving to music.

An important difference that you must recognize is between "presenting" and "teaching." Presenting is generally teacher-centered, whereas teaching focuses on the child. This book provides many suggestions for ways to involve children in successful musical experiences. Chapter 3, which focuses on the fundamentals of music, will help you gain and develop your musical skills so that teaching and learning music is rewarding for both you and your students.

TEACING AND LEARNING IN LOGICAL SEQUENCE

Children learn best when ideas progress logically from simple to complex. As you plan lessons, consider what should come first, second, third, and so on. For example, you can introduce a song by performing it (or playing it on a record or tape player), and then teach students the melody, words, and rhythms by using the rote, rote-note, or note approach.

A second technique you need to develop is presenting the same idea in many different ways. Few of us learn a new idea when it is presented only once. For example, to teach students the rhythm of a specific song:

- Ask students to play the beat (2/4 meter) on the drums.
- Have students experience the strong and weak beats by tapping thighs and clapping hands.
- Have one student play the strong beat on a tambourine and another play the weak beat on the claves.
- Ask students to speak the words in the rhythm of the song, accenting the first beat of each measure.
- Use a rhythm chart with either notes or graphics to help students see the beat.

All or any of these ideas can be used in a logical sequence of events to proceed from the introduction of a song or larger composition to a deeper understanding of the piece.

DECIDING ON LENGTH AND FREQUENCY OF LESSONS

The length of lessons will depend on the age and grade level of your students. In general, younger children will need to have shorter lessons than older students, who have longer attention spans. For kindergarten through third grade, a lesson length of 20 to 25 minutes is recommended. Lessons for students in grades 4 through 6 may be 30 to 40 minutes. The decision about lesson length, however, needs to be carefully tailored to each particular class of students.

When planning, determine the approximate number of minutes needed for each segment of the lesson—for example, 5 minutes for introductory slides and discussion, 10 minutes for singing a song and adding accompaniment. Such guides ensure that the various segments of the plan receive their fair share of time. Further, both teachers and students will be kept on track and will not wander significantly from the major points of the lesson.

Frequency of lessons is another important consideration in organizing music instruction. In general, students need to have lessons scheduled close enough for *continuity of learning* to be maintained. Further, it is generally better to have frequent short lessons than long lessons with considerable time gaps in between. The frequency of lessons is also related to the age and grade level of the students. Younger students need to have instruction more frequently than older students. All students seem to do best with some music instruction as part of each school day.

RELATING MUSIC TO STUDENTS' PERSONAL LIVES

Relating music to the personal lives of students often occurs in preliminary activities as well as in the lesson itself. Many times, preliminary activities will lead students to an understanding of the concept being taught (through repetition of the idea). Preliminary activities normally call for teachers to present something familiar to the students, with the idea of letting that experience act as a bridge to the principal part of the lesson. For example, if you are going to talk about contrast in music, the lesson might have preliminary activities that involve students in looking for "contrast" in the classroom, in clothing, in a poem, in a visual artwork, or in movement. When the concept is clear in the minds of students, you can then involve them in appropriate experiences with sounds. These sounds can be created by the students themselves, recreated from a musical score, or listened to from a recording.

DEVELOPING MULTISENSORY EXPERIENCES

Children often learn more effectively if several of their senses are involved, rather than just one. For example, in an age where television often dominates the lives of children, developing and using the visual sense becomes an important teaching method. A visual cue is often helpful because it does not go away; it remains where you put it, and the student can leave the room either mentally or physically and return to find the visual cue in the same place. On the other hand, music involves sound; it passes through time and is gone. Thus, using the visual sense as well as the aural offers children increased opportunities for understanding and success. The tactile sense is of special interest to students who have some form of visual impairment and provides opportunities to relate sounds with touching. You can compare smooth sounds to silk, or jagged or rough sounds to burlap or hickory bark.

DEVELOPING MULTICULTURAL EXPERIENCES

Through television and a variety of printed material, we are becoming increasingly aware of the closeness of other peoples of the world. Many of the world's cultures are present in the United States, where over a hundred different ethnic groups make up the American cultural mosaic. Studying the multicultural musical environment both of the world and of our own country is a wonderful way for students to learn a variety of new kinds of music. It also provides a distinctive opportunity for students to broaden their understanding of other cultures and to develop sensitivity and tolerance toward each other.

DESIGNING AUDIOVISUAL MEDIA

You will want to use media such as slides, films and videos, transparencies, and recordings. These items will need to be carefully written into the appropriate places of the lesson plan, including such items as tape recorder index numbers and record sides and bands.

BRINGING CLOSURE TO A LEARNING EXPERIENCE

Near the end of a lesson you need to schedule a summary or closing activity in which to pull together the separate parts of the lesson and give students a feeling of finality. Quite often such closure is accomplished by students performing a piece in its entirety after having worked on separate segments during the lesson.

EVALUATING LEARNING

Evaluation tells you how effective you have been in your teaching. Often you will discover that you have been successful with some aspects of a presentation and not as effective with others. By systematically evaluating students, you learn what changes need to be made in materials and teaching strategies to ensure that students make satisfactory progress in all areas of study.

For students, periodic evaluation is crucial in letting them know how well they are progressing in their musical study. Children need to have a sense of accomplishment, and a regular program of evaluation gives them needed feedback. One of the most helpful aspects of evaluation for students is that they become aware of strengths and weaknesses—in effect discovering areas in which they excel and areas to which they need to give special attention.

You will want to evaluate students with respect to musical performance skills, perception and understanding of music concepts, and acquisition and retention of information about music. In performance, evaluation focuses on progress made in singing and playing instruments. For example, is there steady improvement in the students' ability to sing on pitch and with good tone quality? Can the students physically execute duple and triple meter? Are students able to satisfactorily accompany pieces using classroom instruments?

Perception and understanding of musical concepts can be evaluated through such techniques as a listening test chart (see p. 280), in which the students are asked to discriminate between contrasting phenomena (loud and soft, duple and triple, violin and trumpet) as they listen to a piece of music. Understanding is often demonstrated by students actually *doing* something, such as creating a "sound composition" illustrating rondo form. Still another way of demonstrating perception and understanding is to ask students to identify a similar concept (such as unity through repetition) in art forms such as music, painting, and poetry.

You can give periodic quizzes to determine how well students have assimilated and retained information about music presented in the class. In general it is better to give short quizzes at frequent intervals than to wait for long periods of time and give lengthy tests.

WRITING LESSON PLANS

As you begin to write a lesson plan to teach music, you need to ask yourself the following questions:

1. What is the activity?
2. Who is the lesson for? (grade level)
3. What concepts do you want to teach?
4. What materials do you need? (to be completed last)
5. What do you want to do? (objectives)
6. How are you going to do it? (procedures)
   a. Preliminary
   b. Main content
7. How will you tie everything together? (closure)
8. Did you teach what you thought you were going to? (evaluation)

As in all lesson plans, detail is critical, especially at the beginning, so don't leave anything to chance. Following are some sample lesson plans to help you see how a typical lesson might be set up.

"Five Little Pumpkins"

Activity: Performing a song
Grade: 2
Concepts: Ascending and descending patterns

Five Little Pumpkins

Key: F
Starting pitch: C
Meter: 4/4, begin on 1

From *Singing and Rhyming* of OUR SINGING WORLD series. © Copyright, 1959,1957,1950, copyright renewed by Ginn and Company.
Used by permission of Silver Burdett & Ginn, Inc.

OBJECTIVES

Students will

1. Identify the upward motion of the beginning pitches of musical phrases from *one* to *five* little pumpkins.
2. Play the pitches F G A B♭ C on the xylophone as each occurs.
3. Create appropriate motions to song using pumpkins as a guide.
4. Sing with good tone quality.

MATERIALS

Pictures of pumpkins
Recording if necessary
Pumpkin note heads with numbers
Xylophone
Fence or gate

PROCEDURES

Preliminary Activities

1. Ask the children to sit on the floor around you.
2. Ask the children when pumpkins are used (fall, Halloween, Thanksgiving). Show pictures of pumpkins.
3. Announce that "Today we are going to learn a song about pumpkins."

Main Content

1. Sing the song "Five Little Pumpkins" or use a recording. Indicate pitches with hands.
2. Discuss the five pumpkin faces identified in the song.
3. Assign children to groups representing the five pumpkins.
4. Perform the song a second time and ask each group to raise their hands when their particular pumpkin is named.
5. Read all the words of the song together.
6. Perform the song phrase by phrase, asking children to repeat by singing.
7. Ask children to point to the music chart as each pumpkin is referred to (Figure 2.1)

Figure 2.1

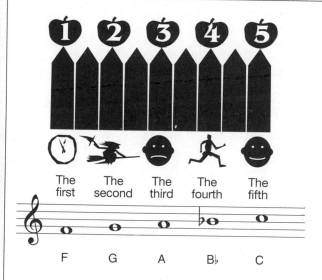

8. Have the class perform the song as a child plays the xylophone notes F G A B♭ C at appropriate times, noting that pitches are ascending.

9. Have the class perform the song as a child points to the appropriate pumpkin face.

10. Ask children to sing the words and music to "Ooo went the wind and out went the light, and the five little pumpkins rolled out of sight." Discuss which way "rolled out of sight" occurs (ascending or descending):

rolled___ out of sight.

11. Ask children to create a motion for "rolled out of sight."

12. Ask children to create motions for each musical phrase. For example, "five little pumpkins" could be five fingers; one finger = watch; two fingers = witch; three fingers = child doesn't care; four fingers = run; five fingers = ready for fun. The ending could be a swish with hands to snuff out the candle, then five fingers, hand over hand.

CLOSURE

Have the class perform the entire song with motions.

EVALUATION

1. Do the beginning pitches of each phrase go up or down? (up)
2. What are the names of these pitches? (F G A B♭ C)
3. Do the last five pitches go up or down? (down)
4. Does the class perform the song with the correct pitches and rhythms?
5. Does the class perform the song with good tone quality?

ADDITIONAL INTEGRATIVE AREAS

Reading, visual art, Halloween

"Magic Penny"

Activity: Performing a song
Grades: 3–5
Concepts: Form: ABA
               Rhythm: Syncopation
               Harmony: Chords

Magic Penny

Key: D
Starting pitch: D
Meter: 4/4, begin on 1

Words and Music by Malvina Reynolds

OBJECTIVES

Students will

1. Diagram the form of "Magic Penny" using colored shapes.

2. Create movements that indicate the form (ABA).

3. Identify syncopated rhythms found in the song:

4. Sing with energy and clear diction.
5. Accompany the song with the following chords:
   D F♯ A
   G B D
   A C♯ E
   E G♯ B

MATERIALS

Song (or a recording)
Autoharp (Omnichord or guitar)
Resonator bells
Tambourine
Colored shapes

Rhythm chart
Master chord chart and individual chord charts: D F♯ A; G B D; A C♯ E; E G♯ B

PROCEDURES

Preliminary Activities

1. Create some "magic" by "holding" and then hiding a magic penny.
2. Compare the magic penny of this song with giving love away. Help children discover that giving is also receiving.

Main Content

1. Play or sing the entire song (or use a recording).
2. Play or sing the entire song and select a child to hold up colored shapes for each section: ABA.
3. Sing or play the entire song and have the children create a movement for part A and a contrasting movement for part B. Sing or play the song and ask the children to perform the movements.
4. Teach the song phrase by phrase. Ask the students to identify rhythms that repeat.

5. Ask two or three children to play the syncopated rhythms on the tambourine when they hear them. (Syncopation is similar to a hiccup—the strong beat is *always* on the off beat.)

6. Lead the class in performing the song. Ask students how many times they sing/hear syncopation in lines 1 and 2. (7)
7. Lead the class in performing the song. Ask students how many times they sing/hear syncopation in lines 3 and 4. (5)
8. What is the total number of times that syncopation occurs? (19)
   Part A = 7
   Part B = 5
   Part A = 7
9. Ask the children to sing or play the entire song. Encourage them to sing with energy, clear diction, and good tone quality.
10. Introduce chords that can be played on resonator bells, Omnichord, or Autoharp (see Chapter 5). Invite the students to play chords as indicated in the musical score (for older students use one bell per student):
    D = D F♯ A A = A C♯ E
    G = G B D E = E G♯ B
11. Practice the accompaniment while the rest of the class sings reinforced by the syncopated pattern played on a tambourine.

CLOSURE
Perform the entire song accompanied by the instrumental ensemble.

EVALUATION
1. What notes are used in the chords D, G, A, and E?
2. Identify the repeated rhythm pattern.
3. What does syncopation mean? Can you find and perform syncopated rhythms in the song?

ADDITIONAL INTEGRATIVE AREAS
Mathematics, reading, "magic."

Fast and Slow Music

Activity: Listening to music
Grades: 1–2
Concepts: Fast/slow

OBJECTIVES
Students will
1. Visually identify objects that move fast and slow.
2. Demonstrate through body movements fast and slow, getting faster, and getting slower.
3. Orally identify sounds that are fast and slow; sounds that move gradually faster and gradually slower.
4. Identify expressive uses of fast and slow, getting faster, and getting slower in the recorded music used.

MATERIALS

Recordings:

Saint-Saëns, "The Swan" from *Carnival of the Animals* (slow)

Rimsky-Korsakov, "Flight of the Bumble Bee" (fast)

Honegger, "Pacific 231" (fast/slow)

"Kalinka," Red Star Army Chorus (fast/slow)

Record, cassette, or CD player

Pictures that suggest fast (auto racing, jogging, airplane taking off) and slow (turtle, person walking, leaf floating to the ground)

Word cards (*fast, slow, getting faster, getting slower*)

PROCEDURES

Preliminary Activities

1. Show pictures that suggest fast and slow.
2. Ask students to move their arms slowly, then faster; have them run and then slow down to a walk.
3. Ask students to dramatize a rosebud gradually opening or a candle melting down; a race horse bursting through the starting gate or a football player running for a touchdown.

Main Content

1. Ask the students to create slow sounds and then fast sounds. Experiment with sounds that start slowly and gradually get faster and fast sounds that gradually slow down.
2. Space students around the room. Ask them to move creatively as you play a fast or slow pattern on a drum. Invite individual students to take turns playing creative drum rhythms (fast-slow, getting faster-getting slower).
3. Play Saint-Saëns's "The Swan." Discuss the composer's choice of a slow tempo to represent a swan swimming on a pond.
4. Play Rimsky-Korsakov's "Flight of the Bumble Bee." Discuss the composer's choice of a fast tempo to represent a bumble bee flying past you.
5. Play Honegger's "Pacific 231." Ask students to place appropriate words on the chalkboard (fast, slow, getting faster, getting slower) as they listen to the music. After they have listened, discuss the composer's use of fast and slow to represent a train starting, traveling down the track, and then slowing down.
6. Play "Kalinka." Ask students to indicate where the music gets faster and slower. Discuss the different language sung by the chorus and tenor soloist. If there is someone in the class who speaks Russian or understands it, ask him or her to share insights with the other students.

CLOSURE AND EVALUATION

Play excerpts from "The Swan," "Flight of the Bumble Bee," "Pacific 231," and "Kalinka." Choose appropriate cards (with captions *fast, slow, getting faster, getting slower*) and ask students to place them on the chalkboard as you play the selections. (It will be a good idea to tape-record your selections so that they occur one after the other.)

REMINDERS FOR PLANNING AND TEACHING LESSONS

- Visuals must be large enough to see from the back of the room. Do not use yellow or orange as a color for printed text; they cannot be seen on white paper. The same is true of black on blue or purple paper.

- Be sure that your lesson is appropriate in content and musical concepts for the maturity level of your students. A song with a very wide range, such as "The Star Spangled Banner," is not suitable musically for young children. They can't sing that high or that low.

- Remember that kindergarten, first-grade, and even second-grade students do not read well and need help in following a chart.

- You are a *leader* in teaching. Be involved in your lesson. Get the children involved in doing something, responding in some way.

- Be involved in the listening; don't just stand and gaze at the floor or look out the window.

- *Always use a mechanical source for the pitch of a song.* Otherwise, most of the time you will pitch the song too low, since adult voices are generally lower than children's voices.

- Be sure that you start the song on the pitch given. If the recorder is difficult for you, use a guitar, Autoharp, or pitchpipe for the starting pitch.

- Avoid using colloquialisms, such as *OK* and *you guys*.

- Be accurate in teaching rhythm and melody.

- If you use a recording of a song, be sure to give the pitch and either mouth or sing the song along with the recording.

- Be sure that your lesson has sequence; don't "leapfrog" from one thing to another.

- Every lesson should have closure; avoid just stopping. Review to find out if you have achieved your objectives.

- Use terms accurately. For example, a *song* must have, or originally have had, words (if it is imbedded in a large piece). *Everything else is a composition or piece.* In other words, Beethoven's Symphony No. 5 is not a song but a piece.

- Know how to work the audio equipment (tape recorder or record player) before you begin your lesson.

- Recognize the cultural diversity that may be in your classroom and include music relevant to Native American, Hispanic, Asian, or other students.

SOME OPTIONS TO USE WHEN TEACHING MUSIC

If you do not play an instrument
1. Sing the song yourself.
2. Play a recording.
3. Ask a child to play the song on the piano. (Many children take piano lessons and are delighted to have a reason to practice.)
4. Ask a friend to tape-record the song (either melody, accompaniment, or both).

If you can't sing in a higher register
1. Use a recorder or melody bells.
2. Play a recording.
3. Use a child to help you start the song.
4. Indicate with your hand when the pitch should be high.
5. Guide children to sing an octave higher than you sing.

If you have a poor sense of rhythm
1. Use a child to help you keep a steady beat.
2. Use a metronome to help you practice the rhythmic and melodic patterns.
3. Use a metronome in class to help keep the class together.

If you have difficulty singing a song in tune
1. Use a recording.
2. Play the song on melody bells or recorder.
3. Use small groups of children as your leaders.

If you can't read music quickly or accurately
1. Teach songs that you have learned accurately by ear. (Save your music reading practice for when you are alone.)
2. Use recordings.
3. Try to feel the contour of the melody with your hands; don't depend on the music notation.

If you feel insecure in finding the starting pitch and getting the children to sing together
1. Practice using melody bells or recorder.
2. Play the key note of the song (D for key of D major, F for key of F major, etc.).
3. Play notes 1, 3, and 5 of the scale (e.g., C, E, and G in the key of C major). You may wish to sing the syllables *do, mi, sol* (1, 3, 5) to establish the tonality.
4. Play the first two notes of the song.
5. Sing the first two notes of the song.
6. Establish the tempo and say "Ready, sing."

If you don't know what to do when children won't sing
1. Be enthusiastic.
2. Give clear directions.
3. Select songs that need a lot of energy and are fairly fast.
4. Select songs that are fun to sing.

5. Select songs that have meaning to them and aren't just silly.

6. Set an example by singing or playing the song.

7. Add instruments as accompaniment (both harmonic—Autoharp, Omnichord, or guitar—and percussion).

8. Be sure the songs are within the children's vocal range.

MAKING GOOD TEACHING GREAT TEACHING

1. Know what you can expect from children at each grade level. Know each child in your classroom. Care about them.

2. Be an example. Students look up to you and seem to have a way of knowing whether you measure up to what they expect of you.

3. Be energetic and industrious. Stay fresh and inspired. Never stop reading and learning. Burnout is a product of an uninspired person. Read! Attend conferences! Give above and beyond yourself. Remember "The only things we really have are those we give away."

4. Learn to motivate both your students and the people you work with.

5. Be a dedicated teacher. Never count your time, and remember that the student is the most important person in the classroom.

6. Give freely of your love and your time.

7. Be the best musician you can be. Learn about music by performing it and attending concerts. There is no substitute for knowing what you are teaching.

8. Be active in teaching organizations. Learn all you can from others.

9. Use activity teaching. Students learn by doing.

10. Use quality music in your classroom. Good music and good materials are the foundation of good teaching.

11. Use good supplementary materials. Develop a library of visuals that will enhance your teaching.

12. Use a variety of musical styles: jazz, folk, electronic, blues, and so on.

13. Build your classroom teaching skills and a program that is educationally sound.

14. Be a firm, fair, and kind disciplinarian. Remember that you are the leader, and you determine what happens in your classroom. Everything begins at the top, and that means you.

15. Reward all good work. Don't make your awards necessarily competitive. Keep it simple—maybe a pat on the shoulder or a star on a good paper. Remember that praise is the very best reward.

16. Show that you care about each student (even those who try your patience). Be sincere and interested in each life.

17. Believe in the value of what you are doing. It is an anchor when the going gets rough.

QUESTIONS FOR REVIEW

1. What are each of the following as applied to music?
   a. Long-term goals
   b. Short-term goals
   c. Musical concepts
   d. Objectives
   e. Preliminary experiences
   f. Main content of lesson
   g. Closure
   h. Evaluation
2. Why is a visual helpful in making a child understand music?
3. Identify various musical expectations for
   a. Preschool-kindergarten
   b. Grades 1 and 2
   c. Grades 3 and 4
   d. Grades 5 and 6
4. How would you decide on the length and frequency of music lessons?
5. How would you develop multisensory experiences?
6. How/why would you develop multicultural experiences?
7. How would you use media in your teaching of music?
8. How can you integrate songs with other classroom experiences?

3

FUNDAMENTALS OF MUSIC:
UNDERSTANDING HOW SOUNDS ARE ORGANIZED IN A MUSICAL COMPOSITION

Music is an aural art form consisting of the organization of sounds in time. An understanding of music begins with the perception of its basic elements, which include melody, rhythm, texture, tone color, dynamics, and form. This chapter explains some of the basic characteristics of each of these elements and provides musical examples. You are encouraged to *experience* each of the characteristics of the elements through actual performance. When you finish this chapter, you should be able to perform or listen to short musical compositions and describe them in terms of the basic elements.

EXPERIENCES WITH MUSIC

A melody is a succession of musical sounds that are perceived as belonging together. Melodies are familiar to all of us. We sing, whistle, and play melodies from the time we are little children. While the rhythm or beat of a piece of music may dominate our physical response to it (toe-tapping, nodding,), we generally recognize a composition by its melody. As you give close attention to the features of melodies discussed here, you will increase your understanding and experience greater pleasure in performing or listening to music.

A MELODY IS BASED ON A SET OF PITCHES

Pitch refers to the highness or lowness of a sound. It is based on the number of vibrations per second. The unit of measurement for pitch is the *hertz. By* playing various pitches on the piano, resonator bells, or guitar, you can soon tell which are high and which are low.

A MELODY MOVES BY STEPS AND SKIPS

The distances between various pitches are called *intervals*. The intervals between the tones of some melodies may be small, while in other melodies the distances between the various pitches are quite large. If melodies move basically by steps, they are called *conjunct*. If, however, melodies move primarily by skips, they are known as *disjunct*.

Steps (conjunct)   Skips (disjunct)

"Join into the Game"

Activity: Performing a song
Grade: 1
Concept: Conjunct melody

Join into the Game

Words and Music by Paul Campbell

Key: C
Starting pitch: G
Meter: 3/4, begins on 3

Phrase 1

Let ev – 'ry - one clap hands like me. (clap hands)
Let ev – 'ry - one whis – tle like me. (whistle)

Phrase 2

Let ev – 'ry - one clap hands like me. (clap hands)
Let ev – 'ry - one whis – tle like me. (whistle)

REFRAIN
Phrase 3

Come on and join in - to the game;_____
Come on and join in - to the game;_____

Phrase 4

You'll find that it's al – ways the same. (clap hands)
You'll find that it's al – ways the same. (whistle)

"Reveille"

Activity: Performing a song

Grades: 2–3

Concept: Disjunct melody

Reveille

U.S. Army Bugle Call

Key: G
Starting pitch: D
Meter: 2/4, begins on "and" of 2

A MELODY HAS SHAPE

Melodies may go up or down. If you look at the first section of "Row, Row, Row Your Boat" and "Joy to the World," you'll notice that the general direction of the first song is upward, while the general direction of the second is downward. Perform those two lines and listen to the melody going up or down.

Row, Row, Row Your Boat

Key: C
Starting pitch: C
Meter: 6/8, begins on 1

Joy to the World

Key: C
Starting pitch: C
Meter: 2/4, begins on 1

Melodies sometimes move in terraces, starting at a low pitch and ascending in graduated levels, or beginning at a high pitch and descending in graduated levels.

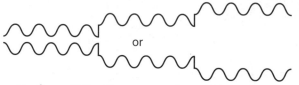

Perform "The Farmer in the Dell" and trace in the air the terraced melody moving from low to high in the first half of the song.

The Farmer in the Dell

England

Key: G
Starting pitch: D
Meter: 6/8, begins on 6

1. The far - mer in the dell,_____ The far - mer in the

dell, Hi! ho! the der - ry oh, The far - mer in the dell._____

Some melodies operate like a pendulum, undulating above and below one or several basic pitches.

Perform "Hickory Dickory Dock" and draw the movement of the melody on paper.

Hickory Dickory Dock

J. W. Elliott

Key: F
Starting pitch: A
Meter: 6/8, begins on 1

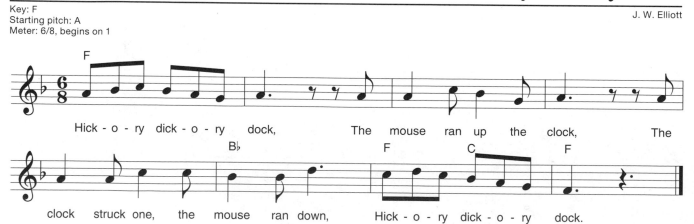

Hick - o - ry dick - o - ry dock, The mouse ran up the clock, The

clock struck one, the mouse ran down, Hick - o - ry dick - o - ry dock.

A MELODY HAS RANGE

As you trace melodies, you will discover that the distance from the lowest to the highest note is sometimes large and other times small. The term *range* is used to describe these distances. Some melodies have a small range, while other melodies have a large range.

Perform "The Star-Spangled Banner," and identify the wide pitch range (low B flat to high F); then perform "Old MacDonald Had a Farm," and identify its narrow pitch range (D to B).

The Star-Spangled Banner

Music by John Stafford Smith
Text by Francis Scott Key

Key: Bb
Starting pitch: F
Meter: 3/4, begins on 3

Proudly, ma non troppo

1. Oh,___ say, can you see by the dawn's ear - ly light what so proud - ly we hailed at the twi - light's last gleam - ing, Whose broad stripes and bright stars through the per - il - ous fight, O'er the ram - parts we watched, were so gal - lan - ly stream - ing? And the rock - ets' red glare, The bombs burst - ing in air, gave proof through the night that our flag was still there. Oh, say, does that___ Star - Spang - led Ban - ner___ yet___ wave___ O'er the land___ of the free and the home of the brave?

Old MacDonald Had a Farm

United States

Key: G
Starting pitch: G
Meter: 4/4, begins on 1

VERSE

1. Old Mac-Don-ald had a farm, E - I - E - I - O! And
2. Old Mac-Don-ald had a farm, E - I - E - I - O! And

on this farm he had some chicks, E - I - E - I - O! With a
on this farm he had some ducks, E - I - E - I - O! With a

Chick, chick here, and a chick, chick there, Here a chick, there a chick, Ev-'ry-where a chick, chick.
Quack, quack here, and a quack, quack there, Here a quack, there a quack, Ev-'ry-where a quack, quack.

REFRAIN

Old Mac-Don-ald had a farm, E - I - E - I - O!

A MELODY IS MADE UP OF PHRASES

Melodies often have several sections, set off from each other by a slight pause or point of rest. These subsections, called *phrases,* function in similar fashion to a phrase in a sentence.

Perform "Shenandoah" and listen to the phrases. Outline the phrases by moving your hand from left to right in the air as you perform the piece. Select different-colored objects, and as each phrase occurs place one object on a flannelboard. Point out that each object (color) represents a phrase in the melody.

Shenandoah

American Sea Chantey

Key: D
Starting pitch: A
Meter: 4/4, begins on 4

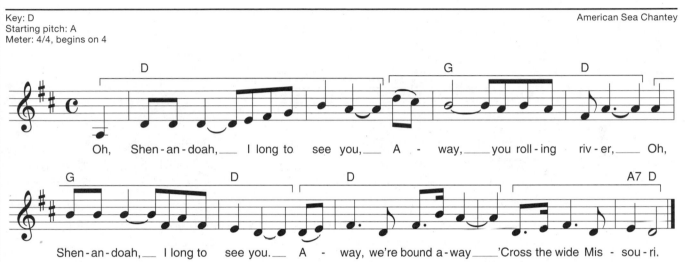

Oh, Shen-an-doah,___ I long to see you,___ A - way,___ you roll-ing riv-er,___ Oh,

Shen-an-doah,___ I long to see you.___ A - way, we're bound a-way___'Cross the wide Mis-sou-ri.

A MELODY MAY BE BASED ON A SCALE

Melodies are often based on scales, which are arrangements of pitches in an order from low to high. The two most common scales in Western music are *major* and *minor.*

Major Scale

ACTIVITIES

1. Place the pitches of the following major scales on a chalkboard. Write the note names beneath each note. Have the students sing the scales with a neutral syllable, such as "loo," and then with note names. Ask students to take turns playing the scales on melody bells.

C major scale

Loo

C   D   E   F   G   A   B   C

F major scale

G major scale

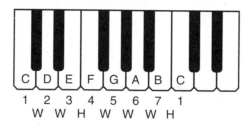

2. Point out that the distinctive quality of the *major* scale is due to its particular pattern of whole and half steps. Place a diagram of a keyboard on the chalkboard. Point out that the keyboard has twelve tones consisting of seven white keys (without any duplication of pitches) and five black keys. Between some notes, such as C and D, is an intervening black key; between others, such as E and F, there is none. If a black key intervenes between two consecutive white keys, the interval is described as a *whole step*. If no key occurs between two consecutive pitches, such as E to F (or C to C♯), the interval is described as a *half step*. The scale shown below has the following whole- and half-step pattern: W-W-H-W-W-W-H. It is described as a *major scale*. All major scales, regardless of the pitch on which they start, have the same pattern of whole and half steps.

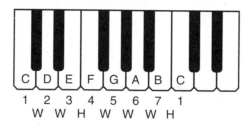

3. Have the students sing songs based on major scales.

Sweet Betsy from Pike

American

Key: C major
Starting pitch: C
Meter: 3/4, begins on 3

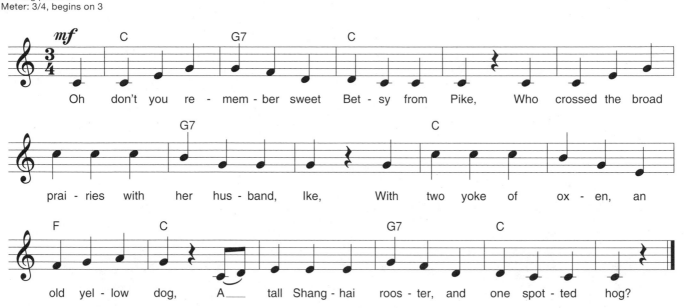

Oh don't you re - mem - ber sweet Bet - sy from Pike, Who crossed the broad
prai - ries with her hus - band, Ike, With two yoke of ox - en, an
old yel - low dog, A___ tall Shang - hai roos - ter, and one spot - ted hog?

Home on the Range

Traditional

Key: F major
Starting pitch: C
Meter: 6/8, begins on 6

1. Oh, give me a home where the buf - fa - lo roam, Where the deer and the an - te - lope play;___ Where
sel - dom is heard a dis - cour - ag - ing word, And the skies are not cloud - y all day.___

B Chorus
Home, home on the range,___ Where the deer and the an - te - lope play;___ Where
sel - dom is heard a dis - cour - ag - ing word, and the skies are not cloud - y all day.___

It's a Small World

Words and Music by Richard M. Sherman and Robert B. Sherman
Arr. by C. A. R.

Key: G major
Starting pitch: B
Meter: Cut-time (2/2), begins on 2

Minor Scale

In addition to the major scale, the other most common scale in Western music is the *minor scale*. The minor scale differs from the major scale in the pattern of whole and half steps. In the following D minor scale, for example, the pattern of whole and half steps is W-H-W-W-H-W-W.

D minor scale

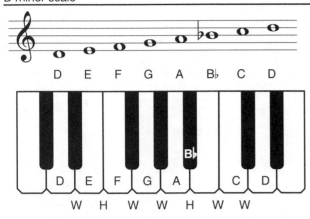

In many songs written in a minor key, the seventh degree of the scale will be raised (sharped) a half step. In the scales below notice that G, the seventh degree, is raised (sharped); when minor scales have the seventh raised, they are known as *harmonic minor scales*.

A minor scale (harmonic minor)   E minor scale

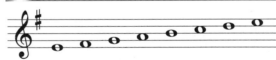

ACTIVITIES

1. Place the pitches of the D minor, A minor, and E minor scales on the chalkboard. Write note names beneath each note. Have the students sing the scales with a neutral syllable and then with note names. Ask students to take turns playing the scales on melody bells.
2. Perform the following songs based on minor scales.

Wayfaring Stranger

United States

Key: D minor
Starting pitch: D
Meter: 3/4, begins on "and" of 2

1. I'm just a poor way - far - ing strang - er, A - trav - 'ling through this world of woe; But there's no sick - ness, toil nor dan - ger in that bright world to which I go. I'm go - ing there to see my fath - er, I'm go - ing there no more to roam; I'm just a - go - ing o - ver Jor - dan, I'm just a - go - ing o - ver home.

Go Down, Moses

Spiritual

Key: A minor
Starting pitch: E
Meter: 4/4, begins on 4

1. When Is - rael was in E - gypt's land, Let my peo - ple go. Op - pressed so hard they could not stand, Let my peo - ple go. Go down, Mos - es, 'Way down in E - gypt's land;___ Tell___ old Phar - aoh, Let my peo - ple go.

Shalom, Chaverim

Israeli Folk Song

Key: E minor
Starting pitch: B
Meter: 4/4, begins on 4

(E minor)

Sha - lom, cha - ve - rim! Sha - lom, cha - ve - rim, Sha - lom, Sha - lom! Le

hit ra____ ot, le hit ra____ ot, Sha - lom, sha - lom.

Pentatonic Scale

In addition to the seven-tone major and minor scales, melodies also consist of other types of scales, such as the five-tone, or pentatonic, scale, which is extremely common in the music of China and Japan. Students can experience a pentatonic scale by playing the five "black" keys on the piano keyboard, such as for "Old MacDonald."

Pentatonic scale

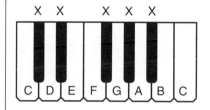

ACTIVITIES

1. Play a pentatonic scale on the white keys of the piano, the pitches C D F G A.
2. Create a melody on a xylophone using only the pitches C D F G A. You may wish to play some pitches more than once, or you can extend the melody higher or lower using the same pitches. The melody will sound more interesting if you place it in a meter.

3. Perform the well-known Korean song "Ahrirang." It is based on the following pentatonic scale:

Ahrirang

Folk Song from Korea
English Words by Alice Firgau

Key: Pentatonic (C D F G A)
Starting pitch: C
Meter: 3/4, begins on 1

Ah - ri - rang, ah - ri - rang, ah - ra - ri - yo.

O - ver the hills of Ah - ri - rang.

Voic - es call me from far a - way.

I must fol - low I can - not stay.

A MELODY MAY CONTAIN ACCIDENTALS

You sometimes encounter the term *accidental*. Accidentals are notes (sharps, flats, or naturals) that are not in the key of the song but are added for a particular effect. For example, in the song "I Like It Here," which is in the key of B♭ major, the notes E natural, F sharp, and G sharp are not part of the key but are used to make the melody more interesting.

B♭ major

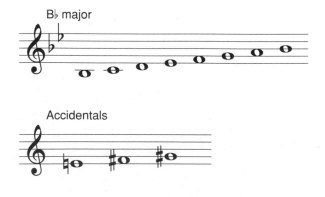

Accidentals

I Like It Here

Words and Music by Clay Boland

Key: B♭
Starting pitch: F
Meter: 2/2, begins on "and" of 1

A MELODY HAS A KEY

If you wish to play or sing a melody, it is necessary to identify the key. If there are no sharps or flats, the song is in the key of C major or A minor.

Major Keys

There are two ways of determining the major key if a song has sharps in the key signature:

1. You can identify the farthest sharp to the right (or a single sharp if there is only one) and move up a half step. The key will be named for that pitch.
2. You can identify the last sharp and then simply name the next letter of the alphabet.

In the example below, either method gives you the key of G major.

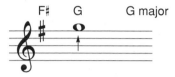

If there are flats in the key signature, you can identify the major key by simply (1) identifying the flat before the last, or (2) counting down four lines and spaces from the farthest flat to the right. If there is only one flat (B flat), you use the second method and count down four lines and spaces to F.

Minor Keys

Minor keys are related to major keys. The relative minor begins three half-steps below the "home tone" of the major key. For example, the song "Zum Gali Gali" is in the key of E minor, which lies three half-steps below G major. Note that both E minor and G major have the same key signature of one sharp.

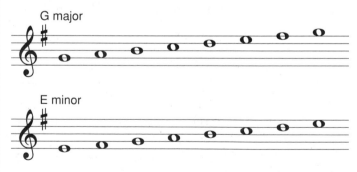

Zum Gali Gali

Israeli Folk Song

Key: E minor
Starting pitch: E
Meter: 2/4, begins on 1

CHORUS

Zum ga-li ga-li, ga-li, Zum ga-li ga-li, Zum ga-li ga-li, ga-li, Zum ga-li ga-li.

1. Pi-o-neers work hard on the land;_____ Men and wom-en work hand in hand.
2. As they la-bor all day__ long,_____ They__ lift their voice in__ song.

ACTIVITIES

1. Sing or play the song "Frère Jacques," which is written in the key of G major.

Key of G major

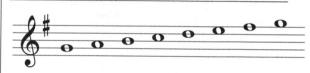

Frère Jacques

Round

Key: G major
Starting pitch: G
Meter: 4/4, begins on 1

ROUND

Fré-re Jac-ques, Fré-re Jac-ques, dor-mez-vous, dor-mez-vous?
Are you sleep-ing, are you sleep-ing, Broth-er John, Broth-er John?

Son-nez les ma-ti-nes, Son-nez les ma-ti-nes, din, dan, don, din, dan, don.
Morn-ing bells are ring-ing, morn-ing bells are ring-ing, Ding, ding, dong, ding, ding, dong.

2. Sing or play the song "Pat-a-Pan," which is written in E minor.

Key of E minor (harmonic)

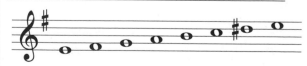

Pat-a-Pan

French Carol
Tr. Janet Tobitt

Key: E minor
Starting pitch: E
Meter: 2/2, begins on 2

1. Wil - lie, take your lit - tle drum; Rob - in, bring your fife, and come; Play - ing on the fife and drum, Tu - re - lu - re - lu, pat - a - pat - a - pan, We'll make mu - sic loud and gay, For our Christ - mas hol - i - day.

3. Sing or play "My Hat," which is written in C major (no sharps or flats in the key signature).

Key of C major

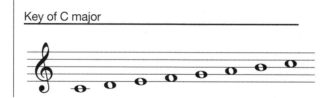

My Hat

Germany

Key: C major
Starting pitch: G
Meter: 3/4, begins on 3

My hat, it has three cor - ners;_____ Three cor - ners has my hat;_____ And

had it not three cor - ners,_____ It would not be my hat._____

4. Sing or play "Fum, Fum, Fum," which is written in A minor.

Key of A minor (harmonic)

Fum, Fum, Fum

Catalonia

Key: A minor
Starting pitch: A
Meter: 2/4, begins on 1

1. On De - cem - ber twen - ty fifth sing fum, fum, fum;
On De - cem - ber twen - ty fifth sing fum, fum, fum. On that day a Child was
born, all pink and white at break of morn, In a sta - ble dark and
drear - y lay the Son of Vir - gin Ma - ry, fum, fum, fum.

5. Sing or play "Home on the Range," which is written in F major.

Key of F major

Home on the Range

Traditional

Key: F major
Starting pitch: C
Meter: 6/8, begins on 6

Oh, give me a home where the buf - fa - lo roam, Where the deer and the an - te - lope play; ___ Where

sel - dom is heard a dis - cour - ag - ing word, And the skies are not cloud - y all day. ___

Chorus

Home, home on the range, ___ Where the deer and the an - te - lope play; ___ Where

sel - dom is heard a dis - cour - ag - ing word, And the skies are not cloud - y all day. ___

6. Sing or play "O Hanukkah," which is written in D minor (natural).

O Hanukkah

Jewish Folk Song

Key: D minor
starting pitch: D
Meter: 4/4, begins on "and" of 4

Reprinted from *Gateway to Jewish Song* by Judith K. Eisenstein, published by Behrman House, Inc., 1261 Broadway, New York, N.Y.

7. Many times composers label their pieces as being in a major or minor key, meaning that they are based on a particular major or minor scale. To hear what this means in terms of the sound of a piece, listen to excerpts from each of the following:

- Major key: Mozart's Horn Concerto No. 3 in E Flat Major, K. 447, "Rondo"
- Minor key: J. S. Bach's "Little" Fugue in G Minor

A MELODY MAY BE ATONAL

Some composers write music in which there is no discernable key at all. Such music is called *atonal*. One of the most distinctive traits of much atonal music is its *dissonant* sound.

As an outgrowth of experimentation in writing atonal music there developed a procedure for constructing music known as the twelve-tone system. In this system, composers construct music by first arranging the twelve tones of the octave in a particular order. The resulting *tone row* is then used as the basis for constructing a musical composition.

Activity: Creating a musical composition
Grades: 5–6
Concept: Atonality

PROCEDURES

1. Use twelve colored cards. Label each one with a note of the scale—that is, C, C♯, D, D♯, and so on.

2. Toss the cards into the air and have students pick them up one at a time at random. Form your own tone row according to the order in which the cards are picked up. Your row might look something like this:

3. Set your tone row into a meter. It might look like this:

4. Perform this "composition" on a keyboard instrument and then try another random toss of the cards. Write your new tone row and decide which you like the best.

5. Play the following twelve-tone row.

6. Listen to the above tone row as Schoenberg placed it in a meter for his *Variations for Orchestra.*

EXPERIENCES WITH RHYTHM

Rhythm refers to the organization of musical sounds in time.

RHYTHM HAS A BEAT

1. Play a recording of "Stars and Stripes Forever" by John Philip Sousa. Call attention to the strongly felt beat in the music. Ask students to clap to it.
2. Sing or play the Brahms "Lullaby" and ask students to sway gently from side to side as if they were attempting to put a baby to sleep. Call attention to the weakly felt beat in the music.
3. Discuss the different moods expressed by music with a strongly felt beat and music with a weakly felt beat. (For example, strong beat conveys feelings of action and excitement; weak beat conveys feelings of peacefulness and restfulness.)
4. Select popular music by such groups as Manhattan Transfer, Aerosmith, or Ten Thousand Maniacs and listen to songs that contain strong and weak beats.

RHYTHM HAS TEMPO

1. The speed with which the beat recurs in music is called *tempo. Compare* the relatively fast tempo of "Stars and Stripes Forever" with the much slower tempo of the Brahms "Lullaby."

Lullaby

Johannes Brahms

Key: C
Starting pitch: E
Meter: 3/4, begins on 3

2. Listen and compare the tempo of "The Elephant" and "Birds" in Saint-Saëns' *Carnival of the Animals*.

3. Sing or play a familiar song, such as "America the Beautiful," and experiment with musical effects created by performing at different tempos (slow, medium, fast).

4. Sometimes the tempo *gradually* gets faster or slower. Listen to Honegger's "Pacific 231," a musical composition about a train. Notice the gradual increase in tempo at the beginning of the composition as the train starts up and the gradual decrease in tempo near the end of the piece as the train slows down.

RHYTHM HAS METER

As the beat recurs in most music, certain pulses are emphasized or accented. The accenting of specific pulses establishes a pattern of strong and weak beats called *meter*. The patterns of beats are divided into measures by bar lines. In the meter signature, the top number indicates the number of beats in a measure and the bottom number indicates the type of note receiving a single beat. In "Hot Cross Buns," for example, the time signature of 2/4 indicates that there are *two* beats in a measure and that the quarter note receives *one* beat.

Hot Cross Buns

Key: G
Starting pitch: B
Meter: 2/4, begins on 1

England

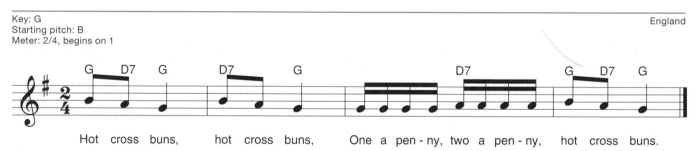

ACTIVITIES

1. In most music, the meter is organized in groups of either two beats (duple meter) or three beats (triple meter). Place the following terms on the chalkboard/flannel board:
   duple = 2
   triple = 3

2. Have the students chant the following in duple meter:

Have them chant the above and play a drum or clap on the strong beats.
Have them slap their thighs on beat 1 and clap on beat 2.

3. Have the students chant the following in triple meter:

Da - vid | and | Jon - a - than | like | to | play | golf | a - gain

Le - roy | and | Chris - to - pher | play | on | the | hock - ey | team

Have them chant the above and play the drum or clap on the strong beats.

Have them slap their thighs on beat 1 and clap on beats 2 and 3.

4. Have students sing "Hot Cross Buns" and then "America," clapping the duple and triple meter, respectively.

America

Traditional
Words by Samuel Francis Smith

Key: F
Starting pitch: F
Meter: 3/4, begins on 1

My coun - try! 'tis of thee, Sweet land of lib - er - ty,

Of thee I sing; Land where my fa - thers died,

Land of the Pil - grims' pride, From ev - 'ry____ moun - tain - side

Let____ free - dom ring!

5. Some music does not have any meter at all. Such sounds may be organized accord-ing to the text (as with Gregorian chants) or duration of a musical idea (such as Varèse's *Ionization*).

6. In music of some cultures, polyrhythms may occur—that is, a number of highly contrasting rhythms performed at the same time. Experiment with the following example of African polyrhythm by dividing the class into five sections and having each perform one of the rhythmic lines over and over. (Have the students count from 1 to 12 and clap on the appropriate notes.) When they perform all five lines simultaneously, they will have created polyrhythm.

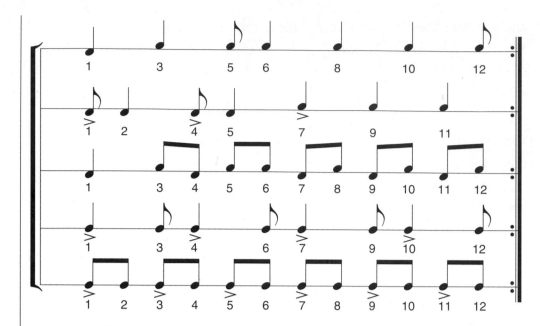

Bruno Nettl, *Folk and Traditional Music of Western Continents*, 2nd ed., © 1973. By permission of Prentice-Hall, Inc., Englewood Cliffs, New Jersey.

RHYTHM MAY HAVE SYNCOPATION

Sometimes in music, beats or portions of beats that would normally be unaccented are instead accented. This is called *syncopation*.

1. Have students clap and count the following pattern, emphasizing the strong portion of the beat:

2. Have students clap and count the following pattern emphasizing the weak portion of the beat:

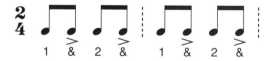

3. Repeat 2 tying together the second and third eighth notes in each measure:

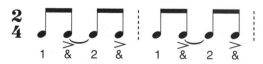

4. Have students clap and count the above rhythm with the tied eighth notes now written as quarter notes. Have them recite "Syn-co-pah" as they clap.

5. Sing the song "Five Little Frogs" and call attention to the syncopated rhythm.
6. Write out the first line of "Five Little Frogs" on the chalkboard or on a transparency; circle the syncopated rhythm.

Five Little Frogs

Words by Louise Binder Scott
Music by Virginia Pavelko

Key: C
Starting pitch: G
Meter: 4/4, begins on 1

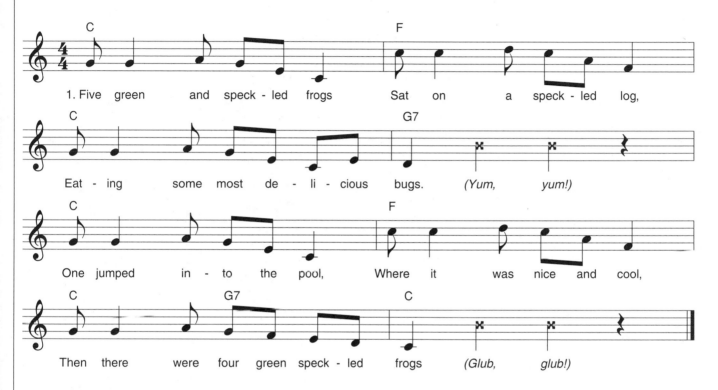

1. Five green and speck-led frogs Sat on a speck-led log,
Eat-ing some most de-li-cious bugs. *(Yum, yum!)*
One jumped in-to the pool, Where it was nice and cool,
Then there were four green speck-led frogs *(Glub, glub!)*

2. Four green and speckled frogs . . .
   Then there were three green speckled frogs. *(Glub, glub!)*
3. Three green and speckled frogs . . .
   Then there were two green speckled frogs. *(Glub, glub!)*
4. Two green and speckled frogs . . .
   Then there was one green speckled frog. *(Glub, glub!)*
5. One green and speckled frog
   Sat on a speckled log,
   Eating some most delicious bugs. *(Yum, yum!)*
   He jumped into the pool,
   Where it was nice and cool,
   Then there were no green speckled frogs. *(Glub, glub!)*

RHYTHM PATTERNS MAY REPEAT

Often a musical composition contains repeated rhythmic patterns. These help to tie together or unify a piece of music.

1. Have students sing "Five Little Frogs" and clap the rhythm of the song.
2. Ask students to identify the rhythmic patterns that repeat. Write them on the chalkboard.

3. Have the students clap the above rhythm or play it on a drum.
4. Sing the song again listening carefully to the repeated patterns.
5. Play several minutes of Beethoven's *Symphony No. 5*, first movement. Have students count the number of times they hear the opening four-note rhythmic pattern.
6. Word rhythms often match the musical rhythms. Have the students recite "My Country 'Tis of Thee" to the following music rhythm:

7. Perform only the rhythm to part 1 (up to the chorus) of "Erie Canal." Then perform only the rhythm to part 2 (chorus) Be sure to keep a steady beat (use Doo or Tah).

Erie Canal

United States

Key: D minor, chorus in F major
Starting pitch: A
Meter: 2/2, begins on "and" of 2

I've got a mule, her name is Sal, Fif-teen miles on the E-rie Ca-nal. She's a good old work-er and a good old pal, Fif-teen miles on the E-rie Ca-nal. We've hauled some barg-es in our day. Filled with lum-ber coal and hay, And we know ev-'ry inch of the way From Al-ban-y___ to___ Buf-fa-lo.___

Chorus

Low bridge, ev-'ry-bo-dy down, Low bridge, 'cause we're com-ing to a town; And you'll al-ways know your neigh-bor, You'll al-ways know your pal, If you've ev-er nav-i-gat-ed on the E-rie Ca-nal.

READING RHYTHMS

Music notation was created (and has evolved over the centuries) to show both the pitch of the sound (whether it is high or low) and how long (duration) it is supposed to continue. Musicians have created a series of symbols to represent how long a sound is to last. Figure 3.1 illustrates this system. Each of these notes has a name based on the idea of a "whole."

Figure 3.1. Symbols of duration: Music notation

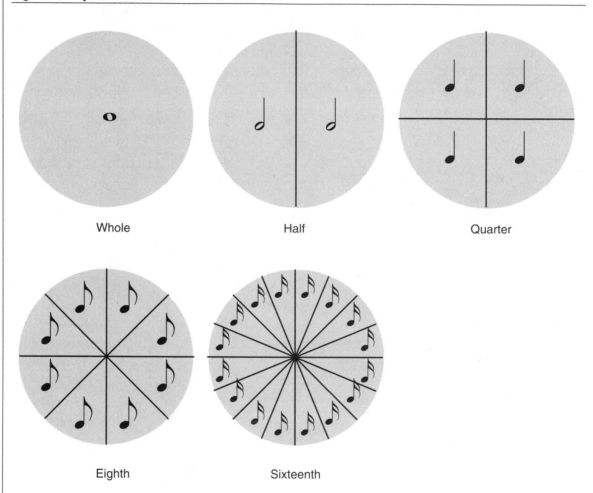

In Figure 3.1, each symbol represents half the value of the previous symbol; thus, two half notes equal one whole note (♩ + ♩ = 𝅝); two quarter notes equal one half note (♩ + ♩ = ♩); two eighth notes equal one quarter note (♪ + ♪ = ♩); and two sixteenth notes equal one eighth note (♪ + ♪ = ♪).

A dot (.) after a note is a symbol that lengthens that note by half its value. Thus, if a half note is to receive a duration of two counts, a dot placed next to it indicates that it will now receive three counts.

Here are some examples for you to try. Remember that 4/4 meter indicates that there are four beats to a measure and that a quarter note (♩) receives one count.

1. Bongo drums or wood block

2. Conga drum or claves

3. Maracas or hand drum

4. Ratchet (twirl) or tambourine

Music would be very dull if we heard only sound and no moments of silence. Silences in music are called *rests*, and there is a rest equal to every note. Examine the following table and note the shapes of the various rests.

Duration of Notes and Rests

𝅝	Whole note/whole rest	𝄻
𝅗𝅥	Half note/half rest	𝄼
♩	Quarter note/quarter rest	𝄽
♪	Eighth note/eighth rest	𝄾
𝅘𝅥𝅯	Sixteenth note/sixteenth rest	𝄿

Here are some other examples for you to try (instruments listed or of your choice):

1. Bongo drums

2. Conga drum

3. Maracas

4. Ratchet (twirl)

You may also create your own rhythm.

EXPERIENCES WITH TEXTURE

Texture refers to the number of lines of music being performed and to the relationship among different musical lines.

TEXTURE MAY BE MONOPHONIC

1. Sing "America" together in unison without accompaniment. Since there is just one musical line, the texture is described as monophonic (*mono* = one; *phonic* = sound).
2. Think of other examples of monophonic texture, such as a boy or a girl walking down the street alone singing a song or a single bird sitting on a tree branch singing.

TEXTURE MAY BE HOMOPHONIC OR HARMONIC

When melodies are accompanied by chords, the texture is described as homophonic or harmonic. In music, harmony is created when more than one pitch sounds at the same time. It most often occurs in the chordal structure of a musical composition.

Normally musicians speak of harmony as occurring within the framework of a major or minor scale. You have already experienced major and minor scales and melodies. Chords can be constructed on every scale degree by arranging pitches a third apart above the principal pitch. For example, in the C major scale the chords are as follows:

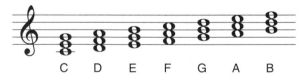

Chords most often consist of three pitches. However, some chords have four pitches. Such a chord is called a "seventh" chord because the distance between its lowest and highest notes is seven scale degrees:

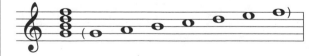

ACTIVITIES

1. Accompany "Merrily We Roll Along" by playing the chords on the piano, resonator bells, Autoharp, Omnichord, or guitar.

Merrily We Roll Along

Traditional

Key: C major
Starting pitch: E
Meter: 4/4, begins on 1

Mer - ri - ly we roll a - long, roll a - long, roll a - long.

Mer - ri - ly we roll a - long o'er the dark blue sea.

2. Play the chords C (C E G) and G_7 (G B D F) to accompany "My Hat" (page 54).
3. Play the chords G (G B D), C (C E G), and D_7 (D# A C) to accompany "Yankee Doodle" (page 475).

TEXTURE MAY BE POLYPHONIC

When music has two or more different lines of music being sung or played at the same time, the texture is described as *polyphonic*.

1. Sing "Row, Row, Row Your Boat" as a three-part round (class divided into three sections). Notice that when everyone is singing, there are three *different* lines of music.
2. Listen to the opening section (exposition) of Bach's "Little" Fugue in G Minor, particularly noticing the several *different* lines of music.

Row, Row, Row Your Boat

Key: C
Starting pitch: C
Meter: 6/8, begins on 1

Traditional

EXPERIENCES WITH TONE COLOR

Musical tones are distinguished from each other by the quality of their sounds. In music this is called *tone color* or *timbre* (pronounced "tam-ber").

TONE COLOR VARIES WITH THE TYPE AND SIZE OF MATERIAL PRODUCING THE SOUND

1. Explore ways to produce different sounds; for example, strike two sticks together, shake pebbles in various-sized cans, blow air across different sizes of pop bottles.
2. Listen to each sound and describe it with words.
3. Make a list on the board of all the different qualities of sounds you make. Notice that the tone color varies with the type and size of the material producing the sound.

EXPLORING TONE COLORS

1. Sing the song "The More We Get Together."
2. Create an accompaniment, first with tone colors created by mouth or body, for example
   a. Oom-pah-pah
   b. Oom-ss-ss
   c. Oom-deedle-eet
3. Perform as an accumulative song, that is
   a. Begin with Oom-pah-pah.
   b. Add Oom-ss-ss.
   c. Add Oom-deedle-eet.
   d. Add the melody, "The More We Get Together."
4. Create an accompaniment with the different tone colors of classroom percussion instruments, for example
   a. Use bongo drums with Oom-pah-pah.
   b. Use sand blocks with Oom-ss-ss.
   c. Use a tambourine with Oom-deedle-eet.
5. Sing as an accumulative song as in step 2.

The More We Get Together

Key: D major
Starting pitch: D
Meter: 3/4, starts on 3

Germany

The more we get to - geth - er, to - geth - er, to - geth - er, The more we get to - geth - er, the hap - pi - er we'll be. For your friends are my friends, and my friends are your friends. The more we get to - geth - er, the hap - pi - er we'll be.

Oom - pah - pah

Oom - dee - dle - eet

TONE COLOR VARIES WITH DIFFERENT TYPES OF INSTRUMENTS

Musical instruments can be classified on the basis of the quality of their sounds. For example, on *stringed instruments*, the distinctive sound is produced by vibrating strings, which are set in motion by being either bowed or plucked. *Wind instruments* produce their distinctive sounds with a vibrating air column, which is set in motion by vibrating a reed, "buzzing the lips," or simply blowing across a notch or other opening. On *percussion instruments*, the sounds are produced by striking the instruments with either the hand or a mallet or by striking several objects together.

ACTIVITIES

1. Find instruments at home or at school, or make your own instruments for the class to listen to and classify.
2. Listen to some examples of musical instruments from throughout the world and describe their distinctive tone colors. Include some electronic instruments such as those found in current popular music.

TONE COLOR VARIES WITH DIFFERENT TYPES OF VOICES

Singers can also be classified according to the tone color or quality of the musical sounds they produce.

ACTIVITIES

1. Listen to different vocal tone colors produced by individuals taking turns singing a familiar song.
2. Listen to recordings of women and men singing. Think of some words to describe the different tone colors of women's and men's voices (women's voices are generally lighter and thinner than the heavier, fuller sounds of men).
3. Play recordings of singers from different areas of the world (such as Africa, China, and India) and listen to differences in tone color.

EXPERIENCES WITH DYNAMICS

The term *dynamics* describes the degree of softness or loudness in music. Different dynamic levels are used by composers to help express various moods in music and to provide variety or contrast in musical works.

DYNAMIC LEVELS MAY BE SOFT OR LOUD

1. Sing the American spiritual "Steal Away," exploring soft and loud dynamic levels. Note that this song was sung by slaves on plantations and that it focuses on an "afterlife" with the words "I don't have long to stay here." Notice how the mood of the piece changes with different dynamic levels for various sections of the text. For example, sing softly the words "I don't have long to stay here" and loudly the words "He calls me by the thunder; The trumpet sounds within a my soul."
2. Use a megaphone (or make one out of cardboard). Talk into the small end for the sound to be louder, or talk into the large end for the sound to become softer.

DYNAMIC LEVEL MAY GRADUALLY GET LOUDER (CRESCENDO) OR SOFTER (DECRESCENDO)

1. Explain that a composer indicates "to get louder" or "to get softer" with similar symbolic shapes:

    (Crescendo)   (Decrescendo)

Draw the shapes on the chalkboard.

2. Sing "Steal Away" again, this time adding the suggested crescendos and decrescendos.
3. Create a short piece of music with classroom instruments, using different dynamic levels to provide variation or contrast.

Steal Away

Spiritual

Key: F minor
Starting pitch: F
Meter: 4/4, begins on 1

EXPERIENCES WITH MUSICAL FORMS

The term *form* refers to how a composition is put together. Most forms are based on repetition and contrast.

REPEATED MUSICAL IDEAS UNIFY COMPOSITIONS AND CONTRASTING IDEAS PROVIDE VARIETY

The most common musical forms are binary, ternary, rondo, fugue, and theme-and-variation.

Binary Form

As the name implies, musical compositions in binary form have two principal sections: The first is often labeled A and the second B.

ACTIVITIES

1. Sing "Greensleeves" and *listen* and *look* for the two contrasting sections, A and B.
2. Diagram the form by having students place sheets of red (A) and blue (B) paper on the board.

Greensleeves

Key: E Minor
Starting pitch: E
Meter: 6/8, begins on 6

England

3. Obtain two colors of transparent plastic and cut circles to fit over the fronts of flashlights. Listen to "Johnny Be Good" featured in the film *Back to the Future*. Have half of the students shine flashlights with one color on the ceiling as they hear the verse, and have the other half shine flashlights with a different color on the ceiling for the chorus.

Ternary Form

In many musical compositions an A section of music is followed by a B section, and then there is a return to the A section. In effect, such compositions consist of three sections, and the form is described as *ternary*.

ACTIVITIES

1. Sing "We Wish You a Merry Christmas."
2. Diagram the form with colored paper.
3. Explain that repeating the A section helps to tie together or unify the piece. The B section is designed to provide contrast or variety.

We Wish You a Merry Christmas

English

Key: A
Starting pitch: E
Meter: 3/4, begins on 3

We wish you a mer-ry Christ-mas, We wish you a mer-ry Christ-mas, We

wish you a mer-ry Christ-mas, and a hap-py New Year! Good

tid-ings to you where-ev-er you are; Good

tid-ings for Christ-mas, and a hap-py New Year! We

wish you a mer-ry Christ-mas, we wish you a mer-ry Christ-mas, We

wish you a mer-ry Christ-mas, and a hap-py New Year!

RONDO FORM

A larger form based on the repetition of a musical idea is the *rondo*. A rondo can be diagrammed in the following way:

Theme	Contrasting Idea	Theme	Second Contrasting Idea	Theme
A	B	A	C	A

ACTIVITIES

1. Using a drum to keep the beat, ask students to walk around the room. On a signal they should change the way they walk (backward, sideways, on tiptoe, on their heels, etc.). On a second signal, they should return to the way they walked at the beginning. On a third signal, they should walk a different way.
2. Repeat having one student hold colored cards marked A B A C A. As each card is held up, students walk in the appropriate fashion.
3. Listen to the third movement of Mozart's Horn Concerto No. 3, having the students make up movements to follow the form. Diagram the form on the board with sections of colored paper and letters.

Paper	Letters	Musical Idea
Red	A	Horn with orchestral accompaniment playing pulsating, driving theme
Blue	B	Contrast provided by smooth, lyrical theme played by horn with orchestral accompaniment
Red	A	Return to pulsating A theme
Green	C	Lyrical, contrasting section
Red	A	Pulsating theme from beginning

FUGUE

The fugue is another musical form based on repetition and contrast. The first section of the fugue is known as the *exposition*. In the exposition, the *subject* (musical idea) is stated in one musical line and then imitated in other musical lines. For example, in Bach's "Little" Fugue in G Minor, the melody begins in the soprano line and then imitatively repeats in the alto, tenor, and bass lines.

Following the exposition, segments of contrasting musical ideas known as *episodes* alternate with periodic returns of the subject. The episodes are particularly important in providing variety in the musical work. The repetition of the subject from time to time helps tie the musical composition together and provides a sense of unity.

ACTIVITY

Play a recording of Bach's "Little" Fugue in G Minor. Follow the diagram of events in the composition (see the table blow). If you wish, have the students provide a visual response to their listening experience by asking half of the class to raise their hands whenever they hear the subject, and asking the other half of the class to raise their hands whenever they hear the episodes.

"Little" Fugue in G Minor

J. S. Bach

Listening Guide to Bach's "Little" Fugue in G Minor

Call No.	Measures	Events
1	1–21	Exposition, main melody (subject) repeats three more times (in alto, tenor, and bass lines)
2	22–24	Episode, section designed to offer variety, contrast
3	25–30	Subject with selected voices in other melodies called counterpoint
4	31–32	Episode
5	33–36	Subject with selected voices in counterpoint
6	37–40	Episode
7	41–45	Subject with selected voices in counterpoint
8	46–49	Episode
9	50–54	Subject with selected voices in counterpoint
10	55–62	Episode
11	63–68	Subject with selected voices in counterpoint; conclusion

THEME-AND-VARIATION FORM

In theme-and-variation form, the theme is generally stated at the beginning. Thereafter it is repeated over and over, but with changes each time for contrast.

ACTIVITIES

1. Explore the theme-and-variation form through the following:
   a. Have students draw circles on the chalkboard or paper and then create many different ways (variations) of changing the circle.

   b. Have students print their names in at least eight different ways (using a different color, a different shape, a different size, curved lines, straight lines, etc.).
2. Sing the song "Simple Gifts." Explore ways of creating variety in the song by singing it faster or slower, louder or softer.

Simple Gifts

Shaker Melody

Key: F
Starting pitch: C
Meter: 2/4, begins on 2

3. Listen to the "Simple Gifts" section from Aaron Copland's ballet *Appalachian Spring*. This orchestral selection, which is based on the "Simple Gifts" melody, is cast in theme-and-variations form. Listen carefully and see if you can identify ways in which the composer changes each appearance of the tune.

Listening Guide to Copland's *Appalachian Spring,* **"Simple Gifts" Section**

Theme	*"Simple Gifts" Played by the Clarinet*
Variation 1	Variation (contrast) in tone color with "Simple Gifts" in oboe and bassoon
Variation 2	Variation (contrast) in tone color with "Simple Gifts" in stringed instruments; theme augmented
Variation 3	Variation (contrast) in tone color with "Simple Gifts" in trumpet
Variation 4	Variation (contrast) in tone color with "Simple Gifts" in clarinet and bassoon
Variation 5	Variation (contrast) in tone color and texture with "Simple Gifts" in the full orchestra

    a. Place pictures of the following instruments on the bulletin board:
      Clarinet
      Oboe
      Bassoon
      Strings (violin, viola, cello, bass)
      Trumpet
      Full orchestra

    b. Ask students to pretend they are playing a clarinet, violin, or trumpet. Have them hum the tune "Simple Gifts" as they "play" their imaginary instruments.

    c. As students listen to Copland's "Variations on Simple Gifts" from the ballet *Appalachian Spring,* have them point to pictures of instruments used in each variation.

4. Have the students listen to *Variations on "Pop Goes the Weasel"* by Lucien Caillet. Use contrasting shapes and colors to represent contrasting sounds in each of the variations.

    a. Listen to this piece again, having the students draw symbols to express each variation.

    b. Discuss each student's creation and mount the most original and best crafted on the bulletin board.

Listening Guide to Caillet's *Variations on "Pop Goes the Weasel"*

Shape	Musical Section	Comments
	Theme (after a short introduction)	The introduction is made up of many repetitions of the first two notes, *sol-do*. The theme is then played almost all the way through. Listen for the sound of the "pop," which the composer directs to be made with a popgun.
	Variation 1 (a five-voice fugue as Bach might have written)	A fugue is similar to a round, with different groups of instruments (or voices) playing the theme one after another. Listen for the pop played on the woodblock, then by a sliding whistle, and finally no pop at all.
	Variation 2 (a minuet as a countermelody with the theme below it)	After a short interlude in 3/4 meter, a new and charming melody is introduced—the minuet. After it gets going, listen for "Pop! Goes the Weasel" played on low pitches with the minuet sounding above it.
	Variation 3 (minor key, played by the violin as a gypsy tune)	Notice the change to a slow tempo and duple meter. Listen for the minor tonality. A long, elaborate violin part leads into the "gypsy" interpretation, with many fancy embellishments to "dress up" the tune.
	Variation 4 (a lively music box tune)	In sharp contrast, the familiar tune is now transformed into a high, twinkling, music box melody in waltz time, with a high-pitched "oom-pah-pah" accompaniment. Listen for the short, crisp, staccato style of playing.
	Variation 5 (a jazz version)	The orchestra swings into a syncopated arrangement of the familiar song. The tempo becomes very fast, and the mood is happy. Notice the accents falling on unexpected beats, giving a syncopated effect. Listen for a final "pop" played by full orchestra, including drums.
	Coda	A very lively coda ends the selection. Listen for the same tones heard in the introduction. They begin very high and then go lower and lower, exactly the reverse of the introduction. The last two tones are the familiar *sol-do*.

QUESTIONS FOR REVIEW

1. What are the following as they apply to music?
    a. Melody
    b. Rhythm
    c. Texture
    d. Tone color
    e. Dynamics
    f. Form
2. Why are "steps" easier to sing in first grade than "skips"?
3. Why is a melody with a wide range easy to sing in grade 6 and hard to sing in grade 2?
4. What is the difference between (a) a major scale; (b) a minor scale; and (c) a pentatonic scale?
5. What are accidentals? Why are they used?
6. What is the difference between tonal and atonal music?
7. Why is a song with a low A  difficult for young children to sing but okay for an adult?
8. Which of the following is an example of syncopation? Why?

9. In what ways are the following examples the same/different?

10. What is the difference between monophonic, polyphonic, and homophonic texture? Give a music example of each.
11. What are examples of different vocal tone colors?
12. What are examples of different instrumental tone colors?
13. What kinds of graphics would you use to teach the following forms?
    a. AB
    b. ABA
    c. Rondo
    d. Fugue
    e. Theme-and-variation

TEACHING MUSIC THROUGH SINGING

From a very young age children express their feelings through play chants and sound patterns that they experience alone or share with other children. Because singing is an intimate, highly expressive experience, it is an important way for a child to convey happiness, love, dreams, joy, and sadness.

Songs provide a rich storehouse of musical and literary treasures. Folk songs tell us of the way people from other cultures, times, and places have lived and worked, while art songs may describe such things as a waterfall or a butterfly. Hymns and chorales provide opportunities to express feelings of awe, inspiration, praise, and thanksgiving.

Children should sing for sheer fun and pleasure in a variety of recreational activities, such as games, folk songs and dances, and musical plays. They should also learn musical concepts like melody, rhythm, and form through the pieces that they perform.

CHARACTERISTICS OF THE CHILD VOICE AND CHILDREN'S SONG INTERESTS

Teachers need to understand children's vocal characteristics and song interests in order to set realistic musical expectations and develop appropriate teaching strategies.

The singing voice of a young child (boy or girl) is relatively high, light in both quality and volume, and often limited to an octave or less in range (lowest note to highest note).

Children singing

A clear, flutelike quality is desirable and should be promoted. Many children in today's television- and movie-oriented society have been greatly influenced by "pop" singers, and some will try to imitate their sounds. However, the teacher should encourage and nurture the beauty of the child voice, not an imitation of the adult voice.

Major differences develop between a girl's voice and a boy's voice as they mature through childhood. Initially the girl's voice is light and thin and has a slightly translucent quality. As she matures, she is capable of creating a bigger sound but retains the same light quality. When a girl enters adolescence, her voice becomes breathy, and she often temporarily loses the ability to sing high notes. By the age of fifteen she begins to develop the mature voice of a woman, and at this time the true soprano and alto qualities start to emerge.

A boy's voice is similar to a girl's voice until the age of nine, when it begins to develop the fullness and power we associate with such musical groups as the Vienna Boys' Choir. A boy's voice reaches its peak of clarity and brilliance *just before it begins to change*. American boys tend to want to sing lower than their European counterparts, and it is not unusual for a young boy, speaking in a high unchanged voice, to announce that he would like to sing bass. Allowing a boy to sing low before he is vocally ready is one of the most harmful things we can do. We need to acknowledge his wish to be "grown up" and can suggest that he sing the "lower" part of the song.

It is generally agreed that children must learn to match pitches and sing short musical phrases before the age of nine if they are to be confident singers as adults. By the age of nine, a child is becoming much more sensitive and self-conscious about singing alone. The ability to sing in tune and to sing increasingly complex melodies depends on carefully constructed singing experiences that follow the basic physical development of the child.

A child's vocal range varies a great deal. The musical term *tessitura* refers to the range in which it is comfortable to sing. Contributing factors include natural talent, maturity, and musical experience.

The appropriateness and interest of songs also varies with the talent and interests of students. Most of the songs in the basal series books have been tried and found to work well throughout the United States in a variety of teaching situations. A teacher should also consider whether a particular song can enhance lessons in other areas, such as social studies, language arts, or science.

As you gain experience in analyzing and teaching songs to children of different ages, you will want to refer frequently to the following outline of musical expectations.

PRESCHOOL AND KINDERGARTEN (AGES FOUR AND FIVE)

Vocal Characteristics and Abilities

- Voices are small and light.
- Children are generally unable to sing in tune.
- Singing range is D–A for most; D–D for some.

- Children can sing play chants and easy tonal patterns.

- Children can sing short melodies in major, minor, or pentatonic scales.
- Children can sing melodies with one note to a syllable.
- Children can sing with an awareness of a steady beat.
- Children can sing repeated rhythmic patterns accurately.
- Children can sing softly and loudly.
- Children can sing melodies with or without a simple accompaniment.

Song Interests

Preschool children like songs that tell a story. Consider how many nursery rhymes are little dramas: "Jack and Jill," "Little Jack Horner," "Polly, Put the Kettle On." Little children enjoy songs that give them an opportunity for natural expression. When they act out "Three Little Kittens Who Lost Their Mittens," they really become the little kittens. They are very much at home in the land of make-believe. Children also like songs that deal with familiar experiences: bedtime and wake-up songs; helping songs; and songs about friends, animals, the seasons, and special occasions.

EARLY PRIMARY: FIRST AND SECOND GRADES (AGES SIX AND SEVEN)

Vocal Characteristics and Abilities

- Most voices are light and high; a few may be low.
- Many children are still unable to sing in tune at age six.
- By age seven most children will be able to sing at least short phrases in tune and will begin to sing alone.
- Children begin to understand high and low pitches.
- Children can sustain a single pitch.
- Range expands from five to six consecutive pitches (D–B) to a full octave (D–D).

- Children understand the difference between a playground-shouting voice and a singing voice.
- Children begin to understand the importance of breath in singing.
- Children can sing melodies in major, minor, and pentatonic scales.
- Children can sing call-and-response songs, as well as songs in two- or three-part form.
- Children sing with attention to dynamics and changes in tempo.
- Children can sing rhythmically, accenting strong beats.
- Children can sing from simple music notation.
- Children can sing melodies with simple harmonic or rhythmic accompaniment.

Song Interests

At six and seven children enjoy songs about animals, community, friends, action (with movement or creative motions), pretending, folk games from around the world, and special occasions.

INTERMEDIATE: THIRD AND FOURTH GRADES (AGES EIGHT AND NINE)

Vocal Characteristics and Abilities

- Most children can sing a song in tune.
- Girls' voices continue being very light and thin.

- Boys' voices begin to develop the rich resonance of the mature boy soprano-alto voice.
- Children can sing rounds, partner songs, canons, and descants. There is little use of alto or lower part.
- Children have much more control over expressive qualities of singing, such as legato, dynamics, and sustained phrases.
- Children are capable of singing melodies or parts from music notation.
- Children can harmonize parts or chords by ear, such as thirds and sixths.
- Children can sing songs with more complex rhythms.

Song Interests

At eight and nine children enjoy songs about early America (Indians, Pilgrims), transportation, geography (New England, the West, the South), the circus, planets, and people and songs that express emotions. Songs from other lands (such as Mexico, Africa, China, Japan) are appealing because of their contrasting styles.

UPPER ELEMENTARY: FIFTH AND SIXTH GRADES (AGES TEN AND ELEVEN)

Vocal Characteristics and Abilities

- Unchanged voices remain clear and light; boys' voices become more resonant.
- Children show greater ability to sing in two and three parts.
- Children have a heightened rhythmic sense and respond to music with strong rhythms.
- Children tend to imitate the quality and style of "pop" singers.
- Some voices begin to change—that is, boys' voices lower, girls' voices become very breathy.
- Children can read simple music notation.

Song Interests

Children enjoy songs related to adventure, work, transportation, history, and feelings such as happiness, sadness, and love, as well as songs from other cultures and countries. Children also enjoy folk songs from America, songs about places or events, and contemporary popular songs. They like to harmonize and accompany songs with classroom instruments, especially guitar, Autoharp, Omnichord, and recorder. They are enthusiastic about dramatics and producing musical plays.

TECHNIQUES FOR TEACHING CHILDREN TO SING

While many children sing naturally, others require guidance and help in learning to use the head voice, singing in tune, and developing good tone quality.

CREATING AN ENVIRONMENT FOR SINGING EXPERIENCES

There are many ways to help children achieve readiness for singing. Songs sung to them by a parent, teacher, or friend provide an effective model for them to follow. Recordings of children's voices found in the many music series books, as well as recordings of children's choirs, should be used during the day, both before and during class periods. Children learn to reproduce tonal sounds by imitation. Hearing songs repeatedly will help the child relate to pitch, melody, and rhythm. In other words, children should be surrounded with many models of good singing and interesting songs.

IMPROVING POSTURE

Because the body is the "instrument" for singing, it must be held upright; that is, a child must sit or stand with shoulders erect, head up, and spine straight. Create games and draw analogies to improve posture. For example:

1. Ask the children to reach for an imaginary bar above their heads and to pull their bodies upward toward it. They should then relax and put their arms down to their sides.
2. Have the children pretend they are puppets and have collapsed on the floor. Then have them pretend they are being pulled up with a string attached to the back of their necks. (Children can take turns being puppets and puppeteers.)
3. Have the children pretend they are inflated balloons just ready to leave the ground.

TEACHING GOOD BREATHING HABITS TO SUPPORT THE TONE

Most children who cannot sing in tune, or in their head voice, have not developed the ability to support a tone with their breath. As they learn to "feel" the pitches, they will be better able to "match" the pitches. Have students follow you in the following exercises:

1. Sip air as if through a soda straw and release it on a hissing sound. Be sure to keep the sound steady and not like a radiator that has sprung a leak.
2. Sip air as if through a soda straw and let the air out on a high "Ooo" sound, descending to a low sound. Use this same technique to imitate sirens.
3. Pretend that your finger is a lighted candle. Fill your lungs with air and blow gently on the "candle," so that the "flame" flickers but does not go out.
4. Inhale quickly, as if you see a fumble on the one-yard line by your favorite football team.
5. Lean over from the waist. Let your arms dangle. Breathe deeply, expanding the ribs. Straighten up, and exhale slowly and steadily.

89

TEACHING MUSIC THROUGH SINGING

FINDING THE HEAD VOICE

Children who cannot sing in tune share a common problem: they are unable to manipulate their voices so that they can match the musical sounds they hear. The mind has to link the motor coordination of setting the vocal cords into action with the tonal image received by the brain. Before a child can sing comfortably, he or she must learn how it feels and sounds to use the head voice.

One way of helping children find their head voice is to strengthen the concept of different "voices." Try the following game:

Teacher: Let's see if you can use your different voices. First, listen to me . . . "This is my whispering voice."

Child answers (in a whisper): This is my whispering voice.

Teacher: This is my talking low voice.

Child: This is my talking low voice.

Teacher: This is my talking high voice.

Child: This is my talking high voice.

Teacher: This is my yelling voice.

Child: This is my yelling voice.

Teacher (on a single pitch): This is my singing voice.

Child (same pitch): This is my singing voice.

A second approach is to help children discover speech inflection. Start with speaking small phrases, such as Good $\nearrow$morn$\searrow$ing. How are$\nearrow$you? Gradually develop these phrases into tonal intervals, like the following (either sing or play pattern on melody bells):

Good Morn - ing. How are you?

A third approach involves imitating familiar sounds, such as the swooping up and down of a siren or the calls of the bobwhite, cuckoo, and cardinal.*

---

*Additional songs and ideas may be found in *One, Two, Three . . . Echo Me!* by Loretta Mitchell (West Nyack, N.Y., Parker Publishing, 1991), pp. 1–28. Especially useful are the ideas for using puppets to teach the difference between singing and speaking.

Developing the Ability to Match Tones

The ability to match tones is directly related to breathing techniques, ear training, a relaxed jaw, and singing with energy. Most children have sung childhood chants, like

Come on ov-er to   my   house

You can use similar chants to help them learn to match tones.

ACTIVITIES

1. Using a few pitches (such as G E A, in the chant illustrated above), create question-and-answer games. Because most adults sing too low for children, it is wise to use a pitch pipe, recorder, or melody bells to give the starting pitch or the beginning melodic phrase. Avoid using the piano. The tone is too heavy for young voices and they have trouble matching it. If a child cannot sing the response in the key in which you play or sing it, try to match his or her range and work from there.

Where is Jim-my? I'm   here.

What hol-i-day is   com - ing?   Val-en-tine's Day is   com - ing.

2. Using two toy telephones, create a telephone game. Play or sing a chant, such as, "Hello, how are you?" Have the child answer, "Hello. I'm fine," for example.

3. In the song "Listen to the Wind," invite children (Grades K–1) to match tones on the pitches C and A on the word *Whoo-ee*:

Whoo - ee

Note that *Whoo* is the easiest sound for children to sing and is most effective in developing the head voice. Playing these two pitches on resonator bells, melody bells, or recorder enables the child to hear the pitch he or she is trying to match. (See Chapter 6, "Teaching Music Through Playing Classroom Instruments" for a detailed discussion and suggested activities.) Many times even a young child can play these two pitches on the bells. You may need to mark the proper pitches with colors to aid in identification.

Listen to the Wind

German Folk Tune: *Cuckoo*
Words by Joy E. Lawrence

Key: F
Starting pitch: C
Meter: 3/4, begins on 1

(ONE CHILD)   (ALL)   (ONE CHILD)   (ALL)

Who - ee!   Who - ee!   hear___ the wind,   Who - ee!   Who - ee!   hear___ the wind,
Pit - ter   pat - ter   goes___ the rain,   Pit - ter   pat - ter   goes___ the rain,

(ONE CHILD)   (ALL)

Comes down the chim - ney,   Goes up the chim - ney,   Who - ee!   Who - ee!___ hear___ the wind.
Here on the win - dow,   There on the win - dow,   Pit - ter   pat - ter___ goes___ the rain.

You may wish to add the following percussion accompaniment to the song:

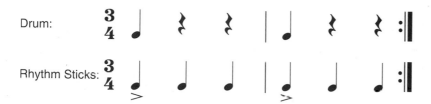

Drum:

Rhythm Sticks:

4. "Hello, There!" is an easy tone-matching song that is especially appropriate for kindergarten children, many of whom have played "echo" in the woods or in a cavern of some kind. Here the teacher sings and the children "echo" to help with the tone-matching process. Have the children sit in a circle, as you sing the song. Choose one child to be blindfolded and sit in the center and another child to be the "echo." The child who is "it" tries to identify the child who sings the echo after the teacher. Continue the game by taking turns with a new child being "it" and a second child singing the echo.

Hello, There!

Traditional

Key: C
Starting pitch: G
Meter: 2/4, begins on "and" of 2

Hel - lo, there! (Hel - lo, there!) How are you? (How are you?) It's so good (It's

so good, To see you (To see you.) We'll sing and (We'll sing and) be

hap - py (be hap - py) That we're all here to - geth - er a - gain._____

5. In "Going on a Picnic," ask children (Grades K–1) to be creative in deciding what to take. Reinforce the two pitches (D and C} by playing them on the piano or resonator bells.

Going on a Picnic

Words and Music by Lynn Freeman Olson

Key: F
Starting pitch: F
Meter: 4/4, begins on 1

Go - ing on a pic - nic in the park to - day— If it does - n't rain there's time to play.

Did you bring the _____ _____? Yes, I brought the _____ _____? Did you bring the _____ _____?

Yes, I brought the _____ _____? Read - y for a pic - nic, here we go!

DEVELOPING THE CONCEPT OF HIGH AND LOW

A basic skill in tone matching is to develop the concept of high and low.

ACTIVITIES

1. Show pictures that illustrate the concepts of high and low, such as a plane and a car, a child stretching upward and one kneeling down, or a bird in a tree and a dog lying on the ground.

2. Create a variety of movements indicating low to high and high to low. For example, children could stand and stretch arms high, then stoop low to feel the ground:

I am down low.   Now I'm up high.

3. Ask the children to be puppets on a string and pretend that their voices are being lifted up. Use a marionette to illustrate. Have different children "work" the voices of each other.

4. Have the children sing "Ooo" as they pretend that they are watching their favorite baseball player hit a home run. Voices should rise as the ball goes into the upper stands.

5. For those who have difficulty hearing their own voice, give the following direction: Cup one hand behind your ear and place the other hand in front of your mouth. (This makes an echo chamber.) Sing "Ooo" into your hand so that it sounds high and then low.

6. Repeat the following simple chant several times:

Dog - gie down low,   Bird - ie up high.

Change keys each time, gradually getting higher.

7. Turn a xylophone so that the lowest pitches are to the left and the highest pitches are to the right. Play low C followed by high C. Play the full scale from bottom to top (C D E F G A B C) then top to bottom (C B A G F E D C). Ask children to sing the ascending scale with syllables (*do re mi fa sol la ti do*). Ask the class if they sang high or low when they began. Compare singing the scale with a plant growing up tall. On a chalkboard or chart, place eight pictures of a plant or tree developing from seed to full maturity. Point to pictures as the children sing the scale.

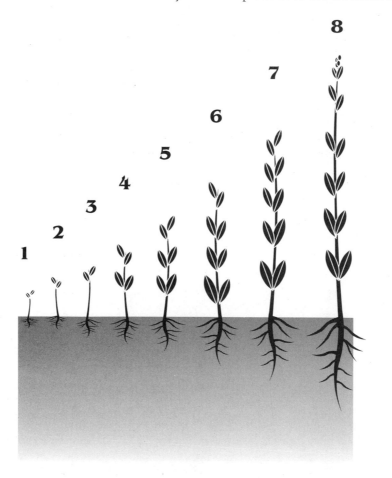

DISCOVERING PATTERNS

All pieces of music have patterns that repeat. These patterns may be melodic, rhythmic, or harmonic. Teaching a child to identify these patterns and then perform them shortens the time required for them to learn to sing songs or to listen perceptively to a larger musical composition.

ACTIVITIES

1. Examine repeated patterns in shirt and blouse material.
2. Show pictures with patterns that occur more than once.
3. Sing the well-known English song "Looby Loo." Point out the two rhythm patterns that are repeated. Have one child play the first rhythm pattern on a classroom percussion instrument such as rhythm sticks:

Pattern I

Have another child play the second pattern on another instrument such as a triangle. Be sure to choose instruments with different tonal colors.

Pattern 2

Ask the children to count how many times each pattern is played. (Pattern 1 is performed six times, including the D.C. repeat, while pattern 2 is performed four times. Notice that exact repetition occurs twice, with the third and fourth times slightly altered.)

Put the following scale pattern on the chalkboard or a chart and point to the notes as the class sings the verse to show how the song moves upward. These syllables correspond to the notes on the staff of F G A B♭ C. (Showing a scale pattern helps children know which way to make their voices go—up or down.)

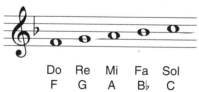

Do	Re	Mi	Fa	Sol
F	G	A	B♭	C

In "Looby Loo," the chorus is different from the verse, both in melody and in rhythm. Give the students flashlights with colored transparencies in them, and have children with one color "dance" their flashlights on the ceiling for the rhythm of the chorus and children with another color "dance" their flashlights for the verse. Of course, most kindergarten children will want to act out the words of the song and create additional verses of their own. This provides an easy link to rhyming and teaching the use of words in a language arts lesson.

Looby Loo

English Singing Game

Key: F
Starting pitch: F
Meter: 6/8, begins on 1

Here we go loo - by   loo,   Here we go loo - by   light.   Here we go loo - by   loo

All on a Sat - ur - day   night.____

fine

1. I   put   my   right   hand   in,____   I   take   my   right   hand
2. I   put   my   left   hand   in,____   I   take   my   left   hand
3. I   put   my   right   leg   in,____   I   take   my   right   leg
4. I   put   my   left   leg   in,____   I   take   my   left   leg

D.C. al fine

out –____   I   give   my   hand   a   shake, shake shake,   And   turn   my - self   a - bout.   Oh,
out –____   I   give   my   hand   a   shake, shake shake,   And   turn   my - self   a - bout.   Oh,
out –____   I   give   my   leg   a   shake, shake shake,   And   turn   my - self   a - bout.   Oh,
out –____   I   give   my   leg   a   shake, shake shake,   And   turn   my - self   a - bout.   Oh,

4. Play or sing other songs with repeated rhythm patterns and have the children clap the pattern or play it on percussion instruments.

The repeated pattern in the song "Jack-o'-Lantern," for example, is

This pattern occurs six times. Clap the pattern or play it on classroom percussion instruments as an ostinato:

Use a drum to keep the steady beat:

Teach the words and melody of the song by imitation.

Jack-o'-Lantern

German Folk Song
Words by Lois Holt

Key: D
Starting pitch: D
Meter: 3/4, begins on 3

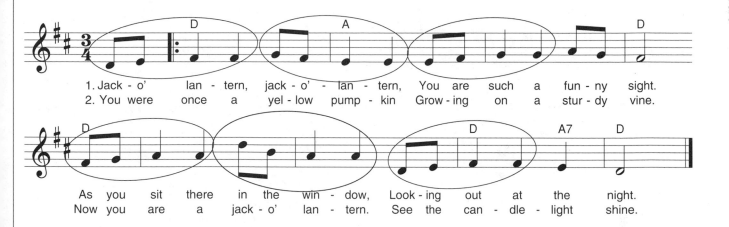

1. Jack - o' lan - tern, jack - o' - lan - tern, You are such a fun - ny sight.
2. You were once a yel - low pump - kin Grow - ing on a stur - dy vine.

As you sit there in the win - dow, Look - ing out at the night.
Now you are a jack - o' lan - tern. See the can - dle - light shine.

PREPARING TO TEACH A SONG

Follow these steps when preparing to teach a song:

1. Choose an appropriate song for a specific class or grade level. Refer to pages 85–87 for musical expectations and song interests of various maturation levels. Choose
   a. A song within a child's vocal capability (range and rhythm)
   b. A song with an interesting and appropriate text
   c. A song that may increase the child's perception and understanding of music as an expressive art form
   d. A song that can be integrated with other activities (when possible)

2. Analyze the musical materials of the song—that is, range of melody, rhythmic patterns, formal structure, harmony, and expressiveness of text (see the sample analysis that follows).

3. Decide on what musical concepts to emphasize, such as skips, rhythmic/tonal patterns, repetition.

4. Decide on what vocal techniques your class needs to work on, such as good breathing, using the head voice, tone matching, posture.

5. Determine the approach you will use to teach the song (rote, rote-note, note). In the sample analysis that follows, "Tinga Layo" will be taught using the rote-note approach for Grades 3–4.

6. Determine how you might integrate the song into other classroom activities, such as movement and social studies.

7. Prepare a lesson plan.

Sample Analysis: "Tinga Layo"

Tinga Layo

West Indies Calypso
English words: Margaret Marks

Key: C
Starting pitch: E
Meter: 2/4, begins on 2

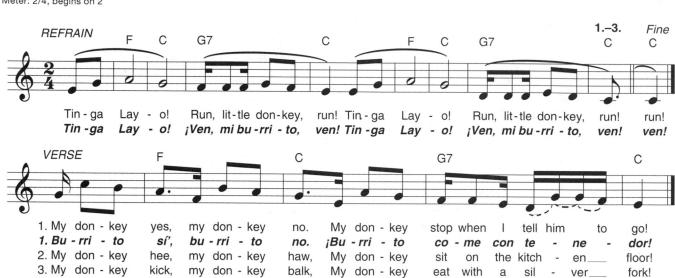

Permission given by Facultad de Artes—Universidad de Chile. Juan Amenabar Ruiz, Vice-Decano

EXPRESSIVENESS OF TEXT

Song should be sung moderately fast with lots of energy. It is important to observe both legato ("Tinga layo") and staccato ("Run little donkey run") as you sing.

MELODY

- There are two phrases in the refrain:

  Tinga layo! Run little donkey run
  Tinga layo! Run little donkey run

- There are two short phrases and one long phrase in the verse:

  My donkey yes
  My donkey no
  My donkey stop when I tell him to go

- The range of the melody is from C to C.

- The melody basically moves stepwise, with larger skips occurring in the verse.

- The melody is in the key of C major.

RHYTHM
- The meter is duple: 2/4.
- The tempo is moderately fast.
- The meter is the same throughout.
- Repeated rhythm pattern occurs in measures 3 and 7.

FORMAL ORGANIZATION
The song is organized in an ABA pattern.

TEXTURE (HARMONY)
The song can be accompanied on the Autoharp, Omnichord, piano, or synthesizer. Classroom percussion instruments can be used to create variety and interest.

Chords are C, F, G_7; or transpose to key of D (D, G, A_7).

Sample Lesson: "Tinga Layo"

Activity: Teaching a song

Grades: 3–4

Concepts: Expressiveness/energy in singing, rhythm in patterns

OBJECTIVES
Students will
1. Sing with good tone quality.
2. Sing with accurate pitches and rhythms.
3. Identify rhythm patterns by sound and notation.
4. Accompany song on Autoharp, Omnichord, or guitar and classroom percussion instruments.

MATERIALS
- Song
- Autoharp, Omnichord, or guitar
- Classroom percussion instruments
- Rhythm chart
- Chord chart

PROCEDURES
1. Emphasize the need for energy in singing. Review several breathing exercises:
   a. Sip through a straw and vocalize "Ooh" downward.
   b. Breathe and blow out two candles, one close to you and one at a distance.

2. Play or sing "Tinga Layo" for the class.
3. Play or sing the song again and ask the children to tap their thighs and clap on beats 1 and 2 (duple meter). Repeat, using a drum or tambourine for meter beats.
4. Sing or play the first two phrases of the song. Accompany yourself on a chording instrument. Ask students to clap the melodic rhythm (the words) and accent as you do. Sing the first two phrases again and have students sing. Emphasize the need for good breathing and energy in singing.
5. Sing or play the verse and have the students repeat after you.
6. Demonstrate the following rhythm:

   Using a rhythm chart, ask students to clap the rhythm.
7. Repeat, using a drum or maracas to play the rhythm pattern.
8. Ask students to find how many times the "musical picture" occurs in the song (four times if you include the repeat).
9. Ask the class to read both the English and Spanish words of the song. Read with expression—or example, legato for "Tinga layo" and staccato on "Run little donkey run."
10. Introduce the chords C, F, and G_7 (on Autoharp or Omhichord) or D, G, and A_7 (on Autoharp or guitar). Provide each student with a chord chart showing where the chords are located on a guitar (see Appendix B).

    Practice singing the song and pushing down an imaginary chord bar (any one will do for this exercise) and strumming at the beginning of each measure. When students can sing and strum at the same time, ask selected students to accompany the song, using only a single chord wherever it occurs. For example, one student might play C, a second F, and a third G_7. As skill increases, each student will be able to play all three chords to accompany the song.

CLOSURE

1. Sing "Tinga Layo" accompanied by a chording instrument (Autoharp, Omnichord, guitar) and rhythm instruments. Emphasize again the importance of posture, good breathing, energy, legato and staccato singing, and the crisp rhythm of

2. Extend use of song into movement activities (see Chapter 8 for ideas) and listen to other examples of Calypso music.

EVALUATION

Ask students the following:

1. Why do you need energy in singing?
2. What is duple meter?
3. What rhythm patterns are used in this song?
4. What chords would you use? (C F G₇)

LEADING A SONG

Before you develop techniques for teaching children to sing songs, you need to be able to *lead* a song. As with all musical skills, this requires practice. The more you do it, the more comfortable you will be in standing before a class and leading them in singing. You need to analyze the song to determine the following:

1. Whether you sing or play the melody accurately or should use a recording
2. The starting pitch and how to find it on an instrument or with your voice
3. The meter of the song (duple or triple)
4. On what beat the song begins and on what beat to say "sing"
5. What the text of the song is about and how it can be performed expressively (e.g., smoothly, loudly, softly, with or without accents)
6. How to end the song together

The following guidelines for leading a song will contribute to your success and will also improve the singing of your students.

1. Check the posture of the students and be sure that they are looking at you. Assume a posture that reflects the mood of the song.
2. Sing the song, perform it on an instrument, or use a recording to establish the key, tempo, dynamic level, and mood. Perform the entire song unless students already know it. Be sure that you reflect energy and pride in your performance, whether you are actually playing or singing the song or using a recording.
3. Return to the starting pitch or pitches and play or sing them for the class. Then say "1, 2, ready sing," or "1, 2, sing," depending on the meter and whether the song begins on an upbeat. Be sure that the speed (tempo) of your "1, 2, . . ." is the same as the tempo of the song, not too fast, and not too slow. It is important for students to begin with the first word rather than drift in along the way.
4. Lift your arm to indicate your breathing so that students will also breathe and sing together. Remember, good breathing, a lot of energy, and the desire to produce a pleasing sound are major factors in achieving good singing. The act of singing is *physical*, not *mystical*.
5. Give students a signal with your hand when they are to sing. You are *leading* a song, not just *singing along* with them. If you use a recording, be sure that you know the introduction extremely well and that you can count the beats accurately.

Figure 4.1. Conducting patterns

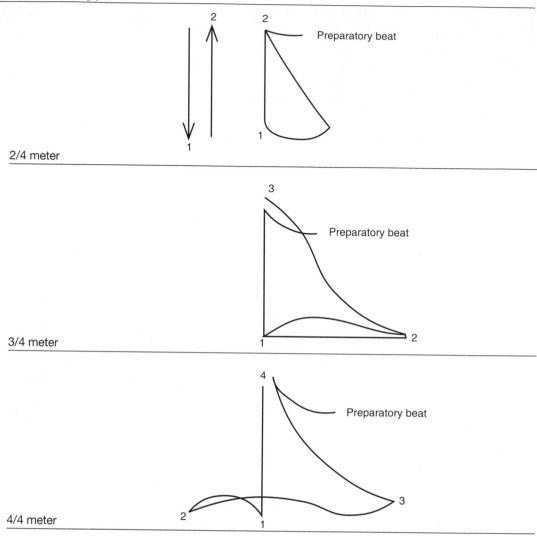

2/4 meter

3/4 meter

4/4 meter

6. Use the conducting patterns in Figure 4.1 to keep the singing together. Be sure that the "downbeat" is always on 1.

7. You may also consider "mapping" the melody—that is, raising or lowering your hands with the melody. Be sure that the style of the gesture fits the mood of the song.

8. So that they end together, give a clear signal to stop students at the end of the song.

9. Look at the students and be supportive. Praise students if they did well, but don't say "good" when the singing was poor. Give them specific suggestions for improvement and then try the song again.

10. Use imagination when leading a song. If students miss the meaning of the song and just "sing along" any old way, try different ways of singing so that students can express themselves with different moods.

11. Show pride in what you are doing. Become an actor or actress. Leave your troubles outside the classroom. Enjoy the music and make it fun. Both you and the students will enjoy it.

12. Practice leading the following songs, suitable for Grades 3–5.

We Wish You a Merry Christmas

English words: Margaret Marks

Key: G
Starting pitch: D
Meter: 3/4, begins on 3
Introduction to tempo: 123 / ready sing

We wish you a mer-ry Christ-mas, We wish you a mer-ry Christ-mas, We wish you a mer-ry Christ-mas, and a hap-py New Year.

Jingle Bells

Pierpont

Key: G
Starting pitch: D
Meter: 2/4, begins on 1
Introduction to tempo: (2 measures) 12 / ready sing

Dash-ing through the snow in a one-horse o-pen sleigh, O'er the fields we go, Laugh-ing all the way. Bells on bob-tail ring mak-ing spi-rits bright. What fun it is to ride and sing a sleigh-ing song to-night. Jin-gle bells, jin-gle bells, jin-gle all the way! Oh, what fun it is to ride in a one-horse o-pen sleigh! Jin-gle bells, jin-gle bells, jin-gle all the way! Oh, what fun it is to ride in a one-horse o-pen sleigh!

TEACHING SONGS TO CHILDREN

There are many ways to teach songs. The three that will be discussed here are rote (both nonconceptual and conceptual), rote-note, and note. You will find many ideas in the basal series textbooks. Most of these are not structured in perfect order for either you or your class, and you will find that adapting the activities may be the most suitable for your teaching skills and style. You may also wish to combine various methods with different songs. Remember that a multisensory approach, in which students hear, see, and physically respond, is one of the most effective.

Teaching students to read music is not very different from teaching them to read poems or stories. Teachers sometimes say, "But I don't read music," as if that is a permanent condition. You can learn to read music, and so can your students. The more songs you teach, the more confident and proficient you will become. While the saying "Practice makes perfect" may not be totally true, it is a fact that practice can improve one's musical skill.

TEACHING A SONG BY ROTE (NONCONCEPTUAL)

When you teach a song by rote, students learn through imitation. There are no materials in the hands of students; they learn the tune, rhythms, and words through aural memory. Short songs are usually taught in their entirety (whole song approach); longer songs require teaching single sections or phrases, putting the sections together, and singing the entire song. The following activities are intended simply to teach the song.

1. Perform the song phrase by phrase and have the students imitate each phrase in turn. Use your hands to "map" the melody, which gives students a visual reference that indicates whether their voices should be high or low and whether the duration is long or short.
2. Ask students to imitate the motions or actions you perform as you sing the song. Relate your actions to the words of the song so that they become cues to remembering the words. This method is appropriate for students in early childhood classes or primary grades.
3. As you perform the song several times, have students do a dance or play a game. Often students can perform the song quite soon because they have heard it many times.
4. Perform the song and leave out a little motion, pattern, or word. Ask students to fill it in at the proper time.
5. As students listen to a performance of the song, ask them to arrange, in order, pictures or charts specified in the song.

GUIDELINES FOR TEACHING SONGS TO CHILDREN

As you teach songs to children it is important to remember the following:

1. All children can experience some degree of success in singing activities.
2. If a child cannot match a pitch, it doesn't mean that the child cannot *hear* any difference in pitch; it probably means that the child doesn't know what it *feels* like to match a pitch. Conduct tone-matching activities regularly and frequently.
3. Good singing, like good speech, requires controlled breath.
4. Good singing, like good speech, requires clear diction and articulation.
5. Choose songs with a limited range for young children and beginning singers.
6. Pitch songs for the children, not for the teacher. Generally an adult voice is much lower than a child's voice. Use a mechanical source to find the pitch (a pitch pipe, recorder, piano, or Autoharp). Transpose melodies that are too high or too low. (See p. 210 for specific activities involving transposition.)
7. Male teachers should use melody instruments as an aid in leading and teaching songs. They should *not* sing falsetto but in their own range. Children will sing one octave higher.
8. Choose a variety of songs representative of different moods, tempos, tonalities, forms, rhythms, and melodies.
9. Choose songs representative of different cultures—both Western and non-Western. Include folk, art, patriotic, "fun," ethnic, popular, and children's songs.
10. Choose songs "for the moment" as well as songs of permanent value.
11. It will be helpful if you can answer the following questions when deciding to use a particular song:
    a. Is it musically expressive? Does it have a sense of completeness and beauty?
    b. Is the melody easily singable? Does it have a comfortable singing range? Are the intervals between notes easily singable?
    c. Is the rhythm interesting?
    d. Is there sufficient repetition and contrast to make the song interesting?
    e. Are the text and length of the song appropriate for a child's maturity and musical level?
    f. Do the words appropriately fit the melody and rhythm?
    g. Does the song fit the objectives for the lesson? For example, if your aim is to develop an awareness of ascending and descending melodies, the song must have these characteristics.

Sample Lesson Plan: Nonconceptual Rote Learning

Activity: Singing the song "Michael Finnegan"

Grades: 3–4

Concepts: Rhythm: Duple meter

Harmony: Chords F, C

Melody: Repeated phrases

Michael Finnegan

Children's Game Song

Key: F
Starting pitch: C
Meter: 2/4, begins on upbeat

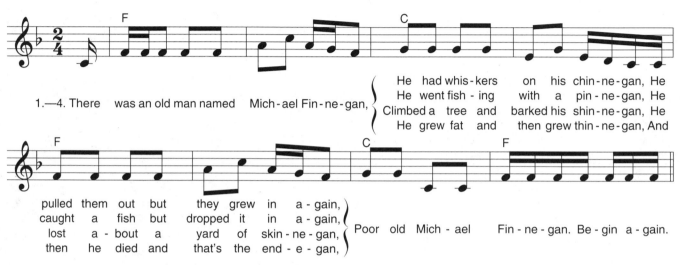

Silver Burdett Music, © 1981. By permission of Silver Burdett Company.

OBJECTIVES

Students will sing the song expressively with

1. Good tone quality.
2. Correct pitches.
3. Correct rhythms.
4. Correct words.

MATERIALS

Recorder or melody bells, piano, Autoharp, or Omnichord, or a recording of the song

PROCEDURES

1. Sing or play (recorder, melody bells, piano, Autoharp, or Omnichord, recording) the first verse.
2. Read the words to verse 1. Ask students to identify words that rhyme: Finnegan, chinnegan, in again, begin again.
3. Discover rhythm patterns that are repeated:

4. Sing or play the song again. This time, ask children to clap the meter with you. It is in duple meter with two pulses per measure.

5. Sing each phrase and ask students to imitate. (There are four phrases; repeat each as necessary.)

6. Sing again combining phrases 1 and 2, then 3 and 4.

7. You are now ready to have students sing the entire song. Do the following in order:

a. Play the F major triad (to set the tonality or key feeling): F A C A F.

b. Play the first two notes of the song: C, F.

c. Think the tempo of the song (remember to keep the same tempo). Play four F major chords on Autoharp or piano, and at the same time say "1, 2,1, sing." (Note that the song begins on an upbeat.)

8. Follow the same procedure to teach each verse.

CLOSURE

Sing the song and accompany on appropriate instruments.

EVALUATION

1. Identify those melodic phrases that are the same.

2. Name the words that rhyme. Where do you find them?

3. What does 2/4 mean?

4. Create a pattern and clap it in duple meter. Create a second pattern and clap it in triple meter.

5. Play an F chord on a chording instrument.

TEACHING A SONG BY ROTE (CONCEPTUAL)

In teaching a song by rote with a conceptual emphasis, you focus on some aspect of the song, such as ascending or descending melody, duple meter, beat, or repetition of melodic or rhythmic pattern. While no notation as such is used, students participate in many activities of an imitative nature. For example, you might clap the duple meter of the song, accenting the first beat. Or you might have students raise their hands when the melody goes up, and lower their hands when the melody goes down. The following teaching strategies focus on a particular concept.

• **Rhythm:** Focus the students' attention on an aspect of rhythm. For instance, you could clap a rhythm pattern from the song and ask the children to echo it. This could be extended to saying the words or playing the particular rhythm on a classroom percussion instrument.

• **Pitch:** Focus the students' attention on an aspect of pitch. You could "map" the melody, indicating where it goes high or low or has long or short durations. Tone matching might be included as you ask students to imitate a high pitch or a short pitch pattern. You could also ask students to sing the melody patterns or play them on resonator bells or xylophone.

• **Dynamics:** You could sing the song inappropriately and ask students what purpose loud and soft serves. They can discover which dynamics are most suitable for a particular song or phrase.

• **Form:** Focus the students' attention on an aspect of form. Guide the students in discovering the form of the song, such as AB or ABA. Some of the activities in the following sample lesson plan will help students discover which sections of the song are the same and which are different. Perceiving how a song is put together can contribute to speed in learning.

Sample Lesson Plan: Conceptual Rote Learning

Activity: Singing the song "Michael Finnegan"
Grades: 2–4
Concepts: Rhythm: Duple meter
       Harmony: Chords F, C

OBJECTIVES
Students will
  1. Sing with good tone quality.
  2. Sing with correct melody and rhythms.
  3. Identify and perform duple meter.
  4. Accompany the song on a chording instrument using the F and C chords.

MATERIALS
  • Autoharp, Omnichord, or guitar
  • Classroom percussion instruments

PROCEDURES
  1. Perform the song "Michael Finnegan" in its entirety.
  2. Read the words to verse 1. Ask students to identify words that rhyme: Finnegan, chinnegan, in again, begin again.
  3. Ask students to identify rhythm patterns that are repeated. Have students echo you as you chant them:

Mich - ael   Fin -ne -gan;   on   his   chin -ne -gan;   they   grew   in   a -gain

  4. Sing the words to the song phrase by phrase. (There are four phrases.) Ask students to sing each phrase after you.
  5. Sing or play the song again. This time ask students to clap the meter with you. (It is in duple meter with two pulses per measure.)

6. Assign half of the class to sing the song while the other half claps the duple meter, accenting the first beat. Switch assignments and sing through again. Add percussion instruments such as rhythm sticks or claves.

7. Play the two accompaniment chords (F, C) on the Autoharp or Omnichord. Use a plastic card to make a louder sound. Ask an individual student to strum these chords.

CLOSURE

Have the class sing "Michael Finnegan" accompanied by Autoharp or Omnichord and percussion instruments.

EVALUATION

1. Identify those melodic phrases that are the same.
2. Name words that rhyme and find them in the music.
3. Name, play, and sing the melodic/rhythmic pattern.
4. What does duple meter mean? What does triple meter mean? Which is in the time signature of this song? How do you know?
5. Why would you choose the chords F and C to play and accompany this song?

TEACHING A SONG BY ROTE-NOTE

Teaching a song by the rote-note method involves not only imitating what is heard but also recognizing short melodic or rhythm patterns. You can combine media such as flash cards or posters with the playing or singing of melodic and rhythmic patterns to introduce experiences with music notation.

Sample Lesson Plan: Rote-Note Learning

Activity: Singing the song "Michael Finnegan"
Grades: 2–4
Concepts: Melody: repetition of phrases and pitches

OBJECTIVES

Students will

1. Recognize repeated phrases of the melody.
2. Recognize repeated pitches of the melody.

MATERIALS

- Accompanying instrument (Autoharp, , Omnichord, guitar, or piano)
- Charts with repeated patterns
- Colored strips of paper
- Coloring materials
- Copies of song

PROCEDURES

1. Sing or play the song "Michael Finnegan."
2. Use colored strips of paper to represent each phrase—for example, use red for phrase 1, "There was an old man named Michael Finnegan"; yellow for phrase 2, "He had whiskers on his chinnegan"; red for phrase 3, "He pulled them out but they grew in again"; green for phrase 4, "Poor old Michael Finnegan, Begin again." Ask students which phrases are repeated (1 and 4).
3. Use copies of the song so that students can mark the music with colors. Ask them to mark the music with colors that correspond to the strips of paper.
4. Compare the notation of the contrasting phrases. What is different? What is similar? What is the same?
5. Play the five repeated pitches in the first measure of the song (F F F F F). Call attention to their being the same. Play the four repeated pitches in the second phrase (G G G G). Repeat procedure for the third (F F F F) and fourth (F F F F F F F) phrases.
6. Sing or play song again. Give the starting two pitches (C and F) and ask students to sing the song, tracing in the air the outline of the melody as they sing.

CLOSURE AND EVALUATION

1. Play or sing "Michael Finnegan" again. Invite students to raise their hands when they hear four or more pitches that are the same. Ask them to locate these repeated pitches on their copies.
2. Have students locate phrases of the song where the pitches are not the same.

TEACHING A SONG BY NOTE: THE KODÁLY APPROACH

Teaching a song by note means to teach students to read the music notation. This requires preparation in understanding and conceptualizing the abstract symbols that represent the various elements in music, such as melody, rhythm, and harmony. In teaching most songs to elementary-age children, you will rely heavily on the rote or rote-note approach, but you should introduce the reading of music notation at an early age.

It is important that a child's experience with the sounds of music precede contact with visual symbols. Symbols of musical notation take on meaning only when they can be connected to a tonal or rhythmic grouping that has been sung or played. The approach to music reading in this book is based on the Kodály system of tonal and rhythm syllables as practiced in American schools. It is an adaptation of a method of music education developed by the Hungarian composer/educator Zoltán Kodály (1882–1967), who created a method based on the Hungarian language and folk music. The method stresses good singing and music literacy—the ability to read music. While rhymes and children's game songs are important, body movement is also an important means of learning.

The Kodály approach focuses on a balance of singing, listening, playing, moving, thinking, and creating. In the Kodály method, pitch discrimination and the concepts of high and low are taught first. Hand signs (adapted from John Curwen's approach in England) contribute to learning music through a combination of eye (seeing), ear (hearing), and body (moving). The philosophy of the Kodály approach is as follows:

1. All people capable of lingual literacy are also capable of musical literacy. Learning to read music, like learning to read words, is a taught skill. Knowing how to read this language increases the quality of life itself.
2. Singing is the best foundation for musicianship. Singing is as natural an activity as speaking. It is through singing that musical knowledge can be internalized.
3. To be most effective, music education must begin with the very young child. It is in his or her early years that a child acquires discrimination in pitch as well as language.
4. The folk songs of a child's own linguistic heritage constitute a musical "mother tongue" and therefore should be the vehicle for all early instruction. The natural patterns of rhythm and melody are found in folk music of all cultures. Through folk music, children can gain a sense of identity with the present and continuity with the past.
5. Only music of the highest artistic value, both folk and composed, should be used in teaching. All music used with children should have intrinsic value, for it is from this heritage that the child will learn to value good music.
6. Music should be at the heart of the curriculum: a core subject used as a basis for education. Music contributes to all phases of a child's development: emotionally, intellectually, physically, and aesthetically.

The tools of the Kodály method are (1) the tone syllables *do, re, mi, fa, sol, la, ti, do;* (2) hand signs; and (3) rhythm duration syllables.

The first tool, tone syllables, is based on tonality, and one purpose of this approach is to develop the ear to hear and perform tonal patterns (see Figure 4.2).*

Figure 4.2. Tonal syllables: Movable do

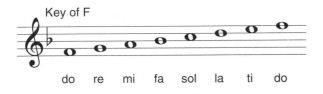

*Lawrence Wheeler and Lois Raebeck, *Orff and Kodály Adapted for the Elementary School,* 3rd ed. (Dubuque, Iowa: Wm. C. Brown, 1985).

Figure 4.3. Curwen-Kodály hand signs

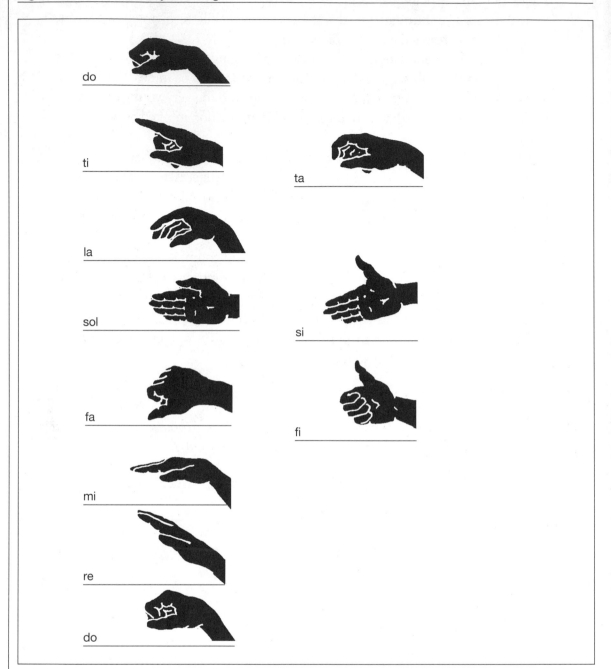

The second tool of the Kodály approach is the use of hand signs. Originally developed by John Curwen in England in 1870, and somewhat altered and changed for use in Hungarian schools, these hand signs have become an invaluable teaching aid (see Figure 4.3).

The third tool of the Kodály method is rhythm duration syllables. Rhythm is taught by patterns and by relative durations over the beat. The rhythm syllables (see Figure 4.4) are used widely in North America. For a detailed discussion of Kodály methodology, see Nye and Nye, *Music in the Elementary School,* 6th ed. (Englewood Cliffs, N.J.: Prentice-Hall, 1992), and Choksy and Abramson, *Teaching Music in the Twentieth Century* (Englewood Cliffs, N.J.: Prentice-Hall, 1986).

Figure 4.4. Chart of rhythm syllables (Kodály)

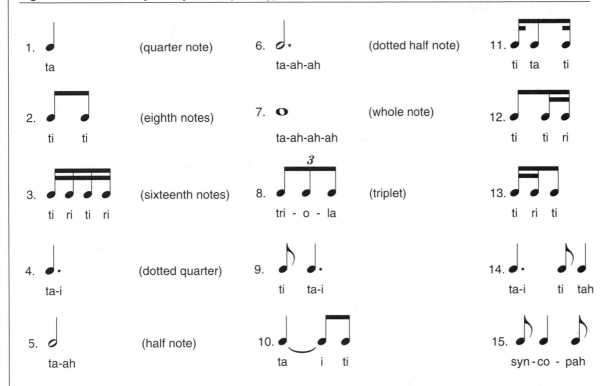

Sample Lesson

Activity: Singing the song "Michael Finnegan" by reading music notation
Grades: 3–5
Concepts: Tonal syllables (do, re, mi, fa, sol, la, ti, do)

   Rhythm syllables: ♩♩ Ti-ti; Ti-ri-ti-ri

OBJECTIVES

The student will

1. Sing the song by reading the correct pitches using tonal syllables.
2. Sing the song by reading the correct rhythms using rhythm syllables.
3. Sing the song with energy and enthusiasm.

MATERIALS

   • Charts with tonal syllable patterns such as *do mi sol, mi re do, sol do, re sol do, ti la sol*
   • Chart with tonal scale
   • Chart with rhythm syllables
   • Autoharp, Omnichord, or guitar; resonator bells

PROCEDURES

1. Discuss the value of reading music and compare it to reading words. For example, reading music saves time and allows the student to learn many more songs. Reading music also provides the student with a skill that can enhance all music experiences and activities.
2. Review the meter (2/4) and the key (F major).
3. Sing the F major scale from *do* to *sol* (not the full octave). Practice singing the intervals using charts showing the patterns of the song.
4. Create a game using any combination of *do, re, mi, fa, sol.* Appoint a student as leader and have the rest of the class echo. Use resonator bells or xylophones in place of singing if you wish.
5. Play or sing the song and have students clap the meter beats (1 2 1 2).
6. Introduce rhythm patterns by playing or singing the following for students and having them imitate:

7. Introduce rhythm syllables used in the song:

8. Place the following patterns on charts and ask students to read them using rhythm syllables:

9. Place a copy of the song on a transparency and ask students to read the rhythm using syllables.
10. Sing the F major scale (*do re mi fa sol la ti do*) and then the descending scale (*do ti la sol fa mi re do*).
11. Practice singing tonal syllables from the chart. Locate similar patterns in the song.

12. Sing the song using tonal syllables.
13. Speak the words of the song in rhythm.
14. Sing the entire song from notation.
15. Emphasize the need for singing with good tone quality, enthusiasm, and energy.

CLOSURE

Sing the song using tonal syllables and then sing it using rhythm syllables. Finally, sing the song using words.

EVALUATION

1. Where is *do*? Where is *re, mi, fa, sol*?
2. What are the rhythm syllables for eighth notes? for sixteenth notes?
3. What advantage do you have when you know tonal syllables? rhythm syllables? How do they help you learn a song?
4. What tonal syllables are used in this song?
5. What is the difference between singing a song with a lot of energy and singing one just because the teacher tells you to do it?

TEACHING PART SINGING

Singing in parts adds an exciting dimension to musical experiences. It is important, however, that a child be able to sing a simple song in tune before trying to sing harmony; thus, part singing is seldom attempted before third grade. Each of the following approaches or songs can be used singly or in combination with a variety of age levels to teach this important skill.

LINING OUT A SONG

Lining out is a technique for learning a song in which each line is given out by a leader and, in turn, repeated by a group. If the note at the end of each phrase is sustained (with the voice or an instrument), lining out is a good first step in developing part singing. This is appropriate for Grades 3–6.

1. Sing the song phrase by phrase, each time sustaining the pitch of the last note. Ask the students to imitate each phrase after you sing it.
2. Divide the class in half, and ask one half to begin the song and the other half to answer.

Old Texas

American Cowboy Song

Key: G
Starting pitch: D
Meter: 2/4, begins on "and" of 1

SINGING DIALOGUE SONGS OR ECHO SONGS

Dialogue or echo songs use repetitive phrases in a second voice. "Go, Tell It on the Mountain" and "Follow Me" are suitable for Grades 3–6. "The Keeper" is appropriate for Grades 5–6.

Go, Tell It on the Mountain

Spiritual

Key: F
Starting pitch: A
Meter: 4/4, begins on 1

A VERSE *Freely*

1. When I was a seek-er, I sought both night and day. I
2. He made me a watch-man Up-on the cit-y wall. And

asked the Lord to help me, And He showed me the way.
if I serve Him tru-ly, I am the least of all.

B REFRAIN *(in rhythm)*

Go tell it on a moun-tain, O-ver the hills and ev-'ry-where.

Countermelody

Go, tell it on a moun-tain,

Go, tell it on a moun-tain, Our Lord in heav-en is born.

Go, tell it on a moun-tain, our Lord is born.

A Drum

B Tambourine

The Keeper

English Folk Song

Key: D
Starting pitch: A
Meter: 4/4, begins on 4

VERSE

A keep-er would a - hunt-ing go, And un-der his cloak he car-ried a bow,

All for to shoot at a mer-rie lit-tle doe, A - mong the leaves so___ green, O!

CHORUS

1 Jack-ie boy! Sing ye well? Hey down, Der-ry, der-ry down! A -

2 Mas - ter? Ver - y well! Ho down! A -

mong the leaves so___ green, O! To my hey, down, down!

mong the leaves so___ green, O! To my ho down, down!

Hey down, Der-ry, der-ry down! A - mong the leaves so___ green, O!

Ho down! A - mong the leaves so___ green,___ O!

Jingle sticks

Tambourine

(Chorus only)

Jingle sticks

Tambourine

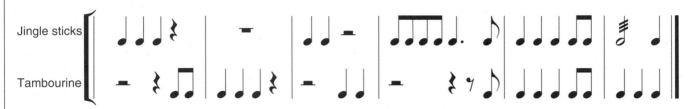

Follow Me

Key: F
Starting pitch: F
Meter: 2/4, begins on 2

Traditional

Come a - long,   Sing a song,   Fol - low me;

Come a - long,   Sing a song,   Fol - low

me;   It is eas - y, you can see.   Ev - 'ry day,   In this

me;   It is eas - y, you can see.   Ev - 'ry day

way,   Just re - peat,   'Til the tune's com - plete.

In this way,   Just re - peat, com - plete.

ADDING DESCANTS

A descant is a melody that is always sung or played above the primary melody. A simple descant can be created by using the roots of the chords with a passing tone here and there. In the following songs, a basic descant has been created from the chord roots. "Did You Ever See a Lassie?" is appropriate for Grade 4, "It's a Small World" for Grade 5.

Did You Ever See a Lassie?

Key: F
Starting pitch: F
Meter: 3/4, begins on 3

German Folk Song
Arr. by Joy E. Lawrence

The descant in "Did You Ever See a Lassie" has been created from the following chords. The bottom pitch is the root. (See Chapter 6 for more detailed discussion and suggestions for instruments.)

It's a Small World

Words and Music by Richard M. Sherman and Robert B. Sherman
Arr. by Joy E. Lawrence

Key: G
Starting pitch: B
Meter: 2/2, begins on 2

1. It's a world of laugh - ter, a world of tears; it's a world of
2. There is just one moon and one gold - en sun; and a smile means

hopes and a world of fears. There's so much that we share, that it's
friend - ship to ev - 'ry - one. Though the moun - tains di - vide and the

time we're a - ware. It's a small world, af - ter all.
o - ceans are wide. It's a small world, af - ter all.

REFRAIN

It's a small world, af - ter all. It's a small world, af - ter all.

It's a small world, af - ter all, it's a small, small world.

Chords

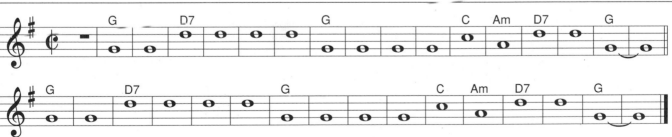

Descant created from these chord roots

Percussion pattern

You can also create harmony by singing the verse and chorus at the same time, as you would do in a partner song.

He's Got the Whole World in His Hands

Key: D

Starting pitch: A

Meter: 4/4, begins on "and" of 3

Spiritual

He's go the whole world____ in his hands____ He's got the

whole world____ in his hands____ He's got the whole world____

in his hands____ He's got the whole world in his hands._____

2. He's got the wind and rain in his hands. (3 times)
   He's got the whole world in his hands.
3. He's got you and me brother in his hands. (3 times)
   He's got the whole world in his hands.
4. He's got everybody in his hands. (3 times)
   He's got the whole world in his hands.

Descant (created from chord roots)

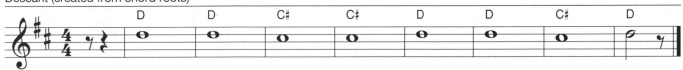

Percussion

Drums

Shaker
(Rattle)

ADDING COUNTERMELODIES

A countermelody is a second melody, which may be above or below the main melody.

1. Start by having the students sing the melody of "Oh, Be Joyful."
2. Play the two countermelodies on the next page. You may use a recorder, melody or resonator bells, or xylophone.
3. Ask the class to sing the melody as you play the countermelody.
4. Sing each countermelody with the suggested words. Ask individual students to reinforce on the instruments.
5. Play and sing the entire song, adding the accompaniment ensembles.

You may wish to perform the song in the following order:

• Verses 1 and 2 sung in unison, accompanied by the Autoharp or Omnichord.

• Verse 1 sung a second time with countermelody 1 sung or played on piano, resonator bells, or xylophone. Autoharp or Omnichord plays chords.

• Verse 2 sung a second time with countermelody 2 sung or played on piano, recorder, resonator bells, or xylophone. Autoharp or Omnichord plays chords.

• Instrumental interlude played by instrumental ensemble only. Autoharp or Omnichord plays chords.

• Verse 3 sung in unison with instrumental ensemble accompanying. Autoharp or Omnichord plays chords.

Oh, Be Joyful

From Gaudeamus Hodie
Words and Music by Natalie Sleeth

Key: C
Starting pitch: C
Meter: 4/4, begins on 1

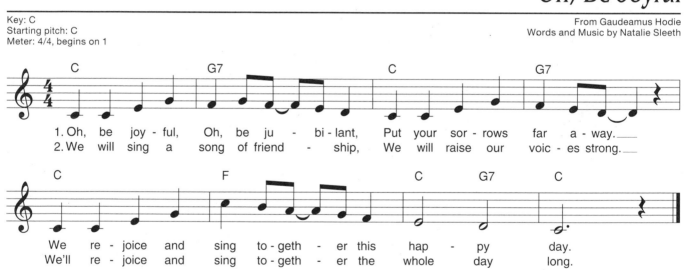

1. Oh, be joy - ful, Oh, be ju - bi - lant, Put your sor - rows far a - way.___
2. We will sing a song of friend - ship, We will raise our voic - es strong.___

We re - joice and sing to - geth - er this hap - py day.
We'll re - joice and sing to - geth - er the whole day long.

Countermelody 1

Oh, be joy - ful, Oh, be joy - ful on this day.

Countermelody 2

Oh, be joy - ful, Oh, be joy - ful, Oh, be joy - ful, put your sor - rows a - way.

Bells or recorders

SINGING OSTINATO CHANTS

An ostinato is a repeated melodic or rhythmic pattern. "The Cuckoo" is suitable for Grades 4–5. "Zum Gali Gali" is appropriate for Grades 4–6.

The Cuckoo

Key: G
Starting pitch: B
Meter: 3/4, begins on 3

Austrian Folk Song
Ostinato: Joy E. Lawrence

1. O I went to Pe - ter's flow - ing spring Where the wa - ter's so good, And I
2. Af - ter Eas - ter come sun - ny days That will melt all the snow; Then I'll
3. When I've mar - ried my maid - en fair, What then can I de - sire? O a

heard there the cuck - oo As she called from the wood.
mar - ry my maid - en fair, We'll be hap - py, I know.
home for her tend - ing And some wood for the fire.

REFRAIN

Ho - li - ah, Ho - le - rah - hi - hi - ah, Ho - le - rah cuck - oo! Ho - le - rah - hi - hi - ah

Ho - le - rah cuck - oo! Ho - le - rah - hi - hi - ah, Ho - le - rah cuck - oo! Ho - le - rah - hi - hi - ah - ho!

OSTINATO

Ho - le - rah cuck - koo - koo, Ho - le - rah cuck - koo - koo, Ho - le - rah cuck - koo - koo Ho - le - rah cuck - koo - koo,

Ho - le - rah cuck - koo - koo, Ho - le - rah cuck - koo - koo, Ho - le - rah cuck - koo - koo Ho.

1. Have the class sing the song.
2. Accompany on Autoharp, Omnichord, or guitar while the class sings the song.
3. Chant the word rhythms of the ostinato. Ask the class to imitate.
4. Sing the ostinato on pitches. Ask the class to sing the ostinato.
5. Have half of the class sing or play the ostinato, while the other half sings the refrain.

Rhythm ostinato

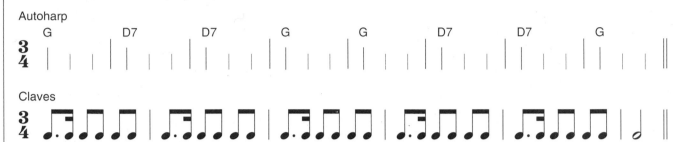

Zum Gali Gali

Israeli Folk Song

Key: E minor
Starting pitch: E
Meter: 2/4, begins on 1

1. Sing or play the ostinato used in "Zum Gali Gali."
2. Play the E minor chord on Autoharp, Omnichord, or guitar while the class sings the ostinato.
3. Perform the song with accompaniment. Have part of the class sing the ostinato while the rest sing the melody.
4. Add the following rhythms on drum, claves, and tambourine:

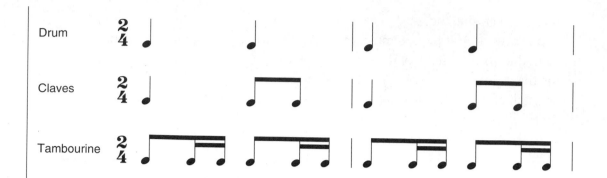

SINGING ROUNDS

A round consists of exact imitation of a given melody sung one or two measures later. Singing rounds can help a child begin to comprehend the concept of harmony. There are several steps to follow for such singing to be successful:

1. The melody must be learned very well.
2. As children sing the song, play the melody as a round (that is, beginning a measure or two later). Use melody bells or a recorder, which will enable the child to hear the melody as a second part while singing.
3. Choose the best singers to sing the second part of the round. Encourage them to be on their own.
4. Do not try a three- or four-part round until children are secure with two parts.

Sing the following rounds. Begin with two parts, gradually adding a third or fourth part. "Kookaburra" is appropriate for Grades 3–4; "Sing Together" and "Praise and Thanksgiving" are appropriate for Grades 3–6.

Kookaburra

Key: D
Starting pitch: A
Meter: 2/4, begins on 1

Australian Folk Song

Sing Together

England

Key: G
Starting pitch: G
Meter: 6/8, begins on 1

Sing, sing to - geth - er, mer - ri - ly, mer - ri - ly sing; Sing, sing to - geth - er,

mer - ri - ly, mer - ri - ly sing; Sing, sing, sing, sing.

Praise and Thanksgiving

Traditional Round

Key: G
Starting pitch: D
Meter: 3/4, begins on 1

ROUND

Praise and thanks - giv - ing let ev - 'ry - one bring Un - to our

Fath - er for ev - 'ry good thing. All to - geth - er joy - ful - ly sing!

QUESTIONS FOR REVIEW

1. What are the main characteristics of the child voice?
2. What differences are there in vocal characteristics between children in Grade 1, Grade 3, and Grade 6?
3. What are three techniques for teaching children to sing in tune?
4. What physical activities are involved in singing parts?
5. Why is it best to begin part singing with a high countermelody or descant rather than a lower part?
6. Why is discovering patterns helpful in learning a song?
7. What kinds of visual, movement, and literature experiences involve patterns?
8. Why are percussion instruments useful in teaching the rhythm of a song?
9. What is the difference between leading a song and teaching a song?
10. What is meant by conceptual versus nonconceptual rote learning?
11. What are rote, rote-note, and note learning? Give a musical example of each.
12. Who was Kodály? How can teachers use his approach to teach music?

3 INTEGRATING SONGS WITH OTHER SUBJECTS AND ACTIVITIES

Music should be an integral part of a child's daily life. One of the unique opportunities that the classroom teacher enjoys is to introduce many musical experiences into the day's activities. Songs can be used to develop physical coordination; teach phonics; provide opportunities for creative dramatics; contribute to a greater understanding and appreciation of people, places, and cultures; and bring new meanings to the study of history. Special days such as Halloween, Thanksgiving, Christmas, and Hanukkah have traditionally used songs to express feelings appropriate to the celebration. Other areas in the elementary curriculum that lend themselves to the use of music include the study of animals, learning about community helpers, and expressing ideas about nature (spring, summer, fall, winter).

The following integrative categories are of special interest to elementary-age children:

- Action
- Animals
- Circus
- Geography
- History (famous people/events)
- Holidays
    Halloween
    Thanksgiving
    Christmas

Hanukkah

Martin Luther King, Jr. Day

Valentine's Day

Presidents' Day (George Washington/Abraham Lincoln)

- Patriotic songs of the United States
- Getting acquainted
- Human relationships/emotions
- Language arts
- Mathematics
- Science
- Transportation

Representative songs have been selected for these categories, and materials and suggestions for planning lessons are provided. Sample lessons are included for five of the integrative categories. You are encouraged to create your own lessons from the suggestions that follow each song. You will also find a list of songs at the end of each integrative unit that are appropriate for a variety of grade levels. You are encouraged to teach these songs, which can be found in the basal music series of your school, to add to the list of integrative categories, and to create other interesting ways of including songs in the classroom.

INTEGRATIVE CATEGORY: ACTION

Sample Lesson: "The Hokey Pokey"

Grades: K–1

Integrative Area: Action/coordination

Concepts: Melody: Narrow range

                         Rhythm: Steady beat, duple meter, repeated patterns

The Hokey Pokey

American Folk Song

Key: G
Starting pitch: D
Meter: 4/4, begins on "and" of 3

Moderately and rhythmically

You put your
{ right hand in,_____
left hand in,_____
right foot in,_____
left foot in,_____
whole self in,_____ }
You take your
{ right hand out,_____
left hand out,_____
right foot out,_____
left foot out,_____
whole self out,_____ }
You put your

{ right hand in_____
left hand in_____
right foot in_____
left foot in_____
whole self in_____ }
And shake it all a-bout. And then you do the ho-key po-key and you

turn your-self a-bout; And that's what it's all a-bout. Hey!

OBJECTIVES

Students will

1. Sing the song with good tone quality.
2. Indicate their knowledge of a narrow melodic range.
3. Clap the steady beat.
4. Clap in duple meter.
5. Perform repeated rhythmic and melodic patterns.
6. Perform appropriate movements.

MATERIALS

- Chart showing narrow and wide range
- Individual charts: D E F♯ G and sample keyboard (either a cardboard keyboard, a piano, or an electronic keyboard)
- Chart showing a steady beat
- Chart showing the following repeated rhythmic pattern:

 (4 times)

- Charts with D, E, F♯, and G written out individually
- Drum, tambourine

PROCEDURES

1. Warm up voices by using techniques for developing head voice (see p. 89).
2. Sing the song or play a recording. Ask students to clap the steady beat as they listen.
3. Sing the song or play a recording and ask students what word they might say or sing for the highest note.
4. Show the chart that indicates a narrow range of sound. Match with the appropriate word.
5. Play D and G on the xylophone and show children that these pitches are close together, meaning this music has a narrow range.
6. Select students to hold each letter and ask other students to count the number of letters in between. Use this visual to reinforce the sound of a narrow range.
7. Sing or play a recording of the song again. Ask students to clap the steady beat and accent the first and third beats. Reinforce this concept by clapping a steady beat and duple meter.
8. Perform the song again. Ask students how many times they can hear the following rhythmic pattern:

   ♩. ♩ (10)

9. Ask students to sing the song, and select one student to play the repeated pattern on the tambourine.
10. Have students stand and imitate your motions as you sing the song or play a recording.

CLOSURE

Ask students to form a circle and as they sing the song do the motions suggested by the words. Accompany on the drum (steady beat) and tambourine (repeated pattern).

EVALUATION

1. Review the concept of narrow range by asking students to define the term and point to it on the appropriate chart.
2. Ask a student to illustrate steady beat and duple meter by clapping.
3. Ask a student to play on the tambourine the rhythm pattern that was repeated.
4. Ask students what motions were referred to in the words of the song.
5. While still in the circle, ask children to sing the song and do the motions. Ask two children to accompany on drum and tambourine.

"If You're Happy"

Grades: K–1
Integrative Areas: Action: Movement, coordination
Concepts: Melody: Steps-skips, repetition
Rhythm: Duple
Tone color: Rhythm sticks, drum

If You're Happy

Key: F
Starting pitch: C
Meter: 4/4, begins on 4

Traditional

Rhythm sticks

Drum (keep the beat)

Suggestions for Lessons

1. Have children act out the directions in the song.
2. Discuss things we do when we're happy (smile, clap hands, and so on). Identify many words that describe happiness.
3. Play the game "Simon Says" to encourage the use of right and left ("Simon says, raise your right hand," etc.).
4. Add rhythm instruments (rhythm sticks, drum) to accompany song.

More Songs: Action

"Che Che Koolay" in Silver Burdett *Music* 3, p. 34; Silver Burdett *Music* 2, p. 55; Macmillan *Music and You* 2, p. 257; Macmillan *Music and You* K, p. 217

"How D'ye Do and Shake Hands" in Silver Burdett *Music* 3, p. 144; Holt, Rinehart and Winston *Music Book* 1, p. 4

"Little Red Caboose" in Silver Burdett and Ginn *World of Music* K, p. 72

"Little Tommy Tinker" in Macmillan *Music and You* 2, p. 231; Macmillan *Music and You* 2, p. 238

"One Finger, One Thumb" in Macmillan *Music and You* K, p. 109; Silver Burdett and Ginn *World of Music* K, p. 120

INTEGRATIVE CATEGORY: ANIMALS

Sample Lesson: "My Big Black Dog"

Grades:	K–1
Integrative Areas:	Improvisation, creativity, movement, coordination, farm, chickens, dramatics, vocabulary
Concepts:	Melody: Steps and skips
	Tempo: Moderate
	Rhythm: Steady, mostly quarter and eighth notes

My Big Black Dog

English Play Song
Piano accompaniment by William N. Simon

Key: F
Starting pitch: F
Meter: 4/4, begins on 4

Who - ev - er took my big black dog, I

wish they'd bring him back! He chased the big chicks

o - ver the fence and the lit - tle chicks through the

crack! The big chicks o - ver the

fence and the lit - tle chicks through the

crack! Who - ev - er took my

big black dog, I wish they'd bring him back!

MATERIALS

- Picture of dogs
- Recording of song (optional)

OBJECTIVES

Students will

1. Identify melodic steps and skips.
2. Decide on an appropriate tempo.
3. Identify walking (quarter notes) and running notes (eighth notes).
4. Sing with energy and correct words, pitches, and rhythms.

PROCEDURES

1. Show pictures of various kinds of dogs, ending with a picture of a big black dog.
2. Ask whether anyone in the class has a "big black dog."
3. Where would you find chicks? (On a farm)
4. What is the difference between a "crack" and a "fence"?
5. Sing the song or play a recording.
6. Teach the song by rote—using your hand to indicate skips.
7. Ask students which words and music are the same. ("Whoever took my big black dog")
8. Have students sing the song with you or with the recording.

9. Guide students in creative motions for the following phrases:
   a. Big black dog
   b. Bring him back
   c. Big chicks over the fence
   d. Little chicks through the cracks
10. Ask half the class to sing the song. Ask the other half to do motions. Then have them change roles.

CLOSURE

When the students know the song and motions very well, ask them to do both.

EVALUATION

1. Is the song mostly steps or skips?
2. What are some words that skip with the music? ("Whoever took my big black dog")
3. How would you decide how fast to sing the song?
4. Do you sing mostly quarter notes (walking) or eighth notes (running)?
5. What is the song about? What is the main character?

Sample Lesson: "The Elephant"

Grades:	K–2
Integrative Areas:	Zoo study, circus study, dramatics, visual art, vocabulary
Concepts:	Melody: Low register, mostly steps
	Tempo: Slow/fast, contrast
	Form: ABA

The Elephant

Words and Music by Hap Palmer

Key: A
Starting pitch: C#
Meter: 4/4, song begins on "and" of 4

Very slowly and ponderously

The el - e - phant moves ver - y slow - ly, oh so ver - y slow - ly. He does - n't like to move too fast, be - cause he is so big and fat.

But should he see a ti - ger or spy a mean old hun - ter, he will start to run and shake the ground, and make them all fall down.

Rum - ble, rum - ble, rum - ble, hear the jun - gle rum - ble. Rum - ble, rum - ble, rum - ble, hear the jun - gle rum - ble. Trees shake and sway as the bird - ies fly a - way; li - ons run and hide with their ba - bies by their side. Rum - ble, rum - ble, rum - ble, hear the jun - gle rum - ble. Rum - ble, rum - ble, rum - ble, hear the jun - gle rum - ble.

OBJECTIVES

Students will
1. Identify the low register of the song as distinctive from a high register.
2. Identify the frequency of steps with occasional skips.
3. Perform appropriate tempos: slow, fast.
4. Define the meaning of ABA form.

MATERIALS

- Pictures of elephants, lions, birds
- Charts with words: *elephant, lion, bird, jungle, rumble, hunter*
- Recordings of Saint-Saëns's *Carnival of the Animals* and Debussy's "Jimbo's Lullaby" from *The Children's Corner Suite*
- Chart or transparency with song
- Cards marked A, B, and A
- Autoharp or Omnichord

PROCEDURES

1. Show pictures of elephants. Discuss their size and slow movements.
2. Play the recording of Saint-Saëns's "The Elephant" from *Carnival of the Animals*. Discuss the character of sound that the composer selected to represent an elephant. Follow the same procedure with Debussy's "Jimbo's Lullaby" from *The Children's Corner Suite*.
3. Sing the song or play a recording. Identify other animals mentioned in the song (tigers, lions, birds).
4. Sing the song or play a recording. Ask students to identify whether the song is mostly high or mostly low.
5. Sing the song or play a recording. Ask students to identify where the song gets faster and slower. What words indicate the faster tempo of the song?
6. Teach the melody by imitation (rote) as follows. Hold up appropriate vocabulary card as needed.
   a. The elephant moves very slowly, oh so very slowly, He doesn't like to move too fast, because he is so big and fat. (Cards: *elephant, slowly, fast, big, fat*)
   b. But should he see a tiger or spy a mean old hunter, he will start to run and shake the ground, and make them all fall down. (Cards: *tiger, hunter, shake, fall*)
   c. Rumble, rumble, rumble, hear the jungle rumble. Rumble, rumble, rumble, hear the jungle rumble. (Cards: *rumble, jungle*)
   d. Trees shake and sway as the birdies fly away; lions run and hide with their babies by their side. (Cards: *trees, birdies, lions, babies*)
   Sing a and b a second time.
7. Show a chart or transparency with the words of the song. Ask students to map the direction of the melody with their hands as they sing the entire song. Repeat as necessary.

8. Indicate with cards marked ABA that the song has three sections. Sing or play a recording of the song. Ask students to indicate when the A section begins and when the B section begins by pointing to the appropriate card.

9. Ask students to sing the song with you. While all sing, ask half the class to stand on the slow part and the other half to stand on the fast part.

10. Ask students to sing the song again, and in the first phrase identify which words move by step and which move by skips. Follow the same procedure for subsequent phrases.

CLOSURE

Sing the entire song accompanied by Autoharp or Omnichord.

EVALUATION

1. Ask students which words are in the low register.
2. Ask students to identify where the music moves by steps or skips (words).
3. Ask students to identify where the music goes faster and where it goes slower.
4. As you perform the song, ask students to identify by pointing to the appropriate card when the song is in the A section, when it is in the B section, and when it is in the A section again.

"Six Little Ducks"

Grades:	K–2
Integrative Areas:	Dramatics, movement, visual art, science, vocabulary
Concepts:	Rhythm: Steady beat, duple meter
	Melody: Large skips

Six Little Ducks

Traditional American

Key: F
Starting pitch: A
Meter: 4/4, begins on 1

Moderately fast

Six lit - tle ducks that I once knew,
Down to the riv - er they did go;

Fat ones, skin - ny ones,
Wib - ble wob - ble wib - ble wob - ble

Fuz - zy ones, too, But the one lit - tle duck with a feath - er in his back,
to____ and fro.

He ruled the oth - ers with a quack, quack, quack; quack, quack, quack.

Suggestions for Lessons

1. Dramatize "Six Little Ducks" with movements.
2. Draw pictures of ducks in a pond or walking toward a pond. Show pictures of baby ducks and mother duck.
3. Discuss characteristics of ducks, such as they swim, have wings, have webbed feet, and so on. Combine with a science unit on animals found around water, such as frogs and fish.
4. Create stick puppets to represent the ducks. Dramatize the song.

More Songs: Animals

"All the Pretty Little Horses" in Silver Burdett *Music* 3, p. 48; Holt, Rinehart and Winston *Music Book 2*, p. 79

"Animal Farm" in Macmillan *Music and You* 3, p. 144

"Baby Chicks" in Silver Burdett and Ginn *World of Music* K, p. 126

"Barnyard Song" in Macmillan *Music and You* 2, p. 52; Holt, Rinehart and Winston *Music Book* 2, p. 120

"Cat" in Holt, Rinehart and Winston *Music Book* 2

"The Cat" in Silver Burdett and Ginn *The World of Music* 2, p. 110

"Doggie Song" in Holt, Rinehart and Winston *Exploring Music* 5, p. 140

"Ducklings" in Macmillan *Music and You* 1, p. 216; Macmillan *Music and You* K, p. 187

"Frog in the Bog" in Holt, Rinehart and Winston *Music Book* 2, p. 118

"Frog in the Pond" in Silver Burdett and Ginn *World of Music* K, p. 130

"One Little Elephant" in Macmillan *Music and You* 1, p. 230

INTEGRATIVE CATEGORY: CIRCUS

Sample Lesson: "Circus Parade"

Grades:	3–5
Integrative Areas:	Creative dramatics, visual art
Concepts:	Rhythm: Duple meter; 4/4, steady beat
	Melody: Skips, contour, contrasting second melodic phrase, accidental (F♯)
	Form: Two-part: AB

Circus Parade

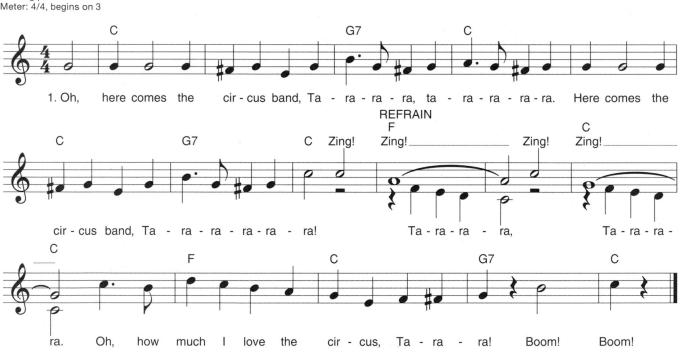

Key: C
Starting pitch: G
Meter: 4/4, begins on 3

Words and Music by Milton Kaye

Reprinted by permission of Milton Kaye.

OBJECTIVES

Students will
1. Perform the song while clapping or tapping a steady beat.
2. Identify the use of an accidental (F♯) throughout song, both visually and aurally.
3. Demonstrate an understanding of second contrasting melodic phrase through singing or playing an instrument
4. Identify the two sections of the song (verse and refrain) through charts (AB).

MATERIALS

- Pictures of circuses
- Written score of song for each student or transparency of song for use with overhead projector (be sure that you own the books or you are in violation of the copyright law)
- Xylophone, resonator bells, drums
- Individual cards in two colors and marked A and B
- Charts showing steady beat and the word *duple*

PROCEDURES

1. Show pictures of a circus and a circus band.
2. Discuss the events, people, and animals found in the circus.
3. Sing or play a recording of "Circus Parade." Ask students to clap a steady beat, accenting the first beat as they listen.
4. Ask students to circle each F♯ on their copies, or ask a student to circle the F♯ on the transparency.
5. Point out that the F♯ is only a half step below G, and that is very close. Sing or play the distance from G to F♯. Ask how many times this pattern occurs in the song. (six times)
6. Have students read the words from their scores or from a chart or transparency.
7. Sing or play a recording of the song. Ask students to sing the verse and top melody of the chorus.
8. Read the verse of the song with Kodály rhythm syllables: Ta-ah = ♩, Ta = ♩ Ti = ♪, Ta-ah-ah-ah = o, Ta-i = ♩. Ask students to listen to the melody as you sing or play a recording. Sing the verse of the song and the refrain (top melody only) using rhythm syllables.
9. Ask the class to sing the entire song with words.
10. Ask a student to play on the xylophone or resonator bells the four pitches that make up the descending melodic phrase: F E D C. These are found in the refrain. The rest of the class should map the direction of these pitches with their hands.
11. Ask students to sing the top line and selected students to play the contrasting melody on instruments.
12. Use a drum for the last "Boom, boom." Sing the refrain again using xylophone and resonator bells for the descending melody and the drum for the final two notes.

CLOSURE

Ask the class to sing the song with instruments used at appropriate places.

EVALUATION

1. Sing or play a recording of the song. Ask students which chart shows a steady beat and whether they tap two or four beats in each measure.
2. Show a chart of the interval G–F♯ and ask a student to demonstrate the sound of these two pitches by singing or playing an instrument.

3. Ask students to locate G–F♯ in their musical scores. Discuss how many times this pattern appears.

4. Sing or play a recording of the song and ask which charts they might use to diagram the form (AB) or (ABA).

More Songs: Circus

"Circus Band" in Holt, Rinehart and Winston *Exploring Music* 7, p. 134

"Circus Parade" in Silver Burdett and Ginn *World of Music* 2, p. 14

"He's a Clown" in Silver Burdett and Ginn *World of Music* 3, p. 172

"Carrousel" in Holt, Rinehart and Winston *Exploring Music* 2, p. 64

INTEGRATIVE CATEGORY: GEOGRAPHY

"Gatatumba"

Grades:	3–6
Integrative Areas:	Culture, vocabulary, dramatics
Concepts:	Rhythm: Steady beat, mostly eighth notes
	Melody: Narrow range, repeated phrases
	Harmony: Mostly thirds

Gatatumba

Spanish Folk Song
Arr. Francis Girard
English version Rosemary Jacques

Key: C
Starting pitch: G
Meter: 2/4, begins on 2

Hur - ry, hur - ry, Ga - ta - tum - ba, Bring the tam - bour - ine and drum. Hur - ry,
Ga - ta - tum - ba, tum - ba, tum - ba, Con pan - de - ras y so - najas, Ga - ta -

hur - ry, Ga - ta - tum - ba, All is read - y, won't you come? Hur - ry,
tum - ba, tum - ba, tum - ba, No te me - tas en las pajas, Ga - ta -

hur - ry, Ga - ta - tum - ba, Strike the bell and let it ring. Hur - ry,
tum - ba, tum - ba, tum - ba, To - ca el pi - to y el ra - bel. Ga - ta -

hur - ry, Ga - ta - tum - ba, Ev - 'ry - bod - y wants to sing!
tum - ba, tum - ba, tum - ba, Tam - bo - ril y cas - ca - bel.

The Spanish words of "Gatatumba" are pronounced as follows:

Ga-ta-tum-ba, tum-ba, tum-ba,
Gah-tah-toom-bah toom-bah toom-bah

Con pan-de-ras y so na-jas,
Kohn pahn-deh-rahs ee soh-nah-hahs

Ga-ta-tum-ba, tum-ba, tum-ba,
Gah-tah-toom-bah toom-bah toom-bah

No te me-tas en las pa-jas,
Noh teh meh-tahs en lahs pah-hahs

Ga-ta-tum-ba, tum-ba, tum-ba,
Gah-tah-toom-bah toom-bah toom-bah

To-ca el pi-to y el ra-bel.
Toh-kahl pee-toh yehl rah-behl

Ga-ta-tum-ba, tum-ba, tum-ba,
Gah-tah-toom-bah toom-bah toom-bah

Tam-bo-ril y cas-ca-bel.
Tahm-boh-reel ee kahs-kah-behl

Instrumental ensemble

Bass xylophone

Recorder (as a drone)

Drum (throughout)

Suggestions for Lessons

1. Locate Spain on a world map. Notice its relationship to surrounding areas (southern Europe, bounded by sea).
2. Discuss what Spanish instruments could be used to accompany the song (guitar, castanets).
3. View pictures of Spanish dress, cathedrals, and dances.
4. Discuss the use of Spanish language in the United States (southern and southwestern states). Point out that this song is sung as part of Spanish Christmas celebrations.

"Roll On, Columbia"

Grades:	4–6
Integrative Areas:	Geography, science
Concepts:	Rhythm: Steady beat, 3/4 meter, repeated patterns
	Melody: Moves mostly by steps, narrow range
	Texture/harmony: Descant on top provides harmony, harmony mostly in thirds or sixths, chords: F, B♭, C$_7$
	Form: Two sections: verse and refrain, AB

Roll On, Columbia

Words by Woody Guthrie
Music based on "Goodnight, Irene" by Huddie Ledbetter and John Lomax

Key: F
Starting pitch: C
Meter: 3/4, begins on 1

1. Green Doug-las fir where the wa-ters cut through, Down her wild
2. Oth-er big riv-ers add pow-er to you: Yak-i-ma,
(3.) Bon-ne-ville now there are ships in the locks. The wa-ter has
(4.) on up the riv-er is the Grand Cou-lee Dam: The big-gest thing

moun-tains and can-yons she flew, Ca-na-di-an North-west to the
Snake, and the Klick-i-tat, too. San-dy, Wil-lam-ette, and the
ris-en and cov-ered the rocks. Ship-loads a-plen-ty are
built by the hand of a man To run the great fac-t'ries and

o-cean so blue,
Hood Riv-er, too
soon past the docks,
wa-ter the land.

Roll on, Co-lum-bia, roll on.

3. At
4. And

REFRAIN
Countermelody

Roll-ing a-long, roll-ing a-long, roll-ing a-long, Co-lum-bia, roll on. Your

Roll on, Co-lum-bia, roll on. Roll on, Co-lum-bia, roll on. Your

pow-er is turn-ing our dark-ness to dawn. Roll on, Co-lum-bia, roll on, roll on.

pow-er is turn-ing our dark-ness to dawn. Roll on, Co-lum-bia, roll on.

Suggestions for Lessons

1. Review the location of the Columbia River and the function of the Grand Coulee Dam.
2. Perform the rhythm of the song by clapping a steady beat and accenting the first beat of each measure (triple meter).
3. Play or sing the harmony (countermelody) found in the refrain.
4. Ask students to read pitches using solfège or rhythm syllables.

More Songs: Geography

"Crescent Moon" (China) in Silver Burdett and Ginn *World of Music* 5, pp. 76–77

"Going to Boston" in Macmillan *Music and You* 5, p. 15

"Hawaiian Rainbows" in Silver Burdett and Ginn *World of Music* 2, p. 40

"Land of the Silver Birch" (Canada) in Silver Burdett and Ginn *World of Music* 5, pp. 80–81

"Laredo" in Silver Burdett and Ginn *World of Music* 5, pp. 72–73

"Lone Star Trail" in Silver Burdett and Ginn *World of Music* 2, p. 17

"My Home's in Montana" in Macmillan *Music and You* 3, p. 48; Silver Burdett and Ginn *World of Music* 3, p. 20; *World of Music* 6, p. 88

"On Top of Old Smokey" in Holt, Rinehart and Winston *The Music Book* 5, p. 97

"Rio Grande" in Silver Burdett and Ginn *World of Music* 5, pp. 6–7

INTEGRATIVE CATEGORY: HISTORY

"Shenandoah"

Grades:	4–6
Integrative Areas:	Transportation, geography, social customs, visual art
Concepts:	Rhythm: Mixed meter, syncopation
	Melody: Wide range
	Dynamics: ◁‾ ‾▷

Shenandoah

Traditional

Key: D
Starting pitch: A
Meter: 4/4, begins on 4

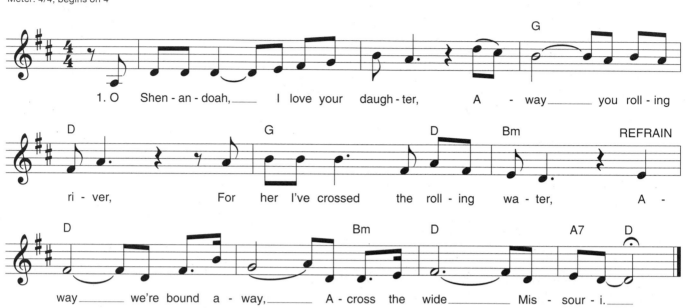

1. O Shen-an-doah, I love your daugh-ter, A - way you roll-ing ri - ver, For her I've crossed the roll-ing wa-ter, A - way we're bound a - way, A-cross the wide Mis - sour - i.

2. The trader loved this Indian maiden,
   Away, you rolling river,
   With presents his canoe was laden.
   Refrain.
3. O Shenandoah, I'm bound to leave you,
   Away, you rolling river,
   O Shenandoah, I'll not deceive you.
   Refrain.
4. O Shenandoah, I long to hear you,
   Away, you rolling river,
   O Shenandoah, I long to hear you.
   Refrain.

Suggestions for Lessons

1. Ask students where the highest note is (D) and where the lowest note is (A). Circle them on a transparency. Ask students whether this is a wide or a narrow range.
2. Perform the song or use a recording. Ask students to read the words.
3. Teach the song by rote using the phrase method. Ask students to sing the entire song.
4. After the class has sung the song, ask on what words there is syncopation (daughter, ri-ver, wa-ter, Mis-sour-i). Circle these words on the transparency.

5. Sing the song again with emphasis on syncopation.

6. Study the Shenandoah Valley region and trace the Shenandoah River. Note the distance to the Missouri River and discuss the hazards of taking such a trip by wagon train.

7. Present images, draw pictures, or create a diorama of wagon trains as they moved westward and crossed the Missouri River.

More Songs: History

"Columbus Sailed with Three Ships" in Macmillan *Music and You* K, p. 44

"George Washington" in Macmillan *Music and You* K, p. 156

"Greatest American Hero" in Silver Burdett and Ginn *World of Music* 5, p. 105

"In My Merry Oldsmobile" in Silver Burdett and Ginn *World of Music* 5, pp. 58–59

"Johnny Has Gone for a Soldier" in Silver Burdett and Ginn *World of Music* 5, p. 26

"Chester" in Holt, Rinehart and Winston *The Music Book* 5, p. 67

INTEGRATIVE CATEGORY: HOLIDAYS

HALLOWEEN

Halloween is one of our oldest festive holidays. Its origin dates back to long before the Christian era. It was held on what is now the last day of October. Giant fires were lit in honor of the sun god, whose spirit, so it was believed, deserved recognition and honor for the important role it played in growing crops. The ceremony was a solemn, devout religious rite around the roaring flames of the fire.

It was not until the Middle Ages that ghosts and witches were introduced into the Halloween celebration, which was now celebrated on All Hallow's Eve, the night before the Christian festival established in memory of the saints and called All Saints' Day. All sorts of pranks and mischievous antics were performed. The pranksters continued their mysterious ghostly deeds until midnight. When the midnight church bells would ring, ushering in the holy day, the Halloween celebrations ceased. Over the years the customs of Halloween celebrations have changed from time to time and place to place. Today we celebrate with costumes, parties, and trick or treating.

"The Witch Rides"

Grades: K–1

Integrative Areas: Dramatics, movement

Concepts: Rhythm: Duple meter

Melody: Wide range, repeated pitches, ascending/descending

The Witch Rides

Key: D minor
Starting pitch: D
Meter: 6/8, begins on 6

Music by Grace M. Meserve
Verses I and 3 by Grace M. Meserve
Verses 2 and 4 by Mary Joy

Reprinted by permission of Silver Burdett.

Suggestions for Lessons

1. Dramatize "The Witch Rides" by galloping on phrases 1, 2, and 4. Stop on "Oo, Oo," and tip the imaginary broomstick down on the second beat of the measure.
2. Ask the students to map the melody in the air as they hear it.
3. Play the steady beat (two beats to a measure) on rhythm sticks.
4. Add creative verses to the song.

"Let's Make a Jack-o'-Lantern"

Grades: 1–3
Integrative Areas: Visual art, candles, creative dramatics
Concepts: Rhythm: Repetition, steady beat

Let's Make a Jack-o'-Lantern

Key: F
Starting pitch: C
Meter: 4/4, begins on "and" of 3

Words and Music by Daniel Hooley
Piano accompaniment by Kryste Andrews

Reprinted by permission of Daniel S. Hooley.

Suggestions for Lessons

1. Using pumpkins, make several jack-o'-lanterns. Scoop them out and cut faces.
2. Place candles in the pumpkins. Turn out the lights so pumpkins can glow.
3. Place the jack-o'-lanterns around the classroom.

More Songs: Halloween

"Black and Gold" in Macmillan *Music and You* K, p. 47; Holt, Rinehart and Winston *Music Book* 1, p. 45

"Five Little Pumpkins," p. 26.

"How Did You Know?" in Silver Burdett and Ginn *World of Music* 2, pp. 200–201

"On Halloween" in Silver Burdett and Ginn *World of Music* 2, p. 198

"There Once Was a Witch" in Silver Burdett and Ginn *World of Music* 2, p. 199

"This House Is Haunted" in Silver Burdett and Ginn *World of Music* 8, p. 136; Holt, Rinehart *Exploring Music* 2, p. 47

THANKSGIVING

Thanksgiving is an American holiday on which people of all faiths give thanks in their own individual ways for freedom to work, play, and worship. It is a time when the classroom teacher will want to impress on children the founding of our country, the trials and tribulations that brought the first settlers to our shores, and the rugged individualism that has characterized our society. Use not only the traditional "turkey" songs but also songs of thanksgiving.

"Mister Turkey"

Grades:	K–1
Integrative Areas:	Creative dramatics, visual art
Concepts:	Rhythm: Steady beat
	Melody: Short phrases, repetition
	Form: AA

Mister Turkey

Key: G
Starting pitch: G
Meter: 4/4, begins on 1

Music by Robert W. Gibb
Words by L. E. Ashley

See him strut-ting all a-round, Fat Mis-ter Tur-key!

Hear the gob-ble, gob-ble sound, Fat Mis-ter Tur-key.

From *Listen and Sing*, Copyright © 1943, 1936, by Ginn and Company (Xerox Corporation). Used with permission of Silver Burdett and Ginn.

Suggestions for Lessons
1. Dramatize the song with appropriate actions—strut, fat, gobble, gobble, etc.
2. Draw pictures of turkeys.

"Five Fat Turkeys"

Grades:	K–2
Integrative Areas:	Number sequences, creative dramatics
Concepts:	Duple meter, steady beat, short phrases

Five Fat Turkeys

Key: G
Starting pitch: G
Meter: 2/4, begins on I

Traditional

G D7 G7 G G D7 G D7
Five fat tur-keys are we.___ We slept all night in a tree.___ When the
G D7 G7 C C D7 G
cook came a - round, we could-n't be found, So that's why we're here, you see.___

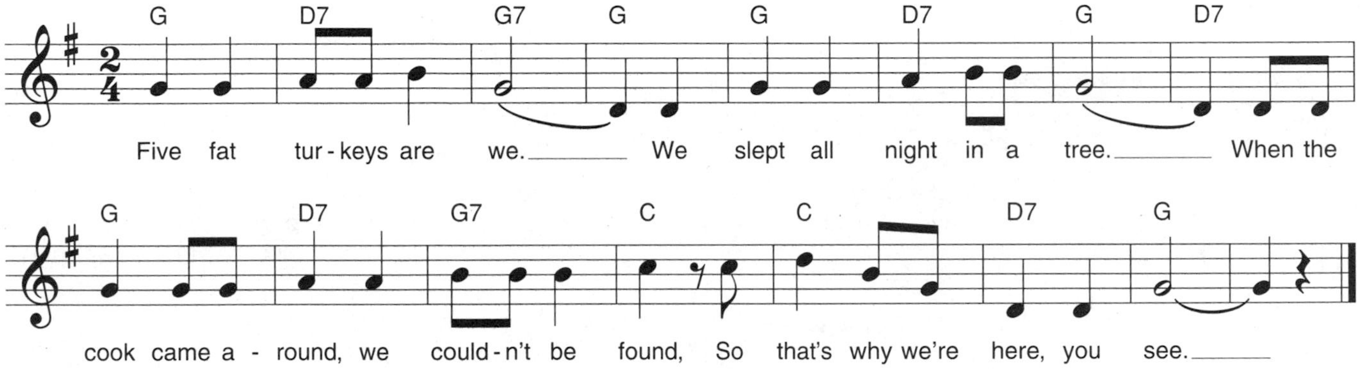

Suggestions for Lessons

1. Dramatize the short story of the five fat turkeys.
2. Select a student to keep a steady beat with a drum.
3. Invite students to stand tall on the highest note (last line).

"Over the River and Through the Wood"

Grades:	4–6
Integrative Areas:	Social studies—history, geography; weather, visual art
Concepts:	Rhythm: Repetition
	Form: ABAC
	Melody: Range of one octave

Over the River and Through the Wood

Lydia Maria Childs

Key: C
Starting pitch: G
Meter: 6/8, begins on 1

1. O - ver the riv - er and through the wood, To grand - fath - er's house we go._____ The
2. O - ver the riv - er and through the wood and straight to the barn - yard gate,_____ We
3. O - ver the riv - er and through the wood, now soon we'll be on our way._____ There's

horse knows the way to car - ry the sleigh through the white and drift - ing snow._____
seem_____ to go so ver - y slow, and it's so_____ hard to wait._____
feast - ing and fun for ev - er - y - one, for this is Thanks - giv - ing day._____

O - ver the riv - er and through the wood, Oh, how_____ the wind does blow!_____ It
O - ver the riv - er and through the wood, now grand - moth - er's cap I spy._____ Hur -
O - ver the riv - er and through the wood, get on,_____ my dap - ple gray!_____ The

stings the toes and bites the nose, As o - ver the ground we go.
rah for the fun! The pud - ding's done. Hur - rah for the pump - kin pie!
woods will ring with songs we sing, for this is Thanks - giv - ing day.

Suggestions for Lessons

1. Study pictures by Currier and Ives of early rural American scenes. Focus on pictures of sleighs and winter scenes. Discuss or dramatize what it might have been like to ride in a sleigh. Ask children to bring replicas of sleighs that they might have at home, such as those often used as Christmas decorations.

2. Create scenes in art class that express the verses of the song.

3. Play and clap the duple pulse: ♪♪♪ ♪♪♪

4. Identify the repeated pitches and rhythm patterns.

"We Gather Together"

Grades: 4–6
Integrative Areas: Social studies—history, language arts—vocabulary
Concepts: Rhythm: Triple meter, repeated patterns ♩. ♪ ♩
                       Melody: Wide range
                       Dynamics:

We Gather Together

Key: C
Starting pitch: G
Meter: 3/4, begins on 3

Netherlands
Trans. Theodore Baker

Suggestions for Lessons

1. Read and study stories or pictures of the first Thanksgiving in America.
2. Discuss the role of Pilgrims, Native Americans, and traders.
3. Locate Plymouth, Massachusetts, on a map of the United States. Using an atlas, locate other cities in the United States that have the name Plymouth. Point out the coastal area of Plymouth, England, and discuss the use of English and Dutch names for American regions or cities, such as "New" England, "New" York.
4. Dramatize the first Thanksgiving. Sing "We Gather Together" as students reenact the Pilgrims gathering around the table to celebrate an abundant harvest. Teach the meaning of such words as *chasten*, *oppressing*, *ordain*, *maintain*, *extol*, and *tribulation*. Emphasize the seeking of freedom from oppression, and freedom to worship, as reasons for coming to America.

More Songs: Thanksgiving

"Come Ye Thankful People Come" in Silver Burdett and Ginn *World of Music* 5, p. 231

"Grandpa's Turkey" in Holt, Rinehart and Winston *Music Book* 1, p. 186

"Tallis Canon" in Silver Burdett and Ginn *World of Music* 3, p. 20

"Thanksgiving" in Silver Burdett and Ginn *World of Music* 2, pp. 202–203

"Thanksgiving Hymn" in Holt, Rinehart and Winston *The Music Book* 6, p. 222

"Turkey Song" in Silver Burdett and Ginn *Music* 1, p. 122

CHRISTMAS

Christmas is a time when Christians celebrate the birth of Jesus Christ. The scene often recreated is called the Nativity. Christmas Eve is a time of special music and pageantry in many Christian churches. While there is much secular celebration, Christmas remains a religious celebration featuring the giving of gifts and a time when thoughts turn to peace on earth, goodwill toward men. Some of the most wonderful musical treasures we have found are in the Christmas carols from countries around the world.

"Jolly Old Saint Nicholas"

Grades:	K–2
Integrative Areas:	Creative dramatics, customs of Christmas
Concepts:	Rhythm: Duple meter, mostly eighth notes, steady beat
	Melody: Narrow range, repeated pitches, repeated phrases

Jolly Old Saint Nicholas

Key: G
Starting pitch: B
Meter: 2/4, begins on 1

Carol

1. Jol - ly old Saint Nich - o - las, Lean your ear this way;___ Don't you tell a
2. When the clock is strik - ing twelve, When I'm fast a - sleep,___ Down the chim - ney
3. John - ny wants a pair of skates; Su - sy wants a dol - ly; Nel - lie wants a

sin - gle soul What I'm going to say;___ Christ - mas Eve is com - ing soon,
broad and black With your pack you'll creep;___ All the stock - ings you will find
sto - ry book; She thinks dolls are fol - ly. As for me, my lit - tle brain

Now you dear old man, Whis - per what you'll bring to me; Tell me, if you can.
Hang - ing in a row; Mine will be the short - est one; You'll be sure to know.
Is - n't ver - y bright; Choose for me, Dear San - ta Claus, What you think is right.

Suggestions for Lessons

1. Read the following story of Saint Nicholas: "According to an old legend, Saint Nicholas was the Bishop of Myra in the fourth century. Because of his great love for children, he was designated the patron saint of children. There were many tales of his kindness to the poor and the gifts he took to them. The custom of giving gifts is carried on in our exchange of Christmas presents."

2. Have a child act as Saint Nicholas, with other members of the class whispering to him something special they would like for Christmas.

3. Dramatize the text of the song. For example, on "lean your ear this way," cup your ear; on "don't you tell a single soul," shake your finger; on "when I'm fast asleep," hold hands to ears, and so on.

"Las Posadas Songs"

Grades:	3–4
Integrative Areas:	Creative dramatics, customs of Christmas
Concepts:	Rhythm: Steady beat, duple and triple meter, repeated patterns
	Melody: Repeated phrases, narrow range
	Form: AB

Las Posadas Songs

Key: C
Starting pitch: G
Meter: 2/4, begins on 1

Words by Louis C. Adelman
Mexican Christmas Songs
Collected by Natividad Vacio

1. See the bright pi - ña - ta, hang - ing high a - bove you,
2. Break the bright pi - ña - ta, send the can - dy fly - ing,

Swing un - til you find it, swing and break it o - pen.
Break the gay pi - ña - ta, send the can - dy fly - ing.

1. Pick up the can - dy, wrapped in red pa - per.
2. Red jel - ly ap - ples, pea - nuts, and chest - nuts,

Fill up the bas - kets with all kinds of good - ies.
Pass them a - round, all eat and have fun now.

Music Through the Day, © 1962. By permission of Silver Burdett Company.

Suggestions for Lessons

1. Describe Mexican customs of celebrating Christmas. Every night, during the weeks before Christmas, candlelit processions go from house to house seeking lodging (posadas), as Mary and Joseph did in Bethlehem. Merrymaking follows the worship before the creche (manger scene) and the breaking of the piñata, a decorated pâpier-maché animal or object filled with candy and nuts. Someone is blindfolded and the piñata is dangled out of reach of the person's stick. After the person swings wildly, the piñata is placed so that it can be broken, and everyone scrambles for its contents.

2. Dramatize the breaking of the piñata.

3. Create a piñata in art class.

4. Compare the Mexican custom of celebrating Christmas with customs from other parts of the world.

"Deck the Halls"

Grades: 3–6

Concepts: Rhythm: Duple meter, steady beat, repeated patterns

Melody: Repeated phrases, wide range, mostly steps

Tonality: Major

Form: AABA

Deck the Halls

Wales

Key: D
Starting pitch: A
Meter: 4/4, begins on 1

1. Deck the halls with boughs of hol - ly,
2. See the blaz - ing Yule be - fore us,
3. Fast a - way the old year pass - es,
Fa la la la la la la la la.

'Tis the sea - son to be jol - ly,
Strike the harp and join the cho - rus,
Hail the new, ye lads and lass - es,
Fa la la la la la la la la.

Don we now our gay ap - par - rel,
Fol - low me in mer - ry mea - sure,
Sing we joy - ous all to - geth - er,
Fa la la la la la la la la.

Troll the an - cient Yule - tide car - ol,
While I tell of Yule - tide trea - sure,
Heed - less of the wind and weath - er,
Fa la la la la la la la la.

Suggestions for Lessons

1. Study pictures from the age of Charles Dickens.
2. Create simple costumes and a "caroling" scene around a lamppost.
3. Discuss the use of *falala* as a refrain-type response in the song. Many joyful songs use nonsense syllables as a refrain.

"O Come, All Ye Faithful"

Grades:	5–6
Integrative Areas:	Language arts—Latin, visual art
Concepts:	Rhythm: Steady beat, duple
	Melody: Wide range, mostly steps, long phrases
	Form: AB

O Come, All Ye Faithful (Adeste, Fideles)

Key: G
Starting pitch: G
Meter: 4/4, begins on 4

Arr. by John Francis Wade
Trans. F Oakley

Suggestions for Lessons

1. Explain that during the Middle Ages, Latin was the only accepted language in the Christian church. Introduce students to singing Latin with the verse found in "Adeste, Fideles" ("O Come, All Ye Faithful").

Pronunciation key for Latin words:

a = ah

i = ee

e = eh

ae = ay

u = oo

g = soft g

2. Dramatize the song with students taking the role of monks.
3. Create a stained-glass window and cathedral atmosphere.

More Songs: Christmas

"Christmas Is Coming" in Macmillan *Music and You* 4, p. 69; Holt, Rinehart and Winston *Exploring Music* 2, p. 73

"Frosty the Snowman" in Silver Burdett and Ginn *World of Music* 2, pp. 208–209

"Fum, Fum, Fum" in Macmillan *Music and You* 5, p. 263; Silver Burdett and Ginn *World of Music* 4, p. 244; Holt, Rinehart and Winston *Music Book* 6, p. 226

"Here Comes Santa Claus" in Silver Burdett and Ginn *World of Music* 1, p. 197

"The Huron Carol" in Silver Burdett and Ginn *World of Music* 5, p. 243.

"I Am So Glad on Christmas Eve" in Silver Burdett and Ginn *World of Music* 2, p. 21

"In a Manger" in Silver Burdett and Ginn *World of Music* 2, p. 212

"Little Drummer Boy" in Holt, Rinehart and Winston *Exploring Music* 2, p. 80

"Rise Up, Shepherd, and Follow" in Silver Burdett and Ginn *World of Music* 5, p. 238

HANUKKAH

Both Christmas and Hanukkah celebrations occur in December. Children should experience the beautiful music of these seasons for, while one is Christian and the other Jewish, both occasions reflect joy.

Hanukkah is a Hebrew word meaning "dedication." Known as the Feast of Lights, it is an eight-day celebration commemorating the rededication of the Temple at Jerusalem (165 B.C.) after the Maccabees had defeated the Syrian Greek armies. During the festival, a candle is lit for each day. Hanukkah is celebrated with parties and the exchange of gifts. The menorah, a candelabra that holds the eight candles, may be found in many Jewish homes.

"Hanukkah Is Here"

Grades:	K–1
Integrative Areas:	Cultural heritage, social studies—history
Concepts:	Rhythm: Duple meter, steady beat
	Melody: Narrow range, repeated phrases
	Tonality: Minor

Hanukkah Is Here

Key: D minor
Starting pitch: D
Meter: 4/4, begins on 1

Words and Music by Suzanne Clayton

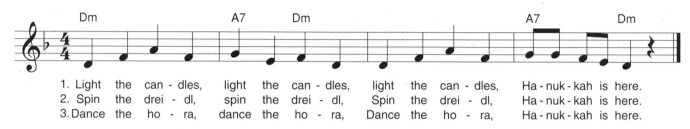

1. Light the can - dles, light the can - dles, light the can - dles, Ha - nuk - kah is here.
2. Spin the drei - dl, spin the drei - dl, Spin the drei - dl, Ha - nuk - kah is here.
3. Dance the ho - ra, dance the ho - ra, Dance the ho - ra, Ha - nuk - kah is here.

Reprinted by permission of Suzanne Clayton, Pittsford Recreation ORFF.

Suggestions for Lessons

1. Ask a Jewish student to bring a menorah to class and tell how his or her family celebrates Hanukkah.
2. Draw menorahs in art class.
3. Discuss the use of Hebrew in Jewish worship. Invite a Jewish student to sing a song in Hebrew for the class.

"O Chanukah"

Grades:	3–5
Integrative Areas:	Cultural heritage, Hanukkah, social studies—history
Concepts:	Melody: Repetition, steps and skips
	Symbols: Use of repeat sign; first and second endings
	Harmony: In thirds
	Rhythm: Duple
	Descant: Melodic and rhythmic repetition

O Chanukah

Jewish Folk Song
English Words by Judith Eisenstein

Key: D minor
Starting pitch: D
Meter: 4/4, begins on last half of 4

O Cha - nu - kah, O Cha - nu - kah, come light the me - no - rah.
Let's___ have a par - ty, we'll all dance the ho - rah.

Gath - er round the ta - ble, we'll give you a treat.

Shin - ing tops to play with and pan - cakes to eat;

And while we are play - ing, The can - dles are burn - ing___ low,

One for each night, they___ shed a sweet light to re -

1. mind us of days long a - go,

2. mind us of days long a - go.

Alto glockenspiel or alto xylophone

Finger cymbals

Drums

More Songs: Hanukkah

"Candles of Chanukah" in Silver Burdett and Ginn *World of Music* K, p. 170

"In the Window" in Silver Burdett and Ginn *World of Music* 2, p. 206

"Joyous Chanukah" in Silver Burdett and Ginn *World of Music* 2, p. 207

MARTIN LUTHER KING, JR. DAY

"We Shall Overcome"

Grades: 3–6
Integrative Areas: Social studies—history, social problems, nonviolent protest
Concepts: Melody: Mostly steps, legato, repetition
                              Form: AB

We Shall Overcome

Key: C
Starting pitch: G
Meter: 4/4, begins on 1

Civil Rights Song

Suggestions for Lessons

1. Review the events leading to the emergence of Martin Luther King, Jr. as a civil rights leader.

2. Read the descriptions of the famous gathering at the Lincoln Memorial in 1963, and have students study the speech "I Have a Dream" given by Dr. King at this event.

I Have a Dream

. . . I say to you today, my friends, that in spite of the difficulties and frustrations of the moment, I still have a dream. It is a dream deeply rooted in the American dream. I have a dream that one day this nation will rise up and live out the true meaning of its creed: "We hold these truths to be self-evident, that all men are created equal." I have a dream that my four children will one day live in a nation where they will not be judged by the color of their skin but by the content of their character.

I have a dream today. When we let freedom ring, when we let it ring from every village and every hamlet, from every state and every city, we will be able to speed up that day when all of God's children, black men and white men, Jews and Gentiles, Protestants and Catholics, will be able to join hands and sing the words of the old Negro spiritual "Free at last, free at last, thank God Almighty, we are free at last."

3. Discuss the appropriateness of the setting, the Lincoln Memorial. Show pictures of this well-known national monument.

4. Dramatize the gathering of people from all over the United States and appoint a student to read the speech as the rest of the class hums and then sings "We Shall Overcome."

"Martin Luther King"

Grades:	2–4
Integrative Areas:	Social justice, history, protest, leadership
Concepts:	Rhythm: steady beat, 4/4 meter, repeated patterns
	Melody: Mostly steps, range within an octave
	Form: ABCA

Martin Luther King

Key: D major
Starting pitch: D
Meter: 4/4, begins on "and" of 3

Words and Music by Theresa Fulbright

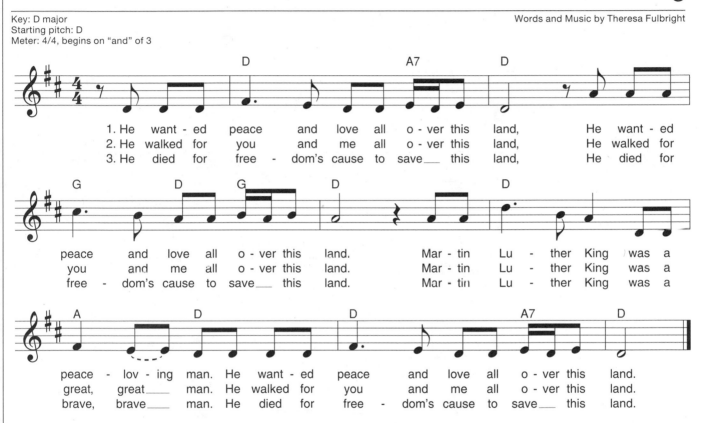

Reprinted by permission of Theresa Fulbright.

Suggestions for Lessons

1. Ask students to discover the repeated words and repeated rhythms as they view the song from a transparency or their books.
2. Discuss the meanings of such words as *peace, love, freedom.* Place these words on cards.
3. Show pictures of Martin Luther King, Jr. Discuss his role as a leader for freedom.
4. Use red, green, yellow, and red strips of paper to diagram the song.

VALENTINE'S DAY

"Somebody Loves Me"

Grades: K–2
Integrative Areas: Friendship, visual art
Concepts: Rhythm: Syncopation, repetition, duple meter, rests (percussion only)
                      Melody: Repetition, range

Somebody Loves Me

Words and Music by Gaynor Jones

Key: C
Starting pitch: C
Meter: 4/4, begins on 1

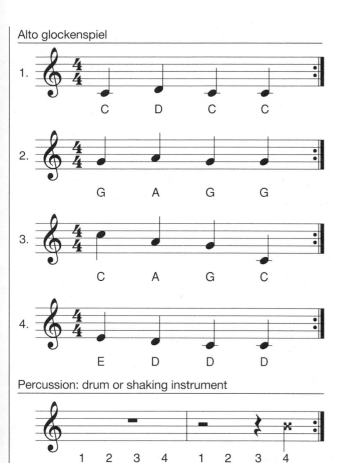

Alto glockenspiel

1. C D C C

2. G A G G

3. C A G C

4. E D D D

Percussion: drum or shaking instrument

1 2 3 4   1 2 3 4

"I Made a Valentine"

Grades:	K–1
Integrative Areas:	Visual art, friendship
Concepts:	Meter: Triple meter
	Melody: Repetition, melodic contour

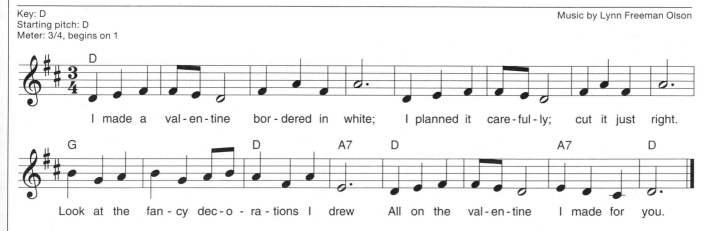

I Made a Valentine

Music by Lynn Freeman Olson

Key: D
Starting pitch: D
Meter: 3/4, begins on 1

I made a val-en-tine bor-dered in white; I planned it care-ful-ly; cut it just right.

Look at the fan-cy dec-o-ra-tions I drew All on the val-en-tine I made for you.

Suggestions for Lessons

1. Read one of the many stories about the origin of Valentine's Day: "St. Valentine was a Roman priest who made friends with children. The Romans imprisoned him when he refused to worship their gods. Children missed their friend and tossed loving notes between the bars of his cell window. In A.D. 496 Pope Gelasius named February 14 as St. Valentine's Day and the custom of sending messages of love and friendship spread throughout Europe and America."
2. Make valentines in art class to give to parents and friends.
3. Create short rhymes in language arts that focus on love and friendship.

More Songs: Valentine's Day

"Be My Valentine" in Silver Burdett and Ginn *Music* 2, p. 148

"Valentine, Valentine" in Holt, Rinehart and Winston *Music Book* 2, p. 152

"Best Friends" in Silver Burdett and Ginn *World of Music* 2, p. 182

"You and Me" in Silver Burdett and Ginn *World of Music* 2, p. 186

PRESIDENTS' DAY: GEORGE WASHINGTON

"Columbia, the Gem of the Ocean"

Grades:	4–6
Integrative Areas:	Social studies—history, government, freedom/independence; language arts—vocabulary; visual art; listening
Concepts:	Rhythm: 4/4 meter, repeated patterns ♫ ♩
	Melody: Octave skips, accidentals, descending scale melody

Columbia, the Gem of the Ocean

United States

Key: F
Starting pitch: C
Meter: 4/4, begins on 4

O Co-lum-bia, the gem of the o-cean, The home of the brave and the free,___ The shrine of each pa-triot's de-vo-tion, A world___ of-fers hom-age to thee. Thy___ man-dates make he-roes as-sem-ble, When___ lib-er-ty's form stands in view, Thy___ ban-ners make tyr-an-ny trem-ble, When___ borne___ by the red, white and blue! When___ borne by the red, white and blue! When___ borne by the red, white and blue! Thy___ ban-ners make tyr-an-ny trem-ble, When___ borne___ by the red, white and blue.

"Old Colony Times"

Grades:	4–6
Integrative Areas:	Social studies—history, government, freedom/independence; language arts—vocabulary; visual art; listening
Concepts:	Rhythm: Fermata, duple meter
	Melody: Mostly steps, narrow range, repetition phrases
	Form: AB

Old Colony Times

American Song

Key: F
Starting pitch: C
Meter: 4/4, begins on 4

Suggestions for Lessons

1. Show pictures of Mount Vernon, home of George Washington. Explain that it is open to the public as a national monument.

2. Study the Revolutionary War period and the events that led to George Washington's election as the first president of the United States.

3. Display *Washington Crossing the Delaware* by Currier and Ives.* Observe the use of vertical and horizontal lines to create stability, and also the red, white, and blue colors.

4. Show a picture of *George Washington* (the sculpture) by Greenough. Note how he has been cast as a Roman statesman.

5. Read the words to "Columbia, the Gem of the Ocean." Discuss the meaning of such words as *Columbia, gem, shrine, patriot, homage, mandate, tyranny.* Relate the name "Columbia" to the American space shuttle *Columbia.*

6. Discuss the relationship of the United States to England before the Revolutionary War. Dramatize the song "Old Colony Times."

7. Read stories about George Washington:

   Suzanne Hilton, *The World of Young George Washington* (New York: Walker Publishers, 1987)

   May Yonge McNeer, *The Story of George Washington* (Nashville: Abingdon, 1973)

   Robert M. Quackenbush, *I Did It with My Hatchet: A Story of George Washington* (New York: Pippin Press, 1989)

---

*100 Currier ancl Ives Favorites (New York: Crown Publishers, 1978), p. 43.

PRESIDENTS' DAY: ABRAHAM LINCOLN

"On Springfield Mountain"

Grades:	4–6
Integrative Areas:	Social studies—history, geography, politics, Civil War; poetry; visual art
Concepts:	Rhythm: Triple meter, rhythm patterns: ♩ ♩ ♫
	Tempo: Slow
	Melody: Melody centers around G and D (*do* and *sol*), many skips

On Springfield Mountain

American Folk Song

Key: G
Starting pitch: D
Meter: 3/4, begins on "and" of 2

On Spring-field Moun-tain there did dwell A love-ly youth, I knew him well. Too roo-de-nay too roo-de-noo, Too roo-de-nay too roo-de noo.

"Battle Hymn of the Republic"

Grades:	4–6
Integrative Areas:	Social studies—history, geography, politics, Civil War; poetry; visual art
Concepts:	Rhythm: Duple meter, strong beat, repetition of rhythm patterns: ♪.♪
	Melody: Wide range, mostly steps, a few skips
	Dynamics: Loud
	Form: AB

Battle Hymn of the Republic

Key: Bb
Starting pitch: F
Meter: 4/4, begins on 4

Music by William Steffe
Words by Julia Ward Howe

Mine eyes have seen the glo - ry of the com - ing of the Lord; He is

tramp - ling out the vin - tage where the grapes of wrath are stored; He hath

loosed the fate - ful light - ning of His ter - ri - ble swift sword; His truth is march - ing on.

Chorus

Glo - ry, glo - ry hal - le - lu - jah! Glo - ry, glo - ry hal - le - lu - jah!

Glo - ry, glo - ry hal - le - lu - jah! His truth is march - ing on.

Suggestions for Lessons

1. Read the poem "Lincoln" by Carl Sandburg. Discuss how the poet portrays the spirit and background of the man who was the sixteenth president of the United States.
2. Read the Gettysburg Address. Have students study the events that led to this occasion. Dramatize the event by asking a student to read the speech while the rest of the class sings "Battle Hymn of the Republic."
3. Show slides of the Lincoln Memorial in Washington, D.C. Point out that this monument is modeled after the famous Parthenon in Athens, Greece. Discuss the power and stillness represented in the figure of Lincoln.
4. Listen to *Lincoln Portrait* by Aaron Copland. Identify the theme "On Springfield Mountain." Sing the song in class.

5. Read stories about Abraham Lincoln:

Russell Freedman, *Lincoln: A Photobiography* (New York: Clarion Books, 1987)

Carol Greene, *Abraham Lincoln: A President of a Divided Country* (Chicago: Children's Press, 1989)

Jim Hargrove, *Abraham Lincoln: The Freedom President* (New York: Ballantine, 1989)

Rebecca Stefoff, *Abraham Lincoln, 16th President of the United States* (Ada, Okla.: Garrett Educational Corporation, 1989)

More Songs: Presidents' Day

"Abraham Lincoln" in Silver Burdett and Ginn *World of Music* 4, p. 119

"George Washington" in Macmillan *Music and You* K, p. 156

INTEGRATIVE CATEGORY: PATRIOTIC SONGS OF THE UNITED STATES OF AMERICA

Patriotic songs of the United States express the hopes, desires, and feelings of pride American people have for their country and its heroes. They embody the history and feelings of the American people as they have struggled through wars, famine, depression, and victories to build a better life for themselves and their children. These songs have become favorites because they appeal to people in a direct but simple manner and because there is a vitality that inspires us generation after generation

"I Like it Here"

Grades:	4–6
Integrative Areas:	Patriotism, freedom
Concepts:	Melody: Accidentals, half and whole steps
	Rhythm: Duple meter, steady beat
	Symbols: Repeat sign, first and second endings

I Like It Here

Words and Music by Clay Boland

Key: B♭
Starting pitch: F
Meter: 2/2, begins on "and" of 1

1. I like the U - nit - ed States of A - mer - i - ca,_____ I like the
2. I am so luck - y to be in A - mer - i - ca,_____ And I am

way we all live with - out fear._____ I like to vote for my choice,
thank - ful each day of the year._____ For I can do as I please,

_____ speak my mind, raise my voice. Yes, I like it here.
_____ 'cause I'm free as the breeze. Yes, I

like it here._____ I'd like to climb to the top of a moun - tain so high,_____

_____ Lift my head to the sky_____ and say how grate - ful am I_____ For the

way that I'm liv - ing, I'm work - ing and giv - ing And help - ing the land I hold

dear._____ Yes, I like it, I like it, I like it here.

Suggestions for Lessons

1. Have the students play a drumbeat on their knees as they listen to and then sing the song.
2. Read the poem "I Hear America singing" by Walt Whitman:

I Hear America Singing
I hear America singing, the varied carols I hear,
Those of the mechanics, each singing his as it should be blithe and strong,
The carpenter singing his as he measures his plank or beam,
The mason singing his as he makes ready for work or leaves off work,
The boatman singing what belongs to him in his boat, the deck hand singing on the steamboat deck,
The shoemaker singing as he sits on his bench, the hatter singing as he stands,
The wood-cutter's song, the ploughboy's on his way in the morning, or at noon intermission or at sundown,
The delicious singing of the mother, or the young wife at work, or the girl sewing or washing,
Each sings what belongs to him or her and to none else,
The day what belongs to the day—at night the party of young fellows, robust, friendly,
Singing with open mouths their strong melodious songs.

More Songs: Patriotic Songs

"America," p. 61

"The Star-Spangled Banner," p. 41

"Yankee Doodle," p. 475

"America the Beautiful" in Silver Burdett and Ginn *World of Music* 3, p. 189

"We'll Find America" in Holt, Rinehart and Winston *Exploring Music* 7, p. 7

"Pledge of Allegiance to the Flag" in Holt, Rinehart and Winston *The Music Book* 5, p. 1

"Fifty, Nifty, United States" in Holt, Rinehart and Winston *The Music Book* 5, p. 4

INTEGRATIVE CATEGORY: GETTING ACQUAINTED

"How Do You Do?"

Grades:	K–1
Integrative Areas:	Talking to others, self-image
Concepts:	Melody: Repetition of phrases, narrow range
	Rhythm: Duple meter, steady beat, repetition of rhythmic patterns
	Form: AABA

How Do You Do?

Folk Tune from Germany
Words Adapted

Key: F
Starting pitch: C
Meter: 2/4, begins on "and" of 2

1. As I was walk - ing down the street,
2. Now when I'm walk - ing down the street,

I saw the peo - ple walk - ing;
And met some friends out walk - ing,

And when they met some - one they knew,
I smile at them, and one they smile too,

They start - ed in a - talk - ing:
And then we start a - talk - ing:

"How do you do?" "How do you do?"
"How do you do?" "How do you do?"

And when they met some - one they knew,
And ev - 'ry - one is smil - ing, too,

They start - ed in a - talk - ing.
And ev - 'ry - one is talk - ing.

Suggestions for Lessons

1. Discuss what you say when you meet someone new. Examples include "How do you do?" "Pleased to meet you," and so on.

2. Discuss what you say when you make a new friend. Examples include "How about coming over to my house?"

3. Play a game. Teacher picks a child and sings "How are you today?"

How are you to - day?_____

Child answers by singing "I am fine today." (can be improvised also)

I am fine to - day._____

4. Use a song pattern to call the roll and ask the child to sing a response with his or her own name. Examples:

What is your name?_____

My name is Lu - bel - la

What is your name?_____

My name is An - ton.

5. Sit in a circle and sing a question, then point to a child in the circle who must sing an answer. This same game can be played with teams and points given to the side that sings correctly.

6. Begin teaching the song by rote with line 5, "How do you do?"

7. Ask a child to play the xylophone whenever the class sings "How do you do?"

8. Sing the verse and stop on "walking," asking students what the word should be. Continue through the song stopping at the end of each phrase ("walking," "a-talking").

9. Point out that the first two lines repeat, then the class sings "How do you do?" and lines 6–7 repeat.

INTEGRATIVE CATEGORY: HUMAN RELATIONSHIPS AND EMOTIONS

"Magic Penny"

Grades:	3–4
Integrative Areas:	Getting along with others, love, developing positive self-image, aspiration
Concepts:	Rhythm: Syncopation, repetition of patterns, duple meter
	Melody: Repetition of phrases, wide range
	Form: ABA

Magic Penny

Words and Music by Malvina Reynolds

Key: D
Starting pitch: D
Meter: 4/4, begins on 1

Suggestions for Lessons

1. Discuss the text of the song "Magic Penny." Ask students for examples of those feelings of pleasure they experience when they have shared something with someone else.

2. Create a class project in which students share with those less fortunate, such as reading to older persons who have lost their sight, or sending get-well cards to a child in the hospital who has no parents.

More Songs: Human Relationships and Emotions

"Happiness" in Macmillan *Music and You* 6, p. 264

"Loneliness Song" in Macmillan *Music and You* 5, p. 65; Holt, Rinehart and Winston *Music Book* 5, p. 210

"Look to the Rainbow" in Silver Burdett and Ginn *World of Music* 3, p. 159

"You Can't Buy Friendship" in Silver Burdett and Ginn *World of Music* 2, pp. 194–195

INTEGRATIVE CATEGORY: LANGUAGE ARTS

"Old MacDonald Had a Farm"

Grades:	K–2
Integrative Areas:	Linking sight and sound, effect of accumulation in music and in poetry, creativity, word/phrase sequencing
Concepts:	Rhythm: Mostly ♩ and ♪ notes, repetition of patterns
	Melody: Short phrases, repetition of pitches, narrow range
	Harmony: Chords: G, C, D$_7$

Old MacDonald Had a Farm

United States

Key: G
Starting pitch: G
Meter: 4/4, begins on 1

1. Old Mac - Don - ald   had   a   farm,   E - I - E - I - O!   And
2. Old Mac - Don - ald   had   a   farm,   E - I - E - I - O!   And

on this farm he had some chicks,   E - I - E - I - O!   With a
on this farm he had some ducks,   E - I - E - I - O!   With a

Chick, chick here, and a   chick, chick there,   Here a chick, there a chick,   Ev-'ry-where a chick, chick.
Quack, quack here, and a   quack, quack there,   Here a quack, there a quack,   Ev-'ry-where a quack, quack.

REFRAIN

Old Mac - Don - ald   had   a   farm,   E - I - E - I - O!

Suggestions for Lessons

1. Have each child choose a particular animal or sound and remember where it is in the verse sequence.

2. Read poems that use the same type of sequencing, such as "The House That Jack Built" or "The Twelve Days of Christmas." Discuss the effect of such a technique (it lengthens the poem or song, increases its complexity, etc.).

More Songs: Language Arts

"Mister Frog Went A-Courtin'" in Silver Burdett and Ginn *World of Music* 2, p. 18

"Who Built the Ark?" in Silver Burdett and Ginn *World of Music* 2, p. 52

"Turn, Turn, Turn" in Silver Burdett and Ginn *World of Music* 5, pp. 62–63

INTEGRATIVE CATEGORY: MATHEMATICS

"Five Little Frogs"

Grades:	K–3
Integrative Areas:	Nature, numbers, number relationships
Concepts:	Rhythm: Duple meter, syncopation, repetition
	Melody: Direction of phrases

Five Little Frogs

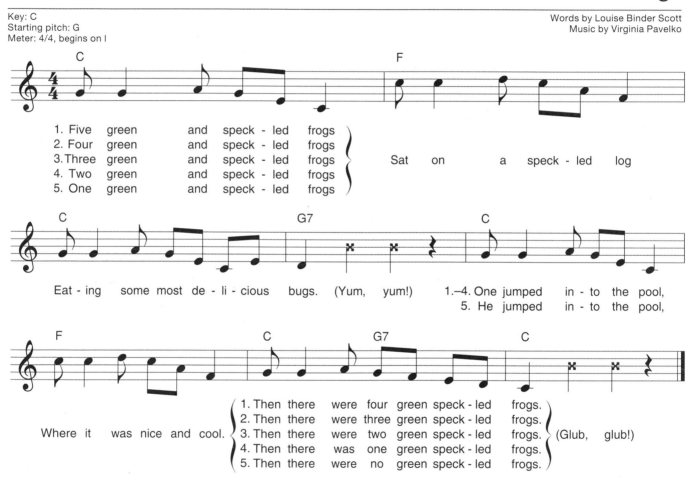

Key: C
Starting pitch: G
Meter: 4/4, begins on I

Words by Louise Binder Scott
Music by Virginia Pavelko

1. Five green and speck-led frogs
2. Four green and speck-led frogs
3. Three green and speck-led frogs
4. Two green and speck-led frogs
5. One green and speck-led frogs

Sat on a speck-led log

Eat-ing some most de-li-cious bugs. (Yum, yum!)

1.–4. One jumped in-to the pool,
5. He jumped in-to the pool,

Where it was nice and cool.

1. Then there were four green speck-led frogs.
2. Then there were three green speck-led frogs.
3. Then there were two green speck-led frogs.
4. Then there was one green speck-led frogs.
5. Then there were no green speck-led frogs.

(Glub, glub!)

Suggestions for Lessons

1. Dramatize the words of "Five Little Frogs."
2. Chart repeating phrases with colors.
3. Map the direction of the melody.
4. Emphasize breath for octave skips.
5. Use fingers or charts showing 5, 4, 3, 2, 1 to indicate the number of frogs remaining.
6. Emphasize subtracting one from each set of frogs.

More Songs: Mathematics

"Counting Song" in Macmillan *Music and You* 1, p. 213; Silver Burdett and Ginn *World of Music* 2, p. 31

"Five Fat Turkeys," p. 157

"Five Little Pumpkins," p. 26

"Twelve Days of Christmas" in Macmillan *Music and You* 5, p. 266

INTEGRATIVE CATEGORY: SCIENCE

"Follow the Drinkin' Gourd"

Grades:	4–6
Integrative Areas:	Astronomy, Civil War (underground railway)
Concepts:	Rhythm: Duple meter, syncopation, triplets
	Melody: Repetition of phrases, narrow range
	Form: AB

Follow the Drinkin' Gourd

Key: E minor
Starting pitch: E
Meter: 2/2, begins on "and" of 2

Spiritual
Arr. by Paul Campbell

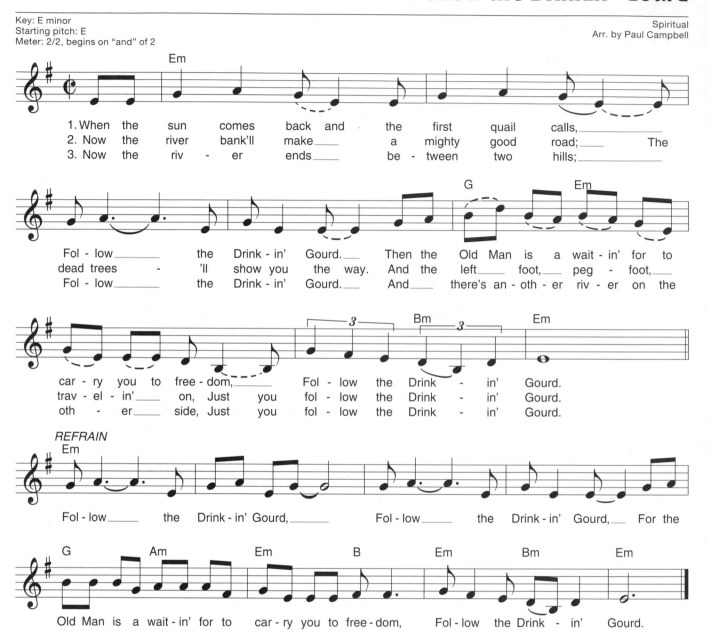

1. When the sun comes back and the first quail calls,_____
2. Now the river bank'll make____ a mighty good road;____ The
3. Now the riv - er ends____ be - tween two hills;_____ The

Fol - low_____ the Drink - in' Gourd.____ Then the Old Man is a wait - in' for to
dead trees - 'll show you the way. And the left____ foot,____ peg - foot,____
Fol - low_____ the Drink - in' Gourd.____ And____ there's an - oth - er riv - er on the

car - ry you to free - dom,_____ Fol - low the Drink - in' Gourd.
trav - el - in'____ on, Just you fol - low the Drink - in' Gourd.
oth - er____ side, Just you fol - low the Drink - in' Gourd.

REFRAIN

Fol - low_____ the Drink - in' Gourd,_____ Fol - low_____ the Drink - in' Gourd,____ For the

Old Man is a wait - in' for to car - ry you to free - dom, Fol - low the Drink - in' Gourd.

New Words & New Music adaptation by Paul Campbell. TRO. Copyright © 1951 Folkways Music Publishers, Inc. New York, N.Y. Used by permission.

Suggestions for Lessons

1. Study the origins and placement of selected constellations in the galaxy, such as the Big Dipper and Orion.
2. Visit a local planetarium to learn more about astronomy.
3. Create charts showing some of the most common constellations and stories about them. Discover at what seasons of the year they are most clear.
4. Use a compass to discover the magnetic pull to the north. Show students the location of the North Star and the Big Dipper. Discuss ways that a traveler could find his or her way home without a compass.
5. Have students read stories about the Civil War and the underground railway. Be certain that they do not confuse this with a bona fide train. Explain that the North Star and Big Dipper showed slaves the way to freedom.
6. Place the words on a chart. Have students read the words to each verse of the song. Explain what each means.
7. Listen to a recording of (or sing) "Follow the Drinkin' Gourd." Have students read the words as they listen.
8. Teach the song starting with the chorus followed by the verses. Pay particular attention to the repetition of the syncopated rhythmic pattern.
9. Sing the entire song through.

More Songs: Science

"April Showers" in Silver Burdett and Ginn *World of Music* 6, p. 251

"Aquarius" in Holt, Rinehart and Winston and Winston *Exploring Music* 7, p. 188

"Autumn Leaves Now Are Falling" in Holt, Rinehart and Winston *Exploring Music* 1, p. 40

"Clouds" in Silver Burdett and Ginn *Music* 4, p. 55

"Moon Is Coming Out" in Macmillan *Music and You* 1, p. 225

INTEGRATIVE CATEGORY: TRANSPORTATION

"Erie Canal"

Grades:	4–6
Integrative Areas:	History, geography, visual art, poetry, vocabulary, science
Concepts:	Rhythm: Duple meter, syncopation, repetition of patterns
	Melody: Repetition of phrases, many skips
	Tonality: Minor/major
	Form: AB

Erie Canal

United States

Key: D minor
Starting pitch: A
Meter: 2/2, begins on "and" of 2

Robustly

1. I've got a mule, her name is Sal, Fif-teen miles on the E - rie Ca - nal. She's a
2. We'd bet-ter get a - long, old pal. Fif-teen miles on the E - rie Ca - nal. You can

good old work - er and a good old pal, Fif-teen miles on the E - rie Ca - nal. We've
bet your life I'd nev - er part from Sal. Fif-teen miles on the E - rie Ca - nal. Get

hauled some barg - es in our day. Filled with lum - ber, coal and hay, And
up there, mule,___ here comes a lock. We'll make Rome___ by six - o' - clock. Then

we know ev - 'ry inch of the way From Al - ban - y___ to___ Buf - fa - lo.___
one more trip, and back we'll___ go,___ back we'll___ go to Buf - fa - lo.___

Chorus

Low bridge, ev - 'ry-bod - y down, Low bridge, 'cause we're

com - ing to a town; And you'll al - ways know your neigh - bor, You'll

al - ways know your pal, If you've ev - er nav - i - gat - ed on the E - rie Ca - nal.

Suggestions for Lessons

1. Present the following background on the Erie Canal: The Erie Canal, authorized in 1817 and completed in 1825, connected Lake Erie (Buffalo) and the Hudson River (Albany). A 363-mile waterway, it was of immense significance in the development of commerce in the United States. This cheap, all-water route provided transportation for agricultural produce from the west to the east and manufactured products from the east to the "new" west. The canal teemed with boats and barges as pioneers swarmed to find new lands. Songs of the mule skinners who drove the mules along the towpath as they hauled the flat-bottom boats echoed through the countryside both day and night. Since low bridges occurred at frequent intervals along the canal, the mule skinners would shout a warning to the passengers on the boat so that they could duck. This song is about a mule skinner and his mule Sal. It tells of the produce carried and the friendliness of the passengers.

2. Study the canal as a means of transportation. Use encyclopedias for reference. Locate Albany and Buffalo on a map of New York and determine how long the canal was. Find Lake Erie and place it in relation to the other Great Lakes. When was the Erie Canal considered part of the "new" west? (1825) Discover when other cities in this area (Cleveland, Cincinnati, and Columbus, Ohio) were founded. What was the Western Reserve? Have students learn about other canals, such as the Panama Canal, the Canal at Corinth (Greece), and the Suez Canal.

3. Using the dictionary, explore the meanings of words such as *barge*, *mule skinner*, and *navigation*.

4. Listen to the two parts of the song: Part A is in the minor mode and Part B is in a major mode. Part B is also called the *chorus*.

5. Teach the song starting with the chorus (Part B). Note the repetition of the rhythm, ♪♩, then teach the verses.

"The John B. Sails"

Grades:	4–6
Integrative Areas:	History, geography, vocabulary, visual art, science
Concepts:	Rhythm: Duple meter, syncopation, ties
	Melody: Narrow range, repetition of phrases
	Harmony: Mostly thirds and sixths
	Chords: G, C, D$_7$

The John B. Sails

Calypso Folk Song from the Bahamas

Key: G
Starting pitch: D
Meter: 4/4, begins on 4

1. Oh, we came on the sloop *John B.* My grand - fath - er and me, A -
2. The___ first mate___ he got sad, Feel - in' aw - f'ly bad,
3. The___ poor cook___ he got fits, And throw 'way all___ the grits, Then he

round Nas - sau Town___ we did roam._____ Walk - in' all night
Captain come a - board,___ took him a - way.___ Please let me a - lone
took and___ eat up all of the corn.___ Please let me go home.

Just see - in' the sights, Well, I feel so break - up, I want___ to go home.
And let___ me go home, Well, I feel so break - up, I want___ to go home.
I want___ to go home, Well, this is the worst___ trip Since I___ was born.

REFRAIN

So hoist up the *John B.* sails, See how the main - s'l sets,

Send for the Cap - tain a - shore, Let___ me go home. Please let___ me go home,

I want___ to go home. Well,___ I feel so break - up, I want___ to go home.

Suggestions for Lessons

1. Read several sea chanties (also spelled "shanties"), such as "Yeo, Heave Ho."
   Discuss the meaning of the words used, such as *capstan* and *anchor*.

   Yeo, Heave Ho
   Yeo, heave ho! 'Round the capstan go—
   Heave, men with a will, Tramp, and tramp it still!
   The anchor must be weighed, The anchor must be weighed.
   Chorus:
      Yeo ho! Heave ho!
      Yeo ho! Heave ho!
   Yeo, heave ho! Cheerily we go,
   Heave, men with a will, Tramp, and tramp it still
   The anchor grips the ground, The anchor grips the ground.
   Chorus:
      Yeo ho! Heave ho!
      Yeo ho! Heave ho!
   Yeo, heave ho! raise her from below,
   Heave, men, with a will,
   Tramp, and tramp it still;
   The anchor's off the ground
   And we are outward bound.
   Chorus:
      Yeo ho! Heave ho!
      Yeo ho! Heave ho!
   Yeo, heave ho! round the capstan go,
   Heave, men, with a will,
   The anchor now is weighed, The anchor now is weighed.
   Chorus:
      Yeo ho! heave ho!
      Yeo ho! heave ho!

2. Write your own poem or short story about sailing ships.
3. Listen to a recording of sea chanties: *Sea Shanties*, RCA Victor LSC 2551 (Robert Shaw).
4. Listen to *Windjammer*, by Morton Gould (original sound track for the film *Windjammer*, Columbia CL 1158).
5. Study how various artists have expressed their feelings about sailing and sailing ships, and show these scenes by Currier and Ives:*
   The Clipper Yacht "America"
   Clipper Ship "Nightingale"
   The Wreck of the Steam Ship "San Francisco"
   Summer Scenes in New York Harbor
6. Locate the Bahama Islands on a map. Discuss the meanings of Calypso and the cultural background of the Bahamian people. Identify Latin American instruments, such as maracas, claves, and bongo drums, that seem appropriate to accompany the song.

*100 Currier and Ives Favorites (Museum of New York, N.Y.: Crown Publishers, 1978).

7. Present principles of sailing in science class. Compare the terminology with that found in traditional sea chanties. Children could also study fishing activities of sailing vessels, such as whaling and fishing for mackerel, porpoise, smelt, herring, cod, and flounder.

"I've Been Working on the Railroad"

Grades:	2–5
Integrative Areas:	History, geography, social change, passenger/shipping, visual art, poetry
Concepts:	Rhythm: Duple meter, steady beat, repetition patterns:

Melody: Short phrases, repetition of phrases
Tonality: Major
Form: AB

I've Been Working on the Railroad (Dinah)

Traditional

Key: G
Starting pitch: G
Meter: 4/4, begins on 1

Di - nah won't you blow, Di - nah won't you blow, Di - nah won't you blow your horn?

Some-one's in the kitch - en with Di - nah, Some-one's in the kitch - en, I know,_____

Some-one's in the kitch - en with Di - nah, Strum - ming on the old ban - jo.

Fee fie fid - dle - ee - i - o, Fee fie fid - dle - ee - i - o,_____

Fee fie fid - dle - ee - i - o, Strum - ming on the old ban - jo.

"Casey Jones"

Grades:	4–6
Integrative Areas:	Trains, history
Concepts:	Rhythm: Duple, steady beat, repetition of rhythm patterns, syncopation
	Melody: Repetition of phrases, range from B flat to D
	Form: Verse and refrain: AB

Casey Jones

Key: B♭
Starting pitch: B♭
Meter: 4/4, begins on 1

Words by T. Lawrence Seibert
Music by Eddie Newton

1. Come, all you round-ers, if you want___ to hear___ A
2. Put in your wa-ter and___ shov-el your coal. Put your
3. Ca-sey pulled up___ at___ Re-no hill.___ He

sto-ry___ a-bout___ a___ brave en-gi-neer, And Ca-sey Jones___ was the
head out___ the win-dow, watch them driv-ers roll. I'll run her till___ she___
toot-ed for the cross-ing with an aw-ful shrill. The switch-man knew___ by the

round-er's name. On a six-eight___ wheel-er, boys, he won___ his fame. The
leaves the rail, 'Cause I'm eight hours___ late___ with the west-ern mail. He
en-gine's moans That the man at the throt-tle was___ Ca-sey Jones. He

call-er called Ca-sey at a half___ past four. Ca-sey
looked at his watch,___ and his watch___ was slow. He___
pulled up with-in___ two___ miles of the place, And___

Suggestions for Lessons

1. Review what is known about the character Casey Jones. He was known for the speed at which he could make a train travel and for the wonderful sound he could get out of the train whistle. Some stories tell us that the people who worked in the fields near the railroad track could tell when Casey was at the throttle by the sound of the whistle.

2. Review the difference between a "diesel" and a "locomotive." Show pictures of each.

3. Discuss the meaning of a ballad (story) and read the words of the song as a story.

4. Teach the syncopated patterns by playing and singing the rhythm patterns.

5. Use colored charts for repeating phrases.

6. Create an overlay for the overhead projector with repeated phrases in "Casey Jones."

7. Dramatize the story as students sing the song.

8. Invite students to bring in toy trains (steam locomotives, diesels). Discuss how train travel has changed during the past century.

9. View pictures of trains and train travel:

   Claude Monet, *The Saint-Lazare Railroad Station*

   Currier and Ives, *The "Lightning Express" Trains* (*100 Currier and Ives Favorites*, p. 57)

10. Listen to musical compositions about trains, such as Villa-Lobos, "The Little Train of Caipira"; Honegger, "Pacific 231"; Glenn Miller, "Chattanooga Choo-Choo," "Orange Blossom Special."

11. Read the following poem by David McCord about a train.

Song of the Train*
Clickety-clack,
Wheels on the track,
This is the way
They begin the attack:
Clickety-clack,
Click-ety-clack,
Click-ety, clack-ety,
Click-ety
Clack
Clickety-clack,
Over the crack,
Faster and faster
The song of the track:
Clickety-clack,
Clickety-clack,
Clickety, clackety,
CLACKETY
Clack.
Riding in front,
Riding in back
EVERYONE hears
The song of the track:
Clickety-clack,
Clickety-clack,
clickety, CLICKETY,
Clackety
CLACK.

More Songs: Transportation

Ships

"Cape Cod Chantey" in Macmillan *Music and You* 5, p. 251; Silver Burdett and Ginn *World of Music* 4, p. 29

"Gallant Ship" in Holt, Rinehart and Winston *Exploring Music* K, p. 129

"Blow the Wind Southerly" in Silver Burdett and Ginn *World of Music* 5, pp. 70–71

Railroad

"Clickety Clack" in Macmillan *Music and You* K, p. 184

"Wabash Cannonball" in Silver Burdett and Ginn *World of Music* 5, pp. 14–15

Automobile

"Car Song" in *Silver Burdett Music* 1, p. 34; Silver Burdett and Ginn *World of Music* 1, p. 16

---

* David McCord, *Far and Few*. New York: Little, Brown, 1952.

QUESTIONS FOR REVIEW

1. What can music share with history?
2. What can music share with visual art?
3. What can music share with mathematics?
4. What can music share with social studies?
5. What can music share with dance?
6. What are some other areas in which music can be integrated into the classroom?
7. What types of evaluation techniques would you use as you develop lessons from the suggestions made?
8. What other integrative ideas do you have for teaching
   a. "Six Little Ducks" (K–2)
   b. "Circus Parade" (3–5)
   c. "Gatatumba" (3–6)
   d. "The Witch Rides" (K–1)
   e. "Martin Luther King" (2–4)
   f. "Somebody Loves Me" (K–2)

TEACHING MUSIC THROUGH PLAYING CLASSROOM INSTRUMENTS

Students are usually enthusiastic about performing music on instruments, and you will generally find them highly motivated and very responsive. As with singing, playing instruments involves students directly in making music, spontaneously or from a musical score, alone or with a group. Experience is often the best teacher; students learn to listen attentively both to the music they are playing themselves and to the music performed by the total ensemble. Individual players come to rely on others and to respect their roles in the creative process of performing music together.

Development of motor coordination is essential in playing classroom instruments. Through such activities many students improve the effective use of their arms, hands, fingers, legs, and feet.

Classroom instruments function in a variety of ways. Some are used to play melodies (recorder, melody bells, xylophone, and glockenspiel), others to play harmony (Autoharp, guitar, synthesizer, Omnichord), and still others to play both melody and harmony (piano and resonator bells). The many percussion instruments, such as drums, tambourines, claves, and triangles, are used to play rhythms.

As students learn to play instruments, they should develop

1. The ability to choose appropriate instruments for such musical concepts as
   a. Steady beat
   b. Differences in dynamics
   c. Musical form
   d. Pitch and melody

2. The ability to discriminate and select appropriate rhythm instruments for various types of music

3. An awareness of the expressive potential of different instruments

4. The ability to select and play instruments that can add to the expressiveness of music through accompaniment

Teachers need to learn the physical and musical characteristics of some of the most common classroom instruments and to develop basic playing skills that will enable them to demonstrate, and guide students in playing, these instruments.

The following guidelines will contribute to students' successful experiences with playing instruments:

1. Provide many aural experiences before using instruments.

2. Provide many opportunities for immediate success.

3. Reinforce each playing skill before going on to a new one.

4. Give *all* students an opportunity to play instruments.

5. Use instruments on a regular basis.

6. Encourage students to improvise.

7. Use instruments in musical ways.

8. Keep directions simple.

9. Avoid giving out all of the instruments at once.

10. Avoid asking students to "experiment" in creating sounds indiscriminately.

11. Avoid letting students mistreat instruments.

12. Avoid allowing students to "abuse" music by unmusical playing or behavior.

13. Ask students to "play" the instrument not "hit" the instrument.

Careful attention to these guidelines will reward both you and your students with musically satisfying experiences.

This chapter focuses on a general description and functions of melody, harmonic, and percussion instruments and techniques for teaching students to play them. It deals with selecting an appropriate instrument, playing rhythm accompaniments to songs, developing a rhythm ensemble, making your own instruments, and integrating instrumental experiences into the classroom. The chapter concludes with sample lessons.

MELODY INSTRUMENTS

A melody instrument is any instrument that can produce enough different pitches to play a melody. Classroom instruments that meet this criterion are piano, melody bells, resonator bells, xylophone, glockenspiel, and recorder. The functions of these melody instruments include (1) playing melodies, (2) playing ostinato melodic patterns, and (3) playing descants and "harmony" parts.

Piano

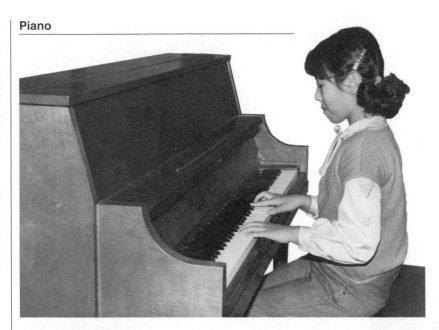

Electronic keyboard

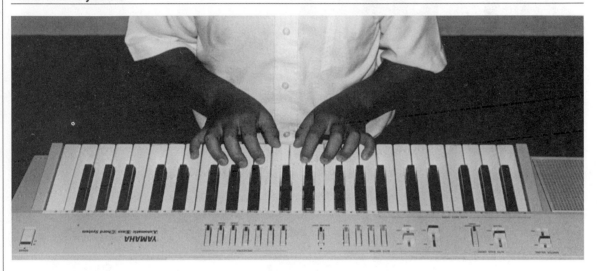

PIANO AND ELECTRONIC KEYBOARDS

The piano and electronic keyboards (such as those made by Casio, Yamaha, and Suzuki) are used primarily for playing melodies and simple accompaniments.

When you play the piano, depressing the keys causes hammers to strike strings. You can sustain the sound by depressing the right "damper" pedal, which raises the felt pads (called dampers) from the strings and allows them to continue to sound. When you release the pedal, the "dampers" return to the strings and stop the sound. When playing the following simple exercises and tunes, try playing a pitch on the piano and then pressing downward on the pedal. Remove your finger from the key and listen to it continue to sound. Then release the pedal with your foot and notice that the tone stops. Careful use of this pedal will allow you to play melodies smoothly. Too much pedal—that is, playing a melody with the pedal depressed throughout—will cause the tones to blur together. A little experimentation will make this principle clear to you.

Although the keyboard on the electronic keyboard is laid out in the same way as on the piano, it offers a variety of tone colors to choose from. That is, the electronic keyboard can sound somewhat like a harpsichord, a piano, an organ, a violin, and so on. In this way electronic keyboards differ dramatically from the piano.

The Form of the Keyboard

Since the "form" of the keyboard (pattern of black and white notes) is also found on melody and resonator bells, you will want to become familiar with it.

Position yourself in the center of the keyboard. You will notice white keys and black keys grouped into twos and threes. This pattern is repeated throughout the keyboard:

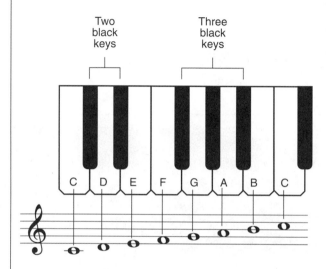

Each white key has a letter name that corresponds to a line or space on the staff. Thus, the pitch name E represents the white key E on the keyboard. The piano keyboard is divided into a series of eight pitches to the octave; there are eight octaves. The lowest pitch (to your left) is A. Play this note and then move up the keyboard playing only the white notes. The pitches are A, B, C, D, E, F, and G; then you start over again.

The octave A, B, C, D, E, F, G, A is divided into twelve semitones or half steps. Raising a pitch a half step is called a sharp (♯) (for example, F, F♯), and lowering it a half step is called a flat (♭) (for example, G, G♭). Notice in the following example that a single black note may have two names (for example, F♯ and G♭).

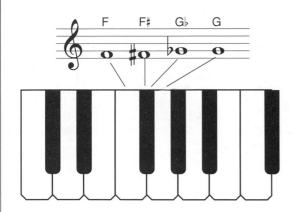

The pitch to the left of the two black keys in the center of the piano keyboard is called *middle C.* Place your right thumb on A (below middle C) followed by your third finger on A♯. Play the chromatic scale (half steps) alternating finger and thumb with each pitch. Next, play from A to B. Notice that this is a whole step (A♯ is in between). Play from C♯ to D♯. Notice that this is a whole step with D in between. Locate and play other half and whole steps.

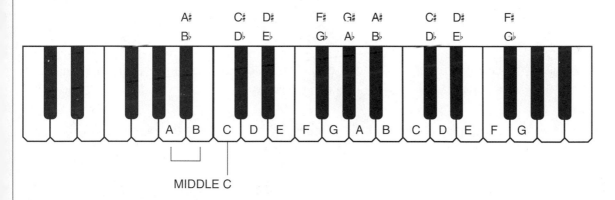

Fingering

To play a melody on a keyboard, you need to use the correct fingers. Follow these steps, and you will soon be able to play a melody.

1. Place your right hand on the keyboard with your thumb on middle C.
2. Curve your fingers above the keys, cupping your hand slightly as if over an orange, with the wrist flat.
3. Raise your thumb and "drop" it to the bottom of the key. Do not try to "push" the key down. The pitch should sound bright and clear.
4. Follow this same procedure with each of your five fingers playing successive pitches.
5. Now play the following exercise with your right hand, using the fingers indicated:

   thumb = 1

   index = 2

   middle = 3

   ring = 4

   little = 5

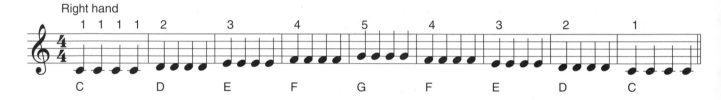

6. Now place your hand so that the thumb is on G and the fifth finger is on D. Repeat the above pattern with your hand in this position.

Now you are ready to play the following melodies. Be sure to count the beats out loud as you play to ensure correct rhythm.

Mary Had a Little Lamb

Sara J. Hale

Key: G
Starting pitch: B
Meter: 4/4, begins on 1

Good News

Spiritual

Key: G
Starting pitch: B
Meter: 4/4, begins on 2

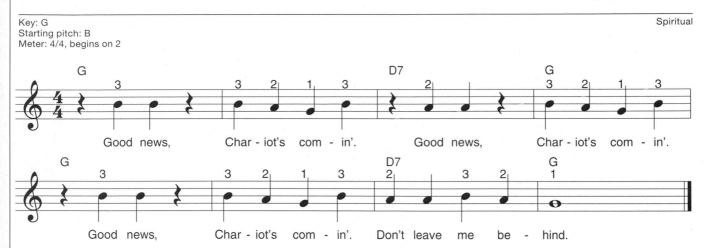

Good news, Char - iot's com - in'. Good news, Char - iot's com - in'.

Good news, Char - iot's com - in'. Don't leave me be - hind.

Lightly Row

Germany

Key: G
Starting pitch: D
Meter: 2/4, begins on 1

Light - ly row, Light - ly row, O'er the shin - ing waves we go.

Smooth - ly glide, smooth - ly glide on the si - lent tide.

Michael, Row the Boat Ashore

Spiritual

Key: C
Starting pitch: C
Meter: 4/4, begins on 3

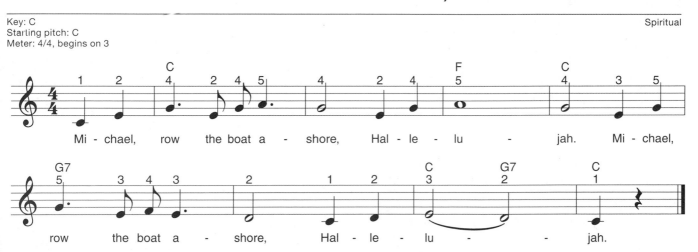

Mi - chael, row the boat a - shore, Hal - le - lu - jah. Mi - chael,

row the boat a - shore, Hal - le - lu - jah.

TRANSPOSITION

Sometimes it is necessary to transpose a piece of music from one key to another. This often occurs because of a need to lower the pitch level of a song in order to make it easier to sing or to make an accompaniment for a song easier to play.

The following song is shown first in the key of G major and then transposed down one whole step to the key of F major.

The Farmer in the Dell

England

Key of G

The far -mer in the dell,_____ The far -mer in the dell,

Hi! ho! the der - ry oh, The far -mer in the dell._____

Key of F

The far -mer in the dell,_____ The far -mer in the dell,

Hi! ho! the der - ry oh, The far -mer in the dell._____

Notice that the chordal accompaniment is also transposed.

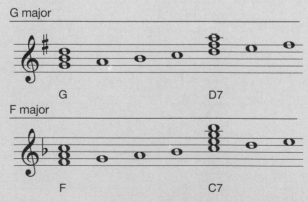

G major

G   D7

F major

F   C7

Sing and accompany the song first in G major and then in F major.

MELODY BELLS

A set of melody bells consists of a series of chromatically tuned metal bars mounted horizontally on a frame in the form of a piano keyboard. The smaller set contains pitches that range from C to G. Larger sets consist of two complete octaves. The lower pitches are to the left and higher pitches are to the right.

Twenty-five-note chromatic bells

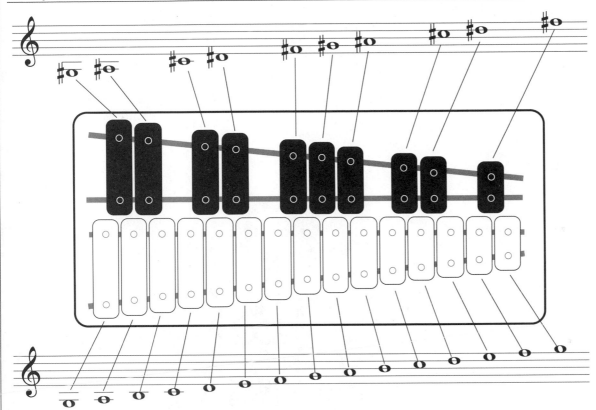

Melody bells

Eight-note diatonic step bells

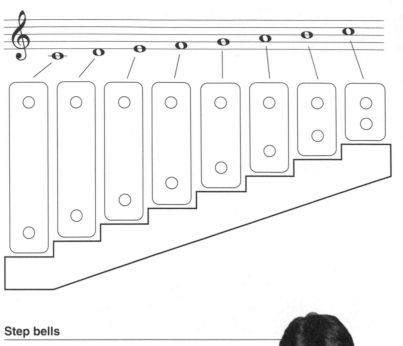

Step bells

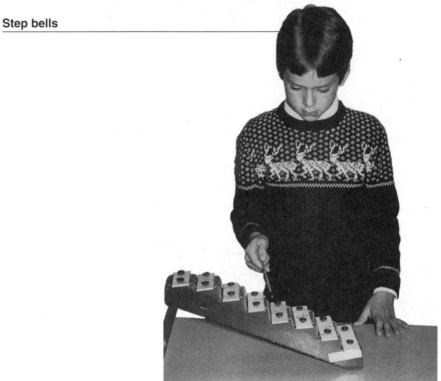

A smaller set of melody bells constructed vertically as "steps" encompasses only one octave (eight notes) without sharps or flats. The pitches go higher as the bells go "up the ladder." Many use a different color tone bar for each pitch.

Melody bells are played with a short stick with a mallet head made of wood, hard rubber, string, yarn, or soft rubber. The choice of mallet head determines the tone quality. A hard mallet will produce a bright, loud tone, while a soft mallet will produce a quiet, mellow tone.

To play melody bells, grasp the mallet with your thumb and one or two fingers. Keep your wrist flexible and strike the bell near the center, letting the mallet rebound instantly. If you hold the stick too tightly, the tone will lack any resonance or brilliance.

Have students practice striking the bells holding the mallets in either hand until they can alternate L-R-L-R-L-R as they move up or down a melody pattern. It is important for students to develop the technique of playing with two mallets. A little practice will reward the student with a musically satisfying sound.

RESONATOR BELLS

Resonator bells are tuned metal bars mounted individually on a block of wood or plastic that serves as its own resonator. When played as a melody instrument, resonator bells function in the same fashion as melody bells. However, because they are not fastened to one another, individual bells can be removed and can also be used to play harmony as well as melodies.

Resonator bells

Xylophone

XYLOPHONES

Xylophones are pitched instruments made from tuned wooden bars mounted individually on a frame. They do not have black bars (keys) like piano keyboards or melody bells but generally have the B flat and F sharp accidentals. You can purchase other accidentals to make it possible to play in several keys. Xylophones are especially useful in playing ostinato melodies, harmonic patterns, and descants. They are available as soprano, alto, and bass instruments.

You play xylophones with the same technique as melody bells, but you use soft instead of hard mallets.

GLOCKENSPIELS

Glockenspiels, whose tones are clear and brilliant, are similar to melody bells in that they are tuned metal bars mounted horizontally on a frame. Like xylophones, glockenspiels do not have sharps or flats. But the tone bars are removable, and you can purchase and add the B flat and F sharp accidentals. You can also add other accidentals in order to play melodies in several keys. Glockenspiels are generally played with wooden or rubber mallets. There are both alto and soprano glockenspiels.

Glockenspiels

Metallophones

METALLOPHONES

Metallophones are large diatonic instruments that include the chromatics B flat and F sharp. The tone bars are of aluminum and are tuned for perfect pitch and harmonics. They provide a full and resonant sound to the ensemble. The soprano and alto metallophones are smaller than the large metallophone, which has a deep bass sound.

RECORDER

The recorder has become increasingly popular as a melody instrument in elementary classes. It has a clear, pure tone that blends well with young voices. Any song is a potential recorder piece, and many music series books provide simple ostinato patterns and descants that can be played on either the soprano or alto recorder.

The two kinds of recorders—baroque and German—are identified by their fingering patterns. You can determine which kind your recorder is by comparing the size opening of the fourth fingerhole with the fifth. If the fifth hole is larger than the fourth, it is a baroque recorder and you should use baroque fingering (as in this book). If the fourth hole is larger than the fifth, it is a German recorder and you must use German fingering. Recorder instruction texts generally provide both fingerings.

Children age nine and older are most successful at playing recorders. Younger children do not yet possess the finger dexterity and coordination to play this instrument. The photo below illustrates the correct way to place the instrument in the mouth.

When playing the recorder, it is necessary to

1. Place the tip of the mouthpiece between your lips and in front of your teeth. Never place the mouthpiece between your teeth.
2. Blow gently.
3. Whisper the sound "too" or "doo" into the mouthpiece. Avoid a "whoo" sound. Use the tongue to stop or release the air.
4. Begin with a few pitches and gradually add notes. Avoid songs that contain middle C until students have perfected the technique of covering the holes tightly. (Middle C is a difficult pitch to play on the recorder.)

Fingering

The fingers of the left hand control the upper tone holes, while the fingers of the right hand cover the lower holes.

1. The thumb of the left hand has three positions:
   a. Covers the thumbhole
   b. Does not cover the thumbhole
   c. Covers only half of the thumbhole
2. The bottom two holes have double openings so that the player can play C sharp and D sharp.
3. You play pitches by covering the holes completely with your fingers. The slightest "leak" will create the wrong pitch or a high-pitched squeal. Minimize finger movements, since the higher you raise your fingers, the greater the possibility that a hole will become uncovered.
4. A simple thumb rest can be made from a piece of eraser and taped to the back of the recorder. This provides for greater stability in holding the instrument.

Recorder

Soprano recorder fingerings (baroque system)

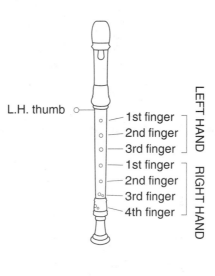

Experiences

1. Introduce the recorder to students by having them play the following pitches:

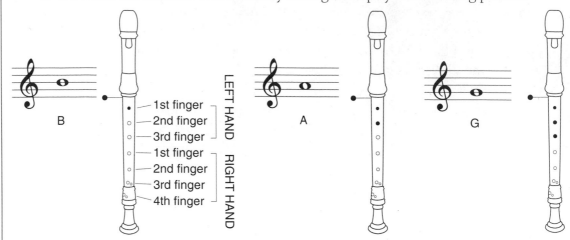

2. Sing "Hot Cross Buns" (p. 60) and then play it by ear on the recorder. Play "Au Clair de la Lune" from notation.

Au clair de la lu - ne, Mon a - mi Pier - rot.

3. Use the same three pitches to create a simple descant to "America" (p. 61).

4. Compose and perform additional tunes using these three pitches. Use titles such as "BAG" or "GAB," which reflect the occurrence of these three pitches in the tune.

5. Gradually add the following pitches:

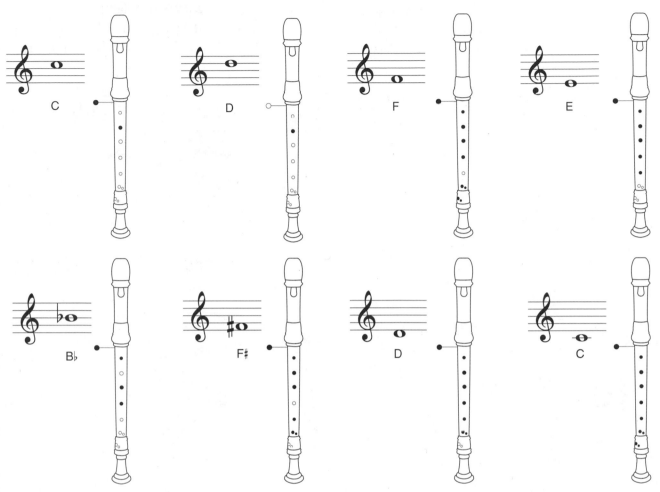

6. Try playing some simple melodies, such as the "Ode to Joy" theme from Beethoven's Ninth Symphony (below), "Jolly Old Saint Nicholas" (p. 160) and "Merrily We Roll Along" (p. 69).

Ode to Joy (Ninth Symphony)

Ludwig van Beethoven

Key: G
Starting pitch: B
Meter: 4/4, begins on 1

USING MELODY INSTRUMENTS IN THE CLASSROOM

Students should be encouraged to use classroom instruments to play familiar songs and simple melody patterns by ear. Short childhood chants are effective for developing the ear and for vocal tone matching. As children sing the chants, they should match them on the melody or resonator bells.

Rain, Rain

Rain, rain, go a - way, Come a - gain some oth - er day.

Starlight, Starbright

Star - light, star - bright, First star I see to - night.

Wish I may, Wish I might Have the wish I wish to - night.

Golden Bells

Folk Song from China

Key: Pentatonic
Starting pitch: A
Meter: 4/4, begins on 1

Hear the gold-en bells sound a-cross the wa-ters blue.

Gen-tle winds that blow sing their sweet___ song for you;

Oo___   Oo___

Sing their sweet song for you.   Oo___

From *New Dimensions in Music,* Book 4 © 1970 American Book Company. Reprinted by permission of D. C. Heath and Company.

Drums

Finger cymbals

Xylophones

(Lines 1 and 2)

(Lines 3 and 4)

One of the advantages to using melody or resonator bells is that the letter names of the notes are stamped on each tone bar; thus students can be guided to relate a letter name with each pitch. Because it is difficult to read music and play melody bells at the same time, however, teachers should encourage children to improvise melodies and play songs by ear. Descants and ostinatos can be taught from notation but are best performed from memory.

Melodic Ostinato

An ostinato is a repeated pattern that occurs throughout a composition. Select one of the following patterns to play on the xylophone or glockenspiel to accompany "Row, Row, Row Your Boat" (p. 39). The ostinato should be played initially by ear only, and later from music notation.

1.

2.

The song "Colorful Boats" (p. 416) is composed on the following pentatonic (five-note) scale. Play the following melodic ostinato or have students create their own. Any combination of pitches may be used.

Pentatonic scale

Melodic ostinato

Play or sing "Good News" (p. 209), "Lightly Row" (p. 209), "Mary Had a Little Lamb" (p. 208), or "Sweet Betsy from Pike," adding the suggested accompaniments. You may wish to create your own rhythm pattern and choose different instruments.

Sweet Betsy from Pike

Traditional

Key: C
Starting pitch: C
Meter: 3/4, begins on 3

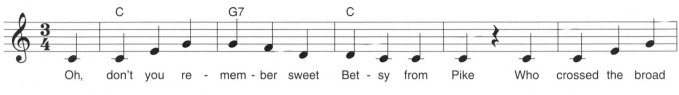

Oh, don't you re - mem - ber sweet Bet - sy from Pike Who crossed the broad

prai - ries with her hus - band, Ike, With two yoke of ox - en, an

old yel - low dog, A___ tall Shang - hai roost - er and one spot - ted hog.

Descant: Glockenspiel

Bass xylophone/metallophone

Using Melody Instruments to Play Harmony

Resonator bells can be used to play simple chords as harmonic accompaniments. Individual students can be assigned a single note of the chord, such as D, F, or A; thus, three students can play at the same time. Sing the following songs accompanied by chords played on the resonator bells.

The Peddler (Korobushka)

Key: D minor
Starting pitch: A
Meter: 2/4, begins on 1

Russian Folk Song
English Words Adapted by Linda Williams

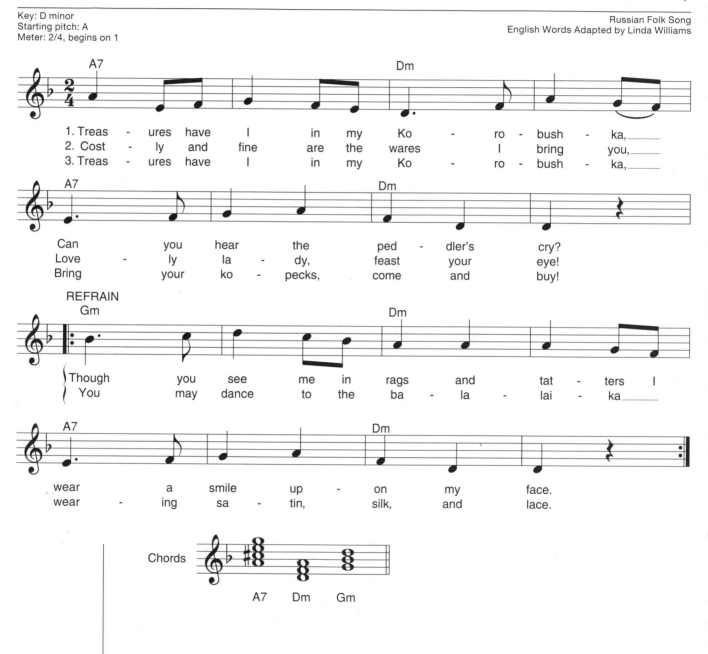

1. Treas - ures have I in my Ko - ro - bush - ka,_____
2. Cost - ly and fine are the wares I bring you,_____
3. Treas - ures have I in my Ko - ro - bush - ka,_____

Can you hear the ped - dler's cry?
Love - ly la - dy, feast your eye!
Bring your ko - pecks, come and buy!

REFRAIN

Though you see me in rags and tat - ters I
You may dance to the ba - la - lai - ka_____

wear a smile up - on my face.
wear - ing sa - tin, silk, and lace.

Chords

A7   Dm   Gm

America

Arr. Henry Carey
England c. 1690–1743

Key: G
Starting pitch: G
Meter: 3/4, begins on 1

My coun - try, 'tis of thee, Sweet land of lib - er - ty, of thee I sing. Land where my

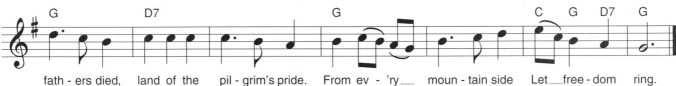

fath - ers died, land of the pil - grim's pride. From ev - 'ry___ moun - tain side Let___free - dom ring.

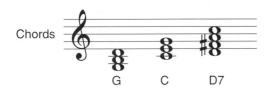

Chords: G C D7

This Old Man

Nursery Rhyme

Key: F
Starting pitch: C
Meter: 2/4, begins on 1

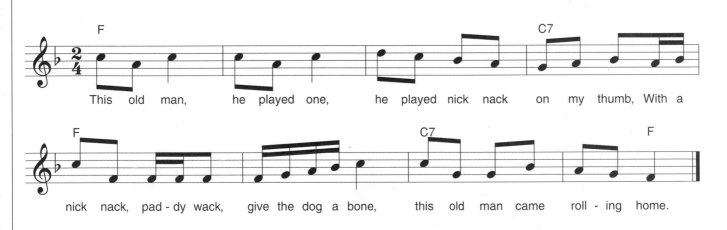

This old man, he played one, he played nick nack on my thumb, With a

nick nack, pad - dy wack, give the dog a bone, this old man came roll - ing home.

Chords: F C7

Other types of harmony that can be played on melody instruments include descants (a second contrasting melody), rounds, and simple alto or tenor harmony parts. After experimenting with different melody instruments, choose the one that is most satisfying to you and that produces the best musical result for each of the following:

- Descants

    "Did You Ever See a Lassie?" p. 120

    "It's a Small World," p. 121

- Rounds

    "Sing Together," p. 129

    "Row, Row, Row Your Boat," p. 39

- Simple harmony

    "Swing Low, Sweet Chariot," p. 375

    "Hahvah Nahgeelah," p. 362

    "The John B. Sails," p. 194

    "I've Been Working on the Railroad," p. 196

HARMONIC INSTRUMENTS

Instruments such as the Autoharp,* Omnichord, and guitar can be used to play harmonies or drones as accompaniments to songs or to provide an introduction, interlude, or coda (ending) to a composition.

THE AUTOHARP

The Autoharp is a small stringed instrument that is easy to carry and to play. It has a range of nearly four octaves, which can be divided into three registers: low, medium, and high. The special sounds of each register can be used to create a variety of rhythmic and tonal effects.

Autoharp: Appalachian position

Autoharp: Table position

Autoharp: Lap position

*Autoharp is the registered trademark of Oscar Schmidt International, Inc., Garden State Road, Union, New Jersey.

Low register   Middle register   High register

The Autoharp can be played with one pick in a lap or table position or the upright, "Appalachian style," position. By using a set of finger picks in the upright position, you can play melodies as well as chords.

The Autoharp may have twelve, fifteen, twenty-one, or more chord bars. This discussion is limited to the fifteen-bar Autoharp, which is diagrammed as follows:

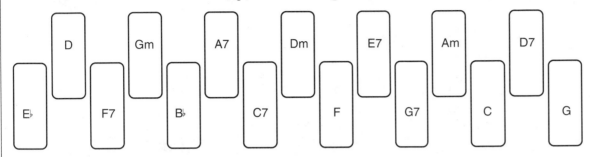

Each bar carries a chord name. When you press the chord bar, the pitches (strings) that are not part of that chord are blocked off by felt strips; thus, the only pitches that sound are the ones that are part of that chord. Experiment by pressing the C chord bar. While it is depressed, pluck each string. You will discover that only C, E, and G will sound; however, they will sound in more than one octave, which gives a rich texture to the tone when you strum. Press the chord bar firmly for the duration of the strum, or the pitches will not be blocked off and the sound will "run together."

Place the instrument on a table with the longest strings closest to you. Press the C chord bar with your left index finger, cross over with your right arm, and strum your pick across the strings from low (closest to you) to high (away from you). You should grasp the pick loosely between your thumb and index finger. Play several chords while keeping a steady beat. Place the third finger of your left hand on the G_7 chord bar and your ring finger on the F chord bar. Now play the following harmony pattern:

(Strum)   / / / /   / / / /   / / / /   / / / /
        C C C C   F F F F G_7 G_7 G_7 G_7 C C C C

You can obtain different sound qualities by changing the material of the pick (e.g., plastic card, eraser, coins) or by strumming the right end (short strings) or left end (long strings) of the instrument.

By moving your left index finger to the right and up, you can play a D_7 chord. Directly to your right is the G chord. Practice various combinations until you feel comfortable.

   / / / /   / / / /   / / / /   / / / /
   G G G G   C C C C D_7 D_7 D_7 D_7 G G G G

   / / / /   / / / /   / / / /   / / / /   / / / /   / / /
   C C C C D_7 D_7 D_7 D_7 G G G G   C C C C   F F F F   C G_7 C

Try accompanying the song "Galway Piper" on the Autoharp by using two chords: D and A_7.

Galway Piper

Traditional Irish Folk Song

Key: D
Starting pitch: D
Meter: 4/4, begins on 1

Lively

Ev - 'ry per - son in the na - tion,___ Of a great or hum - ble sta - tion,___

Holds in high - est es - ti - ma - tion, Pip - ing___ Tim of___ Gal - way. Loud - ly___ he can play, or low.

He can___ move you fast or slow, Touch your___ hearts or stir your toe, Pip - ing___ Tim of Gal - way.

Alternating playing in the low and high registers of the autoharp adds variety and interest to the accompaniment. Play and sing "The Cuckoo" (p. 126), playing the first beat in the low register and the second and third beats in the upper register.

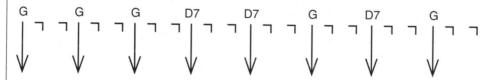

G   G   G   D7   D7   G   D7   G

Follow this chord diagram:

G G G D₇ D₇ G G D₇ D₇ G (Repeat)

G D₇ D₇ G G D₇ D₇ G

Play the following songs. Try holding the Autoharp upright and placing it in the lap or table position. Experiment with various strum patterns.

"This Old Man," p. 223

"Jolly Old Saint Nicholas," p. 160

"We Wish You a Merry Christmas," p. 76

"Gatatumba," p. 147

Tuning the Autoharp

It is important that the Autoharp be kept in tune. Like all musical instruments, the Autoharp is affected by weather and atmospheric conditions, so frequent tuning is necessary. If you have trouble hearing chords, ask a music teacher or perhaps a teacher who plays piano or guitar to help you.

One of the more difficult ways of tuning an Autoharp is to match each pitch with that of the piano. Since the piano is often out of tune, the result may be less than pleasing. A better way is the following:

1. Begin with an F major chord. Find the pitches F, A, and C. Tune them to a set of tuned bells or a pitch pipe. Use the hammer provided to tighten the string and raise the pitch; loosen it to lower the pitch. If you have trouble finding the right tuning peg, trace your finger along the string. Once the F major chord is in tune, you are ready to tune other chords.

2. Press the C major chord bar and tune the C chord (C, E, G). Remember that you have to tune all the pitches throughout the Autoharp, not just the three in the middle register.

3. Continue as above with the G major chord bar, followed by:

   D_7 F♯ strings to be tuned

   B♭   B♭ strings to be tuned

   E_7 G♯ strings to be tuned

   A_7 C♯ strings to be tuned

   E♭   E♭ strings to be tuned

4. Touch up as needed.

THE OMNICHORD

The Omnichord is similar to an Autoharp in that you can push down marked buttons and play chords, but it can play rhythms, too. It can automatically execute chord combinations with a rhythm or a walking bass line. You can play the Omnichord in traditional Autoharp style by using chords only. The Omnichord is self-contained with a built-in amplifier and is completely portable.

There are many major, minor, and seventh chords on the Omnichord, as well as such preset rhythm patterns as waltz, march, and rock. Separate tempo and volume controls are provided for both chords and rhythms. The performer, however, must be careful to release each chord completely before moving to a different one or the chords will not change.

Omnichord

The electronic component enables you to select from the following tone colors: piano, guitar, banjo, organ, flute, chimes, brass, vibes, and synthesizer.

The SonicStrings, a unique feature of the Omnichord, encompass four full octaves. These SonicStrings play pitches of the chord selected. Thus, if the student plays a C major chord, the SonicStrings can also be strummed to sound the pitches C, E, and G at more than one octave. If all rhythms and sustained chords are turned off, the SonicStrings can be played as an Autoharp; however, the general volume control must be on. Any song that can be accompanied with chords on the Autoharp can be accompanied on the Omnichord. Because the Omnichord does not need tuning, it is frequently used in place of the Autoharp.

THE GUITAR

The guitar is a popular instrument with children, and, by third grade, many have physically matured enough to hold it and begin to play simple chords.

There are many different types of guitars, including Hawaiian, twelve-string, folk, classical, steel string, and electric. The two types of guitars most used in the classroom are the classical guitar with nylon or gut strings, and the steel string flattop guitar.

Contemporary rock groups use electric guitars. Both classical and steel string guitars are acoustic (not amplified). The basic difference is in the tone quality, the classical nylon string guitar having a more mellow quality and the steel string flattop guitar having a bright and brassy sound. Because nylon strings are easier on the fingers, the classical guitar is usually recommended for beginners.

Classical guitar

Flattop guitar

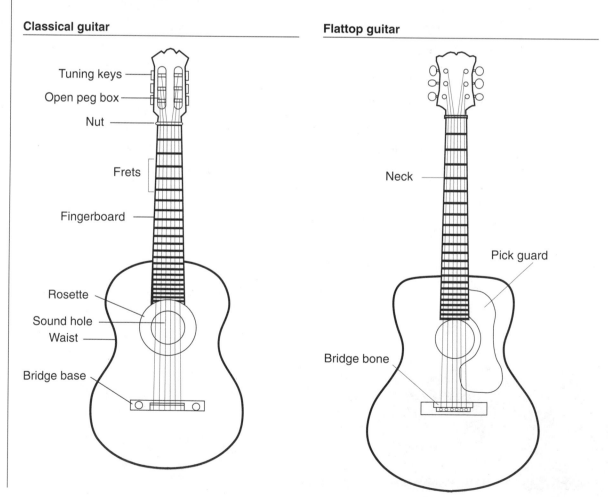

The basic function of the guitar in the classroom is to accompany songs. Like the Autoharp, the guitar can provide an introduction, interlude, or ending to a song. The guitar's great advantages are that there are only six strings to tune and, since many students may own guitars, more instruments may be available for use in the classroom. A guitar player can move freely around the classroom. This chapter provides an introduction to basic guitar skills that will enable you to accompany songs. Materials are limited to the use of eight chords (as used in the key of D, G, E, and E minor). For detailed discussions and more advanced techniques, consult one of the many excellent publications that teach one how to play the guitar.

The six strings of the guitar are E A D G B E. The following diagram shows the matching pitches on the piano keyboard:

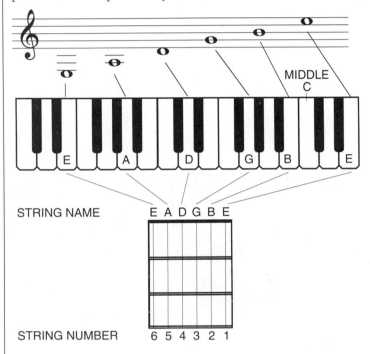

STRING NAME   E A D G B E

STRING NUMBER   6 5 4 3 2 1

Tuning the Guitar

Tune the open strings to a piano that is in tune. If no piano is available, use a pitch pipe and tune the lowest string (E). Notice that the strings of the guitar are numbered from the highest pitch—1—to the lowest pitch—6. Guitar pitches are notated one octave higher than they actually sound. The pitch of each string is adjusted by turning the tuning peg. To lower the pitch, turn a peg toward you; to raise the pitch, turn it away from you. The following diagram shows which strings are controlled by each tuning peg:

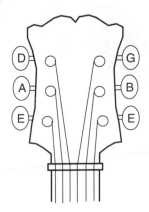

By following the steps listed below, you will be able to tune your guitar accurately.

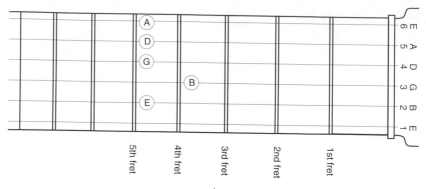

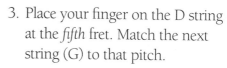

5th fret   4th fret   3rd fret   2nd fret   1st fret

1. After you have tuned the bass E string, place your second finger (left hand) on that same string at the *fifth* fret. Match the next string (A) to that pitch. The open fifth string is now A.

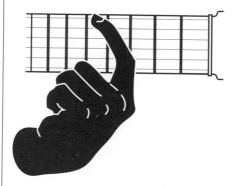

2. Place your finger on the A string at the *fifth* fret. Match the next string (D) to that pitch.

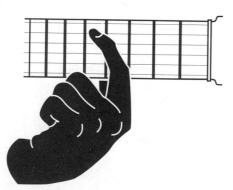

3. Place your finger on the D string at the *fifth* fret. Match the next string (G) to that pitch.

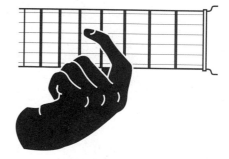

4. Place your finger on the G string at the *fourth* fret. Match the next string (B) to that pitch.

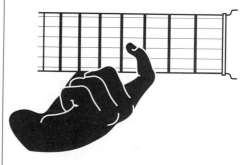

5. Place your finger on the B string at the *fifth* fret. Match the next string (E) to that pitch.

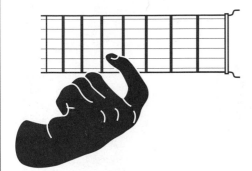

Now that you have tuned the guitar, you can try some simple chords. Chords are created by placing one or more fingers on designated frets. Place your index finger (1) on the third string, first fret; second finger on fifth string, second fret; and third finger on fourth string, second fret. Strings 1, 2, and 6 are open. Strum the E major chord.

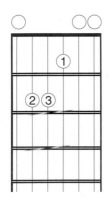

Place your second finger on fifth string, second fret, and third finger on the fourth string, second fret. Strings 1, 2, 3, and 6 are open. Strum the E minor chord.

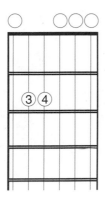

Each fret on the neck of the guitar represents a half step in the chromatic scale. Pluck the highest string (E). Now, place your index finger (first finger) on the string between the metal strips (frets) and pluck the string. You will now hear F. Move your finger up each fret and you will hear the pitch go up by half steps.

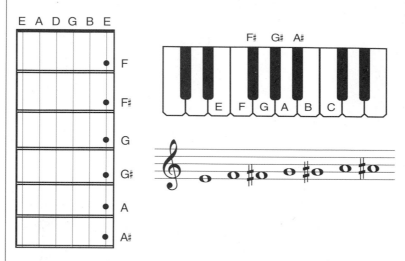

Follow the same procedure for each string and listen for the half steps.

Playing the Guitar

There are three basic positions for playing the guitar: (1) classical style, in which the player is seated and places a foot on a small stool or platform; (2) folk style, in which the player is seated and balances the guitar on a crossed leg; and (3) standing, where the player uses a neck strap. Regardless of the position you choose, the back of the guitar should remain flat against your body. Avoid tipping it downward to see the strings more clearly, thus creating an "Autoharp" playing effect. In addition, do not allow the neck of the guitar to drop below the horizontal position.

Classical-style position   **Folk-style position**   **Standing position**

To play the guitar, you need to know how to strum with your right hand and form chords with your left hand. The notation, called tablature, indicates which strings are to remain open and which strings are to be fretted. X indicates that the string is not sounded, while O indicates that the string is open. The circle on the fretboard indicates where the fingers are to be placed. Left-hand fingers are identified as follows:

1 = index finger

2 = middle finger

3 = ring finger

4 = little finger

The thumb is not used in playing the guitar. You must use the tips of your fingers to press down the strings. They should be close above the frets that stop the string but should not touch the frets. Diagram for E major and E minor chords appear on p. 231. Here are the diagrams for the other chords used in this book. (See Appendix A for a complete chord chart.)

G major   **D major**

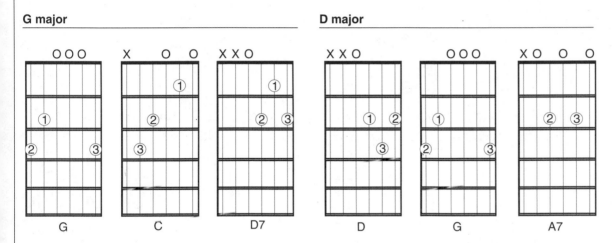

G   C   D7   D   G   A7

Strum Patterns

The *sweep strum* is created by a downward motion of the thumb across all the strings. It can be used on accented beats as well as unaccented beats. The *brush strum* is created by using the backs of the fingernails across the strings. It is used on unaccented beats. A combination of sweep and brush strum can be used for duple meter (sweep-brush) and triple meter (sweep-brush-brush). The *pluck-sweep strum* involves plucking the root of the chord and strumming on the remaining chords. It is often done with a plastic pick.

Using a Capo

A *capo* (capotasto) is a device that clamps over the strings of a guitar and holds them down tightly at a new pitch level, instantly transposing a song into a higher key. When the capo is in place, chord fingerings are the same but the sounds are at a new pitch level. For example, if the capo is installed on the second fret (one whole step higher) and a D chord is played, it will sound like an E chord. If the capo is put on the third fret, chords will sound one and a half steps higher. Thus, if you know two chords in the key of D major, D and A_7, you could place the capo on the third fret and play in the key of F. The two chords would now sound as F and C_7 using the same fingering. Experiment with key changes by placing the capo on the appropriate fret to match the key you wish to play in.

Guitar capo

Playing Song Accompaniments

1. Play and sing "Shalom, Chaverim" accompanied by one chord (E minor). (Another one-chord song you might play is "Zum Gali, Gali" on pages 53 and 127.)

Shalom, Chaverim

Israeli Folk Song

Key: E minor
Starting pitch: B
Meter: 4/4, begins on 4

Sha - lom, cha - ve - rim! Sha - lom, cha - ve - rim, Sha - lom, Sha - lom! Le

hit ra____ ot, le hit ra____ ot, Sha - lom, sha - lom.

2. Practice changing back and forth from the G chord to the D₇ chord (see p. 233). Then try accompanying "Clementine," "La Raspa," or "Old Texas" (p. 116).

Clementine

United States

Key: G
Starting pitch: G
Meter: 3/4, begins on 3

Oh, my dar - lin', oh, my dar - lin', Oh, my dar - lin' Clem - en - tine, You are

lost, and gone for - ev - er, Dread - ful sor - ry, Clem - en - tine.

La Raspa

Mexico

Key: G
Starting pitch: D
Meter: 4/4, begins on "and" of 4

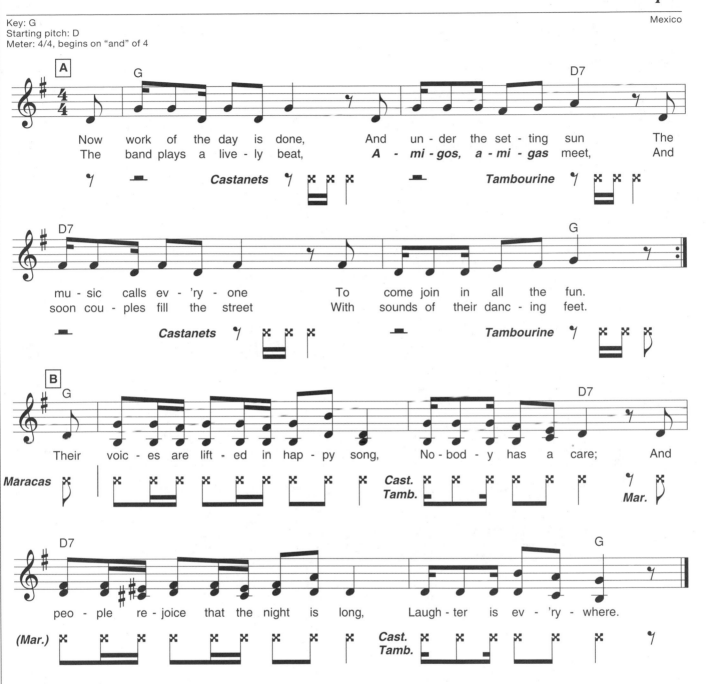

Now work of the day is done, And un-der the set-ting sun The
The band plays a live-ly beat, A - mi-gos, a - mi-gas meet, And

mu - sic calls ev - 'ry - one To come join in all the fun.
soon cou - ples fill the street With sounds of their danc - ing feet.

Their voic - es are lift - ed in hap - py song, No - bod - y has a care; And

peo - ple re - joice that the night is long, Laugh - ter is ev - 'ry - where.

TEACHING MUSIC THROUGH PLAYING CLASSROOM INSTRUMENTS

3. Use the C and G chords to accompany "Mary Ann."

Mary Ann

Calypso

Key: C
Starting pitch: E
Meter: 4/4, begins on 1

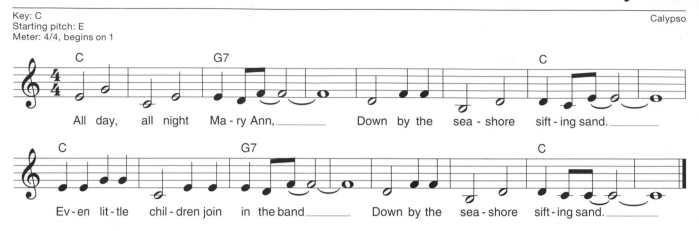

All day, all night Ma - ry Ann,_____ Down by the sea - shore sift - ing sand._____

Ev - en lit - tle chil - dren join in the band_____ Down by the sea - shore sift - ing sand._____

4. Use the D and A$_7$ chords to accompany "He's Got the Whole World in His Hands" and "Six Little Ducks" (p. 143).

He's Got the Whole World in His Hands

Spiritual

Key: D
Starting pitch: A
Meter: 4/4, begins on "and" of 3

He's got the whole world____ in his hands, ____ he's got the whole world____ in his hands,____

He's got the whole world____ in his hands, ____ he's got the whole world in his hands. ____

5. Use the G, C, D, and D_7 chords to accompany "Muffin Man."

Muffin Man

England

Key: G
Starting pitch: D
Meter: 4/4, begins on 4

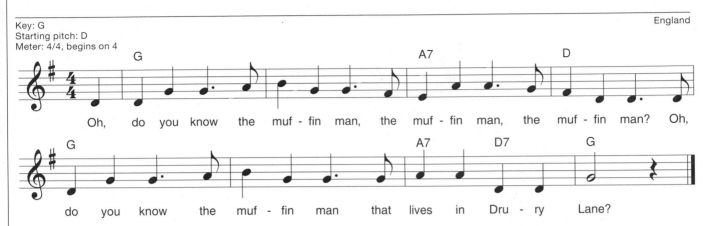

Oh, do you know the muf-fin man, the muf-fin man, the muf-fin man? Oh,
do you know the muf-fin man that lives in Dru - ry Lane?

6. Practice the following progression (D, A_7, D), using the pluck-sweep strum until it is smooth, and then play "Down in the Valley" using this technique.

Down in the Valley

Traditional

Key: D
Starting pitch: A
Meter: 3/4, begins on 1

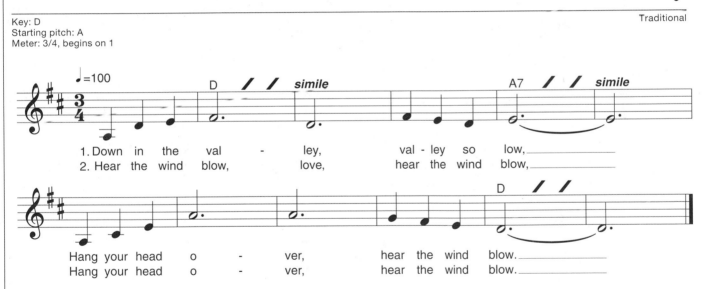

1. Down in the val - ley, val - ley so low,_____
2. Hear the wind blow, love, hear the wind blow,_____

Hang your head o - ver, hear the wind blow._____
Hang your head o - ver, hear the wind blow._____

(You can transpose this song into the key of G and use the chords G and D_7.)

PERCUSSION INSTRUMENTS

A third group of classroom instruments, percussion instruments, are used primarily to provide rhythmic accompaniments to songs. These instruments can also be used in ensembles and to play original musical compositions. They are divided into woods, metals, and skins.

While most percussion instruments are commercially available, later in the chapter we include suggestions for the innovative teacher who wishes to make such instruments. Before using percussion instruments in the classroom, you should have a thorough knowledge of the types of musical effects that can be produced by each instrument. In the sections that follow, you will find brief descriptions of frequently used instruments, directions for playing them, and some functions they might serve.

WOODS

Wood instruments include rhythm sticks, claves, wood blocks, maracas, sand blocks, and the güiro.

Rhythm Sticks

Description: Sticks with both a smooth surface and "ribbed" surface. They are usually 12 inches in length, and round.

Function: Beat, meter, special effects.

Playing: Hold one stick in each hand and strike them together. They may also be scraped (over the "ribbed" surface). Sticks may also be used to tap other objects, such as a desk, chair, book, or drum.

Claves

Description: (pronounced *clah*-vays) Cylindrical hardwood blocks. They are generally about 6 inches long and 1 inch in diameter, and are made from resonant material.

Function: Rhythms (particularly Latin American), beat, syncopation.

Playing: Hold one clave loosely in a partly closed hand and strike the clave held in the other hand. Tap out the rhythm.

Wood Blocks

Description: Hollow blocks of wood that create an interesting "clip-clop" sound.

Function: Beat, meter, syncopation, special effects.

Playing: Strike blocks with a hard mallet.

Maracas

Description: Dried gourds whose seeds have dried, making a crisp, swishing sound.

Function: Rhythm patterns, Latin American music, syncopation.

Playing: Usually played in pairs by shaking.

Sand Blocks

Description: Small blocks of wood covered with varying grades of sandpaper. Handles for each are attached.

Function: Meter, beat, swishing effects.

Playing: Rub two blocks together.

Rhythm sticks

Claves

Maracas

Wood block

Sand blocks

Güiro

Description: (pronounced gwee-*ro*) An elongated wooden instrument with resonating holes and a serrated surface that is scraped with a stick to produce the sound.

Function: Used to accentuate rhythms in Latin American music.

Playing: Hold instrument in one hand while scraping the serrated surface with a stick held in the other hand.

METALS

Metal percussion instruments include cymbals, finger cymbals, triangles, tambourines, jingle bells, and jingle sticks.

Cymbals

Description: Discs of brass with a depression in the center of each.

Function: Accents, crescendos, climax.

Playing: (1) Strike together in a "slicing" manner and "stop" sound against the body; (2) strike together and let sound continue on, such as in a cymbal "crash"; (3) hold onto cymbal and play with a soft mallet.

Finger Cymbals

Description: Tiny replicas of large cymbals.

Function: Special effects, soft accompaniment patterns.

Playing: Touch the rim of one with the rim of another, rather than trying to "clap" them together.

Triangle

Description: A steel rod bent in the form of a triangle with one angle open. It is suspended on a string and played by striking it with a metal stick.

Function: Meter, accents, sustained sound, special effects.

Playing: Hold triangle by string and tap with metal striker. Be sure not to touch triangle with your hand, or the sound will be muted or stopped.

Tambourine

Description: A miniature drum with small metal discs attached to the wooden rim. The discs vibrate when the instrument is struck or shaken.

Function: Sustain sounds, accents, special effects, meter.

Playing: Shake, tap with a hand on the drumhead (if there is one), tap the side of the rim with a hand.

Jingle Bells

Description: Bells mounted on sticks or small frame.

Function: Rhythmic effects in American Indian music; sleigh ride, beat, meter.

Playing: Shake or wear around wrists or ankles.

Güiro

Cymbals

Finger cymbals

Triangle

Tambourine

Jingle bells

Jingle Sticks

Description: Two metal discs attached to a stick.
Function: Meter, sustained sounds, beat, special effects.
Playing: Tap the wooden handle against the palm of the hand.

SKINS

Instruments based primarily on striking stretched skins include the hand drum, bongo drums, and conga drum.

Hand Drum

Description: Metal band covered with a head made of leather (or plastic). The head is struck from one side only.
Function: Meter, beat, accents, tempo.
Playing: Strike with a mallet (hard or soft), a stick, or the hands.

Bongo Drums

Description: Two small drums of different pitches—one high, the other low. The head may be a membrane or plastic.
Function: Often used in Latin American music to play syncopated rhythms.
Playing: Place bongos between the crossed legs of the seated player. Use fingertips and palms of hands to strike the heads. Striking the center of the drumhead or the rim produces different pitches and timbres.

Conga Drum

Description: A tall, barrel-type drum with a membrane head. It has a deep, resonant tone quality. The drum may be placed on the floor or suspended from the shoulder by a strap.
Function: Used in both Latin American and African music for rhythm accompaniments.
Playing: Strike with fingertips, palms of hands, or even elbows. Striking the center of the drumhead, the rim, or the shell produces different pitches and timbres.

Jingle sticks   **Hand drum**

Conga drum

Bongo Drums

HOW TO SELECT AN APPROPRIATE INSTRUMENT

The ability to play a musical instrument is directly related to a student's physical growth and coordination. Some questions to be considered in the choice of instruments include:

1. What is the degree of eye-ear physical coordination required? Playing melody bells from written notation requires a high degree of skill and coordination (ages ten to eleven), while playing a two- or three-note melodic pattern by ear or by letter or number is a task young children (ages five to nine) can handle.

2. Is a large hand required? Many chords on the guitar require a large hand and the ability to stretch the fingers. A student must also be big enough to hold the instrument.

3. What instruments use large muscle movements? Such instruments as drum, tambourine, cymbals, and rhythm sticks are appropriate for use by young students (ages five to seven).

4. Can students move their fingers quickly from one chord bar to another while strumming chords on an Autoharp or Omnichord (ages nine to eleven)?

5. Have students developed sufficient eye-finger dexterity and coordination to play the recorder? They must also have hands large enough to cover all the finger holes (ages nine to eleven).

Just as a composer must decide on what instruments to use in a composition, so teachers must guide students in selecting and playing instruments appropriate to the expressiveness of the music. The following questions will serve as guidelines in determining this selection:

1. Is there an ethnic (such as a Spanish or Latin American) influence in the music?
2. What is the style of the music (march, waltz, calypso, rock)?
3. Is the melody most expressive when played on a percussive instrument, such as melody bells or xylophone, or on a sustaining instrument, such as recorder or piano?
4. Is a harmonic accompanying instrument (such as Autoharp or guitar) needed to maintain the tonality of the song?
5. Can percussion instruments be used to create variety and interest through playing rhythm patterns or ostinatos?
6. What is the nature of the text of the song? Does it portray, for example, a quiet mood, activity, or joyousness?
7. What instruments can best be used to (a) keep a steady beat; (b) express loud and soft; (c) show contrast in texture, mood, and tempos; or (d) illustrate musical form (such as AB, ABA, rondo)?

PLAYING RHYTHM ACCOMPANIMENTS TO SONGS

The following steps will contribute toward successful experiences in using percussion instruments to accompany songs:

1. Ask students to pat their thighs to keep the tempo beat (speed of song). Repeat using selected rhythm instruments such as rhythm sticks.
2. Ask students to pat their thighs and clap their hands in duple or triple meter. Add selected rhythm instruments and accent the first beat of each meter group.
3. Improvise patterns and ask students to imitate by clapping or playing instruments.
4. Ask students to improvise rhythm patterns on instruments within the meter beat pattern, such as triple meter:

5. Decide on patterns to use for a selected song. Choose appropriate instruments. Apply these steps to "Rock-a My Soul," using the instruments indicated.

Rock-a My Soul

Spiritual

Key: D
Starting pitch: F♯
Meter: 4/4, begins on 1

6. The following song (suitable for Grades 1–3) is scored for a small ensemble of three rhythm instruments and voices. Each instrument emphasizes a different aspect of the rhythm. The top line shows the "melodic rhythm." The second line shows the meter beat, while the third line indicates the tempo beat. Use piano, melody bells, or recorder to provide a short introduction and coda.

Baa, Baa, Black Sheep

Mother Goose Rhyme
France

Key: D
Starting pitch: D
Meter: 2/4, begins on 1

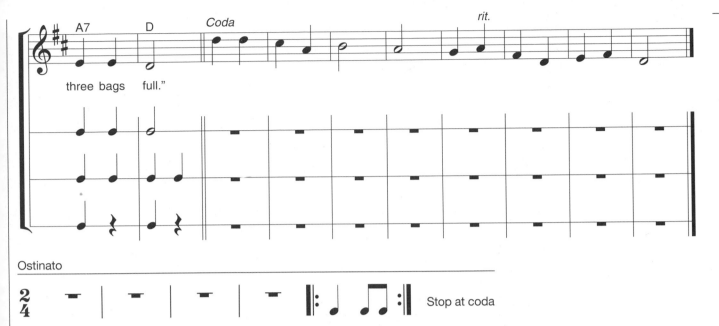

three bags full."

Ostinato

Stop at coda

DEVELOPING A RHYTHM ENSEMBLE (GRADES K–3)

You can organize a classroom percussion ensemble to perform a musical composition. The choice of instruments will depend on such musical characteristics as high-low, strong beat–weak beat, dynamics, and accents. Expressiveness may be further achieved by: (1) alternating the total ensemble with a smaller group of instruments; (2) alternating the total ensemble or a smaller group of instruments with a solo instrument; (3) contrasting different timbres (such as jingle sounds with wood sounds). Leadership skills may be developed by having individual students conduct the ensemble.

Rhythm ensemble

Students should listen to a selected composition many times. After each hearing, they should make decisions regarding their choice and use of instruments. The entire experience should be one of developing aural skill in hearing expressive changes in music. The following guidelines will assist you in this task:

1. Select a musical composition that has a strong rhythm and clear use of instruments.
2. Have students determine the meter (duple/triple).
3. Determine whether there are accents and if they are on the beat or off the beat (such as syncopation).
4. Decide on instrumentation that is expressive of the composition.
5. Create a playing guide (as appropriate to grade level).

Musical compositions that are effective with a rhythm ensemble include:

- Sousa marches
- Elgar: *Pomp and Circumstance*
- Mozart: Symphony No. 40 (Third movement: Minuet)
- Bizet: "Farandole" from *L'Arlésienne Suite*
- Polkas: "Over the Waves," "Carnival of Venice," "Varsoviana"
- Grieg: "In the Hall of the Mountain King" from *Peer Gynt Suite*
- Schubert: *Marche Militaire*

METHODS AND MATERIALS FOR INTEGRATING INSTRUMENTAL EXPERIENCES INTO THE CLASSROOM

Playing instrumental accompaniments adds interest and variety to many songs and contributes toward perceptual and motor skills. The choice and use of appropriate instruments in musical experiences can enrich the study of history, geography, culture and people, poetry, feelings and moods, and holidays. Use the following suggestions as you plan your lessons.

LANGUAGE ARTS (GRADES 4–6)

Use classroom instruments to express ideas and sounds in poems or stories, as in the following two examples.

1. Select classroom instruments to express appropriate sounds in a Halloween story or poem, such as the one by Kay Maves on the next page. Encourage students to be creative in their choice of playing techniques.

Gargoyles*

Gargoyles perch by day on the rooftops,
With frozen stone smiles, and long, lolling mouths ajar,
No movements no sound 'til dark, and then GARGOYLE!
Zipping, slipping through the night air!
Laughing, leering tearing through the quiet air!
Scaring cats, chasing bats 'til dawn
When each one flits to his rooftop
And stares with his cold stone eyes at the busy streets
Through the only bright day,
And knows that night will come when GARGOYLE!
Laughing, leering tearing through the quiet air!
Scaring cats, chasing bats,
Reeling, spinning, shrieking, grinning GARGOYLE!

2. Dramatize "Five Little Pumpkins" (p. 26) and use music and text to determine rhythmic accompaniment and pitch relationships. Some suggestions are
   a. Steady beat (rhythm sticks)
   b. Resonator bells (one for each pitch of the phrase):
      1 = F
      2 = G
      3 = A
      4 = B
      5 = C
   c. "Run and run and run" (play on melody bells):

   d. "Ooo went the wind" (glissando on xylophone)
   e. "*Out* went the light" (wood block)
   f. "Rolled out of sight" (jingle sticks)

3. Read the story of *Peter and the Wolf*.[†] Select classroom instruments to represent each character. Decide on a rhythm, melody, or playing technique. Follow up by listening to Prokofiev's *Peter and the Wolf*. Discuss the composer's choice and use of instruments.

4. Read the story *Little Toot* by Hardie Gramatky.[‡] Select classroom instruments to represent the various boat sounds and types of boats. Use them to dramatize the story.

---

* In *New Dimensions in Music*, "Mastering Music," American Book Company, 1970, pp. 107–108. By permission of D. C. Heath & Co.
† Johnson-Sickels-Sayers, *Anthology of Children's Literature* (Boston: Houghton Mifflin, 1970), p. 261.
‡ Ibid., pp. 81–82.

SCIENCE: SOUND (GRADES 4–6)

1. Explore concepts of sound through classroom instruments.
   a. Place the terms *sound*, *vibration*, *pitch*, and *frequency* on the chalkboard. Select a drum; as you strike the head, have the students place their hands against the side of the instrument. They will feel and hear the *sound* produced by the *vibration* of the instrument. Explain that the vibration of the instrument produces the *pitch*, the highness or lowness of musical sounds. Select some instruments, such as the Autoharp, that produce both high and low sounds. Ask individual students to play them; then discuss why high or low sounds are produced (discovering that high sounds are produced by short strings or instruments and low sounds by long strings or instruments). Demonstrate how high to low pitches can be produced by lengthening an instrument. Have a student play a clarinet or flute first with just the mouthpiece and then add

HOW TO MAKE YOUR OWN INSTRUMENTS

Cymbals

Materials: Lids of pans

Directions: Make a hole in the lids with a nail and fasten to a spool or piece of wood for the handle.

Triangle

Materials: Steel rod
            Bolt

Directions: Bend a steel rod into a triangle. Strike with a blunt end bolt.

Hand Drum

Materials: A quart or gallon can
            Two pieces of canvas or leather
            3 to 5 yards of heavy cord
            Enamel or lacquer and brush
            Leather punch

Directions: Remove the ends of the can and smooth the edges. Paint the can. Cut two pieces of rubber or leather about 4 inches larger in diameter than the can. Punch the same number of holes in each piece at least 1 inch from the edge. Place the two pieces of canvas or leather over the ends of the can and lace them together. Tie a cord securely around the ends of the drum and adjust the lacing until you get the desired sound.

Tambourine

Materials: Two paper plates (heavy plastic type)
            Sixteen pop bottle caps
            Thin wire
            Hammer and nail

Directions: Punch two holes in each pop bottle cap. Place the bottom of the plates together. Punch sixteen holes in each plate, spacing the holes evenly to correspond to the holes in the bottle caps. Wire the plates together, placing the bottle caps between the rims of the plates. Decorate the plates with crayons or paint.

Jingle Bells

Materials: 6-inch dowel rod
            Three jingle bells
            Two tacks
            3-inch leather or plastic strap
            Four pieces of thin wire

Directions: Punch holes in the strap and fasten the bells to the strap with the wire. Tack the strap to the dowel (use small tacks to avoid splitting the wood) or drill a hole through the wood and anchor the strap securely with the wire.

sections of the instrument, gradually lengthening the pipe and lowering the pitch. Pitch is directly related to the *frequency* of vibration. Sound vibrations move back and forth in a cycle; the number of cycles of vibration per second is known as the *frequency*. Some instruments produce sounds of low frequency or pitch, while other instruments produce sounds of high frequency or pitch.

b. Explore various types of sounds by making your own musical instruments. Try for both high and low sounds. Also explore how sounds change depending on which material the musical instrument is made of. The accompanying box provides suggestions for making your own instruments.

c. Show the Disney short film *Toot, Whistle, Plunk, Boom* (through animation, Professor Owl traces the origin and development of four classes of musical instruments found in a modern symphony orchestra: brass, woodwinds, strings, and percussion). Discuss how a pitch can be played high or low on different instruments (stringed, brass) and what determines its quality.

Rhythm Sticks
Materials: Hardwood dowels ³/₈ inch to ⁵/₈ inch in diameter
Directions: Cut dowel rods into 12-inch lengths. Carve ridges on one side and paint rods in bright colors.

Claves
Materials: l-inch dowels in hard woods, which will give clear tone when tapped together: beech, mahogany, walnut, cherry, ash, or sycamore
Directions: Cut dowels into 6-inch lengths. Apply several coats of varnish or hard wax.

Wood Block
Materials: Small wooden box (such as a cigar box)
Directions: Fasten lid tightly onto hollow box. Strike box with stick or mallet.

Maracas
Materials: Ball of plasticine
Dowel rod
Tissue paper and newspaper
Paste or glue
Peas, buttons, rice, pebbles
Directions: Shape the desired size of plasticine on a length of dowel rod. Apply small pieces of damp tissue paper and add small pieces of pasted newspaper. Build up layers of white or colored newspaper. When ball is dry, cut in half, and remove plasticine. Join the two halves together and glue. Drop a few hard objects into the shell and replace the dowel rod. Secure with strips of paper and paste. When dry, paint the maraca with bright colors.

Sand Blocks
Materials: 3-inch square blocks of wood, ³/₄ inch to 1 inch thick
Sandpaper
Directions: Cover blocks of wood with various thicknesses of sandpaper (to get the desired effect). Add handles made from empty spools of thread or small doorknobs.

African Rattle
Materials: Large gourd or papier mâché shell mountd on a dowel rod
Buttons
Knotted string
Directions: Fasten buttons on knotted string and form into loose net. Mount on the outside of the gourd or shell.

HISTORY: MEDIEVAL/RENAISSANCE (GRADES 4–6)

1. Create a simple dance to a medieval Ductia (bowing, stepping forward, stepping backward, moving in a circle). Add a hand drum and tambourine for a percussion accompaniment. (See *Exploring Music*, Book 4, 1975, pp. 90–91, Record 10, side B.)
2. Perform the song "Greensleeves" (p. 74) accompanied on an Autoharp.

GEOGRAPHY: AMERICAN WEST (GRADES 4–6)

1. Select songs that describe activities of the American cowboy, such as roping, branding, herding cows, eating around a campfire. Some possibilities are
   "Home on the Range"
   "Red River Valley"
   "Get Along Little Dogies"
   "Old Paint"
   "Night Herding Song"
2. Add guitar, Autoharp, or Omnichord accompaniment to each.
3. Introduce the harmonica and have selected students play the songs by ear as an accompaniment to the singing.

SAMPLE LESSONS

Dynamics

Activity: Experiencing dynamics through playing instruments
Grades: 1–3
Concept: Dynamics: Loud/soft

OBJECTIVES

Students will
1. Increase their perception of the expressive use of dynamics by playing classroom instruments.
2. Demonstrate an understanding of dynamics by their choice and expressive playing of classroom instruments.

TEACHER PREPARATION

1. Listen to *The Rhythm Makers* "Loud and Soft" (Tom Thumb Records Co.* CD-T303).
2. Prepare a chart with symbols:
   f forte   loud
   p piano   soft
   crescendo   <
   decrescendo   >
   accents   >

*Rhythms Production, Whitney Building, Box 34485, Los Angeles, CA 90034.

MATERIALS

Recording "Loud and Soft"

Chart with symbols

PROCEDURES

1. Engage students in an echo game:

   TEACHER: Cup hands and call "Hello . . ."

   STUDENTS: Hello

   TEACHER: Are you there?

   STUDENTS: Are you there? Are you there? Are you there? (each time softer)

2. Echo-clap the following rhythms:

3. Play or sing the echo song "Hello There" (p. 92). Ask students to respond by
   a. Singing an answer using tonal syllables
   b. Playing an answer on melody or resonator bells

4. Explore playing a single instrument loud and soft.

5. Discover instruments that make loud sounds and those that make soft sounds.

6. Choose large cymbals and a pair of finger cymbals. Play an echo game: One child taps the large cymbal with a soft mallet, a second student answers by tapping the finger cymbals (on rim only). Apply to the words, such as "hello," in the song.

7. Invite children to choose instruments that could make a loud sound (drum, cymbals, wood block) and those that might make a soft sound (sand blocks, jingle sticks). Divide class into two groups. Assign loud instruments to Group 1 and soft instruments to Group 2. Loud instruments will play on first *Hello*, soft instruments on second *Hello*. Practice the rhythm:

   Loud

   Soft

8. Have children listen to "Loud and Soft." Play instruments as directed (be sure students do not bang or hit the instrument to make it loud):

   Group 1   Louder instruments

   Group 2   Softer instruments

Proceed by alternating sets of instruments throughout piece. Children without instruments participate with Group 1 (loud—clapping hands) or Group 2 (soft—tapping fingers).

EVALUATION

1. Observe whether children play loud or soft at appropriate time while listening to "Loud and Soft."
2. Play "Kalinka" and ask children to raise their hands as the music gets louder and bow their heads as the music becomes or starts softer. (Help children understand that loud does not always equal fast and soft does not always equal slow.)

Repetition and Contrast

Activity: Playing instruments
Grades: 2–3
Concepts: Repetition
          Contrast

OBJECTIVES

Students will

1. Identify contrasting melodies by playing selected instruments.
2. Demonstrate an understanding of form by creating a rhythm accompaniment involving contrasting timbres for each section.
3. Increase their ability to hear repetition and contrast of musical ideas in music.

MATERIALS

Songs: "We Wish You a Merry Christmas" (p. 103)
        "Home on the Range" (p. 45)

Recordings: Mozart: *Eine Kleine Nachtmusik*, Rondo
             Herb Alpert: "Spanish Flea"*

Geometric forms

Classroom instruments:

  Group 1: Drum, tambourines, sticks

  Group 2: Triangles, jingle sticks, finger cymbals, jingle bells

Bulletin board with pictures of the instruments

PROCEDURES

1. Provide a large table with two signs: *Heavy, Light*.
2. Explore the contrasting timbres of instruments. Each student plays and places an instrument in front of the appropriate sign. After all are in place, invite several students to play one instrument from each section. Ask the class to decide whether the instrument is in the right place or ought to be with the other group.

---

*Herb Alpert and the Tijuana Brass, *Greatest Hits*, A&M Records CD 3267.

3. Play a game in which all of the instruments are placed at the rear of the classroom. Each student has an "Instrument Sheet." (Pictures could also be placed on a chalk or bulletin board.) A selected student chooses and plays an instrument from the back of the room. Students circle the instrument on their worksheet or point to a picture on the board.

4. Select four students to play drum, tambourine, sticks, and cymbals in the following rhythm:

5. Select four students to play the triangle, jingle sticks, finger cymbals, and jingle bells in the following rhythm:

6. Compare the sounds created by the two groups of instruments in 4 and 5.

7. Listen to Herb Alpert's "Spanish Flea." Play a steady beat on the hand drum for the main theme. Have students select categories of instruments to use for the contrasting theme (sticks, wood block, claves; jingle bells, jingle sticks, tambourine, triangle; hand drum, conga drum, bongo drums, snare drum).

8. Select a single instrument to play the main theme and other instruments to play the contrasting sections. Practice playing the following rhythm and changing on cue:

9. Listen to "Spanish Flea" and accompany with the instruments. Alternate heavy and light instruments for the contrasting sections. Invite a student with a keen musical sense to be the director of the ensemble. Involve all of the students in playing the instruments. Provide the leader with a conductor's baton.

CLOSURE

1. Listen to Mozart's *Eine Kleine Nachtmusic,* Rondo and accompany with heavy or light instruments the main melody and the contrasting melodies. Involve all of the students in playing the instruments. Either the teacher or a student may use a baton to conduct with.

2. Select instruments to play the contrasting sections of "We Wish You a Merry Christmas" (p. 103); one possibility would be jingle sticks (A), claves (B), jingle sticks (A).

EVALUATION

1. Identify the contrasting melodies when they occur in Mozart's *Eine Kleine Nachtmusic,* Rondo by raising hands.
2. Identify the main melody of the Rondo by raising hands.
3. Create an ABA form by playing contrasting instruments.
4. Create an AB form by playing contrasting instruments.

QUESTIONS FOR REVIEW

1. What are some differences between harmonic and melodic instruments? Name two or three of each.
2. What are four guidelines to follow in leading children in successful experiences with classroom percussion instruments?
3. What is the difference between the word *acoustic* and the word *electronic*?
4. Why would you transpose a song higher or lower?
5. What are differences between melody bells, resonator bells, and step bells?
6. What is the difference between a xylophone and a metallophone?
7. What are some problems with playing low C on a soprano recorder?
8. What is *patchen*?
9. What is the difference between the Autoharp and the Omnichord?
10. Can you play or write the guitar fingering for the following chords?
    a. D
    b. A₇
    c. E minor
    d. C
    e. G
    f. D₇
11. Name two *two*-chord songs.
    Name two *three*-chord songs.
12. Why is the F chord hard for amateurs to play on the guitar?
13. Why do children often mix up rhythm sticks and claves?
14. What are some ways you can use instruments to integrate music with other subjects?

7 TEACHING MUSIC THROUGH LISTENING

In our society, radio and television, home stereos, and portable players surround us with music. Sometimes music serves as a background of sound while we wait in an office, ride in an elevator, or shop. At other times, when attending a concert, ballet, or opera, we must listen carefully to enjoy it fully. You might say that in the first instance we *hear* music, while in the second we *listen* to music.

Let us consider some differences in each of these experiences. First, *hearing* is one of the five basic senses. Often we hear sounds without consciously identifying what they are: birds chirping, wind moving through trees, rustling leaves, and so on. In a crowd we may hear a lot of talking without distinguishing any particular words or meanings. On the other hand, listening requires aural skills that include focusing attention on the sound source, remembering sounds, perceiving phenomena unique to sounds, and responding. A baby hears sound but must be taught to listen. Many a parent has said, "My child hears me when I speak, but doesn't want to *listen*." Listening to music requires focusing attention on its unique qualities. This takes energy and self-discipline; if our minds wander, we lose the meaning of what we are hearing.

A listening experience is very different from a visual experience. After viewing a picture, we can look out the window, leave the room, or think about something else, and when we return, the picture will be in the same place with the same colors, lines, and shapes. In music, however, unless we use a recording, no two performances are ever exactly the same. Music is also unique in that it passes through time and we hear it both in the present (as it is happening) and in our memory (as it has happened). Memory, then, is an important component of listening, for part of the pleasure derived from a musical experience is in recalling a musical theme, a harmony, or a distinctive tonal color.

Children can be taught to listen to the expressive use of elements of music such as melody, rhythm, texture, tone color, dynamics, and formal structure. As they grow in their ability to perceive and understand musical phenomena, they have a greater potential for deeply satisfying aesthetic experiences.

A related outcome of a listening experience is learning how music expresses the time, place, and people who create it. For example, as children study and listen to "America," "Yankee Doodle," and "Chester," they can become more aware of and sensitive to the events surrounding the American Revolution.

While there are many benefits to developing home listening libraries of music, nothing can really replace the thrill and excitement of attending a live performance. Throughout the United States, many free concerts are given each year by colleges and universities, public and private schools, museums, churches, and others. Many symphony orchestras sponsor educational concerts for children at a nominal cost. It is important for the classroom teacher to seek out such opportunities so that children can attend live performances of music.

This chapter is designed to provide materials and techniques for preparing students to listen to music. It begins with a discussion of the chain of events in musical expression, followed by sections on sound sources for musical listening, how to guide listening, and integrating listening into the classroom.

THE CHAIN OF EVENTS IN MUSICAL EXPRESSION

Musical expression follows a chain of events that runs from composer to performer to listener.

THE COMPOSER

Music begins with an idea in the mind of a person called a *composer*. The idea may be a melody, a rhythmic motif, or a distinctive tone color. The composer must have the skill to organize these musical ideas in a logical and meaningful fashion that can be perceived and understood by the listener. All composers who have created lasting works of art have been able to achieve a high level of imagination and sensitivity in their works.

THE PERFORMER

Written music must be recreated from the musical score into a performance. The quality of the performance depends on (1) the technical skill of the performer, (2) insights into the musical meanings that are expressed, and (3) understanding of the musical style of the composer. While there is always somewhat of a personal stamp on any performance, the goal is to interpret the music as accurately and sensitively as possible according to the directions given by the composer.

THE COMPOSER/PERFORMER

In many kinds of music, such as the oral traditions of Africa and India, as well as American jazz, the performer is often the composer. In such traditions, the musician creates or composes at the instant of performance. That is, the role of composer appears in the improvisations by the performer. These improvisations, while appearing to be spontaneous, are most often based on a catalogue of musical ideas that have been stored in the musician's mind over a period of time. During performances, the musician must organize both stored and newly created sound materials in logical and imaginative ways.

THE LISTENER

The listener is one of the most important links in the chain of events of musical expression. The principal function of the listener is to receive, interpret, and respond to music. Learning to be an effective listener requires early and sustained training.

SOUNDS PRODUCED BY VOICES

People around the world produce a large number of different vocal sounds. Some are full and open, while others are pinched and nasal. In Western music women's voices are classified as soprano and alto, and male voices are divided into tenor and bass. Each of the following compositions can be used to illustrate various voice qualities:

Soprano: Giacomo Puccini, "Un bel di" (One Fine Day) from *Madame Butterfly*

Alto: Felix Mendelssohn, "O Rest in the Lord" from *Elijah*

Tenor: G. F. Handel, "Comfort Ye" from *Messiah*

Bass: Jerome Kern, "Old Man River" from *Showboat*

SOUNDS PRODUCED BY WESTERN ORCHESTRAL INSTRUMENTS

Sounds are produced by instruments in a variety of ways. In general, instruments are classified as stringed, wind, or percussion, depending on how their sounds are produced. In addition, some twentieth-century instruments produce their sounds electronically.

STRINGED INSTRUMENTS

Stringed instruments are usually played with a bow drawn across the strings. Placing the fingers of the left hand on the strings along the fingerboard changes the pitch. Each pitch is produced by a different finger position. Stringed instruments can also be plucked (called *pizzicato*). The pitches are still created with fingers on the strings; however, the fingers of the right hand pluck the string instead of using a bow. This same technique of plucking is used when playing the Japanese koto or Indian sitar. Other instruments that can be plucked include the harp, guitar, and Autoharp.

Cello

Violin

Harp

Viola

String bass

Violin

The violin is the soprano of the string family and is capable of a wide range of dynamics and expression. It has four strings, which are tuned by tightening or loosening pegs at the upper end of the instrument. *Musical example:* Mendelssohn, Violin Concerto in E Minor, Rondo.

Viola

The viola is the alto of the string family. It is somewhat larger than the violin and its strings are slightly thicker; therefore, its sound is lower and somewhat richer than the violin's. *Musical example:* Hindemith, *Der Schwanendreher* (The Swan Catcher).

Cello

The violoncello (usually called the cello) is the tenor member of the string family. Unlike the violin and viola, which are supported by holding the instruments between the chin and shoulder, the cello is placed upright with a peg connecting the base of the instrument to the floor. The cello's tone is warm and mellow. *Musical example:* Mendelssohn, *Sonata No. 1 for Cello and Piano,* Op. 45.

String Bass

The string bass (double bass) is the lowest-sounding member of the string family of instruments. While it is similar to the cello, the string bass is much larger and players must either stand or sit on a high stool to play it. The sounds of the bass are among the lowest in the orchestra. *Musical example:* Saint-Saëns, *The Carnival of the Animals,* "The Elephant."

Harp

The harp is a large instrument with forty-seven strings. These strings are tuned by pegs across the top of the instrument. A series of pedals on the bottom of the harp enable the player to change keys. *Musical example:* Tchaikovsky *The Nutcracker,* "Waltz of the Flowers."

WIND INSTRUMENTS

The wind instruments are played by blowing into a tube whose length is controlled by covering fingerholes, pressing down valves, or, in the case of a trombone, moving a slide. They are divided into the *woodwind* family and the *brass* family.

Woodwinds

The woodwinds can be classified into three groups: those without reeds, those with single reeds, and those with double reeds.

The first group of woodwinds are those without reeds. The flute is the soprano member of this group. Originally made of wood, it is now usually metal. Its tone in the lower register is warm and smooth, but as it proceeds up the scale, the tone becomes brighter. *Musical example:* Griffes, *The White Peacock.*

The other member of the reedless group, the piccolo, looks like a small flute and sounds an octave higher. Composers use it for unusual effects, since its sound can penetrate heavy masses of orchestral tone. *Musical example:* Sousa, *Stars and Stripes Forever,* ending.

The second group of woodwinds are those with a single reed. The clarinet is a single-reed

Piccolo

Flute

Clarinet

Saxophone

Courtesy of United Musical Instruments, U.S.A., Inc.

instrument whose pitch and tone can vary from a low, dark, sonorous quality to brilliant high pitches. *Musical example:* Copland, *Concerto for Clarinet and String Orchestra.*

The saxophone is another single-reed instrument. It differs from the clarinet in that it is larger and is constructed from metal. Saxophones are found predominantly in bands but occasionally are played in orchestras. They come in several sizes, including alto, tenor, and baritone. *Musical example:* Alexander Glazunov, Concerto in *E flat for Saxophone and Orchestra,* Op. 109.

The third group of woodwinds are those with a double reed. The oboe is a double-reed instrument with a bright tone color and a penetrating quality. *Musical example:* Prokofiev, *Peter and the Wolf,* "Duck."

The English horn is larger than the oboe and therefore has a lower pitch and a darker tone color. *Musical example:* Dvořák, *New World Symphony,* second movement.

The bassoon is a still lower-pitched instrument; it is sometimes described as a tenor-sounding instrument. *Musical example:* Prokofiev, *Peter and the Wolf,* "Grandfather."

English horn

Oboe

Contrabassoon

Bassoon

The contrabassoon is the lowest-sounding member of the woodwind family. It is essentially the same as the bassoon, only larger, and sounds an octave lower. Although it is 16 feet long, the instrument is constructed in coils so that it actually stands about 4 feet tall. *Musical example:* Ravel, *Mother Goose Suite*, "Beauty and the Beast."

Brass

A second group of wind instruments are the *brass*, a name that refers to the material from which the instruments are made. There are four main brass instruments: trumpet, French horn, trombone, and tuba.

The trumpet is the soprano of the brass family and has a high brilliant sound. *Musical example:* Purcell-Clark, *Trumpet Voluntary in D.*

Trumpet

French horn

Trombone

Tuba

Sousaphone

Conn Sousaphone. Photo courtesy of United Musical Instruments, U.S.A., Inc.

The French horn is the alto member of the brass family. Its tone is lower and more mellow than that of the trumpet. *Musical example:* Mozart, *Horn Concerto No. 3 in E flat Major,* K. 447.

The trombone is the tenor member of the brass family. This instrument consists of a tube about 9 feet long, doubled on itself to about half that length. The performer uses a slide to alter the length of the tube and, therefore, the pitch. *Musical example:* Rimsky-Korsakov, Concerto for Trombone and Band.

The tuba is the bass member of the brass family and has a low and powerful tone. A special type of tuba, known as the Sousaphone, is designed in circular fashion so that the instrument can be carried more easily in marching bands. *Musical example:* Paul Tripp, "Tubby the Tuba."

PERCUSSION INSTRUMENTS

A fourth family of instruments are those that are struck or shaken. Instruments that have a definite pitch are timpani, chimes, and xylophone. Instruments of indefinite pitch include the snare drum, bass drum, cymbals, triangle, gong, tambourine, and castanets.

Timpani

The timpani (kettledrums) is capable of definite and variable pitch. The player strikes the heads with different types of sticks, from hard to soft, according to the quality of tone required. The drums are tuned for the particular composition. *Musical example:* Prokofiev, *Peter and the Wolf,* "Guns of Hunters."

Chimes

Chimes consist of metal bars suspended on a frame and struck with a mallet. They are tuned to the chromatic scale and the tone is very bright. *Musical example:* Tchaikovsky, *1812 Overture,* ending.

Timpani

Chimes

Xylophone

Bass drum

Snare drum

Cymbals

Gong

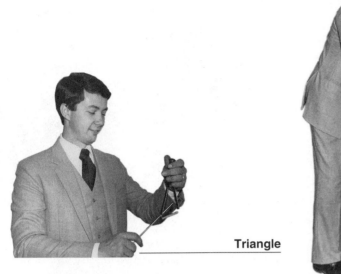

Triangle

Xylophone

The xylophone consists of a graduated series of wooden bars suspended on a frame in two rows representing the white and black keys of the piano. It is played with hard mallets. *Musical example:* Saint-Saëns, *Carnival of the Animals*, "Fossils."

Snare Drum

The snare drum is a shallow cylinder of brass closed at either end by a membrane under tension. Metal strings (snares) are stretched across the lower head so that, when the drum is struck, they vibrate against the membrane, causing the familiar rattling effect. *Musical example:* Bizet, *Carmen*, "Soldier's Chorus."

Bass Drum

The bass drum is made of wood or metal; its pitch is indefinite but very low. It is often used for special rhythmic emphasis. *Musical example:* Verdi, *Requiem*, "Dies Irae."

Cymbals

Cymbals are discs of brass with a depression in the center. They are used in pairs for such rhythmic and tonal effects as keeping the beat and dynamic contrasts. *Musical example:* Ravel, *Mother Goose Suite*, "Laideronette, Empress of the Pagoda."

Triangle

The triangle is a steel rod bent into a triangular shape with one angle open. It is suspended on a string and played by striking it with a metal stick. It has a brilliant, tinkling tone. *Musical example:* Verdi, *Il Trovatore*, "Anvil Chorus."

Gong

The gong is a large, circular, metallic plate suspended by a cord and struck with a mallet. *Musical example:* Ravel, *Mother Goose Suite*, "Laideronette, Empress of the Pagoda."

Tambourine

Castanets

Tambourine

The tambourine is a miniature drum with a single head. In the rim of wood are small metal discs that vibrate when the instrument is struck or shaken. *Musical example:* Verdi, *Il Trovatore*, "Anvil Chorus."

Castanets

Castanets are hollow shells (always used in pairs) that, when clapped rhythmically together, give a sharp, clacking sound. They are often used with dance music of Spain or Latin America. *Musical example:* Bizet, *Carmen*, "Seguidilla."

KEYBOARD INSTRUMENTS

Four keyboard instruments are the pipe organ, piano, harpsichord, and celesta.

Pipe Organ

The pipe organ consists of a set of pipes (one for each key) that sound at different pitches. Stops activate the many pipes (flues, principals, reeds, and strings), and the player can use them to produce an enormous variety of tonal colors. The player sits at a console, which may have several keyboards, including one called the pedal (played with the feet). Each one of these keyboards is connected to a division of pipes. These divisions are called Great, Swell, Positive, Choir, or Solo, depending on the number of manuals. The organist manipulates stops and expression pedals (to get louder and softer) and selects tonal colors from the various divisions to interpret the music. *Musical example:* Ives, *Variations on "America."*

Piano

The piano has eighty-eight notes and a single keyboard. Sounds are produced by hammers that strike strings stretched across the inner framework of the instrument. *Musical example:* Mozart, *Variations on "Twinkle, Twinkle, Little Star,"* K. 265.

Harpsichord

The harpsichord resembles a piano but is smaller and may have two keyboards. Instead of hammers striking strings, small plectrums, activated by the keyboard, pluck strings; thus

Pipe organ, St. Andrews United Presbyterian Church, Olmsted Falls, Ohio

Piano

Harpsichord

Celesta

the harpsichord has a much softer sound than the piano and a more limited dynamic range. *Musical example:* Handel, *The Harmonious Blacksmith.*

Celesta

The celesta looks like a small piano but has only a four-octave keyboard. When the keys are depressed, small hammers strike bell-metal bars. The sounds of this instrument are

Synthesizer

characterized by a light, bell-like quality. *Musical example:* Tchaikovsky, *The Nutcracker*, "Dance of the Sugar Plum Fairy."

ELECTRONIC INSTRUMENTS

Many instruments, such as the piano and guitar, can be electrified. Much popular music today is performed on these electronic instruments.

Another form of electronic instrument is the synthesizer. It is entirely electronic and can perform tasks beyond the capability of traditional instruments. For example, a composer can use a synthesizer to create melodies and rhythms extending beyond the pitch range of a traditional instrument or faster than could be created by a human being. Synthesizers create new sounds and forms of music. *Musical example:* Babbitt, *Ensembles for Synthesizer.*

PERFORMING ENSEMBLES

Both instruments and voices are often grouped into large ensembles such as orchestras, bands, and choruses. Sometimes the ensembles are much smaller, such as duets (two performers), trios (three performers), and quartets (four performers).

ORCHESTRA

The Western symphony orchestra is a large ensemble composed of stringed, brass, woodwind, and percussion instruments. The principal instruments of the orchestra are given in the accompanying table. Figure 7.1 shows a typical seating arrangement.

Instruments of the orchestra are often studied in terms of their general classification (strings, woodwinds, brasses) and their pitch ranges. Thus, there are "soprano," "alto," "tenor," and "bass" instruments, as shown below:

Principal Orchestra Instruments

Range	Strings	Brass	Woodwind
Soprano	Violin	Trumpet	Flute
Alto	Viola	French horn	Clarinet/oboe
Tenor	Cello	Trombone	Bassoon
Bass	Bass viol (double bass)	Tuba	Contrabassoon

The Cleveland Orchestra with its conductor, Christopher von Dohnányi

Figure 7.1. A seating plan of The Cleveland Orchestra

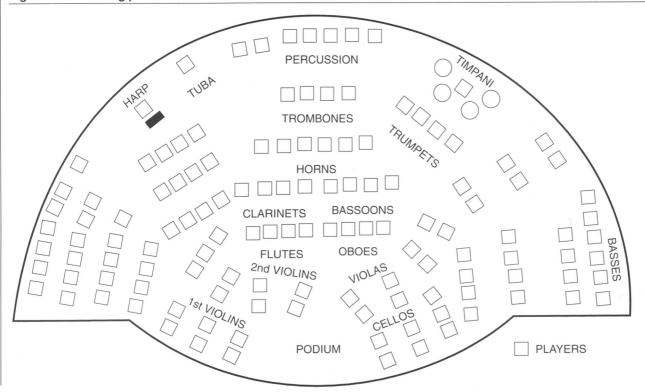

In addition to the instruments listed in the table, orchestras have a variety of pitched and nonpitched percussion instruments with ranges from high to low. Often some keyboard instruments (such as celesta and piano) are also included in the orchestral ensemble.

Suggestions for Lessons

1. Listen to and watch the video *The Orchestra* with Peter Ustinov.* You may wish to teach the instruments over several days since the video has three parts to it.

   Part One includes (a) feelings about music, and (b) the composer. Part Two includes (a) the string family, and (b) the woodwind family. Part Three includes (a) the brass family, (b) the woodwind family, (c) special instruments, and (d) the conductor.

2. Listen to Benjamin Britten's *The Young Person's Guide to the Orchestra*, subtitled *Variations and Fugue on a Theme of Purcell*. (Purcell was an English composer, 1659–1695.) This composition features individual instruments and sections of the orchestra. Place the following diagram on a transparency or on the chalkboard:

---

1. "Purcell theme" played by the entire orchestra

2. Woodwinds play theme

3. Brasses play theme

4. Strings play theme

5. Percussion

6. Entire orchestra plays theme

7. Variations on the theme, each featuring a different instrument or instrument group as follows:
   a. Woodwinds
      Piccolo and flutes
      Oboes
      Clarinets
      Bassoons
   b. Strings
      Violins
      Violas
      Cellos
      Double basses
      Harp
   c. Brasses
      Horns
      Trumpets
      Trombones and tuba
   d. Percussion
      Kettledrums
      Bass drum and cymbals

   Tambourine and triangle
   Snare drum and Chinese block*
   Xylophone
   Castanets and gong
   Whip
   All percussion instruments together

8. A fugue, in which the theme is played by instruments entering one after the other, follows:
   a. Piccolo
   b. Flute
   c. Oboe
   d. Clarinet
   e. Bassoons
   f. Violins
   g. Violas
   h. Cellos
   I. Double basses
   j. Harp
   k. Horns
   l. Trumpets
   m. Trombone and tuba

9. Brass instruments play the "Purcell theme" in a slow tempo, while remaining instruments continue with the fugal style.

---

*Brightly painted, wooden percussion instrument.

*Mark Rubin Productions, Inc. 1990. Available from Friendship House, 29313 Clemens Road, Suite 2-G, Westlake, OH 44145.

BAND

In contrast to the large stringed instrument sections of the orchestra, a band has a large woodwind section consisting of clarinets, saxophones, flutes, piccolos, oboes, English horn(s), and bassoons. Brass instruments of the band include trumpets, French horns, trombones, and tubas. In addition there are many different percussion instruments, particularly bass drum and snare drums. Listen to the sound of a band in Sousa's *Stars and Stripes Forever*.

The Cleveland Heights High School Band

The Burleigh (Wisconsin) Elementary Choir

By permission of the Burleigh (Wisconsin) Elementary Choir, Maria Zellmer, Director.

CHORUS

A chorus is composed of soprano, alto, tenor, and bass voices. Large choruses frequently perform works with an orchestra. Listen to the sound of a chorus in Handel's *Messiah*, "Hallelujah Chorus."

HOW TO GUIDE LISTENING

A teacher must have knowledge about the musical components of a piece of music. He or she needs to decide on the focus of the listening experience, choose materials appropriate to a given maturity level, and develop sequential and imaginative procedures. It is important for teachers to design listening lessons that are multisensory—that is, students need to hear music, see a visual that helps give meaning to the aural experience, be physically involved through movement, and develop skill in verbally describing a musical experience.

LEVELS OF LISTENING

As you explore students' musical needs, it will be helpful to describe four levels of listening, each of which might occur (in differing degrees of complexity) at a given grade level.

1. *What do I hear?* At this most basic level, the student simply hears sounds, which might be created by a voice, an environmental source, or an instrument. No processing of the sounds occurs and no value judgments are made.
2. *How are sounds organized?* Sounds may be organized as melody, rhythm, texture (harmony), timbre (tone color), and form. They may be organized with a distinc-

tive quality, which may be identified as Japanese, or Jazz, or Medieval; or possibly the sounds will reflect the style of a particular composer, such as George Gershwin or Leonard Bernstein. At this level, the listener processes sounds in very general categories and identifies the sounds he or she hears.

3. *What do sounds express?* At this level, the listener processes the sounds heard and both analyzes and judges the effectiveness of the musical components. Thus, a melody may be smooth, have a stepwise motion, have a narrow range, be performed with little dynamic change, or be soothing to the listener. On the other hand, a melody may be jagged, have a wide range, contain different meter patterns, and create a feeling of great excitement. The listener makes a value judgment on the degree to which a composer has effectively expressed an idea or feeling, and how he or she has done so.

4. *What does listening to music do for me?* How can the quality of my life be enhanced by learning to listen to music? This is an affective result of a cognitive process. Knowing and understanding how a composer expresses ideas through musical elements and interacting with them can lead to a change in the listener. This is often called an "aesthetic experience." It may be a feeling of well-being, or it may result in an increased enjoyment of the music. Whatever happens, the listener should feel pleasure and satisfaction as a result of the experience.

THE TEACHER'S ROLE

When you teach a listening lesson, you are actually sharing a piece of music with students—something that was unknown to them before. A piece of music may be familiar to some students. If so, the objective in the lesson could be to further their knowledge or understanding of the music. The same piece might be taught for different reasons at various grade levels. This is known as a "spiral" approach to teaching. Each time students should grow in their understanding and interaction with the piece. Much, of course, depends on the music, for only music that bears repeating and is rich in musical information can be reexperienced with increasing satisfaction and enjoyment.

As you begin to organize and create listening lessons, it is imperative to

1. Have cognitive understanding of the music, such as how the melody moves, where the rhythm patterns are, and whether the melody repeats exactly or repeats with variation.
2. Understand how the music is expressive. For example, is the meaning found simply in the sound and construction of the melody, or is the composer trying to express an outside meaning as well? An example of the latter might be how the composer Paul Dukas expresses, through musical sound, the story of *The Sorcerer's Apprentice* (see p. 278).
3. Write clear objectives that enable students to focus on specific musical concepts or ideas.
4. Carefully and creatively plan steps that will contribute to learning.
5. Develop and implement evaluation tools that will determine whether the objectives have been met.

GUIDELINES FOR PLANNING LISTENING LESSONS

The following suggestions reflect a basic philosophy: Listening to music is *active* listening. The student must focus, concentrate, listen, and respond.

1. Get students' attention. Intrigue them. Provide an exciting and stimulating beginning. Use pictures, charts, puppets, games, or creative experiences.

2. Introduce the music. Remember, once you get students' attention, they want to hear this music that you are excited about. Then don't talk forever. Part of teaching is pacing—knowing when to present an idea and when to hold back another idea.

3. Listen to music with the students. Avoid looking out the window or deciding what you are going to do next. Your interest and enthusiasm will help keep them focused on the music.

4. Get students involved physically and mentally. Ask them to respond in some way. They may clap the beat, trace the melody in the air, stand up or sit down on the verse or chorus, and so on. Repeat the music as necessary; one time is seldom enough.

5. Keep the listening examples relatively short. Give specific directions about the kind of a response you are seeking, such as, "Place the arrows on the chalk board to indicate the direction of the melody."

6. Encourage spontaneous responses to music such as swaying and finger tapping. Try to channel this behavior into desirable musical responses.

7. Use only background information that contributes to musical understanding and is meaningful or important to the listener.

8. Encourage students to listen to the music and not to you. Don't talk when you expect students to listen to music.

9. Sensitivity develops gradually through repeated hearings; don't try to expose students to new music each week. You will probably be providing the first hearing of a piece for many students. You don't want it to be the last. Let them want to hear their "favorite pieces."

10. A class mirrors you. If you show interest and enthusiasm for the music, students are more likely to show interest. If you show insecurity, nervousness, and dislike of the music, they will often begin to talk, exhibit boredom, and perhaps become discipline problems.

11. Fill the room with music. Be certain that students in all parts of the room are hearing a "near live" performance.

12. When explaining a musical element such as form to students, compare it to familiar things. Ideas such as blueprints, patterns in dress or shirt fabrics, and recipes can often help students understand musical form.

TECHNIQUES FOR TEACHING STUDENTS TO LISTEN TO MUSIC

There are many techniques for guiding perceptive listening. Some of these include (1) using visual representations, (2) using written listening guides, (3) learning a familiar song that is found in a composition, (4) moving to music, and (5) playing instruments.

VISUAL REPRESENTATIONS

Visual representations are often highly effective in helping students follow events as they occur in music. For example:

1. AB or ABA form: Use familiar objects to diagram form.

A	B		A	B	A
Cube	Sphere	or	Ping-pong ball	Tennis ball	Ping-pong ball

2. Duple meter or triple meter: Create patterns of shapes or colors and place them on a chalk or bulletin board:

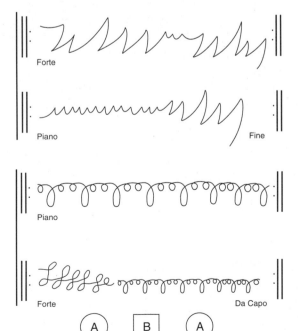

  Duple meter   or   Triple meter

3. Tone color: Create cutouts of animals or instruments and mount them on tongue depressors (readily available from a drugstore or pharmacy). Use stick puppets to identify animals/instruments in selected compositions, such as *Carnival of the Animals* and *Peter and the Wolf.*

Mapping Experiences

Mapping involves developing linear icons for events in a piece of music.

1. Figure 7.2 shows a "musical map" for Mozart's *Eine Kleine Nachtmusik*, third movement. Place this map on a transparency. You may wish to use different colors to illustrate contrasting sections in the music.

Forte

Piano   Fine

Piano

Forte   Da Capo

(A)   [B]   (A)

Figure 7.2.
Mozart: *Eine Kleine Nachtmusik,* **third movement**

2. As you listen to the piece, ask students to move their right hands in the air as they follow the outline. You should guide the movement by following, with a pencil, the outline on the transparency.

3. After the students learn to follow the outline easily, call attention to the repetition, contrast, and then the larger ABA design by placing letters and geometrical shapes on the board.

Integrated Experiences

For an integrated experience, you could incorporate a variety of activities. For example:

1. Read the story of *The Sorcerer's Apprentice*:

A sorcerer (magician) lives in a giant castle above the Rhine River. He spends most of his days preparing magic potions. His secrets are kept in a large book, which is placed in a locked box in his bookcase.

As the sorcerer's work increases, he decides that he needs an apprentice to help him. He hires a boy primarily to carry water from the river up to the castle. The boy has interest in becoming a magician himself but is somewhat lazy. He would rather sit along the river, play his flute, and stroke the sorcerer's cat.

One day, the sorcerer has to be away from the castle on an important mission. He leaves his apprentice to look after things. When he is alone, the boy decides to investigate the magic book. He climbs up the ladder, opens the box, and removes the book. As he thumbs through the pages, he murmurs several of the magic words from the text, and suddenly there is a loud clap of sound that causes him to fall off the ladder. As he lies on the floor, the apprentice suddenly realizes that he has unleashed the magical powers of the book. He looks across the room and, as his eyes catch a glimpse of the broom, he has an idea. He quickly says the words "Abrah cadabrah," commanding the broom to pick up the pail and begin bringing water from the river up to the castle.

The broom obeys and begins to haul water. The apprentice is delighted and frolicks around the castle while the broom continues to work. Everything is fine until suddenly the apprentice realizes that enough water has been brought to fill the huge tub but the broom has not stopped its work. The boy repeats all the magic words but is unable to stop the rising water. He becomes frantic and grabs an axe, chopping the broom in half. To his enormous surprise, each of the resulting splinters of wood becomes a broom, picking up a pail and bringing more and more water.

The situation is now truly frantic, with everything in the castle afloat. All seems lost until the sorcerer suddenly reappears and, seeing the terrible mess, commands the water to recede. The castle is devastated and the angry sorcerer spanks his apprentice. The boy is sad but wiser, now realizing that his laziness and his opening of the magic book without the magician's approval have led to his predicament.

2. Identify the main events in the story:
   a. Mysterious castle
   b. Sorcerer
   c. Brooms
   d. Water rising
   e. Water receding
   f. "Kick in the pants"

3. Discuss how the composer might express these ideas in music, such as
   a. Mysterious castle—soft strings and woodwinds
   b. Apprentice—loud, active melodies

c. Brooms—melody played on bassoon-clarinet
d. Water rising—louder, higher
e. Sorcerer—trumpets and horns, loud chorus
f. "Kick in pants"—sudden loud chord

4. Show the video "The Sorcerer's Apprentice" from *Fantasia* and have students match the pictures in Figure 7.3 with the music.

Figure 7.3 . Images to accompany *The Sorcerer's Apprentice*

1. Mysterious castle: Soft strings and woodwinds

2. Apprentice: Loud, active melodies

3. Brooms: Melody played on bassoon

4. Water rises: Texture thickens

5. Water rises: Dynamics louder; texture thickens

6. Apprentice thinks: Music stops; two brooms: bassoon and clarinet

7. Water rises: Louder; higher; thicker

8. Water rises: Louder; higher; thicker texture

9. Water rises: Louder; higher; thicker

10. Sorcerer: Trumpets herald his return

11. Sorcerer's magic words: Softer; lower; thinner

12. Apprentice disciplined: Solo string; softer

13. Sorcerer kicks apprentice: Sudden loud chord

WRITTEN LISTENING GUIDES

Another effective way of helping students follow events in a musical composition is through a written listening guide. Here are some suggestions for creating a written guide for listening to theme-and-variations form in Haydn's *Symphony No. 94* ("Surprise"), second movement.

1. Listen to the entire piece of music (second movement) and analyze the musical components:
    a. *Melody.* What are some characteristics of the melody (theme) (moves by steps or skips, major or minor, etc.)?
    b. *Rhythm.* What are characteristics of the rhythm (duple or triple meter, repeated patterns, etc.)?
    c. *Tone color (or timbre).* What types of instrumental sounds are heard (strings, brass, woodwinds, etc.)?
    d. *Dynamics.* What types of dynamic changes occur?
    e. *Form.* How is the piece of music put together (e.g., theme with four variations)? How does the composer create each variation (add a second melody, change the tonality, add repeated notes, change the meter, etc.)?

2. From the analysis and discussion, list on the chalkboard the characteristics of each element as it applies to each variation.

3. Construct a listening guide such as the following:

Call Number	Musical Event
1. Theme	Main theme: mostly skips, repeated softly, played staccato
2. Variation 1	Countermelody in the high strings, stepwise melody, legato; contrasts with skips in the main theme
3. Variation 2	Melody changes from major key to minor key
4.	Countermelody added
5. Variation 3	Each melody note repeated as sixteenths; countermelody played by flute
6.	Returns to single-note melody
7. Variation 4	Full orchestra plays main melody; contrasts with ornamented melody (notes above and below the pitches of the main melody)
8.	Ending (Coda), sudden pause
	Return of main theme played by woodwinds

4. Place the guide on a transparency or chart.
5. Select a student to point to the events that will be used to guide students' listening experience.
6. Listen to the piece and follow the guide.
7. Provide each student with an evaluation chart and ask them to circle the appropriate response as they listen to the piece again. Example:

Theme	Melody moves mostly by steps	Melody moves mostly by skips
	Melody is played staccato	Melody is played legato
Variation 1	Countermelody	No countermelody
	Many skips	Mostly stepwise
Variation 2	Major key	Minor key
Variation 3	Melody repeated with sixteenth notes	Melody as at the beginning
Variation 4	No ornamentation of melody	Much ornamentation of melody

THE FAMILIAR SONG IN A MUSICAL COMPOSITION

One of the most effective ways to guide listening is to teach a song that is used by a composer in a musical composition (a list of such compositions appears on pages 285–287). As the student learns to sing the melody, it becomes easier to hear it in a larger context.

Sample Lesson: "American Salute"

Grades: 5–6

Activity: Listening to a piece of music as played by an orchestra; singing a song

Concepts: Theme and variation

Familiar song in larger musical composition

When Johnny Comes Marching Home

Words and Music by Patrick S. Gilmore

Key: E minor
Starting pitch: E
Meter: 6/8, begins on 6

OBJECTIVES

Students will

1. Sing the song "When Johnny Comes Marching Home" with accurate pitches and rhythms.
2. Identify the song as popular during the Civil War.
3. Identify the song as a march.
4. Identify the meanings of the words *jubilee, three times three, laurel wreath.*
5. Exhibit an understanding of form (theme and variations).

MATERIALS

- Musical score for "When Johnny Comes Marching Home"
- Pictures of Civil War
- Chart with words *march, jubilee, three times three,* and *laurel wreath*
- Autoharp, guitar, Omnichord
- Blank 8½" × 11" white or colored paper
- Crayons or Magic Markers
- Chalkboard
- Examples of diminution, augmentation, accelerando, and syncopation on charts

PROCEDURES

1. Teach the song "When Johnny Comes Marching Home."
2. Show pictures from the Civil War and discuss the role (if any) of your state. Make students aware that the Civil War was between "brothers" in our country. "When Johnny Comes Marching Home" was one of the most popular songs to come out of the Civil War (along with "Dixie" and "Battle Hymn of the Republic"). The words were written by Patrick S. Gilmore, a bandmaster attached to General Butler's command in New Orleans. It is a march with a strong beat.
3. Discuss the meanings of words used in the text.
   a. Most soldiers were from small towns where they were well known.
   b. The village church also served as a meeting house and assembly for the community, so the use of the church bell celebrated special events. We still ring bells for national celebrations.
   c. *Jubilee* is another word for *celebration.*
   d. *Three times three* = "Hip, Hip, Hurray! Hip, Hip, Hurray! Hip, Hip, Hurray!"
   e. The laurel wreath was placed on the heads of victorious athletes in the ancient Greek games. It is made of woven leaves.
4. Sing both verses of the song, accompanied by guitar, Autoharp, or Omnichord.
5. Explore the concept of theme and variations:
   a. How many different ways could you "draw" the first letter of your last name? For example:

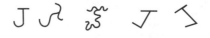

Place examples on chalkboard.

b. How many ways could you draw a circle? For example:

Place examples on chalkboard.

c. Using the "white sound" *chooo* held for five seconds, how many different ways could you alter it? For example:

Staccato: *choo, choo, choo, choo,* etc.

Scoop:

    choo   *choo*

d. How many different ways could you alter the melody of "When Johnny Comes Marching Home"? Examples: faster, slower, higher, lower, different voices, fragments. Experiment by playing the first phrase in different ways on the piano, melody bells, or recorder.

e. Explain musical terms:

Augmentation: Stretching out, for example, ♩ ♩ ♩ becomes 𝅗𝅥 𝅗𝅥 𝅗𝅥

Diminution: Squeezing together, for example, 𝅗𝅥 𝅗𝅥 𝅗𝅥 becomes ♪ ♪ ♪

Fragmentation: Breaking up the melody into small pieces

Acceleration: Getting faster

Syncopation: Emphasizing a weak beat

CLOSURE

1. Listen to Morton Gould's *American Salute.* Follow the listening guide below. You can use individual guides, a transparency, or a large chart. Have a child identify each musical event by pointing to it as it occurs.

Listening Guide: Morton Gould, *American Salute,* "When Johnny Comes Marching Home"

Call Number	Musical Event	Call Number	Musical Event
1.	Introduction is based on rhythmic fragments	9.	Melody: Use of rhythmic syncopation
2.	Melody: Bassoon and bass clarinet	10.	Bridge: Meter changes from 3/4 to 4/4
3.	Bridge: Rhythmic fragments	11.	Part I, melody: Trumpets and trombones (augmentation)
4.	Melody: English horn		
5.	Melody: Strings	12.	Repeats: Pianissimo
6.	Bridge: Brass and timpani play rhythmic fragments	13.	Part II, melody: Woodwinds (diminution)
		14.	Coda: Fragments of theme in imitation
7.	Melody: High woodwinds (ornamentation)	15.	Coda: Accelerando (gets faster)
8.	Bridge: Woodwinds and strings play a crescendo		

2. For children with special needs such as learning disability, dyslexia, hearing impairment: Use pictures of the instruments as a listening guide rather than asking the children to read words.

EVALUATION

1. Listen to *American Salute*. Ask students what the words *jubilee*, *three times three*, and *laurel wreath* mean.
2. Ask students how the composer creates each variation (fragments of the melody, faster, slower, changes in instruments, changes in meter, and so on).

MOVING TO MUSIC

Although Chapter 8 is devoted to techniques for teaching music to children through movement, here are several suggestions for the teacher wishing to use movement as part of the listening experience. Young children in particular are in constant motion. They walk, run, jump, fidget, bounce, mimic, skip, and dance. As teachers you can capitalize on this desire to move.

Suggestions for Lessons

1. Listen to the Rondo from the Mozart *Horn Concerto in E Flat* (third movement). Divide students into pairs and ask each pair to create a movement for A, B, or C. Be sure each pair keeps a steady beat. Practice the movement until students are comfortable with it and then have them perform with the recording. You may assist by pointing to shapes placed on the chalkboard.

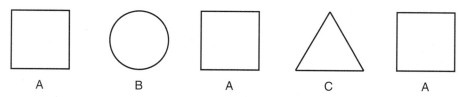

2. Invite children to respond physically to such directions as: "Walk and change direction when you hear a new melody" (Grades 4–6); "Pretend you are a rosebud opening as the music gets louder" (Grades K–3); "Change partners when you hear a different meter or tonality" (Grades 4–6).

PLAYING INSTRUMENTS

Playing classroom instruments is a popular activity with children of all ages.

Suggestions for Lessons

1. Create an ensemble by combining several instruments. Orff instruments (designed by the German music educator Carl Orff) such as xylophones, drums, and glockenspiels can be used by either a few children or many children to interpret larger musical compositions. For example, you may wish to use drums and triangles (or glockenspiels) to interpret the "Anvil Chorus" from the opera *Il Trovatore* by Giuseppe Verdi.

SONGS USED IN LARGER MUSICAL COMPOSITIONS

Song	Composer	Composition*
"America" ("God Save the King") (American hymn)	Ludwig van Beethoven	Wellington's Victory
	Ludwig van Beethoven	Variations on "God Save the King"
	Claude Debussy	Preludes, Book II, No. 9
	Charles Ives	Variations on "America"
	Max Reger	Variations on "God Save the King"
	Niccolò Paganini	Variations on "God Save the King"
Austrian Hymn (Austrian national anthem)	Franz Joseph Haydn	String Quartet, Opus 76, No. 3
	John Knowles Paine	Variations on "Austria"
"The Bear Went Over the Mountain" ("For He's a Jolly Good Fellow")	Ludwig van Beethoven	Wellington's Victory
	Virgil Thomson	Symphony on a Hymn Tune
	Virgil Thomson	Suite from The River, fourth movement
"The Birch Tree" (Russian folk song)	Peter Tchaikovsky	Symphony No. 4, fourth movement
"Camptown Races" (Civil War square dance)	Aaron Copland	A Lincoln Portrait
	Charles Ives	Symphony No. 2, third movement
"Chester" (American Revolution)	William Schuman	New England Triptych, third movement
"Columbia, the Gem of the Ocean" (American Revolution)	Charles Ives	Symphony No. 2, third movement
	Charles Ives	The Fourth of July
"Dixie" (Civil War/Minstrel song)	Ernest Bloch	America
"The Farmer in the Dell" (Play song)	Edwin Franko Goldman	Children's March
	Alec Templeton	Variations on "The Farmer in the Dell"
"Frère Jacques" ("Are You Sleeping?") (French round)	Gustav Mahler	Symphony No. 1, third movement
"Gaudeamus Igitur" (German student song)	Johannes Brahms	Academic Festival Overture
"Git Along Little Dogies" (American West)	Aaron Copland	Billy the Kid
"Goin' Home" (American folk song)	Antonín Dvořák	Symphony No. 9 (New World)
"Goodbye, Old Paint" (American West)	Aaron Copland	Billy the Kid
"Greensleeves" (English folk song)	Ralph Vaughan Williams	Fantasia on "Greensleeves"
	Buryl Red	Greensleeves

* Current recordings, listed in Schwann Catalog, are available in most record stores or in public libraries.

SONGS USED IN LARGER MUSICAL COMPOSITIONS (CONTINUED)

Song	Composer	Composition
"Hail, Columbia" (American Revolution)	Ernest Bloch	*America*
	Charles Ives	"Putnam's Camp" from *Three Places in New England*
"Happy Birthday" (American)	Igor Stravinsky	*Greeting Prelude*
"Hatikvah" (Israeli national anthem)	Bedřich Smetana	*The Moldau*
"Irish Washerwoman" (Irish folk song)	LeRoy Anderson	*Irish Suite*, first movement
"Jesu, Joy of Man's Desiring" (German chorale)	J. S. Bach	Cantata No. 147
	Walter Carlos	*Switched-on Bach*
"Joy to the World" (English Carol)	Charles Ives	Symphony No. 2, fifth movement
"La Marseillaise" (French national anthem)	Robert Schumann	*The Two Grenadiers*
	Peter Tchaikovsky	*1812 Overture*
	Hector Berlioz	*La Marseillaise*
"Land of Hope and Glory" (English)	Edward Elgar	*Pomp and Circumstance March No. 1*
"London Bridge" (English)	Edwin Franko Goldman	*Children's March*
"Londonderry Air" (English)	Percy Grainger	*Irish Tune from County Derry*
"Mack, the Knife" (German opera)	Kurt Weill	*The Threepenny Opera*
	Andre Previn and J. J. Johnson	"Mack, the Knife"
	Louis Armstrong	"Mack, the Knife"
"March of the Three Kings" (French opera)	Georges Bizet	"Farandole" from *L'Arlesienne Suite No. 2*
"Mary Had a Little Lamb" (American)	Edwin Franko Goldman	*Children's March*
"The Metronome" (German)	Ludwig van Beethoven	Symphony No. 8, second movement
"A Mighty Fortress Is Our God" (German chorale)	J. S. Bach	Cantata No. 80
	Felix Mendelssohn	Symphony No. 5 (*Reformation*)
"Ode to Joy" ("Joyful, Joyful") (German)	Ludwig van Beethoven	Symphony No. 9, fourth movement
"Old Chisholm Trail" (American West)	Aaron Copland	*Billy the Kid*
"Old Hundredth" ("The Doxology") (fifteenth-century chorale)	J. S. Bach	Cantata No. 130
	Ernest Bloch	*America*
	Henry Purcell	*Voluntary on "Old Hundredth"*

SONGS USED IN LARGER MUSICAL COMPOSITIONS (CONTINUED)

Song	Composer	Composition
"On Springfield Mountain" (American folk song)	Aaron Copland	A Lincoln Portrait
"O, Susanna" (Civil War/square dance)	Ferde Grofé	Death Valley Suite
"Pop! Goes the Weasel" (English)	Ernest Bloch	America
	Lucien Cailliet	Variations on "Pop! Goes the Weasel"
	Leo Sowerby	Variations on "Pop! Goes the Weasel"
"Sakura" ("Cherry Blossoms") (Japanese)	Eto	Variations on "Sakura"
"Simple Gifts" (Shaker hymn)	Aaron Copland	Appalachian Spring
"The Star-Spangled Banner" (U.S. national anthem)	Edwin Bagley	National Emblem March
	Charles Ives	"Putnam's Camp" from Three Places in New England
"Streets of Laredo" (American West)	Roy Harris	Folksong Symphony
	Virgil Thomson	The Plow That Broke the Plains, cattle movement
"Toreador" (opera)	Georges Bizet	Overture to Carmen
"Twinkle, Twinkle Little Star" (German-French)	Erno Dohnányi	Variations on a Nursery Song
	Wolfgang Mozart	Variations on "Ah, vous dirai-je Maman"
	Camille Saint-Saëns	Carnival of Animals, "Fossils"
"When Johnny Comes Marching Home" (Civil War)	Morton Gould Roy Harris	American Salute Overture, "When Johnny Comes Marching Home"
"Yankee Doodle" (American Revolution)	Ernest Bloch	America
	James Hewitt	Yankee Doodle with Variations
	Charles Ives	Fourth of July
	Charles Ives	"Putnam's Camp" from Three Places in New England
	Roger Sessions	Symphony No. 2, second movement

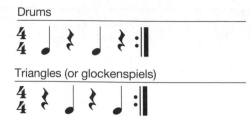

You may wish to alternate between the opening section when all children can play and the "anvil" section where only a few children play selected instruments.

2. A second composition that lends itself to use of instruments is *Pictures at an Exhibition* by Modest Moussorgsky (orchestrated by Maurice Ravel). Students may select classroom percussion instruments that reflect the mood of each of the pictures. For example, heavier instruments such as drums and bass metallophones might be used for the "Promenade" theme. Other parts of this piece that might be selected for use with instruments include

   • Gnomes (a bandy-legged dwarf)
   • The Old Castle
   • Tuileries (famous gardens in Paris)
   • Bydlo (a heavy ox-drawn cart)
   • Ballet of Chicks in Their Shells
   • The Great Gate of Kiev

SAMPLE LESSON PLANS

The following sample lessons and teaching ideas are presented for use with primary-age children.

"Parade of Colors"

Activity: Listening and moving to music
Grade: Kindergarten
Concepts: Steady beat
              Individual response versus all responding together

OBJECTIVES

Students will

1. Respond with proper color.
2. March to a steady beat.
3. Distinguish between individual responses to a single color and entire class marching.

MATERIALS

• Recording: Hap Palmer, "Parade of Colors" (*Learning Basic Skills Through Music*, Educational Activities, Inc. Freeport, N.Y., Vol. II AR 522)

• Colored flags (may be made from remnants; be sure to sew a plastic ring onto one corner to enable physically disabled children to participate more fully)

plastic ring

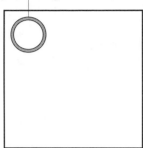

• Two drums, for a student and teacher

• Paper and Magic Markers or crayons to make hats

• Handout: Balloon man with colors printed clearly on each balloon

Making a paper hat

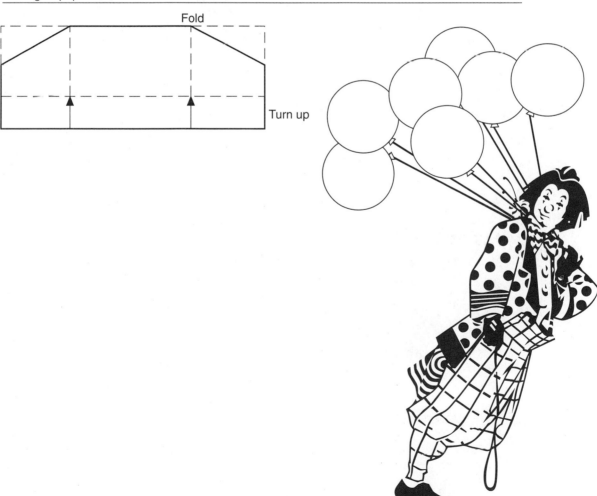

Fold

Turn up

PROCEDURES

1. Have students color the handout of a balloon man.
2. Review colors. Help the children make hats to match colors of flags. Print name of its color on each hat.
3. Play a recording of "Parade of Colors," and invite the children to march to the steady beat of the music. Follow the directions in the song—that is, green stand up, yellow sit down, and so on. All march on the chorus "This is the parade of colors."
4. Play the recording again, asking a selected student to be the leader of the parade and to play the drum to a steady beat. Ask the children to march as in a parade by raising their feet off the floor for each step.

EVALUATION

1. Ask students the difference between "skipping" music and "marching" music.
2. Ask students what colors were used in the "Parade of Colors."
3. Ask students what words indicate the chorus. ("This is the parade of colors")

"Johnny Be Good"

Activity: Listening to music
Grade: 3
Concepts: Form: AB (verse/chorus)
             Meter: Duple

OBJECTIVES

Students will

1. Distinguish between the verse and chorus (AB) of "Johnny Be Good" with creative responses.
2. Identify and respond physically and cognitively to duple meter.

MATERIALS

• Recording: "Johnny Be Good," such as from *Back to the Future* (MCA-39300 [LP] or MCAD-6144 [CD])

• Geometric forms ☐ ○

• Basketball and football

• Cards with the letters A and B

• Chart with the words of the verse and chorus

• Twelve flashlights with colored transparencies (six red and six green) or other contrasting colors mounted over light bulb

PROCEDURES

1. Divide the class in half. Label one group A and the other B. Assign a drum and player for A and another drum and player for B.
2. Divide A into three sections, one for each verse.
3. Give green flashlights to six selected students in B.
4. Give red flashlights to six selected students in A. It is important that three people in A are the leaders for each verse; thus, two will have flashlights for each verse with one a designated leader.
5. Play "Johnny Be Good." Ask Section 1 of A to follow the word rhythms on the ceiling with flashlights. Drums will play the duple meter ♩ ♩ | ♩ ♩ :‖ with accents on 1. Drums only are used on the introduction and interlude.
6. On the chorus, ask Section 2 of B to follow the word rhythms on the ceiling with green flashlights. The tambourine plays in duple meter with accents on 1. Only the tambourine is used on the introduction and interlude. ♩ ♩ | ♩ ♩ ‖
7. Continue alternation of activity with verse and chorus. Drums and tambourine fade out at end.
8. Use the basketball as a label for one group and the football as the label for the other group. Repeat steps 5–7 but play only two verses.
9. Use the shapes A = □, B = ○ to label the two groups. Repeat but play only two verses.
10. Review the concept of verses and chorus: The verses (A) have the same melody but words change, while the chorus (B) has the same melody and words.

CLOSURE

Play "Johnny Be Good." Combine all activities: pointing to balls, letters, and shapes, and flashing flashlights. Students who do not have an assignment should clap the duple meter.

EVALUATION

1. Ask students what AB form in music means.
2. Ask students how contrast was created.

Binary Form

Activity: Listening to binary form

Grades: K–2

Concepts: Binary form (AB)

              Contrasting musical idea

OBJECTIVES

Students will

1. Identify AB as being different.
2. Identify like sounds and different sounds.
3. Identify melodies that are the same and melodies that are different.
4. Identify AB as the form of Herb Alpert's "Spanish Flea," Bach's "Aria" from Suite No. 3 in D Major, and "Johnny Be Good."

MATERIALS

- Pictures showing two contrasting ideas, such as winter-spring; boy-girl; red-green; square-circle.

- Cutout letters A and B to mount on chalkboard

- Classroom instruments: wooden and jingling types

- Recordings: "Spanish Flea" (Herb Alpert and the Tijuana Brass Greatest Hits, A&M CD-3267); "Johnny Be Good" (*Back to the Future*, CD-MCA-6144); Bach, Suite No. 3 in D Major (London CD-430378)

PROCEDURES

1. Show two contrasting pictures. Discuss how they are the same and yet different.
2. Show the letters A and B. Place them on chalkboard.
3. Assign jingling instruments to five students and wooden instruments to a second group of five students.
4. Ask one group to play (either by ear if in K–1 or from chart in Grade 2) the following:

5. Select two children to be machines for A and two others to be machines for B. Children face each other and create a movement that will match the rhythm patterns and then perform.

CLOSURE

Combine instruments and movement to illustrate the A and B sections for each of the following:

- Alpert: "Spanish Flea"
- Bach: "Aria" from Suite No. 3 in D Major
- "Johnny Be Good"

EVALUATION

1. Ask what AB form means.
2. Ask students to identify techniques used in class for each of these sections.

Ternary Form

Activity: Listening to ternary form
Grade: 3
Concepts: Form: Ternary (ABA)
            Repetition and contrast

OBJECTIVES

Students will

1. Identify the repetition of a musical idea.
2. Identify ABA (ternary) form.
3. Use classroom instruments to create a short piece in ABA form.
4. Identify ABA sections in Josquin's "El Grillo"; Chopin's Op. 66, "Fantasie Impromptu"; and "We Wish You a Merry Christmas."

MATERIALS

- Recordings: Josquin's "El Grillo"; Chopin's Op. 66, "Fantasie Impromptu"
- Score of "We Wish You a Merry Christmas"
- Rhythm instruments (jingle sticks; drums)
- Rhythm charts

- Marked spoons (red = A; blue = B)

PROCEDURES

1. Clap the A rhythm and ask children to echo until they tire of it. Discuss why they got bored. (Same thing over and over)
2. Clap the B rhythm.
3. Perform three measures as ABA.

4. Choose rhythm instruments for each measure and play—for example, jingle sticks play A and drums play B.
5. Play "We Wish You a Merry Christmas." (Children without instruments should sing.) Discuss whether it is in AB form or ABA form. Does anything repeat?
6. Select two students to create a movement for A and another two students to create a movement for B. Match the movement to the rhythms. Perform together with instruments.

CLOSURE

1. Listen to each of the listening examples and raise spoons colored red for the A section and spoons colored blue for the contrasting section.
2. Ask students to diagram the ABA form or ternary form as they listen.

EVALUATION

1. Discuss the meaning of ABA form. Ask selected students to create an example of ABA form using mouthed sounds or to rearrange materials in the room to reflect this concept.
2. Ask students the difference between AB and ABA form.
3. Ask students to identify a song in ABA form from the basal music series used in your school.

INTEGRATING LISTENING EXPERIENCES INTO THE CLASSROOM

MUSIC AND DRAMA: OPERA

An *opera* is a story set to music. It incorporates staging, lighting, costumes, and scenery. In opera the dialogue between the characters is sung (in contrast to an *operetta*, where some of the dialogue is spoken). There are contrasts not only in the character roles but also in the types of music each sings. Some of the most significant musical sections are arias (or songs), which are accompanied by the orchestra. A favorite opera of children is Gian-Carlo Menotti's *Amahl and the Night Visitors*, an opera that was written for television.

Sample Lesson: *Amahl and the Night Visitors*

Activity: Listening to an opera

Grades: 4–6 (This lesson should extend over two days)

Concepts: Melody: Direction, legato/staccato, range

Rhythm: Tempo, meter, rubato

Tone color: Female soprano (Mother), boy soprano (Amahl), male trio (Kings)

OBJECTIVES

Students will

1. Exhibit an understanding of opera by dramatizing the story.
2. Identify techniques used by the composer to portray musical events:
   a. Descending musical line when Amahl goes to the door.
   b. Slower tempo when mother goes to the door.
   c. Use of trio when three kings sing.
   d. Duple meter and brass instruments in "March."
   e. Contrast between legato and staccato, loud and soft, high and low.

MATERIALS

- Recording: *Amahl and the Night Visitors* by Menotti (Original, 1951 RCA 6485-2-RG; MCA Classics MCAD-6218)
- Chart with words *descending, ascending, staccato, legato, fast, slow*
- Stick or hand puppets: Amahl, Mother, Kings (Kaspar, Melchior, Balthasar), page, assistants

PROCEDURES

1. Tell the story of *Amahl and the Night Visitors*.

   Amahl, a poor crippled shepherd boy, lives with his mother in a small, sparsely furnished house. He has a wonderful imagination and likes to tell wild "make-believe" stories. As the story opens, Amahl is seated outside the house playing his flute and looking at the sky. After calling him several times, Amahl's mother becomes very angry and demands that he come into the house. Using his crutch, Amahl enters the house and, upon questioning by his mother, tells of seeing an enormous star. She doesn't believe him and tells him to go to bed. During the night Amahl hears singing and goes to the window. Looking out he sees a procession in the distance. Soon there is a knock at his door. His mother tells him to go and see who it is. Amahl goes to the door, looks startled and returns to tell his mother that there is a king outside the door. Again she doesn't believe him and sends him back. After two more trips to the door, he tells her there are three kings. When Amahl's mother looks for herself, she is greeted by the three kings and their page.

   She invites them into the house and soon leaves to find food and bring other shepherds to visit. Amahl asks questions of the kings, Balthasar, Kaspar, and Melchior. After the shepherds return with their gifts of food for the kings, two entertain with a dance. Later, while the kings are asleep, the mother tries to steal the gold for her crippled child. A fight ensues between the mother and the page, who catches her in the act. The kings, however, tell her to keep the gold, for they are on their way to visit the Christ Child and He really won't need their gold. Amahl

announces that he would like to go also, but that he has no other gift to give but his crutch. As he offers his crutch, Amahl is miraculously cured and runs and jumps in excitement. The opera closes as the mother waves to Amahl who joins the kings on their journey.

2. Play the opening section of the opera, through where the mother becomes impatient with Amahl and threatens to spank him.
3. Discuss what is different about this kind of conversation (it is all sung).
4. Point out that in an opera, the story is sung rather than spoken and that an orchestra provides the accompaniment.
5. Play the scene where Amahl is going to the door to see the kings. Students should identify musical events:
   a. Descending melody to the door, ascending melody on return
   b. Staccato
   c. Repetition of "Mother, mother, mother come with me" text and melody
   d. Contrast of slower, legato, heavier sound when mother goes to the door
   e. Smooth, legato singing in harmony by the three kings
6. Use hand or stick puppets to dramatize this scene.
7. Play the scene where Amahl is asking the kings questions. Compare the musical answers of each king:
   Balthasar: Long melodic lines, smooth (bass)
   Melchior: Long, melodic lines, smooth (bass)
   Kaspar (deaf king): Fast, much repetition (tenor)
8. Create a procession of kings, page, and assistants carrying gifts. Play the March and identify the types of instruments used: trumpets, drums, woodwinds. Discuss the use of duple meter and staccato sounds.
9. The entire opera may be performed in 50 minutes. You will want to play a few scenes each day. Keep the students' interest with this continued story.

CLOSURE
Play a recording of the opera and dramatize the events.

EVALUATION
1. Ask the meaning of the word *opera.*
2. Review the story of Amahl and ask students to point out the high voice of the boy soprano Amahl.
3. Ask students what musical techniques were used by the composer to tell the story (direction of melody, speed, legato, staccato, type of instruments used).

MUSIC AND DRAMA: ORATORIO
An *oratorio* is also a large dramatic work, but it is performed in a concert hall without staging, costumes, or scenery. It is always based on a religious text and contains recitatives, arias, and choruses. One of the most famous oratorios is *Messiah* by George Frederick Handel.

Sample Lesson: Handel's *Messiah*

Activity: Listening to music
Grades: 5–6
Concepts: Recitative
           Aria
           Chorus
           Text (word) painting
           Homophonic and polyphonic texture
           Jagged/smooth melody

OBJECTIVES
Students will
1. Identify a recitative.
2. Exhibit an understanding of word painting in the aria "Every Valley Shall Be Exalted."
3. Distinguish between homophonic and polyphonic sections of the "Hallelujah Chorus."

MATERIALS
- Recording of *Messiah* (many are available)
- Chart with the words *aria, recitative, chorus, word painting*
- Graphic listening guide

PROCEDURES
1. Explain to students that in an opera or oratorio most of the conversation or story is sung. Experiment with ideas, letting students create their own recitatives. Notice that there is very little accompaniment.

Autoharp

Jim-my, will you close the door? Yes, I will close the door.

Are an-y of you go-ing to the base-ball game to-day?

2. Listen to the recitative "Then Shall the Eyes of the Blind" from *Messiah*. Notice that it is very short and has little accompaniment.

3. The word *aria* means "song." Handel liked to use musical sounds to express the meaning of certain words. Thus in "Every Valley" the word *crooked* is written with a jagged melody, while *exalted* is a long phrase with many repeated patterns. *Plain* is expressed with a sustained single-note melody:

the crook - ed straight, the crook - ed straight.

Ev - 'ry val - ley, ev - 'ry val - ley_____ shall_ be ex - alt - ed, shall be_

_____ ex - alt - - - - - - - - - -

- - - - - ed,

plain,_____

Write the words *crooked*, *plain*, and *exalted* on the chalkboard.

4. Listen to the aria "Every Valley." Students should follow the musical line with their hands.

5. Play a game in which children follow a leader, all doing the same motion at the same time. Count 1 2 3 4 and create four measures of activity. For example:
   • Slap thighs, slap thighs, clap, clap (1 2 3 4)
   • Tap shoulders (two times), tap top of head (two times) (1 2 3 4)

   Next, have one group do the first activity, and on the count of 3 a second group begin the second activity. Perform in the same fashion as a round. Point out that composers do the same thing with music. Sometimes all of the instruments play the same rhythm at once, and sometimes a melody "chases" after another melody.

6. Listen to the first part of Handel's "Hallelujah Chorus." Decide which performance of the motions would be appropriate, for example, when all do the same thing at the same time.

7. Continue the "Hallelujah Chorus" until the parts "chase one another." Diagram as follows:

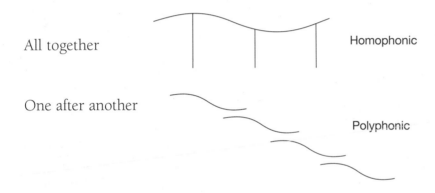

All together .... Homophonic

One after another .... Polyphonic

CLOSURE

Listen to the entire composition and complete a "map" of the sounds. Example:

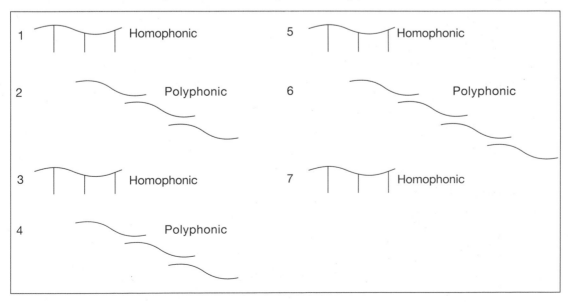

1 Homophonic   5 Homophonic

2 Polyphonic   6 Polyphonic

3 Homophonic   7 Homophonic

4 Polyphonic

EVALUATION

1. What do the terms *recitative*, *aria*, *chorus*, *text painting*, *homophonic*, and *polyphonic* mean?
2. Can you give an example of a jagged melody? a smooth melody?
3. On which words in "Every Valley" would you use a jagged melody, and on which words would you use a smooth melody? Give a reason for your choice.

MUSIC AND DANCE: BALLET

Music and dance are combined in the art form called *ballet*. Even though the music is written for a specific function, it is also exciting to listen to without the visual dimension. As with program music, knowledge of the story adds to the listener's enjoyment.

Sample Lesson: "Hoe-Down"

Activity: Listening to music and dancing a square dance
Grades: 4–6
Concepts: Syncopation
                  Rests
                  Contrasting tonal colors
                  Different phrase lengths

BACKGROUND INFORMATION

Rodeo by the American composer Aaron Copland is a ballet whose story centers on a rodeo in the West. The dancers portray cowboys and cowgirls. In one scene a champion roper displays his roping talents. Another of the principal scenes is a Saturday night dance that the cowboys and cowgirls attend in their finest attire.

OBJECTIVES

Students will

1. Identify accents, syncopation, use of pauses to express a square dance in "Hoe-Down."
2. Identify contrasting instruments such as trumpets, piano, xylophone.
3. Identify repeated patterns that give the piece unity.
4. Identify different length phrases used to create a "jerky" motion.

MATERIALS

- Pictures of rodeos
- Xylophone
- Recording of Aaron Copland, *Rodeo*, "Hoe-Down"
- Cards with terms: *accent, syncopation, pause, repeated pattern, loud, fast, slow*

PROCEDURES

1. Show pictures of a rodeo. Discuss some of the activities, such as roping cattle, riding steers, and chuckwagon races. Use a xylophone to create patterns of sound expressive of these events (wide skips, fast tempo, pauses—rider falls off horse, etc.). Help students create some syncopated patterns.

2. Form eight selected students into partners for a square dance. Have the rest of the class clap a steady beat as the dancers go through some simple motions.

   a. Head couple and foot couple: forward and bow; back to place
   b. Side couples forward and bow
   c. Face partners, right arm swing
   d. Face partners, left arm swing
   e. Couples one and three exchange partners; couples two and four exchange partners
   f. Repeat dance

3. Point out that Copland wrote a piece of music, called *Rodeo*, for a ballet, in which men and women wear costumes and dance. One of the sections is called "Hoe-Down." Review examples of accents, syncopation, pauses, repeated patterns. Play "Hoe-Down" and place these terms, along with others, such as *loud, fast,* and *slow,* on cards.

4. Play "Hoe-Down" a second time. Have students select the terms and place them on a chart as they hear the piece. Any student may choose a card at any time or you may wish to create a competitive game with two teams alternating.

5. Play "Hoe-Down" a third time and make any necessary changes in the cards.

CLOSURE

Listen to "Hoe-Down" from *Rodeo* and choose cards from the chalkboard that are appropriate to music as it is played (for example, syncopation, fast, slow, pauses, and so on).

EVALUATION

1. Ask what is meant by the terms
   a. Accent
   b. Syncopation
   c. Patterns
2. What are some contrasting instruments?
3. Can you identify any melodic or rhythmic patterns that repeat?
4. Are the phrases of the same length?

PROGRAM MUSIC

Sample Lesson: *Carnival of the Animals*

Activity: Listening to program music

Grades: 2–4

Concepts: Identification of low strings, high strings, woodwinds, and brass

Low, high; fast, slow

Wide skips, stepwise melody

Steady beat

Dynamics: Loud, soft

OBJECTIVES

Students will

1. Identify the sound of instruments with an appropriate animal, such as elephant, birds, swan.
2. Identify sounds that are low or high, fast or slow, loud or soft.
3. Identify wide skips, range of melody, steady beat, and dynamics and associate them with appropriate animals.
4. Integrate the study of *Carnival of the Animals* with language arts and visual art.

MATERIALS

- Recording: Saint-Saëns, *Carnival of the Animals*
- Pictures or puppets of the animals described, such as elephant, birds, cuckoo, swan, and fish
- Pictures of the orchestral instruments used in the composition, such as piccolo, string bass, trumpet, oboe, xylophone, violins
- Chalk or bulletin board
- Cards with words *low, high, fast, slow, thick, thin, strings, brass*
- Cassette tape and recorder

PROCEDURES

1. Play the selection "Elephant" from *Carnival of the Animals.* Show a picture of an elephant and discuss its characteristics (big, lumbering, thick skin, large trunk, and so on).
2. Use a puppet of an elephant to show children how to move as an elephant might (slowly, with big steps).

3. Show pictures of instruments: piccolo, string bass, trumpet, oboe. Play recordings illustrating each. Discuss which instrument the composer might use to portray an elephant (string bass). Place the following words on the chalkboard:

low   high
fast   slow
thick   thin
string   brass

Play the selection "Elephant" again. Have children choose appropriate words and place them on a chart with a picture of an elephant at the top.

4. Integrate the lesson with language arts by having children write a poem or paragraph describing an elephant. Integrate it with visual art by having children draw pictures of elephants.

5. Follow this procedure for other animals represented in the work, for example:

• Lions: Low, fast, rise and fall to the melody, punctuates the pacing (steady) beat of the lions' walk, low strings, piano

• Kangaroo: Wide range, staccato (jumpy), many skips, accents, crescendo and diminuendo, suddenly loud, suddenly soft

• Fish: Smooth, harp, glissando, celesta represents rippling water, mostly steps

CLOSURE

Make a cassette tape in which you select five short "animal" pieces from the larger work. (It is easier to make a tape than to hunt for the spot on the record or CD where the animal music appears.) Place five pictures of animals in the front of the room. Divide the class into two teams. Affix all the words to the chalkboard. As each selection is played, have team members decide on the words that best describe the music. One of the team members places them under the proper pictures. The total number of points possible is determined by the number of musical events you have identified.

Additional compositions about animals include:

• Copland, *The Cat and the Mouse*
• Debussy, *Children's Corner Suite*, "Jimbo's Lullaby"
• Griffes, *The White Peacock*
• Hovhaness, *And God Created Great Whales*
• Messiaen, *Oiseaux exotiques* (Exotic Birds, for piano and orchestra)
• Moussorgsky, *The Flea*
• Prokofiev, *Peter and the Wolf*
• Rimsky-Korsakov, *Flight of the Bumble Bee*

EVALUATION

1. Review the composer's use of instruments to represent animals. Discuss ways the composer uses these sounds to represent the animal.

2. Play at random three animal themes from *Carnival of the Animals*. Ask students to identify the instruments used, how they are used, and what animals the music represents.

Sample Lesson: "Spring" from *The Seasons*

Activity: Listening to program music

Grades: 4–6

Concepts: Melody: Repeated patterns, narrow range

Rhythm: Repeated patterns, steady beat, duple meter

Dynamics: Loud and soft, echo effects

Tone Color: Strings

Form: Concerto grosso (small group of solo instruments alternates with the orchestra)

OBJECTIVES

Students will

1. Identify techniques the composer uses to express nature.
2. Identify the contrasting sections of the concerto grosso (small group of instruments and all instruments).
3. Identify different techniques used by string instruments.

MATERIALS

- Poems about spring: birds, flowers, sun
- Paper and markers to draw pictures of budding flowers
- Charts: concerto grosso
- Listening guide
- Recording: Vivaldi's *The Seasons* ("Spring")

PROCEDURES

1. Read poems about spring: birds, flowers, the sun. Discuss how nature, which has been dormant all winter, comes to life again.
2. Draw pictures showing the budding process in trees to full leaf
3. Point out the delicate colors of spring (light green leaves, dogwood).
4. Read the musical events found in the listening guide on page 461. Discuss any that are vague or unknown to the students.
5. Listen to Vivaldi's "Spring" from *The Seasons*. Follow the listening guide (p. 461). Additional compositions about the seasons include
   - Haydn's *The Seasons*, "With Verdure Clad"
   - Vivaldi's *The Seasons*, "Summer," "Fall," and "Winter"

CLOSURE

Compare another season (summer, fall, winter) with "Spring." Discuss the different techniques that the composer might use. How does the music sound different?

EVALUATION

Create an evaluation chart from the listening guide. You may wish to include other musical information that you have learned.

"Pacific 231"

Grades: 1–4

Suggestions for Lessons

1. Show pictures of locomotives. Ask students whether they have ever ridden on a train or whether they have toy trains. Discuss the characteristics of a locomotive: run by coal, begins slowly with a "choo, choo" sound, and so on.
2. For young children, play a game with a leader as locomotive and other children as cars attached behind. They can move their arms as if they are the wheels. Ask one child to be the whistle. Consider how the train might move when going up a hill, down a hill, starting out from the station, coming into the station.
3. Select classroom percussion instruments and accompany the dramatization.
4. Read the story *The Little Engine That Could* by Watty Piper (New York: Platt & Monk, 1980). Discuss the use of tempo in reading the story with expression.
5. Listen to Honegger's *Pacific 231*. Follow this listening guide:

Listening Guide

1. Strings, woodwinds, brass; soft; train starting up
2. Woodwinds and strings joined by low brass; speed increases; becomes louder
3. Steady beat; staccato; imitation; becomes louder
4. Steady beat; staccato; clarinet, bassoon, horn, strings, trumpet, and full orchestra
5. Long theme: staccato, bassoon
6. Orchestra staccato; gradually gets louder
7. Staccato theme with imitation in orchestra
8. Contrasting melody played by clarinet, followed by strings
9. Brass instruments play staccato theme; gradually gets louder
10. Strings play sweeping, contrasting melody; clarinet plays soft running notes
11. Orchestra gradually gets louder; driving beat; imitation
12. Orchestra plays loudly; horns and trumpets play high theme above orchestra melody
13. Gradually slows down as train approaches stop

Additional compositions about machines include

- Anderson: *The Typewriter*
- "Orange Blossom Special"
- Brubeck: "Cable Car" from *Time Changes*
- Schuller: "The Twittering Machine" from *Seven Studies by Paul Klee*

"Cloudburst" from *Grand Canyon Suite*

Grades: 5–6

Suggestions for Lessons

1. Show pictures of the Grand Canyon. Discuss where it is located and its type of climate. Ask students who have visited this "wonder of the world" to describe it to classmates.
2. Discuss what is meant by the word *cloudburst*. Consider ways that a composer might describe such an event through instruments (lightning—loud, crashing cymbals; thunder—roll of drums). Use classroom percussion instruments to create a musical composition that describes a cloudburst. Write an original poem about a cloudburst and draw pictures that express this phenomenon in nature.
3. Listen to Grofé's "Cloudburst" from *Grand Canyon Suite*. Follow this listening guide:

Listening Guide

1. Lyrical melody played softly by strings (canyons with huge rock formations bask in calmness of clear, sunny day)
2. Oboe and strings play lyrical melody with harp accompaniment; crescendo
3. Low strings play long lyrical melody
4. Woodwinds play ornamental melody
5. Full orchestra, strings play melody; crescendo
6. Strings decrescendo; cellos play slow soft melody; repetition of short, melodic fragments
7. Loud splashes of orchestral sound; strings and piano soar up and down; rumbling of timpani represents thunder reverberating through canyons, rain splashing against rocks, and lightning
8. Brass build in tempo and dynamic level as orchestra expresses fury of storm
9. Storm ends with decrease in dynamics and a slower tempo

Additional compositions about nature include
- Beethoven: Symphony No. 6 (*Pastorale*)
- Debussy: *La Mer* (The Sea)
- Smetana: *The Moldau* (a River)

Star Wars

Grades: 4–5

Suggestions for Lessons

1. Show the beginning of the video of *Star Wars*.
2. Discuss the music of the video and consider the demands made on the composer (e.g., music reflecting the characters and interplanetary travel).
3. Listen to a recording of the main theme from John Williams's *Star Wars*, and follow this listening guide:

Listening Guide

1. Introduction: full orchestra
2. Main theme: High brass accompanied by strings, low brass, and percussion
3. Theme 2: Strings, legato, followed by crescendo in brass
4. Main theme: Low brass, joined by strings and high brass
5. Bridge: Rhythmic and melodic fragments; ascending melody
6. Ritard: Solo violin
7. Crescendo: Repeated rhythmic fragments; brass and percussion; ritard
8. Faster: Steady beat in percussion; block chords in high brass
9. Strings: Short melodic patterns played fast
10. Main theme: Low brass; block chords in high brass; main theme repeats
11. Theme 2: Strings
12. Main theme: Low brass, block chords in strings and high brass
13. Theme 3: Low strings, legato, softer; high strings play countermelody
14. Accelerando to main theme: High brass, repeats
15. Theme 2: Altered; strings play ascending melody
16. Block chords in high brass accompanied by strings, percussion; ascending melodies
17. Block chords repeated by violins; slower, softer
18. Full brass, percussion; crescendo; closing loud chords, ends with sustained low strings

Additional compositions about outer space include

- Holst: *The Planets*
- Perrey-Kingsley: *The In Sound Way Out*, "The Little Man from Mars," "Spooks in Space," "Visa to the Stars"
- John Williams: *Return of the Jedi, E.T., Close Encounters of the Third Kind, Empire Strikes Back, Star Trek*
- John Williams: *John Williams Plays John Williams*, "The Star Wars Trilogy" (Sony/classical CD/SK 45947)

1812 Festival Overture

Grades: 4–6

Suggestions for Lessons

1. Read the following background information to the class:

The *1812 Festival Overture* by Peter Tchaikovsky was written to dramatize and commemorate the withdrawal from Russia of the French troops under Napoleon in 1812. Originally the music was to be performed by an enormous orchestra in a public square in Moscow. Arrangements were made for cannon to be included in the percussion section. A large programmatic work, it begins with the Russian hymn "God, Preserve Thy People." A realistic musical description of the Battle of Borodino includes the French national anthem "The Marseillaise" and the Czarist Russian national anthem "God Save the Czar." Chimes and carillon, and bells along with cannon (where possible) provide a fitting climax to the Russian victory.

2. Play the last 4 or 5 minutes (including the cannon) of the *1812 Overture*. Discuss with students various sounds they heard (cannon, bells ringing, large orchestra, and so on).

3. Discuss events for which a cannon might be fired or many bells rung (for example, a battle, a victory, a special national event).

4. Play the last 4 or 5 minutes of the piece again. Ask students to identify instrumental sounds (strings, brass, percussion).

5. After reviewing the background information found at the beginning of this lesson, play or sing the Russian national hymn and French national anthem.

God, Preserve Thy People

Russian Hymn

The Marseillaise

Rouget de Lisle

Ye sons of France, a - wake to glo - ry! Hark, hark what myr - iads bid you
Al - lons, en - fants de la Pa - tri - e, Le jour de gloire est ar - ri -

rise! Your chil - dren, wives and grand - sires____ hoar - y: Be - hold their tears, and hear their____
vé, Con - tre nous, de la ty - ran - ni - e, L'é - ten - dard san - glant est le -

cries, Be - hold their tears,____ and hear their____ cries! Shall hate - ful ty - rants mis - chief____
vé, L'é - ten - dard ____ san - glant est le - vé. En - ten - dez - vous, ____ dans les cam-

breed - ing, With hire - ling hosts,____ a ruf - fian____ band, Af - fright and des - o - late the
pa - gnes, Mu - gir ces fé - ro - ces sol - dats? Ils vien - nent jus - que dans nos

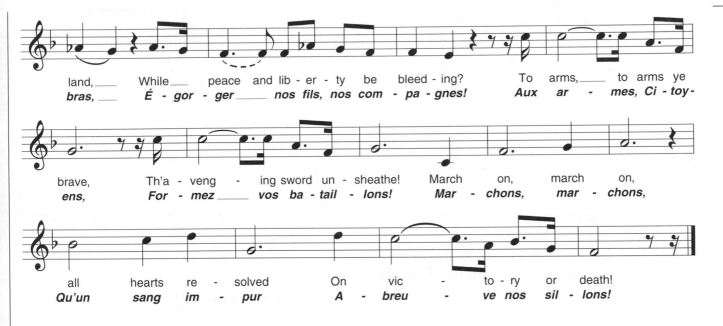

land,___ While___ peace and lib - er - ty be bleed - ing? To arms,___ to arms ye
bras, ___ *É - gor - ger* ___ *nos fils, nos com - pa - gnes!* *Aux ar - mes, Ci - toy-*

brave, Th'a - veng - ing sword un - sheathe! March on, march on,
ens, *For - mez* ___ *vos ba - tail - lons!* *Mar - chons, mar - chons,*

all hearts re - solved On vic - to - ry or death!
Qu'un sang im - pur A - breu - ve nos sil - lons!

6. Play the composition up through the French national anthem.

7. Show the picture "Liberty Leading the People" by Delacroix. Discuss what the artist does to create the feeling of power and victory (focus on female figure in center, upraised arms, mixture of people, many diagonal lines creating movement). Apply these principles of analysis to music. Ask students such questions as

 a. Can you describe what musical ideas would express an army approaching from a distance? (soft to loud—crescendo)

 b. What types of percussion instrument might be used for the clatter of guns? (snare drum)

8. Play sections of the *1812 Overture*. Each time, discuss with students the musical ideas that express the nationalistic event.

9. Play the entire composition. Ask students to choose from the following cards and place them on the chalkboard in the order they hear the corresponding music. (Some may repeat—provide multiple cards.)

Dynamics	*Tone Color*	*Melodies*	*Tempo*	*Range*
Soft	Strings	Smooth	Faster	Gets higher
Loud	Brass	"Marseillaise"	Slower	Lower
Accents	Snare drum	Legato	(Ritard)	
Louder	French horns	"Marseillaise" (fragments)		
Softer	Tambourine	Long descending melody		
	Timpani	"God, Preserve Thy People"		
	Triangle			
	Drum roll			
	Cannon			
	Bells			

Additional compositions about historical events include

- Alford: *Colonel Bogey March* (theme from the film *Bridge over the River Kwai*)
- Beethoven: *Wellington's Victory*
- Ives: *The Fourth of July*
- Ives: *Memorial Day*
- Rodgers (arranged by Robert Russell Bennett): *Victory at Sea*, "Guadalcanal March"

A Lincoln Portrait

Suggestions for Lessons

1. Show pictures of the Lincoln Memorial in Washington, D.C.
2. Play performances of "Battle Hymn of the Republic." Have the class sing the song and discuss its use during the Civil War.
3. Teach the songs "On Springfield Mountain" and "Camptown Races." Discuss the difference in text and style of music (e.g., quiet, lively).

On Springfield Mountain

American Folk Song

Key: G
Starting pitch: D
Meter: 3/4, begins on "and" of 2

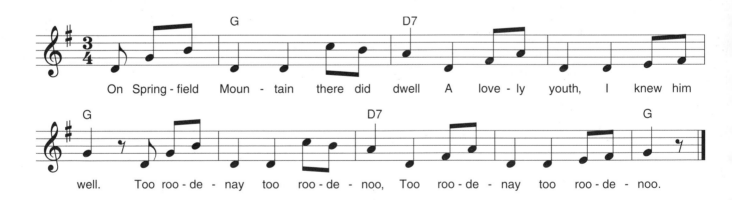

On Spring - field Moun - tain there did dwell A love - ly youth, I knew him well. Too roo - de - nay too roo - de - noo, Too roo - de - nay too roo - de - noo.

Camptown Races

Stephen C. Foster

Key: E♭
Starting pitch: B♭
Meter: 2/4, begins on 4

With humor

The Camp-town la - dies sing this song, do - da, do - da! The Camp-town race track

five miles long, Oh, do - da - day. Oh, see those hors - es round the bend,

do - da, do - da! Guess that race will nev - er end. Oh, do - da - day.

Chorus

Going to run all night, going to run all day, I'll

bet my mon - ey on the bob - tail nag, Some - bod - y bet on the bay.

4. Play Part I of *Lincoln Portrait*. Ask students to identify the musical means by which Copland expresses Lincoln's early life (quiet, melancholy, open harmony, large skips in the melody, thin texture).

5. Review social activities during the middle of the nineteenth century (square dances, Saturday night "military post" parties).

6. Play Part II of *Lincoln Portrait*. Ask students to raise their hands when they hear the fragments of "Camptown Races" in the music. Discuss other ways the composer portrays a Saturday night dance (strong rhythmic beat, use of "fiddles," much syncopation).

7. Play Part I and Part II. Discuss in what ways they are the same and in what ways different.

8. Ask students to read the excerpts from Lincoln's speeches that are heard in the composition:

> *This is what Lincoln said:*
>
> "Fellow citizens we cannot escape history. We of this Congress and this administration will be remembered in spite of ourselves. No personal significance or insignificance can spare one or another of us. The fiery trials through which we pass will light us down in honor or dishonor to the latest generation.
>
> "We even, we here, hold the power and bear the responsibility.
>
> "The dogmas of the quiet past are inadequate to the stormy present. The occasion is piled high with difficulty, and we must rise with the occasion. As our case is new so we must think anew, and act anew. We must disenthrall ourselves, and then we shall save our country.
>
> "It is the eternal struggle between two principles, right and wrong, throughout the world. It is the same spirit that says 'you toil and work and earn bread, and I'll eat it.' No matter in what shape it comes. Whether from the mouth of a king who seeks to bestride the people of his own nation and live by the fruit of their labor, or from one race of men as an apology for enslaving another race, it is the same tyrannical principle.
>
> "As I would not be a slave, so I would not be a master. This expresses my idea of democracy. Whatever differs from this, to the extent of the difference is no democracy."
>
> *Abraham Lincoln, sixteenth President of these United States is everlasting in the memory of his countrymen. For on the battleground at Gettysburg, this is what he said:*
>
> "That from these honored dead, we take increased devotion to that cause for which they gave the last full measure of devotion. That we here highly resolve that these dead shall not have died in vain. That this nation under God, shall have a new birth of freedom, and that government of the people, by the people, and for the people shall not perish from the earth."

Listening Guide (Part I)
1. Introduction: Short melodic fragment (brass; woodwinds; strings)
2. Texture gets thicker and dynamics louder
3. Melody: "On Springfield Mountain" (clarinet)
4. Melody: "On Springfield Mountain" (oboe and strings)
   Melody: "On Springfield Mountain" (trumpet)
5. Fragments of "Camptown Races"
   Faster, lighter (clarinet and oboe alternate with melody)
6. Fragments of "Camptown Races" (trumpets)
7. Melody: "On Springfield Mountain" (fragment) (trumpets and other brass)
8. Melody: "On Springfield Mountain," in imitation between low brass and high brass; strings play a high descant above

PREPARING STUDENTS TO ATTEND A CONCERT

Many communities throughout the United States offer "educational" concerts for students in Grades 4, 5, and 6. These concerts may be performed by such professional orchestras as the Cleveland Orchestra, the New York Philharmonic, or the Philadelphia Orchestra. In smaller communities, local orchestras and college or university ensembles fulfill this function. The cost is usually defrayed by funding from corporations, and sometimes students pay a token ticket charge. While larger communities provide "docents" (volunteers who visit schools to prepare students for what they will hear), most schools rely on the classroom teacher, who may or may not have received audiovisual materials from the orchestra's educational department.

It is not the purpose of these lessons to suggest proper behavior or attire; instead it provides three minilessons based on what students might see and hear at a concert.

SAMPLE CONCERT

Slavonic Dance No. 1 in C Major	Antonín Dvořák
Violin Concerto No. 3 in E Minor, Op. 64	Felix Mendelssohn
Trumpeter's Lullaby	Leroy Anderson
Syncopated Clock	Leroy Anderson
Triplets (xylophone and 3 marimbas)	George Hamilton Green
The Little White Donkey, *Histoires*	Jacques Ibert
The Entertainer	Scott Joplin
Hoe-Down, *Rodeo*	Aaron Copland

Sample Lesson: "Trumpeter's Lullaby"

Activity: Listening to music

Grade: 4

Concepts: Instruments of the orchestra: Strings, brass, woodwinds, percussion, keyboards
Placement of the musicians
Role of the conductor
Role of the concertmaster

OBJECTIVES

Students will
1. Identify by sight and sound instruments of the orchestra.
2. Give reasons for placement of the musicians.
3. Define the role of the conductor.
4. Define the role of the concertmaster.

MATERIALS

- 16mm film: *Toot, Whistle, Plunk and Boom*
- Projector
- Basal music series instruments of orchestras (pictures and recordings)
- Recording: Anderson's "Trumpeter's Lullaby"
- Small cards with words, such as *soft, loud, smooth*
- Large card with title "Trumpeter's Lullaby"

PROCEDURES

1. Show the film *Toot, Whistle, Plunk and Boom* (Disney c. 1953; a cartoon that traces the origin and development of the four families of instruments, as well as the piano, in the modern symphony orchestra).

2. Discuss the characteristics of each instrument and reinforce them with pictures from the basal music series books or large charts showing instrument families.

3. Play the composition "Trumpeter's Lullaby" by Leroy Anderson and ask children to choose the solo instrument either from the book or the chart.

4. Discuss possible reasons for naming the piece a *trumpeter's lullaby* (such as soft, smooth, quiet). Write the descriptive terms on cards and place them on the board under the title of the composition.

5. Show a picture of a large symphony orchestra and ask children to identify the various "families" of instruments. Which sections have the most instruments, and which have the fewest?

6. Ask students to sing a familiar song, such as "Row, Row, Row Your Boat." Do not give any indication of pitch, tempo, or dynamics. Discuss some of the problems they encountered (they didn't sing together, little or no dynamic change, couldn't decide on how fast to sing, and so on).

7. Perform the song again, but invite one student to conduct the performance. Point out that the role of a conductor is important because the conductor controls how the music is played.

8. Invite the students to sing, whistle, or speak "Row, Row, Row Your Boat" whenever they like. The result will be cacophony. Now appoint a student to be the "concert-master" and give the starting pitch. Have everyone in the class tune to (or match) that pitch. After the leader is sure of the pitch, ask the conductor to lead the performance.

9. Dramatize the members of the orchestra and trumpeter playing "Trumpeter's Lullaby."

CLOSURE

Play "Trumpeter's Lullaby" through its entirety.

EVALUATION

1. What is the role of the conductor?
2. What is the role of the concertmaster?
3. How many "families" are there in the Western orchestra, and what are they?
4. What "family" in the Western orchestra has more instruments than any other?
5. What is the name of this piece?
6. What instrument does it feature as a solo?

Sample Lesson: Mendelssohns's *Violin Concerto No. 3 in E Minor* (Rondo)

Grade: 4
Concepts: The orchestra concert
            The string family

OBJECTIVES

Students will

1. Identify the violin as the solo instrument in Mendelssohn's *Violin Concerto No. 3 in E Minor* (Rondo).
2. Identify characteristics of the violin in Mendelssohn's *Violin Concerto No. 3 in E Minor* (Rondo) (can play a wide range, can play very loud and very soft, can play staccato or legato, does not have any frets, has only four strings).

MATERIALS

* Recording: Itzhak Perlman playing Mendelssohn's *Violin Concerto No. 3 in E Minor*
* Pictures of violin, viola, cello, and bass
* Basal music series instruments of orchestra

PROCEDURES

1. Show pictures of violin, viola, cello, bass. Discuss their differences in appearance.
2. Play examples of each.
3. Show and discuss pictures of a violin, including fingerboard, bow, mute, and lack of frets.
4. Indicate that in a concerto, the solo instrument plays both with the orchestra and alone.
5. Play a recording of Itzhak Perlman playing Mendelssohn's *Violin Concerto No. 3 in E Minor* (Rondo). Ask students to diagram the form on the chalkboard (A B A C, etc.).
6. Discuss the relationship of Perlman's talent to his special physical needs due to polio, a disease that affects the nervous system.

CLOSURE

Play "Rondo" and ask students to raise their hands when they hear the main melody.

EVALUATION

1. What instrument is featured as a solo?
2. Name four ways that this instrument can play. (loud, soft, staccato, legato)
3. What instruments do not have any frets (like a guitar does)?
4. What are some parts of the violin? (fingerboard, bow, etc.)
5. What is the form of the rondo that you heard? (A B A C A)
6. What is a concerto?

Sample Lesson: "The Little White Donkey"

Activity: Listening to music

Grade: 4

Concepts: Program music
Mechanism of piano
Jagged melody
Thick chords

OBJECTIVES

Students will

1. Identify the piano as a keyboard instrument and name the mechanical parts that differentiate it from other keyboard instruments.
2. Identify the programmatic qualities of the piano piece "The Little White Donkey" and describe how the composer expresses these qualities in sound.

MATERIALS

- Recordings of "The Little White Donkey" from *Histoires for Piano* by Jacques Ibert (MCAD-25969)
- Pictures of the piano and its mechanism
- Small cards and letters A, B, A for chalkboard or bulletin board
- Large card with title "The Little White Donkey"

PROCEDURES

1. Discuss the characteristics of a piano, such as pedals (damper, sustaining, soft), hammers, size and function of strings, and keyboard.
2. Point out that some music has a story. The piano composition is "The Little White Donkey" from a collection called *Histoires for Piano* by the French composer Jacques Ibert. In this little piece, a donkey is walking along a railroad track when suddenly he hears a train. He gets off the track safely and listens to the whistle warning of the approaching train. After it goes by, he resumes his walk down the track.

3. Play the recording of "The Little White Donkey" and ask students to listen for the composer's musical expression of a train and also of the donkey walking down the tracks. Place the title card of the piece on the board and then place labels that describe the piece under it (such as steady beat = donkey; thick chords in upper register = train).

CLOSURE
Play "The Little White Donkey." Ask students how the composer creates program music.

EVALUATION
1. Ask students what the various parts of the piano mechanism are.
2. Ask students what program music is. Give an example for piano.
3. What is meant by "expressing something outside the music"?
4. What are some of the musical techniques used by the composers of "The Little White Donkey"?

QUESTIONS FOR REVIEW
1. What are the four families of Western orchestral instruments?
2. Who is involved in the chain of events that create musical expression?
3. What are four keyboard instruments?
4. What are two electronic instruments?
5. What are four levels of listening?
6. What are three to four guidelines to follow when planning lessons?
7. What are the titles of three to four songs used in large musical compositions?
8. What are three to four ways that children of different ages and experiences respond to listening to music?
9. What three musical compositions are especially appropriate for young children (Grades K–3)?
10. What three musical compositions are especially appropriate for older children (Grades 4–6)?

8 Teaching Music Through Movement

Rhythm is one of the most basic elements of music. Nature has innumerable rhythmic patterns to which we respond (night and day, changing seasons, ebb and flow of tides); our physical system is subject to rhythm (heartbeat, respiration, digestive system, sleep patterns); and everyday activities require a sense of rhythm (walking, jogging, playing tennis, throwing or catching a ball). Thus rhythm seems to be a widespread phenomenon and an integral part of our human existence.

Children exhibit simple rhythmic movements from infancy. Newborn babies move within their own time and space as they stretch their arms and fingers and kick their legs. Later, as children learn to organize their movements, they walk, run, and jump. With maturation, they develop more complex rhythmic movements for swimming, dancing, playing basketball, or performing on a musical instrument.

This chapter focuses on the use of movement to (1) develop body awareness in space, (2) express musical concepts, (3) interpret musical ideas, and (4) develop skill in folk dancing. It is based on the premise that a child's body, mind, and emotions are integrated into natural rhythmic expression and that through guided experiences involving movement, children will learn to identify what they hear with what they do, thus stimulating their interest in and developing their skill with every facet of musical learning.

Teachers often ask, "How do I begin?" The following guidelines will help you generate ideas and techniques for musical learning experiences through rhythmic bodily response activities:

1. Encourage the child's natural inclination to move.
2. Encourage the natural use of speech, gesture, and body language to express thoughts and emotions.
3. Encourage the use of various levels of energy (dynamics) and timing in movement, speech, and gesture (for example, hurried but forceful speech).
4. Allow children to explore and find ways to "live" particular elements of the music in movement (such as with an ascending melody).
5. Identify elements, concepts, or other aspects of music that children should experience (such as repetition or contrast in music).
6. Pay attention to children's individual responses. Sometimes a child's response is so imaginative that it is worth having the whole class try it.
7. Allow children freedom and opportunities to express music with their bodies in spontaneous ways.
8. Encourage the completion of structured tasks that will, in turn, result in musical learning.
9. Choose music for rhythmic activities that causes children to respond instinctively, by, for example, tapping a foot (Sousa: "Stars and Stripes Forever") or bouncing and catching a ball ("This Old Man").
10. Use a variety of music (jazz, popular, folk, classical, Hispanic, African American, Native American). Begin early to find music you like and make a list of possible ways to move to it.

DEVELOPING BODY AWARENESS IN SPACE*

Some basic tasks involving children with music and movement include (1) developing body awareness, which will enable the child to move freely in space, and (2) developing the rhythmic ability to feel and move to a beat. When children can use their bodies expressively in space and can successfully feel and move to a beat, they are ready to experience movement in more complex musical settings.

In developing the body awareness that allows them to move freely, without inhibition in space, children should be involved in both locomotor and nonlocomotor activities. Locomotor means to move from one place to another, while nonlocomotor means to move within a stationary position. The four stages in developing body awareness are (1) movement as an expression of problem solving, (2) movement as an expression of imagery, (3) movement with no external beat, and (4) movement to a beat with a sense of timing.

MOVEMENT AS AN EXPRESSION OF PROBLEM SOLVING

Expressive movement may be used as a response to challenging statements, questions, or situations. These activities can also reinforce visual aural awareness.

---

* This material is based on the work of Phyllis Weikart in developing rhythmic and spatial concepts for teaching rhythm. See Phyllis S. Weikart, *Teaching Movement and Dance* (Ypsilanti, Mich.: The High/Scope Press, 1982), pp. 31–42.

Suggestions for Lessons

1. Ask the student to respond to such questions as:
   - How can your hand move?
   - How can your foot move?
   - How can your whole body move?
2. Invite students to imitate a leader:
   - My hand can go up or down.
   - My hand can go over and under.
   - My hand can go fast and slow.
3. Draw expressive responses with such statements as
   - Lift your arm slowly.
   - Lower your arm quickly.
   - Draw a square with one foot.
   - Make an "S" with your whole body.
4. Play the game "Simon Says." Create interesting and expressive movements.
5. Play music on a radio and turn the volume down to stop the music. Ask the students to move creatively when they hear the music and "freeze" when it stops.
6. Improvise sounds on the strings of the piano or Autoharp (tap, pluck, glissando). Ask students to respond by moving their hands, feet, bodies, and heads creatively.
7. Using only the black keys on the piano, improvise in the low, middle, and high registers. Ask the students to express the concepts of high and low by moving their bodies.

MOVEMENT AS AN EXPRESSION OF IMAGERY

In movement associated with imagery, the student's imagination is challenged by activities related to something previously experienced. Responses are limited only by the student's frame of reference; thus, "Show me how a snowman melts to the ground" assumes that the student has seen a snowman and has a mental picture of how slowly it melts away.

Suggestions for Lessons

1. Ask students to express the following:
   - Show how a turtle moves.
   - How would you move if you had to carry a heavy pack on your back?
   - How would you move your hand if you (a) touched a warm stove, (b) touched a hot stove, (c) touched a sizzling hot stove?
2. Using musical examples such as the following, ask students to move creatively:
   a. Rimsky-Korsakov: *Flight of the Bumble Bee* (fast)
      Ideas for movements: Move hands in circular motion; fingers "run" across table top.
   b. Debussy: "Jimbo's Lullaby" from *Children's Corner Suite*
      Ideas for movement: Stretch from one side to another, walk slowly with heavy steps, swing arms from side to side.
   c. "Orange Blossom Special" (bluegrass)

Ideas for movement: Rapid circular motion of arms (as for wheels of train), vertical raising of arms to "pull train whistle."

d. "Spooks in Space" from *The In Sound Way Out**

Ideas for movement: Short choppy hand movements, alternating with long sweeping motions of hands and arms overhead. Vertical wave motions with hands for "ghost sounds."

e. Copland: "Hoe-Down" from *Rodeo* (fast, slow, pause)

Ideas for movement: Clap a fast beat, walk slowly, lift knees high, "freeze" on pause with both arms outstretched.

f. "Navaho Gift Dance Song" or "Hopi Basket Dance"†

Ideas for movement: Short choppy movement with drum and (bells); legato movements such as making body and hands both high or low to match melody.

3. Sing the song "The People on the Bus" and have students create appropriate motions that express the words. Create your own verses and additional motions.

The People on the Bus

Key: G
Starting pitch: D
Meter: 4/4, begins on 4

United States

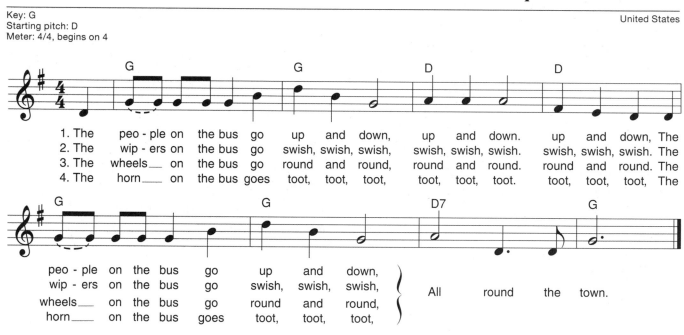

1. The peo - ple on the bus go up and down, up and down. up and down, The
2. The wip - ers on the bus go swish, swish, swish, swish, swish, swish. swish, swish, swish. The
3. The wheels___ on the bus go round and round, round and round. round and round. The
4. The horn___ on the bus goes toot, toot, toot, toot, toot, toot. toot, toot, toot, The

peo - ple on the bus go up and down,
wip - ers on the bus go swish, swish, swish,
wheels___ on the bus go round and round,
horn___ on the bus goes toot, toot, toot,

} All round the town.

---

* *The In Sound Way Out*, Perrey-Kingsley (Vanguard VSD-79222).

† Available on *Authentic Music of the American Indian* (Legacy International, Box 6999, Beverly Hills, Calif. 90212).

4. Sing the song "Little Tommy Tinker" and do the motions of raising hands high into the air on "Oh, Ma."
5. Sing "Eency, Weency Spider." The words of the song suggest movements that children might do. For example, the motion of the spider can be represented by touching the tip of the index finger on one hand to the tip of the thumb on the other, alternating hands as the "spider" goes up the water spout. Both hands, palms down, are lowered for "down came the rain." Have students create movements for the rest of the words.

Little Tommy Tinker

Nursery Rhyme

Key: D
Starting pitch: D
Meter: 4/4, begins on 1

Eency, Weency Spider

Action Song

Key: G
Starting pitch: G
Meter: 6/8, starts on 1

MOVEMENT WITH NO EXTERNAL BEAT

A third type of movement requires the students to move from one space to another freely and successfully according to their own beat or tempo.

Suggestions for Lessons

1. Ask students to walk to the other side of the room as if walking a straight line. Play repeated chords on piano, Autoharp, or Omnichord.
2. Ask students to walk to the other side of the room as if walking a jagged line. Play black keys of the piano only—any series of skips.
3. Ask students to walk, and on your signal, change directions (walk backward, walk sideways, and so on). Follow this same procedure when playing "The Spanish Flea" by Herb Alpert and the Tijuana Brass. For example, every time the first melody repeats, return to the original way of walking.
4. Vary intensity and affect. Play or sing "We Wish You a Merry Christmas"; ask students to walk "happy." Play or sing "Danny Boy"; ask students to walk "sad." Play or sing "I've Been Workin' on the Railroad"; ask students to walk and let their head and arms be happy.

MOVEMENT TO A BEAT WITH A SENSE OF TIMING*

In developing a sense of timing and the ability to move to a beat, it is first necessary to concentrate on the use of a single motion, such as patting the head. Use language as an organizer of movement and concentrate on bilateral motions (such as "Both hands pat your head, both hands tap your shoulders"). Begin with body parts and create other activities. Sitting rather than standing contributes to a child's sense of security and confidence.

Suggestions for Lessons

1. Perform the following simple movements and ask the children to "echo" them.

   TEACHER (says): "Head," points to head with both hands.

   STUDENTS (say): "Head," point to head with both hands.

   TEACHER (say and do): Pat, pat, pat head.

   STUDENTS (say and do): Pat, pat, pat head.

   TEACHER (whisper and do): Pat, pat, pat head.

   STUDENTS (whisper and do): Pat, pat, pat head.

   TEACHER (silently): Pat, pat, pat head.

   STUDENTS (silently): Pat, pat, pat head.

2. After many experiences with bilateral motions, add a drumbeat to a song or musical composition that has a strong and steady beat. Good examples include the recordings *Grease* (RSO Records, Inc.), "Saturday Night Fever Medley," *Saturday Night Fiedler* (Boston Pops, Midsong International Records, Inc.), "Turkey in the Straw" (Roy Clark, *A Festival of Golden Country Instrumentals*, Readers Digest,

---

* Based on the four-step language process developed by Phyllis Weikart, pp. 17–19, 24–27.

1980), and the songs "It's a Small World" (p. 46) and "This Land Is Your Land" (p. 377).

3. As perceptual-motor skills become more developed, create rhythmic sequences from the following more complex sequences of movement.*

   • Alternate motions: One hand or the other; one foot or the other

   • Double alternate motions: Both hands alternate with both feet; two foot taps alternate with two shoulder taps

   • Combined double alternate motions: Right hand to head/left hand to head; both hands to waist; left foot tap, right foot tap/both hands clap

4. Use such motions to express form as in the following example. Phrases of eight or sixteen beats and clear repetition of sections help the students discriminate between their movements.

   • Musical example: Scott Joplin, "The Entertainer" (4/4 meter, quasi-rondo: ABACA)

   • Main theme, A: Pat head, tap shoulders

   • Contrasting melody, B: Slap thighs, clap hands

   • Contrasting melody, C: Tap chest, clap hands

5. Sing "The Little Shoemaker" and ask half the class to tap a steady beat throughout. The other half of the class should tap the word rhythms.

The Little Shoemaker

Words by Janet Gaynor
Music by Alice Riley

Key: F
Starting pitch: A
Meter: 4/4, begins on 4

1. There's a lit-tle, wee man in a lit-tle wee house, Lives o-ver the way, you see. And he sits at the win-dow and sews all day, Mak-ing shoes for you and me. A-

rap-a-tap-tap, a-rap-a-tap-tap. Hear the ham-mer's tit-tat-tee. A-

rap-a-tap-tap, a-rap-a-tap-tap, Mak-ing shoes for you and me.

* Based on the four-step language process developed by Phyllis Weikart, pp. 17–19, 24–27.

EXPRESSING MUSICAL CONCEPTS THROUGH MOVEMENT: THE DALCROZE APPROACH

Emile Jaques-Dalcroze (1865–1951) was a well-known Swiss educator and a pioneer in teaching music based on the premise that rhythm is the primary element. His approach to teaching music consisted of three parts: eurhythmics (rhythmic movement), solfège (ear training), and improvisation. Through his teaching Dalcroze advocated developing the whole child, which he saw as involving physical and muscular control, mental awareness, social consciousness, and emotional health.

The system known as *eurhythmics* (meaning "good rhythm") focuses on developing the child's rhythmic potential through the use of his or her own body. Through experiences with natural movement, eurhythmics offers opportunities for developing keener hearing, concentration, mental alertness to musical elements, rhythmic control, coordination, flexibility, recognition and understanding of musical symbols, and appreciation of expressive qualities of music. Students are also asked to improvise rhythm patterns on a pitch or pitches and to improvise melodies, rondos, and moods using percussion instruments. The study of eurhythmics is based on the following important concepts:

1. The use of the whole body, involving the larger muscle groups, assures a more vivid realization of rhythmic experience than does the more customary use of the extremities, such as the hands in clapping and the feet in tapping.
2. The physical coordinations developed in the well-directed rhythm class give the individual power to control his or her movements in related activities. This is especially true in regard to instrumental skills, where coordination is difficult and specialized.
3. Bodily movement acts as a reference for the interpretation of rhythm symbols, which become truly significant when learned as the result of a vital rhythmic experience.
4. Children develop habits of listening in the process of identifying what they *hear* with what they *do*.
5. Body, mind, and emotion are integrated in rhythmic expression.
6. The freedom of expression that is a cardinal principle in eurhythmics stimulates the creative impulse in every department of musical learning.*

The following section includes some basic concepts of rhythm, with specific suggestions for presentation to children according to Dalcroze's ideas.

CONCEPT: BEAT/METER

As students' perceptions of music are developed, their attention should be focused on the steady beat in music. A beat is a regularly recurring pulse in music, which may be strong, with heavy accents, or weak, with little or no accent. Grouping beats according to accents creates meter, which may be in groups of twos or threes or in combinations of four, five, six, seven, and so on.

---

* Elsa Findlay, *Rhythm and Movement* (Easton, Ill.: Summy-Birchard, 1971), p. 2.

Suggestions for Lessons

1. Feeling the beat: Set a pendulum (or metronome) in motion. Have students say the word *swing* as they move to it. Vary the speed. Add something as simple as a finger cymbal or two pitches on a xylophone for each swing. Use familiar music with a strong beat, and encourage students to speak, chant, swing their arms, and move their whole body to the beat. Examples of appropriate music include "Sing Together" (change words to "Swing, swing together") and current country-western and rock music.

2. Feeling accents:

   a. Sing or play the songs "Yankee Doodle," "I'd Like to Teach the World to Sing," and "Chim-Chimeree" (from *Mary Poppins*). Put a gentle push or weight on the first beat of every measure. Ask students to listen and respond by "lifting a low-hanging cloud back up into the sky" when they feel the music "lift."

   b. Sing or play "76 Trombones" from *The Music Man* by Meredith Willson, or the song "Bicycle Built for Two." Give balloons to small groups of four or five children. Ask them to "lift" the balloons when the music seems to say "lift" (on the accent).

3. Feeling meter:

   a. Use balls for developing coordination and discovering a feeling for beat. Individually or with partners, have students bounce a ball on the accent and then catch it. (You could play beats on drums or chords on piano or Autoharp; caution students not to bounce the ball indiscriminately.) As the students say "One" on the accented beat, they will develop a feeling for groupings of twos and threes.

   ```
   >       >
   1   2   1   2
   >           >
   1   2   3   1   2   3
   ```

   After students can feel duple and triple meter, ask them to bounce the ball to changing meters. Have them say "Bounce, catch" (duple), or "Bounce, catch, hold" (triple).

   ```
       >       >           >               >
       1   2   1   2       1   2   3   1   2   3
   ```

   b. Have students use their arms and upper bodies to find a swing in twos (two beats), then find a swing in threes.

   c. Have students find the accent and move their bodies or bounce balls to the following meters:

   • Duple meter: Current rock, country-western, and such songs as "Consider Yourself at Home" (from *Oliver*), "It's a Small World" (pp. 46), "This Land Is Your Land" (p. 377), "I'd Like to Teach the World to sing" (p. 328), and "The Candy Man."

   • Triple meter: Songs such as "Edelweiss" (from *The Sound of Music*), "Roll On, Columbia" (p. 150), "Silver Bells" (p. 329), and "Did You Ever See a Lassie?" (p. 120).

I'd Like to Teach the World to Sing (In Perfect Harmony)

Key: F
Starting pitch: D
Meter: 4/4, starts on "and" of 4

Words and Music by B. Backer, B. Davis, R. Cook, and R. Greenaway

Moderately

I'd like to build__ the world__ a home__ and fur-nish it with love,__ Grow

ap-ple trees__ and hon-ey bees__ and snow-white tur-tle doves.__ I'd

like to teach__ the world__ to sing__ in per-fect har-mo-ny;__ I'd like to hold it

in my arms__ and keep it com-pa-ny.__ I'd like to see the world__ for once__ all

stand-ing hand in hand,__ And hear them ech-o through__ the hills__ for

peace through-out the land.__ That's the song I hear.__ Let the world sing to-day__

__ A song of peace that ech-oes on__ and nev-er goes a-way.__ I'd

like to build__ the world__ a home__ and fur-nish it with love,__ Grow

ap-ple trees__ and hon-ey bees__ and snow-white tur-tle doves.__ I'd

Silver Bells

Words and Music by Jay Livingston and Ray Evans

Key: B♭
Starting pitch: B♭
Meter: 3/4, begins on 3

CONCEPT: FAST, SLOW, GETTING FASTER, GETTING SLOWER

Suggestions for Lessons: Grades K–3

1. Play "The Little Shepherd" from *The Children's Corner Suite* by Debussy. Ask students to respond with small and larger movements of hands, arms, and bodies as the music varies from slow to fast. Explore other types of physical expression, such as walking fast and then slowly as the music changes. Use fingers to do the walking or running over the desk top.

2. Play "Little Train of the Caipira" by Villa-Lobos. Ask the students to sit in a circle. Pass a large yarn ball to the right when the music gets faster and to the left when the music gets slower.

3. Play a recording of "Kee-Chee" (*World of Music*, CD-2-23, Silver Burdett Book 2, 1991). Ask students to show the beat by tapping it on their knees. Have students indicate if the music gets faster or slower. Ask students to sit in a circle on the floor and to pat their knees one at a time (each quarter note) through the words of the fourth line—"kae ay-na." Then on the rest at the end of the fourth line ask students to cross their hands to the opposite knees with one pat for each measure. Have them resume motions with the beginning of the song.

Kee-Chee

Game from Zaire

Reprinted by permission from *Girl Scout Pocket Songbook.* Copyright 1956, Girl Scouts of the United States of America.

4. Try similar experiences with the following pieces:
   • Saint-Saëns: "The Elephant" from *Carnival of the Animals* (slow)
   • Rimsky-Korsakov: "Flight of the Bumble Bee" (fast)
   • Chopin: *Valse in D Flat Major,* Op. 64, No. 1 (fast)
   • Ibert: "The Little White Donkey" from *Histoires for Piano* (slow, fast, slow)
   • Grieg: "In the Hall of the Mountain King" from *Peer Gynt* Suite No. 1, Op. 46 (slow, becoming fast)
   • "Kalinka" (slow, becomes faster)

Suggestions for Lessons: Grades 4–6

1. Play sections of "Pacific 231" by Honegger. As the tempo changes from slow to fast to slow, ask students to respond by raising or lowering their arms. Point out the tension at both slow and fast tempos.
2. Dramatize the opening train scene from the musical *The Music Man*. Students should illustrate through their movements a train starting slowly, becoming fast, and then slowing down.
3. Many other musical compositions use tempo to express a mood, idea, or feeling. Encourage students to improvise free, creative movements as expressions of slow, fast, or slow-fast-slow, using the following pieces:
   • Chopin: "Fantasie Impromptu," Op. 66 (fast-slow-fast)
   • Prokofiev: Sonata #7 (III) (fast)
   • Mozart: Clarinet Concerto in E flat (II) (slow)
   • Tchaikovsky: "Arabian Dance" from *The Nutcracker* (slow)

CONCEPT: ACCENTS

Many musical compositions use accents as an expressive device. Encourage students to use free, creative movements to express accents as they occur in music.

Suggestions for Lessons: Grades K–3

1. Play the following rhythms on a drum. Ask the students to sit in a circle and raise or lower yarn balls as accents are played.

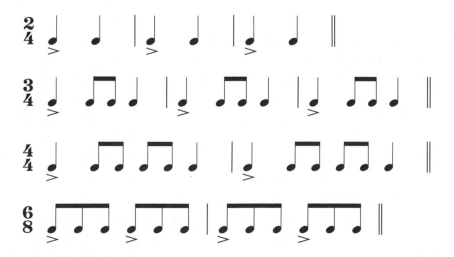

2. Play "Golliwog's Cakewalk" from *The Children's Corner Suite* by Debussy. Ask the students to create tight fists, then open their hands suddenly as they hear accents. Then have them stand and relax their entire body with arms hanging loosely at the sides and to tighten their muscles for the accents.

Suggestions for Lessons: Grades 4–6

1. Invite students to create a designated movement on the accents in each of the following:

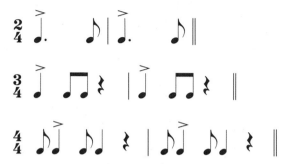

2. Apply the same movements to any of the following pieces:
   - Stravinsky: "Dance of the Adolescents" from *Rite of Spring*
   - Bernstein: "America" from *West Side Story*
   - Bruch: Violin Concerto in G Minor, No. 1, Op. 26 (III—Rondo)

CONCEPT: DYNAMICS

The body is an important means by which a child can be made aware of the role of dynamics in music. Movement experiences should include quiet, slow movements as well as sudden and gradual changes in energy levels.

Suggestions for Lessons: Grades K–3

1. Ask students to draw a big circle when the sound is loud and a small circle when the sound is soft. Play an echo game with movement as the response.
2. Listen to the song "Frosty the Snowman." Discuss how music gets softer when expressing the words *but he waved goodbye*. Have students become "snowmen" and melt to the ground as the music gets softer.

Suggestions for Lessons: Grades 4–6

1. Play portions of Beethoven: "Storm" from Symphony No. 6 (*Pastorale*), or Grofé: "Cloudburst" from *Grand Canyon Suite*. Ask students to decide how to move in their own space in such a way that they show more energy as the storm intensifies, and less energy as the storm recedes. Follow up this activity with a discussion about how students decided on the amount of energy to use, when to change it, and what in the music caused the change (dynamics: loud/soft/accents).
2. Listen to Debussy's "The Sunken Cathedral" from *Preludes Book I*. It begins softly as the mystical cathedral rises through the mist. The music gets louder as the cathedral comes into full view with its bells tolling, and then gradually gets softer as the cathedral vanishes from view. Ask students to interpret the dynamics of this piece with their bodies. You might begin by having them lie on the floor, curled up

tightly to represent the soft dynamics of the beginning. As they stretch and expand their bodies with larger motions, they may express louder dynamics. Returning to the still, quiet position on the floor signifies the return of the cathedral to the hidden depths of the imagination and the soft dynamics of the ending.

CONCEPT: RHYTHM PATTERNS

When long and short sounds are put together and then repeated, a rhythm pattern results. If this pattern is placed in a melody, melodic rhythm is created. For example: ♫ ♩ is a melodic rhythm in the song "Jingle Bells."

Suggestions for Lessons: Grades K–3

1. Use children's names or seasonal words to put note values together.

   Examples: Spring fever ♩ ♩ ♩

   Daffodils, jonquils ♫♩ ♩ ♩

   Rain! 𝅝 or ♩ 𝄾 ▬

   Let the children respond aurally/physically before they are shown the patterns. Then, put patterns together in various combinations.

2. Step characteristic rhythm patterns as students learn songs. The more precisely children can step a pattern with their whole body, the better they feel it in preparation for visual and intellectual understanding.

   Examples: "Jingle Bells"   ♫ ♩

   "Yankee Doodle"   ♩. ♫ ♩ ♩

   "Got a Mule"   ♪ ♩.   ♩

3. Make up word patterns. Practice stepping, clapping, and speaking the patterns, then remove the words and speak the patterns with rhythm syllables.

   Examples: Ice cream cone   ♩ ♩ ♩

   May I have some ice cream?   ♫ ♫ ♩ ♩

   George Washington   ♩   ♫ ♩

   Abraham Lincoln   ♫ ♩ ♩ ♩

4. A 𝄾 is a rest, which is a "silent" pause in music. Help children feel the rest with their bodies but without a sound. An idea for small children is to clap on "walk" and to touch temples gently on the rest.

walk,   walk,   walk,   rest

5. Start a beat ♩ ♩ ♩ ♩ and then add words to help you remember the following patterns. Locate the patterns in familiar songs.

corn   cobs   ap - ri - cot   dou - ble trou - ble   straw - ber - ry   piz - za pie

Suggestions for Lessons: Grades 4–6

1. Present the song "Erie Canal" (p. 65) on a transparency. In Part I of the song ask students to circle the following repeated pattern: ♪ ♩. Count the number of times this pattern occurs (9). Perform Part I of the song for students. Ask them to create a motion for the ♪ ♩ (syncopation).

2. Present Part II of "Erie Canal" on a transparency. Ask students to circle the following repeated rhythmic pattern: ♩. ♩. Count the number of times it occurs (15). Perform Part II of the song for students. Ask them to create a different motion for the rhythmic pattern ♩. ♩ (the motion will need to be short).

3. Divide the class in half. Perform the song again and ask half the class to do the motion for ♪ ♩ and the other half to do the second motion for ♩. ♩.

4. Perform the song with the class singing (without the motions), then perform the song with motions.

CONCEPT: MELODIC CONTOUR

Movement can be a major activity in learning the melody of a song. Moving their hands or "mapping the melody" helps students feel if the melody moves up or down.

Suggestions for Lessons: Grades K–3

1. Ask students to apply movement to the phrase "Oh Ma" in "Little Tommy Tinker" (p. 323). Notice how students can use their head voices better and sing high to low.

2. Ask students to place their hands on feet, ankles, knees, waist, shoulders, jaw, eyes, and top of head as they sing the song "Do-Re-Mi" from *The Sound of Music*.

INTERPRETING MUSICAL IDEAS THROUGH MOVEMENT

Interpreting musical ideas through movement focuses on the simple expressiveness of musical elements, text, or programmatic ideas in music. The bodily movement may be free and creative or carefully planned and either abstract or dramatic. Essential to this type of expression is skill and comfort in using the body in a spatial environment. Many techniques for exploring the use of the body in space can be found on pp. 320–325. Children will find increased pleasure and satisfaction in musical experiences as they become comfortable with physical movement to music and are no longer self-conscious.

WHAT INSPIRES INTERPRETATIVE MOVEMENT?

Inspiration for creating movement patterns or expressiveness comes from the musical elements inherent in the piece of music. Questions to be asked include:

1. What is the rhythm (beat, meter, syncopation)?
2. What is the tempo?
3. What kinds of rhythm patterns are used?
4. What is the text about? Are there programmatic ideas in the music?

5. What are the characteristics of the melody/melodies (steps, skips, contour, legato, staccato, phrases, length)?

6. What is the form (AB, ABA, rondo, theme and variations)?

7. How would you describe the dynamics (loud, soft, gradually getting louder, softer)?

As you study and analyze the qualities of a musical composition, you need to decide how you will use such basic rhythmic activities as walking, marching, clapping, slapping, snapping, stretching, bending, and swaying.

One type of interpretative movement is free and creative, in which children are encouraged to respond in an appropriate way to a given musical composition. Music may contain programmatic ideas to which children relate, or it may be abstract.

- Music examples (programmatic): Moussorgsky's "Ballet of the Chicks in Their Shells" from *Pictures at an Exhibition*; Stephen Sondheim's "Send in the Clowns" from *A Little Night Music*; Grofé's "Sunrise" from *Grand Canyon Suite*

- Music examples (abstract): Chopin's "Fantasie Impromptu," Op. 66; Prokofiev's Classical Symphony, Gavotte; J. S. Bach's "Jesu, Joy of Man's Desiring"

A second type of movement is structured, as determined by the students, the teacher, or both together. The movements are the same from performance to performance and are done together. Structured movement may be abstract or dramatic. In the former, basic rhythmic activities, such as snapping, clapping, and swaying, dominate the interpretation, while in the latter, movements are determined by a literal interpretation of the text or programmatic idea. Songs are popular sources for structured movement. The following general guidelines will help you use movement to involve students in experiencing music.

GENERAL GUIDELINES FOR PLANNING MOVEMENT EXPERIENCES

1. Keep movement within the skill and capability of the student (for example, use bilateral motions for young children). These movements may range from very simple to highly complex.

2. Choose musical compositions that lend themselves through text or programmatic ideas to interpretative movement. Be careful not to impose a story meaning on a simple melody.

3. Plan movements so that they flow freely from one to the other.

4. Plan movements carefully. Sometimes children will improvise movement as a part of the learning process, while at other times you will want them to follow a planned pattern of movements.

5. Ask children to help decide on appropriate interpretative movements and chart them with stick figures and captions that give specific directions, along with the text of the song (if there is one).

6. Make sure children learn each movement well; children must concentrate on the interpretation and not on "what do I do next?"

7. Be sensitive to the children's age. Do not choose a movement that will be awkward or embarrassing to them.

8. For performance experiences, you may wish to use simple costumes.

9. Emphasize important words or syllables. You may choose to do the movement on a strong beat or on a particular word.

10. Enhance the rhythm of the song with coordinated movement (that is, everyone doing the same thing at the same time).

ABSTRACT INTERPRETATIVE MOVEMENT

"Rock-a My Soul"

Activity: Slapping, clapping, and snapping fingers to music
Grades: 4–6
Concepts: Rhythm: Beat, syncopation, melodic rhythm
           Form: ABA

PROCEDURES

1. Sing "Rock-a My Soul" (p. 245).
2. Say the text out loud to feel the beat and develop ideas for movement.
3. Determine the form (ABA) and create two sets of contrasting rhythmic motions as follows:

Measures	Movements
A Section	
Measures 1–8	Slap thighs on beats 1 and 3, clap hands on beats 2 and 4
B Section	
Measures 9–10	Snap fingers on beats 2 and 4, arms in front
Measures 11–12	Snap fingers on beats 2 and 4, arms left
Measures 13–14	Snap fingers on beats 2 and 4, arms right
Measure 15	Arms at side
Measure 16	Clap hands on beats 2 and 3
A Section	
Measures 1–8	Repeat motions for measures 1–7. End with two claps on measure 8

"I'm Gonna Sing When the Spirit Says Sing"

Activity: Stretching, crossing arms, clapping
Grades: 4–6
Concepts: Rhythm: Beat, accent, melodic rhythm

I'm Gonna Sing When the Spirit Says Sing

Spiritual

Key: G
Starting pitch: D
Meter: 4/4, begins on "and" of 3

[Musical notation for "I'm Gonna Sing When the Spirit Says Sing" with lyrics:]

I'm gon-na sing when the spi-rit says sing;___ I'm gon-na sing when the spi-rit says sing;___ I'm gon-na sing when the spi-rit says sing, and o-bey the spi-rit of the Lord.___

PROCEDURES

1. Sing the song.
2. Create movements that follow the text, such as:

   I'm gonna   Hands and arms in ready position

   sing   Both hands and arms stretch out and up

   spirit   Both hands cross chest

   o-bey   Clap

   Lord   Both hands and arms outstretched in front; palms up

3. Chart the movements with stick figures to help students remember them.

DRAMATIC INTERPRETATIVE MOVEMENT

Most children enjoy creative dramatics. They like to be something or someone else and experience great pleasure in acting out a song. Adding some visuals, costumes, and movement can generate a tremendous amount of excitement in the classroom, and, since children have vivid imaginations, the teacher's role is minimized. While dramatic movement can be added to any song, songs that lend themselves especially well to such treatment are those that (1) tell a story (ballad or multiple verses), (2) have contrasting phrases or sections, (3) feature a particular event or time in history, or (4) portray a strong human emotion or action.

In the following songs, ideas for dramatic interpretative movement can be found in the text or musical concepts.

"Little Marionettes"

Activity: Staccato finger movements, clapping, smooth hand motions
Grades: K–2
Concepts: Tempo: Quick
             Melody: Staccato, short phrases, skips
             Rhythm: Steady beat, duple meter

Little Marionettes

French Nursery Song

Key: G
Starting pitch: G
Meter: 2/4, begins on 1

♩=84

Danc - ing, danc - ing fin - gers, Ti - ny mar - io - nettes are danc - ing.

Danc - ing, danc - ing fin - gers, Clap, clap, clap, and three times 'round.

From Music for Early Childhood © 1952 Silver Burdett Company. Reprinted by permission.

PROCEDURES

1. Have students pretend that their fingers are marionettes on strings. Have students dance, stressing the first beat until the words "clap, clap, clap," when they should clap hands.

2. Have students circle one hand with the other in the words "three times 'round."

"I Wish I Were a Windmill"

Activity: Swaying, moving arms up and down

Grades: K–2

Concepts: Rhythm: Steady beat, duple meter

Text: Windmill, move my arms like this

I Wish I Were a Windmill

Key: F

Starting pitch: C

Meter: 4/4, begins on 4

Play Song

I wish I were a wind - mill, a wind - mill, a wind - mill; I wish I were a

wind - mill, I know what I would do. I'd move my arms like this,_____ like

this,_____ like this;_____ I'd move my arms like this,_____ That's what I would do.

PROCEDURES

1. Have students form partners and face each other.
2. Each should clasp right and left hands of his or her partner and raise them overhead to form the "blades" of the windmill.
3. Have each pair move their arms up and down, swaying right and left with the beat.

"Aizu Lullaby"

Activity:	Rocking, swaying
Grades:	K–3
Concepts:	Rhythm: Steady beat, duple meter
	Tempo: Slow
	Melody: Legato
	Text: Rocks her/his sweet little baby

Aizu Lullaby (Aizu Komori Uta)

Key: D
Starting pitch: B
Meter: 4/4, begins on 1

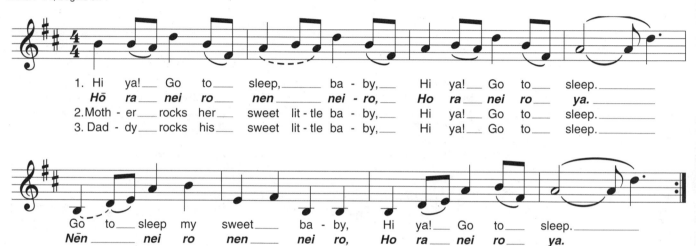

1. Hi ya!__ Go to__ sleep,___ ba - by,__ Hi ya!__ Go to__ sleep._____
Hō ra nei ro__ nen_____ nei - ro, *Ho ra__ nei ro__ ya.*_____
2. Moth - er__ rocks her__ sweet lit - tle ba - by,__ Hi ya!__ Go to__ sleep.__
3. Dad - dy__ rocks his__ sweet lit - tle ba - by,__ Hi ya!__ Go to__ sleep.__

Go to__ sleep my sweet___ ba - by, Hi ya! Go to__ sleep._____
Nēn_____ nei ro nen___ nei ro, Ho ra__ nei ro__ ya.

Betty Warner Dietz and Thomas Choonbai Park, *Folk Songs of China, Japan, and Korea.* © 1964. By permission of Betty Warner Dietz.

PROCEDURES

1. Students take turns rocking a baby doll to sleep.
2. Have them follow the duple pulse and sway right and left on beats 1 and 3.

More complex movements can be used to interpret an entire composition. The following movements can be performed either as a classroom activity or on stage for a school program.

"Catch a Falling Star"

Activity:	Dramatization, snapping fingers
Grades:	5–6
Concepts:	Rhythm:

Accents:

Catch a Falling Star

Words and Music by Paul Vance and Lee Pockriss

Key: B♭
Starting pitch: D
Meter: 4/4, begins on 1

Catch a fall-ing star and put it in your pock - et. Nev-er let it fade a - way.
Catch a fall-ing star and put it in your pock - et. Save it for a rain - y

day. For love may come and tap____ you on the shoul - der some star - less night. And
when your trou - bles start____ in mul - ti - ply - ing— and they just might— It's

just in case you think____ you want to hold her, you'll have a pock - et full of star - light.
eas - y to for - get____ them with - out try - ing with just a pock - et full of star - light.

Catch a fall - ing star and put it in your pock - et; nev - er let it get a -
Catch a fall - ing star and put it in your pock - et;

way. Catch a fall - ing star and put it in your pock - et;
Catch a fall - ing star and put it in your pock - et;

nev - er let it get a - way. Catch a fall - ing star and

save it for a rain - y day. For
put it in your pock - et; save it for a rain - y day. For day.

Save it for a rain - y day.____
Save it for a rain - y day.____

PROCEDURES

1. Practice the rhythm of the song and then decide on appropriate dramatic movements that will express the words.
2. A few students may create a rhythmic ostinato movement while another group of students may dramatize the text.
3. Reinforce learning by asking a select group of students to play the ostinato on percussion instruments.

"Dream a Dream"

Activity: Walking, stretching, holding hands
Grades: 5–6
Concepts: Melody: Phrases, contour, legato
                   Text: Dream, hope, brighter day, find a way, make it happen

Dream a Dream

Ed Robertson (Studio Recordings)

Key: B♭
Starting pitch: D
Meter: 4/4, begins on 4

work   to make them come   true,   we will   sure - ly find   a   way._____

Dream a dream,_____   dare to hope,_____   may - be we_____ can   make   it   hap - pen. Dream a

dream   of a   new   to - mor - row,   may - be   some - day we can see our dreams come   true.

PROCEDURES

1. Sing the song.
2. Create movements that follow text such as

Dream a dream of a new tomorrow	Two steps forward, hands gradually raised, right hand sweeps in arch above head, eyes follow
when the people learn to love their fellow man.	Stop, cross arms over chest, face front
Dare to hope for a peaceful morning	Two steps DS* right, turn, left hand gestures with palm up, body faces L
when we've learned to walk together hand in hand.	All join hands and step forward
If we all will dare to dream dreams	Drop hands, turn to each other in pairs—point to each other; on the word "dreams" outer hand of partners sweeps upward
of a new and brighter day,	Face front, left hand out with palm up on "new," right hand out with palm up on "brighter"
If we work to make them come true	All step four steps DSR
we will surely find a way.	On "surely" turn, face front, both hands front in form of fist
Dream a dream,	Right hand upper sweep
dare to hope,	Left hand upper sweep
maybe we can make it happen.	Face partner—join hands in pairs
Dream a dream of a new tomorrow;	Drop hands, stand as beginning—take two steps forward, gradually raise arms, right hand sweep, eyes follow
maybe someday we can see our dreams come true.	Stop, face front and cross arms over chest

* Stage directions:
DS = Downstage—toward the audience
US = Upstage—away from audience
R = Right
L = Left
C = Center

"Brother, Can You Spare a Dime?"

Activity: Walking, marching, stretching, slapping
Grades: 5–6
Concepts: Text, tempo

This song depicts a railroad man who has become a victim of the Great Depression in the United States during the 1930s and is now waiting in a breadline.

PROCEDURES

1. Select a boy to sing the song as a solo. Dress him in ragged clothing.
2. Create movements that follow the text, such as:

Once I built a railroad, made it run,	Marches forward; hands form wheel, turn on "made it run"
Made it race against time.	Hand straight out in arch "against time"
Once I built a railroad,	Walks downstage (toward audience)
Now it's done.	Hand motions across right, palm down
Brother, can you spare a dime?	Pantomimes holding up tin cup for a "handout"
Once I built a tower, to the sun.	Right hand sweeps upward toward sun
Brick and rivet and lime,	"Brick," slaps hand; "rivet," pantomimes staccato riveting; "lime," smooths hand on other hand as if on brick
Once I built a tower,	Right hand sweeps upward
Now it's done,	Repeat of earlier motion: hand sweeps across, palm down
Brother, can you spare a dime?	Pantomimes holding up tin cup
Once in khaki suits, Gee, we looked swell	Marches, and swings arms vigorously
Full of that Yankee Doodle de-dum	Stops and salutes
Half a million boots went sloggin' through Hell,	Marches as if through mud
I was the kid with the drum.	Pantomimes playing of drum with drumstick (bass drum)
Say, don't you remember, they called me Al	Turns to audience and points to himself with thumb
It was Al all the time	Points to audience, shakes head, takes two steps, turns, points to himself . . .
Say, don't you remember, I'm your Pal!	
(Sings slowly as he sinks to his knees)	
Buddy, can you spare a dime?	Holds up tin cup.

Brother, Can You Spare a Dime?

Music by Jay Gorney
Words by E. Y. Harburg

Key: C minor
Starting pitch: C
Meter: 4/4, begins on 1

Once I built a rail-road, made it run,___ Made it race___ a-gainst time.___

Once I built a rail-road, Now it's done.___ Broth-er, can you spare a dime?___

Once I built a tow-er to the sun:___ Brick and riv-et and lime,_____

Once I built a tow-er, Now it's done.___ Broth-er, can you spare a dime?___

Once in kha-ki suits, Gee! we looked swell, Full of that Yan-kee Doo-dle de dum.

Half a mil-lion boots went slog-gin' through Hell, I was the kid___ with the drum.___

Say, don't you re-mem-ber, they called me Al___ It was Al___ all the time?___

Say, don't you re-mem-ber I'm your Pal?!___ Bud-dy, can you spare a dime?___

PLAYING SINGING GAMES AND DANCING

One of the most enjoyable ways of involving students in moving to music is through singing games and dances. Learning to coordinate body movements and music provides an excellent way for students to improve their listening skills.

Following are some popular singing games and folk dances for various grade levels. While some are accompanied by recorded music, most have songs that are to be sung by the students as they participate in the movement. It is suggested that students learn to sing the songs well before adding appropriate movements.

"Obwisana"

Grades: K–1

PROCEDURES

1. Play a recording of "Obwisana" (Silver Burdett, *World of Music* 2, CD 2-12). The African words mean "Oh Gramma, I just hurt my finger on a rock."

2. Ask students to choose any small object and then bring it with them as you ask them to sit in a circle on the floor. Each child should place the object in front of him or her.

3. As the song is performed on a recording or sung, students should move their object over to their right one person on the first beat of the measure and lay it down on the second beat of the measure. Students continue alternating motions as long as they hear the music.

Obwisana

Folk Song from Ghana

Key: D
Starting pitch: F♯
Meter 2/4, begins on 1

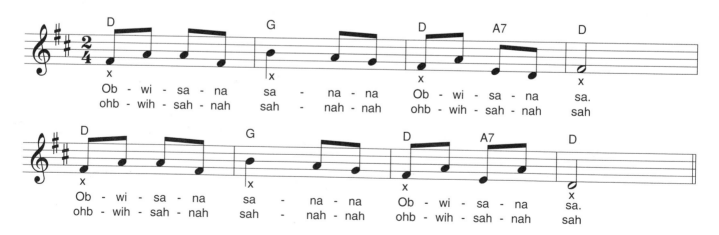

Ob - wi - sa - na   sa - na - na   Ob - wi - sa - na   sa.
ohb - wih - sah - nah sah - nah - nah ohb - wih - sah - nah sah

Ob - wi - sa - na   sa - na - na   Ob - wi - sa - na   sa.
ohb - wih - sah - nah sah - nah - nah ohb - wih - sah - nah sah

"Did You Ever See a Lassie?"

The music for "Did You Ever See a Lassie?" appears on p. 120.

Grades: K–3

PROCEDURES

1. Students form a circle, alternating boys and girls, with hands joined; one student is placed in the center.

2. As the students sing each phrase of the song have them perform the corresponding action:

Did you ever see a lassie, a lassie, a lassie?	Students move to the left four steps in time to the music
Did you ever see a lassie do this way and that?	Students move to the right four steps in time to the music
Do this way and that way, and that way and this way;	Student in center makes some movements while those in the circle stand still
Did you ever see a lassie do this way and that?	Students in circle imitate movements of student in the center

While the students are performing the last phrase, the student in the center points to a student in the circle who will change places with him or her at the end of the phrase. Then the song and dance repeat.

"Wild Bird"

Grades: K–2

PROCEDURES

1. Play a recording of the song "Wild Bird" (Silver Burdett *World of Music*, CD 2–4, 1991).
2. Teach the song.
3. Experiment with listening to various voices in order to determine who belongs to them. (Examples: Jimmy has a low throaty voice; Yolanda has a high thin voice.)
4. Have students form a circle or cage for the bird. (Face inward, hands joined.) One child (the bird) is asked to sit in the center with eyes closed. As students in the circle move to the left, they stop when they sing "free." A single student who is directly behind the bird sings or says the rest of the song as a solo. The student who is sitting in the middle then tries to identify the singer (or speaker). If the student in the center is correct, they change places and play the game again. Otherwise the student in the center remains "the bird."
5. Play the game and ask children who are not "it" to sing.

Wild Bird (Kagome)

Singing Game from Japan

Key: C
Starting pitch: A
Meter: 2/4, begins on 1

Round,   round,   the   wild   birds   fly,
Ka - go - me,   Ka - go - me,
kah - goh - meh   kah - goh - meh

Poor   lit - tle   bird   in   a   cage,   don't____ cry!
Ka - go - no   na - ka - no   to - ri - wa,
kah - goh - noh   nah - kah - noh   taw - ree

Hide   your   eyes   and   soon   you'll____ be
I - tsu,   i - tsu   de - ya - ru?
ee - tsoo   ee - tsoo   day - yah - roo

With   the   wild   birds,   fly - ing   free.
Yo - a - ke - no   ba - n - ni,
yoh - ah - kay - noh   bah - nee

Solo

Who's   stand - ing   back   of   you,   can   you____ say?
Tsu - ru   to   ka - me   to   sub - be - ta.
tsoo - roo   toh   kah - meh   toh   soob - beh - tah

If   you   guess   the   name   you   can   fly   a - way!
U - shi - ro - no   sho - men   da - re?
oo - shee   roh - noh   shoh - mehn   dah - reh

"The Mulberry Bush"

Grades: K–1

The Mulberry Bush

England

Key: G
Starting pitch: G
Meter: 6/8, begins on 1

Here we go 'round the mul-ber-ry bush, the mul-ber-ry bush, the mul-ber-ry bush.

Here we go 'round the mul-ber-ry bush, so ear-ly in the morn - ing.

PROCEDURES

1. Have students form a circle, facing inward, with hands joined.

2. As students sing, have them perform the indicated actions or movements:

Here we go 'round the mulberry bush, the mulberry bush, the mulberry bush. Here we go 'round the mulberry bush, so early in the morning.	Students move counterclockwise in time to the music
This is the way we wash our hands, wash our hands, wash our hands. This is the way we wash our hands, so early in the morning.	Students pantomime each verse of the song

Repeat first verse above.

This is the way we brush our teeth,
brush our teeth, brush our teeth.
This is the way we brush our teeth,
so early in the morning.

Repeat first verse.

This is the way we comb our hair,
comb our hair, comb our hair.
This is the way we comb our hair,
so early in the morning.

Repeat first verse.

This is the way we sweep the floor,
sweep the floor, sweep the floor.
This is the way we sweep the floor,
so early in the morning.

Repeat first verse.

"The Farmer in the Dell"

The music for "The Farmer in the Dell" appears on p. 40.
Grades: K–1

PROCEDURES

1. Have students form a circle facing inward. Boys alternate with girls and join hands. Select one student to be the farmer; he or she stands in the center of the circle.

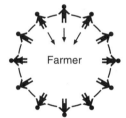

2. As students sing, have them perform the indicated actions or movements:

The farmer in the dell, The farmer in the dell, Hi, ho, the derry oh, The farmer in the dell.	Students walk to right in time to music
The farmer takes a wife, The farmer takes a wife, Hi, ho, the derry oh, The farmer in the dell.	Students walk to right in time to music; "farmer" moves to the circle and takes a "wife"; farmer and wife return to center of circle
The wife takes the child, The wife takes the child, Hi, ho, the derry oh, The farmer in the dell.	Students walk to right in time to music; "wife" moves to circle and takes a "child"; wife and child return to center of circle
The child takes the nurse, The child takes the nurse, Hi, ho, the derry oh, The farmer in the dell.	Students walk to right in time to music; the "child" moves to the circle and takes a "nurse"; child and nurse return to center of circle
The nurse takes the dog, The nurse takes the dog, Hi, ho, the derry oh, The farmer in the dell.	Students walk to right in time to music; the "nurse" moves to the circle and takes a "dog"; nurse and dog return to center of circle

The dog takes the cat,	Students walk to right in time to music;
The dog takes the cat,	the "dog" moves to the circle and takes a "cat";
Hi, ho, the derry oh,	dog and cat return to center of circle
The farmer in the dell.	

The cat takes the rat,	Students walk to right in time to music;
The cat takes the rat,	the "cat" moves to the circle and takes a "rat";
Hi, ho, the derry oh,	cat and rat return to center of circle
The farmer in the dell.	

The rat takes the cheese,	Students walk to right in time to music;
The rat takes the cheese,	the "rat" moves to the circle and takes a "cheese";
Hi, ho, the derry oh,	rat and cheese return to center of circle
The farmer in the dell.	

The cheese stands alone,	Everyone returns to the circle except the
The cheese stands alone,	"cheese"; all stand still facing the cheese
Hi, ho, the derry oh,	
The farmer in the dell.	

3. The above steps can be repeated, with the "cheese" becoming the "farmer."

"Looby Loo"

The music for "Looby Loo" appears on p. 96.

Grades: K–1

PROCEDURES

1. Have students form a circle facing inward with their hands joined.

2. As students sing, have them perform the indicated actions or movements:

(Chorus) Here we go looby loo,	Students walk to the *right* in time to the music; eight steps
Here we go looby light,	
Here we go looby loo,	Students walk to the *left* in time to the music; eight steps
All on a Saturday night.	
I put my right hand in,	Students pantomime words for each verse
I take my right hand out,	
I give my right hand a	
shake, shake, shake,	
And turn myself about.	

Repeat chorus.

I put my left hand in,
I take my left hand out,
I give my left hand a
shake, shake, shake,
And turn myself about.

Repeat chorus.

I put my right foot in,
I take my right foot out,
I give my right foot a
shake, shake, shake,
And turn myself about.

Repeat chorus.

I put my left foot in,
I take my left foot out,
I give my left foot a
shake, shake, shake,
And turn myself about.

Repeat chorus.

I put my head right in,
I take my head right out,
I give my head a
shake, shake, shake,
And turn myself about.

Repeat chorus.

I put my whole self in,
I take my whole self out,
I give my whole self a
shake, shake, shake,
And turn myself about

Repeat chorus.

"Shoemaker's Dance"

Grades: K–2

Shoemaker's Dance

Danish Folk Song

Key: F
Starting pitch: C
Meter: 2/4, Begins on 1

Wind and wind the thread and wind and wind the thread And pull, pull, tap, tap, tap.

Tra la la la la la, la   Tra - la la, la, la, la, la

PROCEDURES

1. Have students form two circles, with boys on the inside and girls on the outside; have partners face each other.

2. As students sing, have them perform the indicated actions or movements:

Wind, wind, wind the thread,	Students pantomime by making fists, which they roll forward around each other four times
Wind, wind, wind the thread,	Reverse fist movement, now backward four times
And pull, pull	Pull twice with both hands as if pulling up shoelaces
tap, tap, tap.	Tap fists together three times
Repeat.	
Tra, la, la, la, la, la, la,	Boys' right hands join with girls' left hands;
Tra, la, la, la, la, la, la,	partners skip *counterclockwise* around
Tra, la, la, la, la, la, la,	the circle in time to the music
Tra, la, la, la, la, la, la.	

"Round and Round the Village"

Grades: 1–3

Round and Round the Village

United States

Key: F
Starting pitch: A
Meter: 2/2, begins on "and" of 2

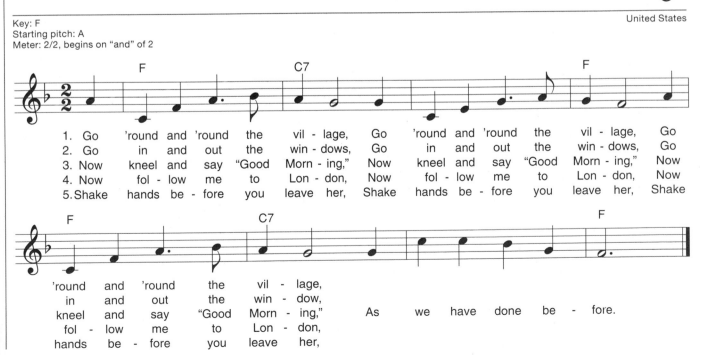

1. Go 'round and 'round the vil - lage, Go 'round and 'round the vil - lage, Go
2. Go in and out the win - dows, Go in and out the win - dows, Go
3. Now kneel and say "Good Morn - ing," Now kneel and say "Good Morn - ing," Now
4. Now fol - low me to Lon - don, Now fol - low me to Lon - don, Now
5. Shake hands be - fore you leave her, Shake hands be - fore you leave her, Shake

'round and 'round the vil - lage,
in and out the win - dow,
kneel and say "Good Morn - ing,"   As we have done be - fore.
fol - low me to Lon - don,
hands be - fore you leave her,

PROCEDURES

1. Have most of the students form a circle alternating boys and girls with hands joined; a few students stand in a line outside the circle.

2. As students sing, have them perform the indicated actions or movements:

Go 'round and 'round the village,
Go 'round and 'round the village,
Go 'round and 'round the village,
As we have done before.

Students on outside of circle move counterclockwise around the circle; students in circle slap hands to beat

Go in and out the windows,
Go in and out the windows,
Go in and out the windows,
As we have done before.

Students in circle join hands and raise arms to form windows; students on outside go *in* and *out* of the windows; at the end they should be *inside* the circle

Now kneel and say "Good Morning,"
Now kneel and say "Good Morning,"
Now kneel and say "Good Morning,"
As we have done before.

Students on inside of circle kneel facing students in the outer circle (this is where the new partner is chosen)

Now follow me to London,
Now follow me to London,
Now follow me to London,
As we have done before.

Students inside of circle skip counter-clockwise (followed by new partners)

Shake hands before you leave her,
Shake hands before you leave her,
Shake hands before you leave her,
As we have done before.

Each student in inside circle shakes hands with student they chose, followed by changing places with each other, inside circle thus returns to outside circle as the dance is repeated

"Pop, Goes the Weasel"

Legend tells us that this song originally did not refer to an animal but to a tool used by old London hatters and tailors called a "weasel," which they would pawn or "pop" when they were short of funds and needed money to tide them over.

Grades: 1–3

Pop, Goes the Weasel

England

Key: C
Starting pitch: C
Meter: 6/8, begins on 1

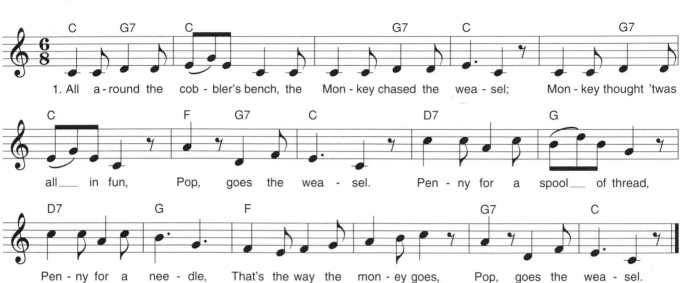

1. All a-round the cob-bler's bench, the Mon-key chased the wea-sel; Mon-key thought 'twas all___ in fun, Pop, goes the wea-sel. Pen-ny for a spool___ of thread, Pen-ny for a nee-dle, That's the way the mon-ey goes, Pop, goes the wea-sel.

PROCEDURES

1. Have children form two lines facing each other.

Head couple

Peel left

Peel right

2. As students sing, have them perform the indicated actions or movements:

All around the cobbler's bench	Head couple join hands and slide to foot of row
the monkey chased the weasel;	Return to original position
Monkey thought 'twas all in fun,	Head couple slides down the row a second time
Pop, goes the weasel.	All clap hands on "Pop"
Penny for a spoon of thread,	From this position, head couple peel off to
Penny for a needle,	right and left; rest of students follow;
That's the way the money goes,	head couple return to head of line and continue down row, becoming new "foot couple"

Pop, goes the weasel.

Game begins again with a new head couple.

"Bow, Belinda"

Grades: 2–3

Bow, Belinda

United States

Key: F
Starting pitch: F
Meter: 2/4, begins on 1

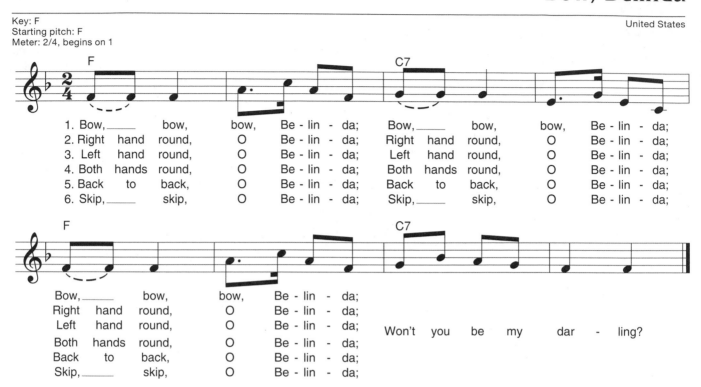

1. Bow,_____ bow, bow, Be - lin - da;   Bow,_____ bow, bow, Be - lin - da;
2. Right hand round,   O   Be - lin - da;   Right hand round,   O   Be - lin - da;
3. Left hand round,   O   Be - lin - da;   Left hand round,   O   Be - lin - da;
4. Both hands round,   O   Be - lin - da;   Both hands round,   O   Be - lin - da;
5. Back to back,   O   Be - lin - da;   Back to back,   O   Be - lin - da;
6. Skip,_____ skip,   O   Be - lin - da;   Skip,_____ skip,   O   Be - lin - da;

Bow,_____ bow, bow, Be - lin - da;
Right hand round,   O   Be - lin - da;
Left hand round,   O   Be - lin - da;   Won't you be my dar - ling?
Both hands round,   O   Be - lin - da;
Back to back,   O   Be - lin - da;
Skip,_____ skip,   O   Be - lin - da;

PROCEDURES

1. Students form two lines, boys in one and girls in the other. Partners in each line face each other.

Head couple ↑   ↑ Foot couple

2. As students sing, have them perform the indicated actions or movements:

Bow, bow, bow Belinda;	Boy takes two steps forward, bows to girl
Bow, bow, bow Belinda;	Boy takes two steps back to original place in line
Bow, bow, bow Belinda;	Boy takes two steps forward, bows to girl
Won't you be my darling?	Boy takes two steps back to original place in line, girl curtsies
Right hand round, O Belinda;	Partners join right hands and turn
Right hand round, O Belinda;	
Right hand round, O Belinda;	Drop hands, face partner
Won't you be my darling?	Boy bows, girl curtsies

Left hand round, O Belinda;	Partners join left hands and turn
Left hand round, O Belinda;	
Left hand round, O Belinda;	Drop hands, face partner
Won't you be my darling?	Boy bows, girl curtsies
Both hands round, O Belinda;	Partners join hands and turn
Both hands round, O Belinda;	
Both hands round, O Belinda;	Drop hands, face partner
Won't you be my darling?	Boy bows, girl curtsies
Back to back, O Belinda (R);	Partners with arms folded move around
Back to back, O Belinda (L);	each other back to back, first right, then left
Back to back, O Belinda;	Face partner
Won't you be my darling?	Boy bows, girl curtsies
Skip, skip, O Belinda;	"Foot couple" join hands to form arch; partners
Skip, skip, O Belinda;	skip under arch and separate to form new lines
Skip, skip, O Belinda;	with a new head couple (the former foot couple)
Won't you be my darling?	

3. Repeat entire dance with new head couple.

"Goodnight, Ladies"

Grades: 2–3

Goodnight, Ladies

Traditional

Key: F
Starting pitch: A
Meter: 4/4, begins on 1

Good night, la-dies!____ Good night, la-dies!____ Good night,

la-dies!____ We're going to leave you now. Mer-ri-ly we roll a-long,

roll a-long, roll a-long. Mer-ri-ly we roll a-long o'er the deep blue sea.

PROCEDURES

1. Have students form two circles, boys on the inside and girls on the outside, with partners facing each other.

2. As students sing, have them perform the indicated actions or movements:

Goodnight, ladies!	Partners bow (boys) or curtsy (girls) to each other; boys move right in circle to next girl, who becomes his new partner
Goodnight, ladies!	Repeat actions
Goodnight, ladies!	Repeat actions
We're going to leave you now.	Boys and girls join inside hands
Merrily we roll along,	Partners skip *counterclockwise* around the circle in time to music
roll along, roll along,	
Merrily we roll along,	
O'er the deep blue sea.	

"O Susanna"

Grades: 3–6

O Susanna

Stephen C. Foster

Key: F
Starting pitch: F
Meter: 2/4, begins on "and" of 2

1. I____ came from Al - a - bam - a with my ban - jo on my knee, I'm____
2. It____ rained all night the day I left, the weath - er, it was dry; The____

going to Lou' - si - an - a my_____ true love for to see.
sun so hot I froze to death, Su - san - na don't you cry.

Chorus

O Su - san - na, O don't you cry for me, For I've

come from Al - a - bam - a with my ban - jo on my knee.

PROCEDURES

1. Have students form a circle alternating boys and girls, facing inward.

2. As students sing, have them perform the indicated actions or movements:

I came from Alabama with my	In time to the music, girls move four steps into the circle; boys clap beat.
banjo on my knee,	Girls move four steps back to their original place in the circle; boys clap beat.
I'm going to Lou'siana my	Boys move four steps into the circle; girls clap beat.
true love for to see.	Boys move four steps back to their original place in the circle; girls clap beat.
It rained all night the day I left, the weather it was dry;	Grand right and left: Boys face clockwise, girls face counterclockwise, join right hands and move around circle, alternating left and right hands. On "me" take new partners.
The sun so hot I froze to death, Susanna don't you cry.	
O Susanna, O don't you cry for me, For I've come from Alabama with my banjo on my knee.	New partners promenade eight walking steps counterclockwise. On the last beat everyone faces inward ready to repeat the dance again.

"La Cucaracha"

Grades: 4–6

PROCEDURES

1. Have students form two circles, boys on the inside and girls on the outside. Students face counterclockwise; boys put their hands on their hips, girls hold their skirts with left hand and castanets in right hand.

La Cucaracha

Mexico

Key: G
Starting pitch: D
Meter: 3/4, begins on "and" of 2

Chorus — G
La cu - ca - ra - cha, la cu - ca - ra - cha, ya no quie - re ca - mi -

D7 — G *fine*
nar, Por - que no tie - ne, por - que le fal - ta di - ne - ro pa - ra gas - tar.

Verse — G — D7
U - na cu - ca - ra - cha pin - ta La di - jo a u - na co - lo - ra - da,

G *D.C. al Fine*
Va - mo - nos pa - ra mi tie - rra A pa - sar la tem - po - ra - da.

2. As students sing, have them perform the indicated actions or movements:

La cucaracha, la cucaracha,	Partners move sideways one step away from each other and back
Ya no quiere caminar,	Partners take six running steps forward, clap on rest
Porque no tiene, porque le falta dinero para gastar.	Repeat side steps Repeat running steps and clap
Una cucaracha pinta La dijo a una colorada,	Partners face each other, left hand behind back, right hand over head. Boy circles left, girl stands still and clicks castanets for twelve counts.
Vamonos para mi tierra A pasar la temporada"	Boy changes direction, circles right, girl clicks castanets for twelve counts.
Repeat chorus.	Repeat actions for chorus

"Hahvah Nahgeelah"

Grades: 5–6

Hahvah Nahgeelah

Jewish Folk Song

Key: G minor
Starting pitch: D
Meter: 4/4, begins on 1

PROCEDURES

1. Have students form a circle alternating boys and girls, facing toward the center, hands joined.

2. Everyone follows these directions:
   a. Move left foot one step to the left; step on right foot crossing behind left foot.
   b. Move left foot one step to left; hop on left foot while swinging the right foot across the front of the left foot.
   c. Move right foot one step to right; hop on right foot while swinging the left foot across the front of the right foot.
   d. Repeat movements.

"Virginia Reel"

Grades: 4–6

PROCEDURES

1. Play a recording of the Virginia reel (such as from Holt, Rinehart's *Exploring Music*, Record 10, Band 5).
2. Have students form two parallel lines about 6 feet apart, boys in one line and girls in the other. The head couple is that one nearest the "head" of the room.

3. The Longways
   a. Boys join hands in their line, girls join hands in their line. All walk forward four steps and backwards four steps. Repeat.
   b. Partners approach each other, join right hands, turn each other completely around, and move back to places. Then they join left hands, turn each other completely around, and move back to places.
   c. They turn with both hands joined.
   d. Now they pass around each other, back to back (do-si-do), arms folded across chest, passing right shoulders, and move back to places.
   e. The head couple (boy and girl) *only* approach each other, grasp both hands, and take eight slides down the middle of the set and eight slides back.

4. The Reel
   a. The head couple reels: Linking right arms, they turn around one and a half times, then the head boy ("gent") turns the second girl ("lady") with his left arm, while the head lady turns the second gent with her left arm. Then the head couple again link right arms and turn once around. They continue down the set alternately linking left arms with each succeeding couple and right arms with each other until all in the lines have been reeled. When the head couple reaches the end of the line, they turn only halfway round and join both hands and slide back to the head of the set on their own sides.

5. The March
   a. The head couple separate, with the gent turning to his right and marching toward the foot directly behind the gents' line, followed by the other gents in single file. At the same time the head lady turns toward her left and marches down behind the ladies' line followed by all the other ladies.
   b. When the head couple reach the foot, they form an arch under which the other couples pass. The head couple remains at the foot of the line and the dance is repeated with a new head couple.

Head couple

"Weggis Song"

Grades: 4–6

Weggis Song

Swiss Folk Song

Key: E♭
Starting pitch: B♭
Meter: 4/4, begins on 1

From Lu - cerne to____ Weg - gis town Hol - di - ri - di - a, hol - di - ri - a Shoes and stock - ings we

don't have on, Hol - di - ri - di - a, Hol - di - a. Hol - di - ri - di - a, Hol - di - ri - di - a

Hol - di - ri - a Hol - di - ri - di - a, Hol - di - ri - di - a, Hol - di - a.

PROCEDURES

1. Have students form a circle alternating boys and girls.

2. As students sing, have them perform the indicated actions or movements:

From Lucerne to Weggis town	Move four steps sideways counterclockwise
Hol-di-ri-di-a, Hol-di-ri-a	Slap thighs/clap hands (2 times)
Shoes and stockings we don't have on,	Move four steps sideways clockwise
Hol-di-ri-di-a, Hol-di-a.	Slap thighs/clap hands (2 times)
Hol-di-ri-di-a, Hol-di-ri-di-a, Hol-di-ri-a.	Face partner, clasp right hands over head and circle eight steps to right
Hol-di-ri-di-a, Hol-di-ri-di-a, Hol-di-a.	Face partner, clasp left hands, and circle six steps to the left; on the last "hol-di-a," slap thighs and clap hands (one time)

3. Repeat dance for each verse.

"Irish Jig"

Grades: 5–6

The music for this dance, "Galway Piper," appears on p. 226

PROCEDURES

1. Have students form two lines, boys in one and girls in the other, with partners facing each other and hands on hips.

2. As students sing, have them perform the indicated actions or movements:

Every person in the nation, Of a great or humble station, Holds in highest estimation, Piping Tim of Galway.	Partners skip four steps forward toward each other, then skip four steps backward from each other returning to places in line (repeat)

Loudly he can play or low.

Each student hops four times on left foot while at the same time tapping the right toe on the floor (forward, side, back, close)

He can move you fast or slow.

Repeat with the right foot while tapping the left toe on the floor (forward, side, back, close)

Touch your hearts and stir your toe, Piping Tim of Galway.

Repeat four hops on left foot as above

Repeat four hops on right foot as above; add a clap on last beat

3. Repeat dance for second verse.

"Cielito Lindo"

Grades: 4–6

Cielito Lindo

Mexican Folk Song

Key: A
Starting pitch: A
Meter: 3/4, begins on 1

De la Sie - rra Mo - re - na, Cie - li - to Lin - do vie - nen ba - jan - do.____
From Si - er - ra Mo - re - na Cie - li - to Lin - do comes____ soft - ly steal - ing____

Un par de o - ji - tos ne - gros Cie - li - to Lin - do, de____ con - tra - ban - do.____
Laugh - ing eyes,____ black and ro - guish Cie - li - to Lin - do, Beau - ty re - veal - ing____

CHORUS

Ay,   ay,   ay,   ay,____   Can - ta y no llo - res.____   Por - que can - tan -
Sing   ban - ish   sor - row____   To   pass the hours____

- do se a - le - gran, Cie - li - to Lin - do, los____ co - ra - zo - nes.____
____ light - ly sing - ing Cie - li - to Lin - do glad - dens the mor - row.____

From *Heritage Songster* by Leon and Lynn Dallin, 2nd ed. (Dubuque, Iowa: Wm. C. Brown, Co., 1980).

PROCEDURES

1. Have students form a circle and join hands.

2. As students sing, have them perform the indicated actions or movements:

De la sierra Morena, Cielito Lindo vienen bajando,	Join hands and walk counterclockwise seven steps; on step eight change direction
Un par de ojitos negros Cielito Lindo, de contrabando.	Walk clockwise seven steps; stop on step eight and face center of circle
Ay, ay, ay, ay,	Take four steps to center, raising arms high
Canta y no llores,	Take four steps backward, lowering arms
Porque cantando se alegran,	Four (two boys, two girls) join right hands and circle four steps to right:

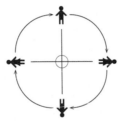

Cielito Lindo, los corazones.	Change hands (left hands); circle four steps to left

3. Repeat dance.

ADDITIONAL SINGING GAMES AND DANCES APPEARING IN OTHER AREAS OF THIS BOOK

- African game song "Tue, Tue," p. 408
- African game song "Kye, Kye Kule," p. 405
- African dance "Salamatu Bansa," pp. 407
- American Indian song "Mos' Mos'" and Round Dance, pp. 435–438
- American square dance, p. 441
- Greek dance, p. 429
- Spanish dance to "La Raspa," p. 443

QUESTIONS FOR REVIEW

1. Why is rhythm one of the basic elements of music?
2. In what ways is movement a natural response of children?
3. What does the phrase "Develop body awareness in space" mean?
4. How can movement be used to help with problem solving?
5. How can movement be used to teach imagery?
6. How can movement express musical concepts?
7. In what ways can movement interpret musical ideas?
8. What is folk dancing?
9. In what grades would you do movement (large/small, fast/slow) and in what grades would you do folk dancing?
10. Why is the word *dancing* difficult to use with fourth or fifth grade students?
11. What are some guidelines to follow in generating ideas and techniques for moving to music?
12. What is the difference between interpretative movement and movement reflective of musical concepts?
13. What are some of the advantages of linking dramatic movement with songs?
14. Who was Emile Jaques-Dalcroze and why is he important?
15. What experiences with movement would you choose for the musical concepts fast-slow and getting faster, getting slower for Grades K–2? for Grades 4–5?
16. Why is it important to include music and movement of other cultures in the elementary curriculum?
17. What do you need to do if students are to sing and move at the same time?
18. What is the difference between a "singing game" and a "dance"?
19. Can you name songs and movement that would be appropriate for Grade 1 but inappropriate for Grade 5? Give reasons for your answer.
20. Can you name songs and movement that would be appropriate for Grade 5 but inappropriate for Grade 1? Give reasons for your answer.

CREATIVE EXPERIENCES WITH MUSIC

Creating music can be an exciting and rewarding experience for students because it is a personal expression of their own feelings and ideas. Being involved in the creative process requires self-discipline, imagination, sensitivity, an understanding of the functions and possibilities of sounds, and the ability to organize materials into logical form. As students explore the realm of sound and focus their efforts on creating a musical work, they experience pleasure and satisfaction in having achieved a goal. Creating a musical composition requires students to use their current music skills and may motivate them to learn new ones.

As in all creative effort, a musical composition must begin with an idea. This may be generated out of a student's interest in innovative ways of creating sounds, mixing instrumental or vocal sounds with environmental sounds, writing a poem and setting it to music, creating a percussion accompaniment for a song, or expressing a dramatic idea or event. The teacher needs to encourage this type of creativity and at the same time set parameters for the musical effort being undertaken.

For instance, after being given an example of playing a drum by tapping the rim, students might be asked to explore three other ways of playing the drum (such as playing in the center of the drum with a drum stick, tapping the drum with fingers, or scratching the drumhead with fingernails). While students are given the opportunity to be creative, their activity has a focus. This is far more desirable than saying, "You have five minutes to play these instruments. Do anything you want to." With this course, chaos is sure to result. Without some sort of direction, it is impossible, for instance, for students to be successful in writing a song. They simply do not know where to begin.

This chapter is directed toward developing skills for creative musical experiences. Students need to (1) have many opportunities to develop techniques for improvising and organizing sounds; (2) produce and use a rich variety of sounds: vocal, instrumental, environmental, body, taped; and (3) create songs, song accompaniments, and musical compositions that express feelings and ideas. The following materials and suggestions may be adapted to planning creative musical experiences for students in Grades K–6.

THE ORFF APPROACH*

Carl Orff (1895–1982) was a German composer/educator who believed it is important that from the very beginning students *physically* experience beat, meter, and rhythm, and that they express these elements by dancing and playing instruments. While Orff agreed with Dalcroze's belief that rhythm is a foundation of musical growth, he developed an approach that begins with speech rhythms already known to the child, such as names and familiar words. These rhythms are used to create original pieces and accompaniment patterns. Orff believed that the study of traditional musical instruments should begin only when the learner can perform simple rhythms on percussion instruments or sing basic tonal patterns and intervals.

The pentatonic (five-note) scale was popular with Carl Orff, because it always gave a pleasant sound and students could not make any mistakes. In the Orff system children are asked to create melodies or accompaniments in major or minor tonalities only after they have learned to create melodies and accompaniments within the pentatonic scale.

Orff advocated asking children to create introductions, codas, and accompaniments for folk songs within the child's ethnic tradition. He designed percussion instruments of high quality to form an ensemble. Some of these instruments are the glockenspiel (soprano and alto), xylophones (soprano, alto, bass), metallophones (soprano, alto, bass), and various assorted drums, jingle bells, and jingle sticks.

The word *process* is paramount in Orff's system, and the keys to this process are *exploration* and *experience*. Students are encouraged to explore space, sound, form, and creativity. The most important instrument in the Orff approach is the body, followed by the voice. The Orff process at every maturity level includes movement, voice and instruments, and improvisation.

IMPROVISING AND ORGANIZING SOUNDS

Improvising involves creating something spontaneously at a given moment. Experiences in improvising rhythms, melodies, and musical forms contribute to a student's confidence and skill in singing, playing instruments, and moving to music, as well as to greater perception and understanding of music created by others. It is essential that the teacher lead students carefully from simple to more complex experiences and provide them with many opportunities to explore sounds (e.g., high/low, fast/slow). Guidelines for improvisation activities

---

* The material in this section is based on Lois Choksy, Robert Abramson, Avon Gillespie, and David Woods, *Teaching Music in the Twentieth Century* (Englewood Cliffs, N.J.: Prentice-Hall, 1986), pp. 96–103.

include providing a "frame" for the activity (examples: given a steady beat, students will improvise rhythm patterns; using only the black keys of the piano, students will improvise a melody). As students gain confidence in improvising with their voices and playing instruments, they will expand their understanding of music and find increased satisfaction and pleasure in the creative process. Following are some techniques for encouraging early experiences with improvisation.

1. Improvise rhythm patterns.
   a. Students keep a steady meter beat in duple meter:
      Pat knees or clap: 1 2 | 1 2 | 1 2 |
      Teacher claps:  to reinforce meter beat.

      As students maintain a steady beat, teacher improvises a different rhythm, such as

   b. Individual students improvise their own rhythm pattern as other students keep a steady beat, such as

   c. Repeat these procedures in triple meter.
2. Select a student to keep the steady beat on a drum. Ask individual students to improvise rhythm patterns on classroom instruments.

RHYTHM IN SPEECH

An excellent way to introduce children to rhythm is through speech patterns.

Suggestions for Lessons

1. Create word phrases and clap them in rhythm, then ask children to imitate. For example:

   Teacher:

   To - day is my birth - day

   Students imitate.

   Teacher:

   Write me a let - ter

   Students imitate.

2. Ask students to create other word phrases that fit a pattern. The pattern may be played by the teacher or a student. For example:

   Leader:

   Student:

   Word rhythms:

   San - ta Claus is com - ing

   Sum - mer time is com - ing

3. Ask students to create a short speech pattern and then a rhythm to go with it. For example:

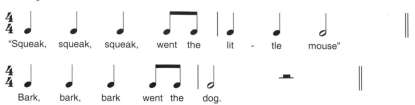

"Squeak, squeak, squeak, went the lit - tle mouse"

Bark, bark, bark went the dog.

4. Experiment with changing the number of beats in a measure according to a speech pattern:

I want to go swim - ming, swim - ming in the pool, in the pool.

5. Play a game in which one student says his or her name and a second student plays the rhythm on a percussion instrument. For example:

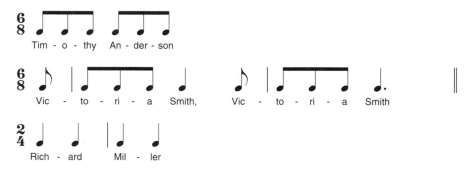

Tim - o - thy An - der - son

Vic - to - ri - a Smith, Vic - to - ri - a Smith

Rich - ard Mil - ler

RHYTHM SPEECH CANONS

A canon is a repeating form in which the same thing is sung or said at a precise interval of time.

Suggestions for Lessons

1. In the following geographic canon, have half the class begin and the second half enter one measure later. Speak the example as a rhythmic speech canon.

Geographic canon

New York, I - da - ho, Mass - a - chu - setts, Maine.

2. Try other types of canons, such as the winter and spring canons on the next page. You might wish to make up your own. Experiment with using instruments instead of your voice and try various types of movement for each measure.

Winter canon

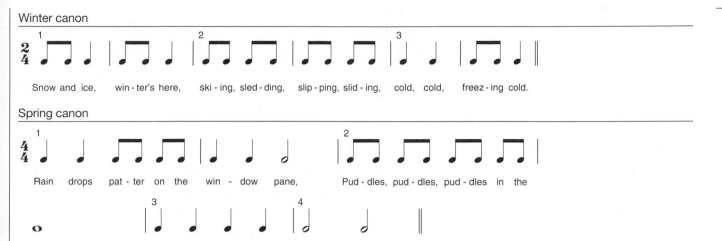

Snow and ice,   win-ter's here,   ski-ing, sled-ding,   slip-ping, slid-ing,   cold, cold,   freez-ing cold.

Spring canon

Rain   drops   pat-ter   on the   win-dow   pane,   Pud-dles, pud-dles, pud-dles   in   the

street.   Splish, splash, splish, splash,   Yuk,   Yuk.

IMPROVISING MELODIES

To improvise a melody, begin improvising using only two notes, such as sol-mi, or G-E (Scale: C D E G A). Create a rap based on these two notes and a set rhythm, such as

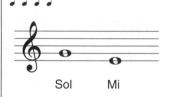

Sol   Mi

Improvise on "We are going to school today" or another phrase of your choice. The music may be different each time. For example:

We   are   go-ing   to   school   to-day

We   are go-ing   to   school   to-day

Try improvising on a three-note scale—sol-mi-la (G E A).

We   are go-ing   to   school   to-day

Next, using a five-note scale (pentatonic), ask students to improvise a melody to a speech pattern or speech canon they have composed.

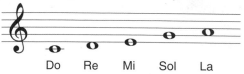

Do   Re   Mi   Sol   La

Play the song on any pitch, but perform to a set rhythm. Any combination of pitches will sound pleasing. For older students, add a freely composed rhythmic accompaniment on classroom percussion instruments. Be sure to keep a steady beat on some instrument, preferably a drum.

OSTINATO PATTERNS (RHYTHMIC AND MELODIC)

An *ostinato* is a melodic or rhythm pattern that is repeated throughout a song or larger musical composition.

Suggestions for Lessons

1. Following are some examples of simple ostinato patterns to "This Old Man." Combine several and play them on classroom instruments, thus creating a small ensemble. (Appropriate for Grades K–2.)

This Old Man

Key: F
Starting pitch: C
Meter: 2/4, begins on 1

2. Following are some ostinati accompaniments on a variety of instruments that can be used to accompany the song "Swing Low, Sweet Chariot." Try these accompaniments and then ask students to create their own ostinati for familiar songs. (This material can be adapted for Grades 3–6.)

Swing Low, Sweet Chariot

Key: F
Starting pitch: A
Meter: 4/4, begins on 4

Spiritual

Swing low, sweet char - i - ot___ com - ing for to car - ry me home. Swing___

low, sweet char - i - ot___ com - ing for to car - ry me home.
                               1. I
                               2. If
                               3. I'm

looked o - ver Jor - dan, and what did I see,___ com - ing for to car - ry me home? A
you get there be - fore I do, com - ing for to car - ry me home, tell
some - times up and some - times down, com - ing for to car - ry me home, but

band of an - gels com - ing af - ter me,___ com - ing for to car - ry me home.
all my friends I'm com - ing, too, com - ing for to car - ry me home.
still my soul feels heav - en - ly bound, com - ing for to car - ry me home.

Laura Wheeler and Lois Raebeck, *Orff and Kodaly Adapted for the Elementary School*, 3d ed. (Dubuque, Iowa: Wm. C. Brown, 1985), p. 272.

IMPROVISING AN ACCOMPANIMENT TO A SONG

Suggestions for Lessons: Grades 3–6

1. Play or sing the chorus of "This Land Is Your Land."
   Tap or clap the beat:

2. Play or sing the song and have students clap the following pattern:

3. Ask students to create other patterns that fit the song. Direct them to stay with the beat. Experiment with several patterns while singing the chorus. For example:

4. Explore the sound possibilities of playing these rhythms on classroom percussion instruments. Select a single instrument for the chorus and a second instrument for the verse. Have the class sing the song and students improvise a rhythmic accompaniment.

This Land Is Your Land

Words and Music by Woody Guthrie

Key: F
Starting pitch: F
Meter: Cut time, begins on "and" of 1

IMPROVING RHYTHMS WITH CLASSROOM INSTRUMENTS

Suggestions for Lessons: Grades K–2

1. Ask students to choose and demonstrate the sounds of classroom percussion instruments by playing simple rhythm patterns, such as

2. Determine instruments that can sustain a sound (such as tambourine and triangle) and those that cannot (such as wood block, rhythm sticks).

3. Divide the class into two groups. Assign Group 1 nonsustaining instruments. Assign Group 2 sustaining instruments.

4. Ask individual students in Group 1 to improvise a rhythm while keeping a steady beat. Give all students a chance to play. Repeat the procedure for Group 2.

5. Create a duet by selecting students from each group to improvise a rhythm together. For example:

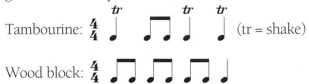

6. Experiment with rhythm in duple and triple meter. Have students who are not playing keep a steady beat, such as
Duple meter: Pat knees, clap
Triple meter: Pat knees, clap, clap

7. As students sing familiar songs, take turns improvising rhythm patterns.

CREATIVE EXPERIENCES WITH VOCAL SOUNDS

Perhaps the most personal and individual sound is the human voice. We can make our voices sound high, low, nasal, or guttural. We can sing any pitch within a one- to two-octave range, and intervals from eighth or quarter tones to skips of an octave or tenth. We can make our voice wail like a siren, bark like a dog, and sigh like the wind, and we can click, cluck, buzz, chirp, pop, and hiss. Almost unlimited vocal possibilities exist within our imaginations.

Suggestions for Lessons: Grades 4–6

1. Have students make a list of sounds that can be made by the human voice and perform them. Vary the pitch from high to low and the speed from fast to slow (tempo). Some suggestions are
   • Sighing
   • Whispering
   • Sneezing
   • Gurgling
   • Screaming

2. Have students use their voices to imitate or express an idea, such as
   - We're going to the circus tomorrow and I can hardly wait.
   - I'm a Martian from outer space.
   - Tonight's the night of Halloween. Boo!

3. Have students write a sentence and explore ways of saying it using different sounds. Possibilities for different sounds include
   - Whisper, shout
   - Shorten a word
   - Lengthen a word
   - Use a different pitch for each word
   - Accent selected words
   - Raise the pitch at the end of a sentence
   - Begin the sentence on a high pitch and end the sentence on a low pitch

4. Introduce a "whoop" sound, along with suggested notation, such as ⌐⌐.
   Ask students to create other ways of saying "whoop" and devise appropriate notation. Continue with other sounds, such as boom, tongue clicks, hiss, whistle.

5. Use four contrasting sounds that can be performed in a variety of ways, such as a high-pitched sound on "Whoop" (may be said/sung on a pitch with a swoop upward—siren effect); a low, heavy sound (poom-poom or boom-boom); tongue clicks with a variety of pitch levels; or hissing sounds (both short and long). Have students organize each set of sounds into a short pattern and perform it. Create symbols expressive of the sounds and use as notation. For example:

Whoop	⌐⌐	Boom	▬ ▬ ▬
Whistle	∿↘	Tongue clicks	× × ×
Siren (whoo)	∿∿	Hiss	Ŝss

CREATIVE EXPERIENCES WITH INSTRUMENTAL SOUNDS

Exploring instrumental sounds involves not only traditional ways of creating sounds (such as playing the keys of a piano or blowing a horn) but also imaginative and nontraditional ways (such as plucking the strings of a piano). You may use not only Western classical instruments but also folk instruments such as the Autoharp, guitar, ukelele, banjo, and dulcimer. If available, explore the sounds of non-Western instruments (Japanese koto, African dono drum, African agogo bells). Encourage students to experiment with a variety of instrumental sounds and to create their own melodies, rhythms, textures, tone colors, and musical forms.

Suggestions for Lessons: Grades 3–6

1. Ask students to explore ways of playing the Autoharp, such as strumming strings with a plastic card, an eraser, fingers, or finger picks; tapping strings with hard and soft mallets; or placing metallic objects (paper clips) underneath the chord bars and sliding a finger along string.

FOLLOW THE LEADER

Joy E. Lawrence

This box contains some icons that might be used with the voice in creating a round.

There are 4 counts to a block, 16 to a line. Divide the class into four groups. Group 1 begins on line 1. When Group 1 begins line 2, Group 2 starts line 1; when Group 1 begins line 3 and Group 2 line 2, Group 3 begins line 1, and so on.

Line 1 (16 counts)	Whoop, whoop, whistle	Whoop, whoop, whistle	Siren	Whoop, whoop, whoop, pause
Line 2 (16 counts)	Boom Boom Boom, Boom boom boom boom, boom boom boom, boom boom	BOOM BOOM BOOM BOOM	Boom Boom Boom Boom Boom Boom Boom Boom Boom Boom	BOOM BOOM BOOM BOOM
Line 3 (16 counts)	Tongue clicks (high/low at random)	Two high clicks, two low clicks	Tongue clicks	High clicks, low clicks
Line 4 (16 counts)	Sssss— Hiss............	SsSsSs Hiss Hiss Hiss	Sssss— Hiss............	SsSsSs Hiss Hiss Hiss
Rhythm pulse:	1 2 3 4	1 2 3 4	1 2 3 4	1 2 3 4

Group 1 performs lines 1–4 two times.
Group 2 performs lines 1–4, then repeats 1–3.
Group 3 performs lines 1–4, then repeats 1–2.
Group 4 performs lines 1–4 once only.

2. Divide the class into small groups. Assign an instrument (such as Autoharp, drums, xylophone, piano) to each group. Ask students to experiment with producing at least four different sounds on each instrument. Decide which sounds are similar among the instruments (if any) and which are the most contrasting. Organize the sounds into duple or triple rhythmic patterns and perform in a sequence, alternating timbre and meter.

First Sound	Second Sound	Third Sound	Fourth Sound
Autoharp	Drums	Xylophone	Piano

(Rhythmic notation in four rows: 3/4, 2/4, 3/4, 4/4 meters with quarter notes, eighth notes, dotted rhythms, and half notes distributed across the four instrument columns.)

3. Divide students into small groups and assign to each a class of instruments (tambourines, jingle sticks; rhythm sticks, wood block; bongo drums, hand drums; maracas, castanets). Tell them to discover at least three ways of creating short sounds and three ways of creating long sounds. Ask each group to demonstrate for the class.

4. Have students explore ways of creating new sounds on the piano (plucking strings, tapping strings with hand in both upper and lower register, using a pencil to "zip" up or down the strings). Play "The Banshee" by Henry Cowell* and ask students to describe some of the unusual sounds.

5. Have students create a musical composition in the form of a rondo: ABACA. Be sure to keep a steady beat and strong sense of rhythm. For example:

Section A:

Piano swoops (ad lib.)

Continues throughout A section

---

*"The Banshee" can be found in *Music and You* (Macmillan Grade 3, Record 2). It is also available on Smithsonian Folkways, CD SF40801.

Section B: Improvise from musical materials such as plucking strings, tapping strings with hand or mallet, "zipping" up or down strings with pencil. Keep a steady beat alternating tone colors and texture (thick/thin). Continue for eight beats.

Section A repeats.

Section C: Improvise from the musical materials but confine sounds to the low register of the piano. Hold pedal down to create blurred sounds. Continue for eight beats.

Section A repeats and gradually gets softer as piece ends.

CREATIVE EXPERIENCES WITH ENVIRONMENTAL SOUNDS

The raw material of music is *sound.* Sounds in our environment often go unnoticed; yet, if we pause to listen, there are many, each with a tone quality and rhythm all its own. Increasing perception of environmental sounds and how they can be used to create a musical composition can be a significant and enriching experience for students.

Suggestions for Lessons: Grades 4–6

1. Ask the class to be completely silent and listen to the sounds around them (clock ticking, a locker door slamming, bird chirping, jet airplane, car engine, coins dropping on the floor, animal sounds). Discuss which of these sounds is long, short, high, low, legato, staccato, loud, soft.

2. Ask students to bring in a written description of the area they pass through on their way to school, along with sound-producing materials to express appropriate sounds—for example, a factory district: whistle, machinery sounds (metal pipes), car horn. See the example in the box on the next page. Discuss differences between sounds produced and heard in the morning and those in the afternoon.

3. Decide on sounds and sound materials you wish to use in the musical composition. Create picture notation for each sound. Place all sounds into a time frame of four beats (see the example in the box).

CREATIVE EXPERIENCES WITH BODY SOUNDS

Another category of sounds are those produced through body percussion. These include such sounds as clapping, tapping, patting, pounding, stamping, and snapping. Sometimes, when only the hands are used, body percussion is referred to as "hand jive." Many times body sounds are used in combination with vocal sounds or in combination with movement. Thus, students might walk in a circle and then stand still and clap a rhythm.

FACTORY DISTRICT IN SOUND

Rhonda Williams

A few blocks from my house are a lot of big factories. They are in operation all day and all night. The early morning and late evening hours are quiet. There is always a light motor hum heard in the morning. After a while, the people begin to come to work. At first there are just a few, then more and more report for work. Occasionally you hear a car horn blow in the parking lot, and greetings of one to another. As the morning continues, the sounds from the factory become louder and more intense, spreading from section to section. In addition, there are sounds of people in the street. At the end of the day, there is a whistle signifying the end of one shift and the beginning of another. Then there is a gradual slowing down of machinery in the factory, since not as many workers are employed on the evening shift. Gradually the parking lot empties of cars and the factory sounds return to the quiet hum of evening.

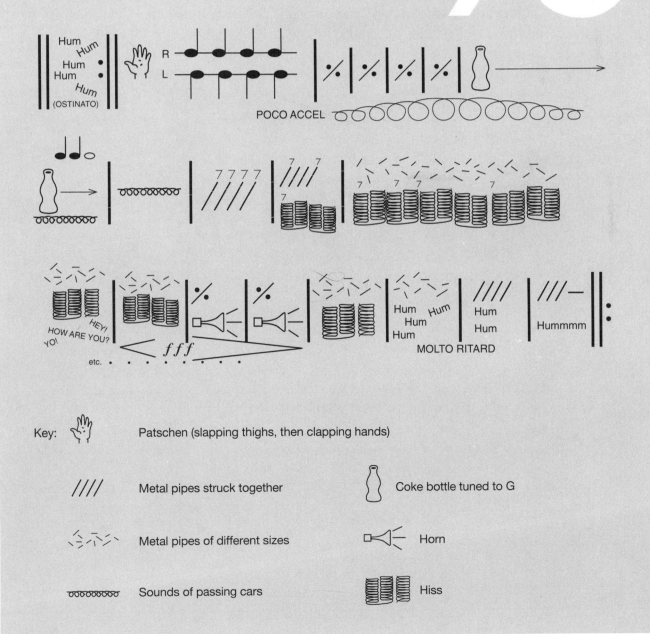

Key:

Patschen (slapping thighs, then clapping hands)

//// Metal pipes struck together

Coke bottle tuned to G

Metal pipes of different sizes

Horn

Sounds of passing cars

Hiss

Suggestions for Lessons: Grades 3–5

1. Ask students to experiment with five ways of using their bodies to make a sound (clap, snap, stamp, slap, tap).

2. Select a rhythm pattern for each sound and have students perform it. For example:

3. Perform two sounds together, such as slap-clap (patschen):

4. Discuss which sounds are heavy and which are light. Experiment with a variety of combinations. Always perform to a steady beat in either duple or triple meter.

5. Sing the Italian folk song "Funiculi, Funicula." Discover the contrasting phrases and "echo" phrases. Ask students to create body sounds for the first half of the song and a second set of sounds for the chorus.

Italian Folk Song

Key: C
Starting pitch: G
Meter: 6/8, begins on 6

CREATING A VIDEO

Suggestions for Lessons: Grades 3–6

1. Listen to the first four variations of Pachelbel's Canon in D.*
2. Decide how the composer created each variation—a high part (called a descant), broken chords in the bass, and so on.
3. Listen to the first four variations again and ask students which variation they would like to be.
4. Divide your class into four groups, each with a tape recorder and a cassette tape containing their chosen variation. Be sure there are not more than five students in each group. If your class is large, you may want to have more groups and cassette tapes.
5. Assign an activity to each group (Group 1—hands or fingers walking; Group 2—using string; Group 3—feet; Group 4—sunflowers, and so on).
6. Ask each group to go into a separate corner of the room or into another space, such as the hall or a vacant room. Each group of five students should listen to its segment and then create a movement that matches the musical variation.
7. Each group should determine what "props" it needs and bring them on a subsequent day (the next day is best).
8. Each group practices the particular variation using the props and activities they have decided on.
9. After each group practices the selected variation, bring students back together and make a sample videotape using a camcorder. Show the tape and allow groups time to make any changes.
10. Make a final videotape using a new tape and an *experienced* camcorder operator. Students like to view their creation.

Caution: This project takes time and cannot be hurried. Often there is organized confusion. Allow at least two weeks (a half-hour per day) to make the musical video. While this project is time consuming, it is well worth the effort.

CREATING A PERCUSSION ACCOMPANIMENT TO A SONG

It is essential in rhythmic experiences to establish the tempo (speed of the beat); early on students must feel and be able to clap (or move) to a steady beat. As students create rhythm patterns to accompany songs, they will need to develop techniques for playing and notating the rhythms.

---

* *The Pachelbel Canon,* RCA Victor 65468-2-RC (there are also many others to choose from).

Suggestions for Lessons: Grades 3–6

Try the following experiences with the African folk song "Tue, Tue" (p. 408):

1. Teach the song "Tue, Tue."
2. Have students tap their knees and clap the beats (duple meter: 1 2 1 2).
3. Decide on an instrument to play the beats, and notate. For example:

4. Explore rhythms that might fit the duple meter and play them on a variety of instruments. Make your choice and notate. For example:

Write as a percussion score:

CREATING A PERCUSSION COMPOSITION

Suggestions for Lessons: Grades 4–6

1. Ask students to improvise a variety of rhythmic patterns in duple or triple meter.
2. Select four different patterns for use in the composition.
3. Discuss how you can extend a composition by repeating an idea or provide interest and variety with a contrasting idea. For example:

4. Have students practice clapping each pattern.

5. Decide on instruments to be used for each pattern. For example:

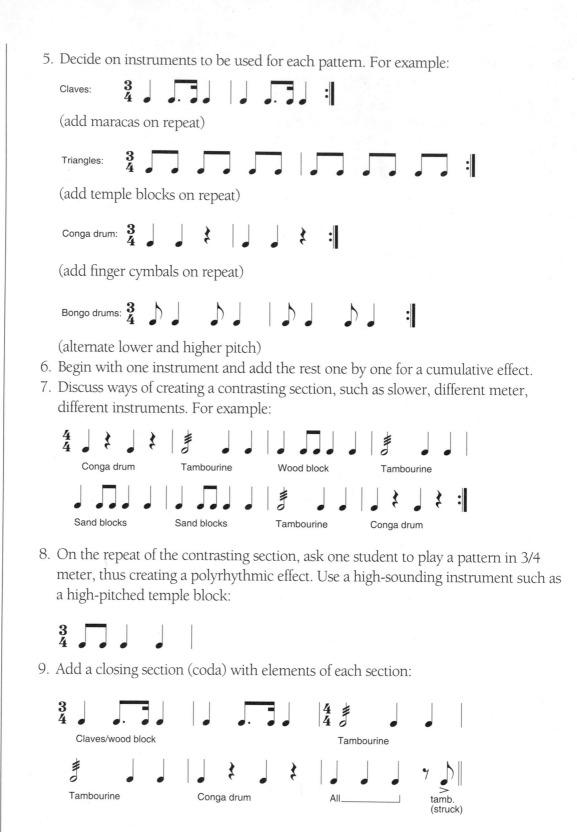

(add maracas on repeat)

(add temple blocks on repeat)

(add finger cymbals on repeat)

(alternate lower and higher pitch)

6. Begin with one instrument and add the rest one by one for a cumulative effect.

7. Discuss ways of creating a contrasting section, such as slower, different meter, different instruments. For example:

8. On the repeat of the contrasting section, ask one student to play a pattern in 3/4 meter, thus creating a polyrhythmic effect. Use a high-sounding instrument such as a high-pitched temple block:

9. Add a closing section (coda) with elements of each section:

CREATIVE EXPERIENCES WITH WRITING MELODIES OR SONGS

Writing an original melody or song involves students in synthesizing their total response to music. It is a major means for developing concepts about melody, rhythm, meter, harmony, and form, as well as for providing opportunities for creating expressive and formal relationships between words and music. All children create melodies. Just listen to them at play and you will hear them sing many chants and short melodic phrases.

As students create melodies or songs, they become involved as composers, performers, and listeners. Musical growth occurs as they become aware of possibilities for sound exploration and pattern development and use these in expressive ways. While the process of composing is most important, the student should also be guided to achieve as expressive a product as possible.

WHAT MAKES AN INTERESING MELODY?

Essentially, two elements contribute to a successful and interesting melody: repetition and contrast. A melody must also have a sense of coming to a rest or close. This discussion focuses on writing a song melody; however, the guiding principles may be used for writing instrumental melodies as well.

The use of repetition can extend the length of a melody, emphasize certain words, create rhythmic interest, and provide unity. Contrast can be achieved by such techniques as alternating melodic skips and steps, changing the direction of the melodic line, changing rhythms, and creating contrasting sections. If a melody is to be sung, one must also consider the range and its appropriateness for a given maturity level.

PREPARING STUDENTS TO WRITE MELODIES OR SONGS

Suggestions for Lessons: Grades 3–6

1. Have the students sing many songs and play classroom instruments to develop a feeling for tonality, rhythm patterns, tone color, and pitch.
2. Help students develop a sense of tonality and beat. Students in Grades 4–6 should be encouraged to write out their responses in rhythm notation.
3. Sing or play a short phrase. Ask students to improvise a second phrase in the same meter, ending on the tonic (keynote of the scale). Explore in several keys, such as G, D, and F. For example:

4. Sing or play melody patterns and ask students to repeat (a) exactly, then (b) as a sequence (beginning on different pitches). For example:

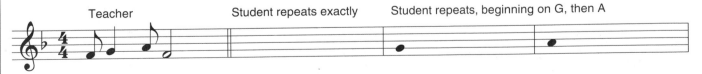

5. Sing or play rhythms and ask students to improvise a response. For example:

Teacher   Student improvises response

6. Sing or play a familiar melody and ask students to create ways of changing it, such as repeating a phrase, adding notes, or changing the rhythm. For example:
Original melody (phrase):

Adding notes, changing rhythm:

Adding notes above and below:

Changing the meter from duple to triple:

Changing the tonality from major to minor:

WRITING A MELODY USING A PENTATONIC SCALE

It is easy to write a melody based on the pentatonic (five-note) scale because every combination will be satisfying to the ear. Some melodies, however, will be more interesting than others.

Suggestions for Lessons: Grades 4–6

1. Have students select a rhythm pattern and improvise a melody. When they have one they like, have them place the notation on a staff. It might look something like this (black keys only):

2. Help students explore the tonal possibilities of other pentatonic scales, such as:

3. Add rhythms appropriate to grade level, such as:

First grade:

Fifth grade:

WRITING A MELODY USING A SEVEN-NOTE SCALE (MAJOR/MINOR)

1. Prepare a handout with (1) a staff showing the C major scale and (2) a staff with a rhythm pattern above it.

2. Tell students to begin on the first note of the C scale (C) and end on the last note (C). Use each pitch only once and place the pitches beneath the rhythm pattern. For example:

do	mi	sol	fa	re		la	ti		do
1	3	5	4	2		6	7		8
C	E	G	F	D		A	B		C

3. Choose a label (syllable, number, or letter) and name each note.
4. Play or sing the four-measure melodies of several students. Discuss the most interesting ones.
5. Experiment with a variety of rhythms for the melodies. Repeat a pitch when necessary to make the melody "fit" the rhythm.

6. Transpose the four-measure melody into different keys, both major and minor. For example:

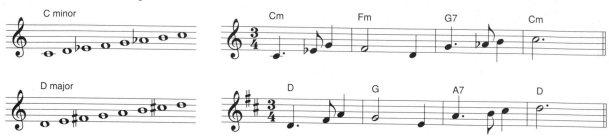

7. Review melodies previously learned (see the box on standard forms, next page) for ideas of what other composers have done.

8. Create a melody of eight measures. Measures 1–4 should end on the dominant (fifth tone of the scale) and measures 5–8 should end on the tonic (first tone of the scale). For example:

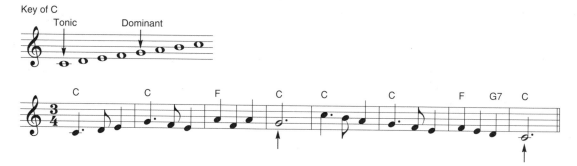

9. Add chords (C, F, G₇) and accompany on the Autoharp. Sing melody on "doo-be-doo" or play on recorders. Explore the possibilities of creating an AB or ABA form by adding a contrasting melody.

SETTING A POEM TO MUSIC

Students in Grades 4–6 will enjoy creating original music to a short poem. The procedure is outlined as follows:

Suggestions for Lessons: Grades 4–6

1. Select a favorite poem of the students and explore some rhythm possibilities suggested by the text. For example:

Firefly*
A little light is going by,
Is going up to see the sky,
A little light with wings.

I never could have thought of it,
To have a little bug all lit,
And made to go on wings.

---

* Elizabeth Madox Roberts, *Under the Tree* (New York: Viking Press, 1950). Reprinted by permission.

STANDARD MELODY FORMS

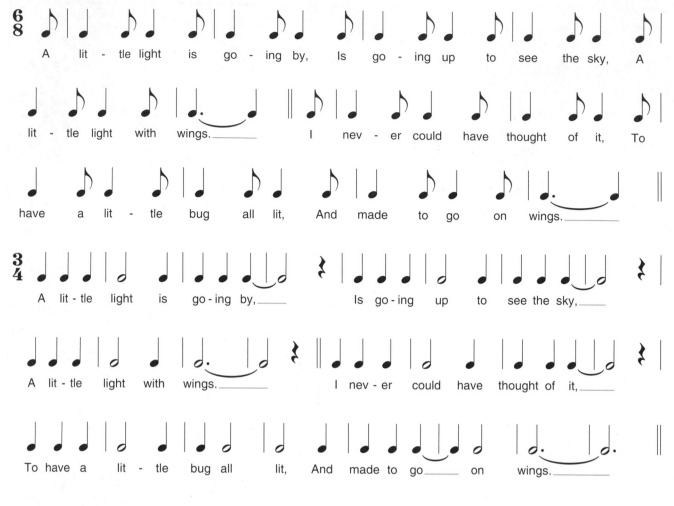

2. Using either duple or triple meter, explore some other rhythm ideas using the same poem.

3. Reread the text of the poem. Consider the following:
   a. Appropriate directions for the melody
   b. Words or phrases that might be repeated
4. Use melody bells and ask students to explore various pitch and rhythm combinations of the pentatonic scale for each phrase assigned. Suggest that they might repeat words or add more than one note per syllable. Limit the range of the melody to one octave. For example:

Pentatonic scale used in the song "Firefly"

 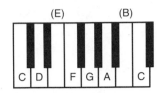

Let the meaning of the words, the rhythm patterns, and the concepts of repetition and contrast be your guide.

5. Provide a transparency with a music staff for each group. Have them write the words beneath the staff and then the corresponding pitches and rhythms above. Each group performs a phrase for the class. Students should make changes in the melody or rhythm of each phrase until they are satisfied with their song.

6. Place the entire song on the transparency and sing.

7. Use the same procedure to explore other types of tonal organization (for example, major, minor); however, be sure that these songs end on the tonic (keynote of the scale).

8. After the song has been completed, add a percussion accompaniment. You may want to create a short introduction and a closing section (coda) to extend the composition. For example:

Introduction: Begin with xylophone (two measures), add wood block (two measures), and triangle (two measures).

Coda: All three instruments join in (two measures), then wood block and triangle (two measures), then just triangle (one measure).

Firefly

Key: pentatonic
Starting pitch: F
Meter: 4/4, begins on "and" of 4

Music by Joy E. Lawrence
Words by Elizabeth Madox Roberts

A lit - tle light___ is go - ing by,___ is go - ing by,___ is go - ing by,___ is

go - ing up___ to see the sky, A lit - tle light___ with___ wings. I nev - er could have

thought of it.___ To have a lit - tle bug all lit___ And made to go___ on___ wings.

From *Under the Tree* by Elizabeth Madox Roberts. Copyright 1922 by B. W. Huebsch, Inc. Copyright renewed 1950 by Ivor S. Roberts. Copyright 1930 by The Viking Press, Inc. Copyright renewed 1958 by Ivor S. Roberts. Reprinted by permission of Viking Penguin Inc.

WRITING AN ORIGINAL POEM AND SETTING IT TO MUSIC

Suggestions for Lessons: Grades 4–6

1. Choose a subject for a poem, such as nature, an event, an idea, or a person. Be sure that it has a strong rhythmic pulse. Following is an example of a poem (later set to music) by a fifth and sixth grade class:*

   We're America's children and we're here to celebrate.
   Living, learning and growing in a land that's really great.
   Our land consists of different people each unique in his own way,
   It matters not if you're short or tall, black or white, great or small—
   We're America's children and we're here to celebrate.
   Living, learning and growing in a land that's really great,
   We all have a chance to see, to be the best that we can be,
   Sing it loud, sing it proud, really great, celebrate.
   America, we love you.

2. After you have written a poem, mark the rhythmic pulses above the text. If necessary, adapt or change the text to fit this pulse:

       /   /   /   /   /   /   /   /
   We're A-mer-i-ca's | chil-dren and we're | here to cel-e- | brate. |
       /   /   /   /   /   /   /   /
   Liv-ing, learn-ing and | grow-ing in a | land that's real-ly | great, Our |
       /   /   /   /   /   /   /   /
   land con-sists of dif-f'rent | people, each u-|nique in his own | way. It |

---

* Written for the eightieth birthday celebration of the Cleveland Heights–University Heights School System, Ohio, 1982.

/ / / / / / / / /
mat-ters not if you're | short or tall, | black or white, | great or | small, |
/ / / / / / / /
We're A-mer-i-ca's | chil-dren and we're | here to cel-e-| brate |
/ / / / / / / /
Liv-ing, learn-ing and | grow-ing in a | land that's real-ly | great, We |
/ / / / / / / /
all have a | chance, you see, to | be the best that | we can be |
/ / / / / / / /
Sing it loud, | Sing it proud, | real-ly great, | cel-e-brate |
/ / / / / /
A-mer-i-ca, | we love | you. |

3. Before you begin composing the melody, note the repeated phrases (such as "We're America's children and we're here to celebrate. Living, learning, and growing in a land that's really great"). You will want to use the same melody for each.

4. Select a key (such as the key of C) and write the pitches on the chalkboard.

5. Experiment with different rhythm patterns within the two-pulse tempo beat and then notate your choice.

6. Using the pitches of your chosen scale, explore various tonal patterns and create a melody for each phrase. For example:

7. When you have completed the song, add accompaniment. Simple chords played on the Autoharp or guitar might be appropriate, or perhaps a music teacher could arrange a piano accompaniment.

We're America's Children

Dolores Blackburn
Taylor School
5–6 grade classes 1982

Key: C
Starting pitch: C
Meter: 4/4, begins on 1

QUESTIONS FOR REVIEW

1. Who was Carl Orff? What were his primary contributions in teaching music to children?

2. Why is it difficult to use the same creative activities for Grade 5 as you might use for Grade 1? Give a musical example.

3. Students in magnet schools for the arts or students who have a great deal of musical talent are very creative. They also get bored easily. Why do you think this is so?

4. What is a logical sequence to learning how to improvise?

5. What kinds of problems do you encounter when you tell students to make up a piece in ABA form?

6. What is the difference between playing by note and improvising a response?

7. Is the process or the product more important or are they of equal importance? What other ideas do you have?

8. What is rhythmic speech? Give a musical example.

9. What is a canon?

10. What is an ostinato pattern?

11. What does the term pentatonic mean?

12. Why is it better to begin improvising using only two notes rather than five notes? Which two would you choose and why?

13. What is a "frame of reference" and why is it important in creating music?

14. What differences can be identified in vocal sounds? Instrumental sounds? Environmental sounds? Body percussion sounds?

15. What are some ways you could create a percussion accompaniment to "La Raspa"? To "When the Saints Go Marching In"? To "This Land Is Your Land"?

16. What steps should be followed in creating a melody? Is it possible to do this with students in Grades K-3 as well as students in Grades 4–6? What kinds of problems do you encounter at each level? What kinds of advantages do you encounter at each level?

INTEGRATING MUSIC WITH THE STUDY OF PEOPLES, PLACES, AND CULTURES

Students today are truly living in an international age. Almost every day they encounter cultures from other areas of the world through television, radio, movies, books, or magazines. Through new technology in communications satellites, a single part of our globe can be in almost instant contact with another. In many regions of our country, children are also coming to know large numbers of foreign peoples who now permanently reside in the United States. From its beginnings, our country has been a refuge for peoples from throughout the world, and demographic surveys of the United States today quickly reveal that while we are indeed one nation, we comprise many cultures.

American schools traditionally have encouraged study and appreciation of different cultural groups. Social studies, geography, and history curricula have directed attention to the contributions of many peoples of the world, and teachers at every grade level have sought to bring multicultural viewpoints to their classrooms. Reflecting this concern for keeping in touch with the international age in which we live, teachers have increasingly endeavored to present a greater variety of music representative of many different cultural groups. This trend has paralleled the work of music scholars, who have documented that music is a worldwide phenomenon occurring among all known peoples.

We now know that our planet contains a number of highly developed musical systems of which the European-American classical tradition is just one. Such findings have clearly challenged many traditionally held views. Today it is evident that while music is an international phenomenon, it most certainly is not an international "language." Music systems in other areas of the world are often constructed in very different ways from our own. If we wish to understand these musics, we must learn how they are constructed. Thus, one of the primary objectives in studying a variety of musics is to help students understand that there are many *different but equally logical* ways for organizing sonic events.

This chapter is devoted to providing music experiences for the classroom from selected places or cultures of the world. We will begin in Africa, move to Asia and Europe, and then to the Americas. For each of these large continental geographic areas, musical examples and teaching strategies are provided. While the experiences suggested may serve as a basis for musical study alone, the intent is to help children perceive music as interrelated with other aspects of culture. Thus, as students study some examples of traditional Japanese music, they will also study other aspects of Japanese life and culture. Children enjoy learning about other peoples of the world, their customs and crafts, and their architecture, dance, literature, painting, sculpture, and music. Through an integrated study of many aspects of a culture, children develop new and important understandings of other peoples. They begin to realize the integral place of the arts in other world societies. Many teachers have also found that a combined study showing the interrelationships of culture and arts significantly enhances a child's interest in investigating and performing music.

SOME SUGGESTED CLASSROOM EXPERIENCES

Along with studying the musics of various ethnic groups, you may wish to introduce the cultural backgrounds through the following:

1. Prepare a bulletin board on each country studied. Place a map on the board and have the students use pins to "tag" the major cities, mountains, rivers, deserts, and so on. Have the students look for pictures of people, examples of the visual arts (architecture, sculpture, painting, dance, puppet theater), and photos of musicians. Arrange them in an attractive design on the board.

2. Invite guests from various countries and ethnic groups to speak to the class. Ask them to bring "native" items (especially musical instruments) to show to the students.

3. Show films on different peoples and cultures.

4. Take a field trip to a museum to see examples of the visual arts of various cultural groups.

5. Investigate the beliefs of various groups. For example, Buddhism is a major religion in China and Japan. Have the class explore the topic "What does it mean to be a Buddhist?"

6. Ask the physical education teacher to help teach dances from various cultures.

7. Have the students look for stories from the various areas being studied. Read them in class and perhaps plan short dramatizations.

8. Plan imaginary trips to different countries. Make an itinerary of things you hope to see and do.

9. Have your school plan a Multicultural or International Festival. Include dress, dance, visual arts, food, and music.

MUSIC OF AFRICAN PEOPLES

BACKGROUND INFORMATION FOR THE CLASS

Africa is the second largest continent in the world (see Figure 10.1), with a land mass stretching approximately 3,500 miles from north to south and almost 2,000 miles from east to west, an area approximately equal to Europe, China, and the United States combined.

The continent contains some of the most diverse land in the world. Its vast stretches of terrain contain the world's largest desert (Sahara) and longest waterway (Nile River). Dense rain forests, receiving up to 8 feet of precipitation each year, result in vegetation so lush that the sun is almost totally obscured, while in bitterly cold regions such as the mountain peaks of the Atlas and Ruwenzori ranges, snow falls for most of the year.

Africa is characterized by enormous ethnic diversity, which is clearly evident in the many countries and languages on the continent. Some ethnic groups, such as the Bantu, who reside in a number of countries south of the equator, primarily raise cattle and cultivate the land. Other groups, such as the Sudanese living between the equator and the Sahara, have built large metropolitan areas. One of the most powerful influences to affect the continent resulted from the development of Islam and the migration of the Arabic peoples along the northern and eastern areas of the continent.

Figure 10.1. Africa

SOME GENERAL CHARACTERISTICS OF AFRICAN MUSIC

A great variety of music is found throughout the African continent. Music is a part of almost every aspect of life from birth to death. It is closely tied to festivals, work, politics, courtship, and recreation. Multi-art productions involving music, dance, and drama (with the latter two often involving brilliant visual effects in costuming and masks) frequently occur throughout the continent.

Because of the vast geographical and cultural differences on the continent, one can expect a considerable amount of diversity in music. The following general outline identifies characteristics of African music south of the Sahara and provides a resource for organizing a study of music for the classroom. It should be noted, however, that these are general characteristics, and that there are regions where a particular characteristic may not be present. The following list of characteristics is designed as an introductory guide to some of the features that make African music distinct among musical systems of the world.

1. Much music is communal and functional; it is often associated with dance and games. While there are some exceptions, the emphasis is on group rather than solo performance.

2. Melodies are often short; longer melodies are often composed of short phrase units. A variety of scales are used: four-, five-, six-, and seven-note scales are common; intervals are predominantly seconds and thirds. Melodies tend to be syllabic.

3. There is a strong beat in much music—often a "driving," pulsating beat with steady tempo throughout. Polyrhythms and syncopation predominate.

4. Texture is both monophonic and polyphonic. Harmony occurs in thirds, fourths, fifths, sixths; thirds are most common. Both stratification of melodic-rhythmic lines and imitation are common.

5. Form is often related to function (e.g., game songs, work songs); the call-and-response form is prevalent. The use of ostinato (repetition of melodies and rhythms) is common.

6. Timbre is characterized by a wide variety of tone colors in the voice. There is generally an open, relaxed quality in singing, while there is a "buzzy" quality in some instruments (xylophone and mbira).

7. Many percussion, stringed, and wind instruments are used; percussion instruments predominate. Music is dominated by percussion quality; individual tones are attacked strongly; stringed instruments are most often plucked. An important xylophone tradition is present.

TEACHING AFRICAN MUSIC: SUGGESTIONS FOR LESSONS*

The overall goal of the suggestions for lessons on African music that follow is to acquaint students with some of the many types of vocal and instrumental music present on the continent and to have them study these types in terms of the elements of music: melody, rhythm, texture, timbre, and form. Objectives are given for each of the lesson suggestions, along with performance and listening selections, some of which are coordinated with dance.

A number of songs are included in the lessons, and it is suggested that they be taught by

---

* In designing lessons for different school settings, you may wish to rearrange the order of materials and teaching strategies given.

rote. Teachers will need to practice the pronunciation of texts before presenting the pieces to the class.

African instruments, such as the mbira, can be purchased in a number of music stores. Where authentic instruments are not available, suggestions for substitutes are given. Teachers and students may also wish to make some instruments, such as drums.

"Kye, Kye Kule" and "Twa-Mu-Sanga"

Grades: 1–2

OBJECTIVES
Students will
1. Be introduced to some geographical characteristics of the continent of Africa.
2. Perform the song "Kye, Kye Kule," add dance movements, and identify the following musical characteristics: short melodic phrases, five-tone or pentatonic scale, syncopation, and call-and-response form.
3. Perform the song "Twa-Mu-Sanga," and identify its musical characteristics: short phrases, "undulating" shape of melody, medium range, and syllabic nature of melody.

Kye, Kye Kule

Ghana

Starting pitch: F
Meter: 4/4, begins on 1

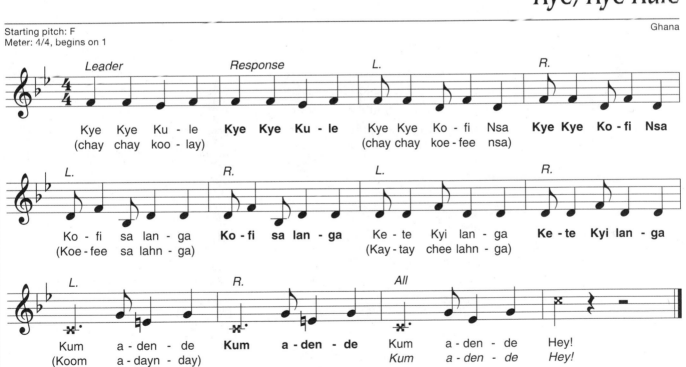

Mona Lowe, *Singing Games from Ghana*, © 1970. By permission of MM Publications, 19603 Jacob, Cerritos, California.

Twa-Mu-Sanga

Starting pitch: D
Meter: 2/4, begins on 1

Twa - mu - sa - nga ng'a - zi - na;   twa - mu - sa - nga ng'a - lo - ga!

Joseph Kyagambiddwa, *African Music from the Source of the Nile* (New York: Frederick Praeger, 1955), p. 107.

MATERIALS

- Globe or map of the world
- Rattle or shekere (pronounced shā-kă-rāy)

PROCEDURES

1. Using a globe or map, have the students find the continent of Africa, then have them locate various countries on the continent. Have them compare the countries in size with each other and with the United States.

2. Have the class perform "Kye, Kye Kule."
   a. Sing the song in call-and-response style, with the leader singing the first portion of the melody and the group providing the response. This is especially good in teaching tone-matching skills.
   b. This song generally accompanies dance. Use the following gestures to accompany the dance: Hands placed on top of the head ("Kye, Kye Kule"), hands placed on top of the shoulders ("Kye, Kye Kofi Nsa"), hands on the waist ("Kofi sa langa"), hands on the knees ("Kete Kyi langa"), hands on the ankles ("Kum adende"). Children should let their bodies sway in time to the music.
   c. Call attention to some of the important musical characteristics:
      - Short melodic phrases passed back and forth in *call-and-response* form
      - Five-tone or *pentatonic* scale:

      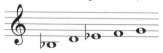

      - Syncopation (third measure):

3. Have the students sing "Twa-Mu-Sanga."
   a. Clap the beat as you sing.
   b. Follow the beat with a rattle. If you do not have an African rattle (shekere), use a maraca or make your own rattle.
   c. Notice how the song you are singing repeats over and over. This repeating melody is known as an *ostinato*. Much African music uses ostinato form.

d. While singing ask the students to move their arms in an arch to indicate the two phrases in the piece. Are the phrases short or long?

Length of phrases

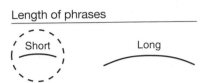

e. Have the students "draw" an outline of the melody. Then ask them to look at these melodic shapes and choose one that most closely matches their drawings:

Melodic shapes

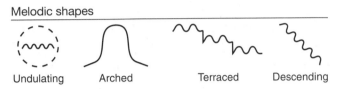

f. Ask: What is the *range* of the melody? In your drawing did you move a large distance or a small distance between the lowest and highest points?

Ranges

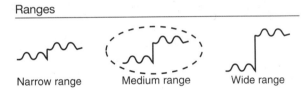

g. Have the class sing the song again, particularly noticing the relationship between notes and text.

Many notes to   *or*   One note per
one syllable   syllable

                    (circle one)

"Salamatu Bansa" and "Tue, Tue"

Grades: 3–4

Salamatu Bansa

Kwasi Aduonum

Starting pitch: G
Meter: 2/4, begins on "and" of 2

Tue, Tue

Starting pitch: C
Meter: 4/4, begins on 1

Ghana

Tu - e Tu - e   ba - ri - ma   tu - e tu - e   Tu - e tu - e   ba - ri - ma
(Too - ay Too - ay   ba - ree - ma   too - ay too - ay   Too - ay too - ay   ba - ri - ma)

tu - e tu - e   A - bo - fra   ba A - ma da - wa da - wa   tu - e tu - e   A - bo - fra
(too - ay too - ay   A - boe - fra   bah Ah - mah dah - wah dah - wah   too - ay too - ay   A - boe - fra)

ba A - ma da - wa da - wa   tu - e tu - e Hai ba - ri - ma   tu - e tu - e Hai ba - ri - ma
(bah Ah - mah dah - wah dah - wah   too - ay too - ay Hey ba - ree - ma   too - ay too - ay Hey ba - ree - ma)

Mona Lowe, *Singing Games from Ghana*, © 1970. By permission of MM Publications, 19603 Jacob, Cerritos, California.

OBJECTIVES

Students will

1. Sing the song "Salamatu Bansa" add dance movements, and identify the following musical characteristics: strong feeling for the beat, call-and-response, and ostinato.
2. Perform the song "Tue, Tue," add a rattle accompaniment and body percussion, and identify the following musical characteristics: strong beat, syllabic melody, and pentatonic scale.

MATERIALS

- Rattle or shekere

PROCEDURES

1. Make a "Characteristics of African Music" chart on the chalkboard or bulletin board. As you study each piece of music, list the predominant characteristics under each musical element (melody, rhythm, and so on).
2. Have the class sing the African song "Salamatu Bansa" in call-and-response style. The teacher either acts as the leader and sings the first phrase ("call"), with the class responding in unison on the second phrase ("response"), or divides the class, having one half sing the first phrase and the other half sing the second phrase.
   a. The song repeats over and over in *ostinato* style. Have the students follow the *beat* by clapping as they sing.

b. As you sing, have students perform the following dance:
- Form a circle—facing forward.
- Bend your knees and let your shoulders and arms hang forward.
- Move in a circle in time to the beat. Let your body rhythmically sway as you clap and move to the beat.
- For variety, as you move in the circle form a chain by placing your hands on the shoulders of the person in front of you.

3. Have the class sing the song "Tue, Tue."
   a. While singing have the group keep track of the beat by clapping. Notice the strong feeling for the beat.
   b. Keep the beat with a rattle (African rattle with a gourd covered with beads or a substitute, such as a maraca).
   c. Add body percussion to the piece. Have the class divide into pairs. Place two pairs together and have them clap in the following manner: Clap partner's hands on beats 1 and 2; hands against the thighs on beats 3 and 4; repeat the pattern for measure 2; change partners for measure 3 and as before clap hands on beats 1 and 2 and then clap hands against thighs on beats 3 and 4; in measure 4 repeat the pattern of measure 3.

   d. Draw attention to the fact that every syllable in the text of the song has *one* note. This gives a "percussive effect" to the music.
   e. Have the students write out the pitches present in the song. Since there are five pitches, the scale is described as *pentatonic*. Children may play these pitches on a xylophone or melody bells as they sing the song.

"Ma Lo We"

Grades: 5–6

Ma Lo We

Adesanya Adeyeye

Starting pitch: A
Meter: 4/4, begins on 1

Ma lo we l'o - kun mo___   Ma lo we l'o - kun mo___   Ma lo we l'o - kun mo o   on - gbe won lo
(Mah lō way lō - koon mo___   Mah lo way lo - koon mo___   Mah lō way lo kŏon mo ō   ŏon - bā wŏn lo)

OBJECTIVES

Students will

1. Sing the song "Ma Lo We," and identify the following musical characteristics: strong feeling for the beat, repetitive melody (ostinato), five-tone scale, and syncopation.
2. Play "Ma Lo We" on the mbira.
3. Perform an example of African polyrhythm.
4. Identify polyrhythm in a recorded musical example.

MATERIALS

- Mbira (also known as kalimba or sanza), a plucked percussion instrument
- Agogo (also known as gankogui) bells, two sizes
- Shekere rattle
- Large and small drums*

PROCEDURES

1. Have the students sing "Ma Lo We."
   a. Students learn the song by rote.
   b. Students clap the beat.
   c. Students can also keep the beat by playing a rattle.
   d. Point out the general characteristics in the song:
      - Strong feeling for the beat
      - Syllabic melody
      - Repetitive melody; ostinato
      - Five-tone scale:

      - Syncopation

2. Have students play "Ma Lo We" on the mbira.
   a. Students should practice finding the different notes on the instrument.
   b. Have the class sing the song slowly while one student plays the melody. As the melody becomes more familiar, the tempo of the piece can be increased.
   c. Call attention to the "percussive quality" created by plucking the mbira.
3. Have the students count each line of the following set of numbers, clapping on the boldface figures. Practice until the class can perform the entire example correctly, keeping a steady tempo throughout. Practice the example at several tempos: slow, medium, fast.

---

*African instruments may be purchased from The House of Musical Tradition, 7040 Carroll Avenue, Takoma Park, Maryland 20912.

African mbira

Percussion instruments for African music

1	2	3	4	5	6	7	8	9	10	11	12
1	2	3	4	5	6	7	8	9	10	11	12
1	2	3	4	5	6	7	8	9	10	11	12
1	2	3	4	5	6	7	8	9	10	11	12
1	2	3	4	5	6	7	8	9	10	11	12

4. Divide the class into five sections and have each section clap one line over and over in ostinato fashion. When all sections are combined, the class is performing polyrhythm.

5. Following is an example of the above rhythm in Western notation. Ask the entire class to clap the five lines one at a time; then divide the class into sections and have them clap all five lines at the same time. The students can hear and see the polyrhythm.

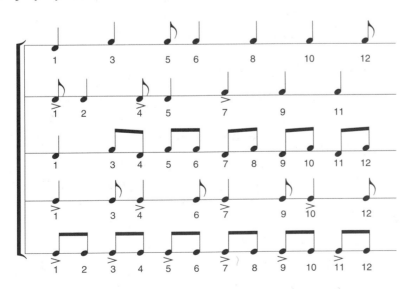

6. Play the following example with instruments.

   a. The first line is played on the metal percussion instrument known as an *agogo* (ah-go-go) or *gankogui* (ghăn-ko-gwee). This instrument has two bell-shaped projections, one producing a lower pitch and the other a high pitch.

   b. The second line of music is played on a larger and, therefore, lower-sounding, agogo.

   c. The third line is played with a *shekere*. The agogo and shekere may be purchased in the United States, but teachers and students may wish to create their own instruments (see p. 250).

   d. Lines four and five are played with small and large drums, respectively.

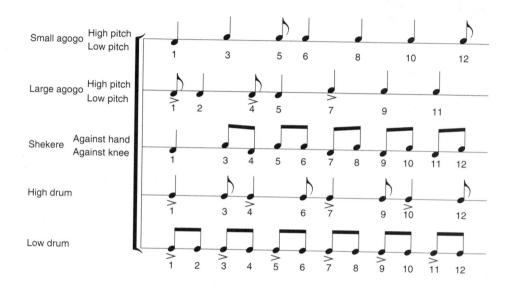

Bruno Nettl, *Folk and Traditional Music of Western Continents*, 2nd ed., © 1973. By permission of Prentice-Hall, Inc., Englewood Cliffs, New Jersey.

7. Perform the entire polyrhythm example several times, giving different students a chance to play instruments. Other students in the class can clap along on a part while the instruments are being played. Perform the example at different tempos; each tempo must be consistently maintained throughout.

8. Listen to an example of polyrhythm (*Mustapha Tettey Addy: Master Drummer from Ghana*, Lyrichord, LLCT 7250, band 3).

   a. This is music that accompanies the Agbeko (Ahg-bek-o) dance of the Ewe (ā-wāy) people of Ghana. You will hear a master drum, a supporting drum, and an agogo.

   b. As the students listen to the music, have them clap the rhythm played on the agogo:

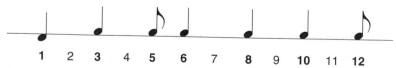

The Music of Ghana

Grades: 5–6

OBJECTIVES

Students will

1. View the videotape or film *Discovering the Music of Africa.*
2. Describe the instruments, their sounds, and how they are used.
3. Identify characteristics of African music.

MATERIALS

• Film *Discovering the Music of Africa* (BFA Educational Media, 2211 Michigan Avenue, Santa Monica, CA 90404; also available in videotape format from West Music Company, P.O. Box 5521, Coralville, Iowa 52241)

PROCEDURES

1. The 22-minute videotape/film is on the music of Ghana. Have the students find Ghana on a map of Africa.
2. Show the film, particularly noticing the drums, bells (gankogui), and rattles (shekere), and the distinctive singing style and dance.
3. On the chalkboard, place the following characteristics of African music as seen in the film:
   • Emphasis on percussion instruments and sounds
   • Call-and-response form
   • Open, relaxed quality of singing
   • Singing in harmony
   • Polyrhythm
   • Ostinato

MUSIC OF ASIAN PEOPLES: CHINA AND JAPAN

BACKGROND INFORMATION FOR THE CLASS

Among the largest and smallest countries of Asia are China and Japan, respectively (see Figure 10.2). China extends 2,700 miles from east to west and 2,600 miles from north to south, encompassing approximately the land mass of the United States and Mexico together. Within its border live over 1.1 billion people, more than in any other country in the world, and four times the population of the United States. In contrast, the islands of Japan stretch 1,250 miles from north to south, but in total land area encompass only approximately that of Iowa and Minnesota. Within this relatively small land mass live over 124 million people.

China and Japan have rich historical traditions, and over many centuries their peoples have made major contributions to the world. The Chinese invented paper and printing and have given to the world silk, porcelain, and the compass, while the Japanese have increasingly demonstrated their technological accomplishments in electronic and manufacturing industries.

Many aspects of life in China and Japan have been subtly affected by the religions and philosophies of their peoples. Particularly evident in the arts have been (1) the Buddhist emphasis on simplicity of lifestyle, contemplation, peace, and tranquillity; (2) the rules of order and personal conduct stemming from the philosopher Confucius; and (3) the religions of Taoism and Shintoism, which have stressed the importance of humans being in communion with nature. The tangible outcomes of these beliefs are present in several major thematic emphases in the arts.

One of the most persistent themes is *nature*. From the very earliest times artists have sought to put themselves and their audiences in harmony with the great "spiritual realities" of the natural world. The theme of nature is evident in Asian architectural settings and building designs; in the visual arts of painting, sculpture, and flower arranging; in literature; and in music.

Another common tenet in both Chinese and Japanese arts is an emphasis on *understatement*. Artists seem to be directed toward simplicity, disciplined control, and attention to detail. In paintings bare outlines are often used to depict such natural objects as mountains and trees. Muted, pastel colors complement the delicacy and simplicity of the lines, and there are many open, blank spaces that viewers are left to fill in in their minds. It seems clear that many Chinese and Japanese artists wish to suggest through understatement with the hope of achieving maximum effect with minimal materials.

Figure 10.2. A portion of Asia

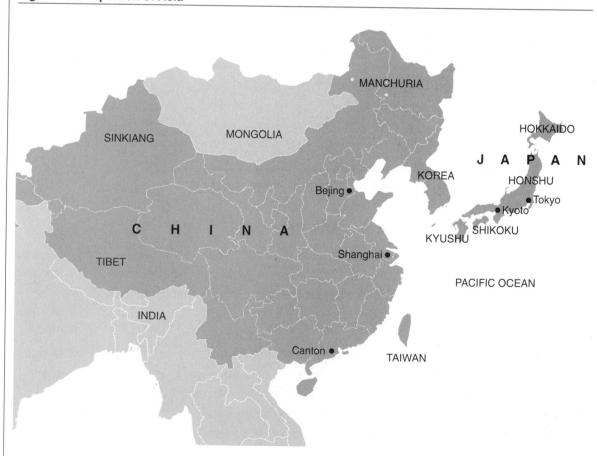

SOME GENERAL CHARACTERISTICS OF CHINESE AND JAPANESE MUSIC

Music has been an important part of Chinese and Japanese life from the beginnings of their recorded history. Several highly developed systems of traditional music are present today and are represented in a number of vocal and instrumental forms. Some general characteristics of these musics include:

1. There is much use of pentatonic scales, although six- and seven-tone scales occur. Melodic lines often contain subtle ornamentation.

2. Meter is predominantly duple.

3. Monophonic (one-line) and heterophonic (simultaneous variations on a single line) textures occur frequently. There is much emphasis on distinct, delicate lines of music, unlike the thick, homogenous sounds of much Western orchestral music. Some harmony is present, however.

4. Both soft and loud dynamic levels are found. However, since much music is composed for small ensembles, dynamic levels are often soft. The predominant use of soft and medium dynamic levels reflects a general tendency toward understatement and delicate refinement in the music. However, within any single performance group a full range of dynamic levels, from soft to loud, is present.

5. A variety of instrumental and vocal tone colors are present. These include stringed, percussion, and wind instruments, with stringed instruments predominating. The tone color of singers sometimes has a pinched, nasal quality.

6. Many compositions are programmatic. Theme-and-variation and ternary forms are common.

TEACHING CHINESE AND JAPANESE MUSIC: SUGGESTIONS FOR LESSONS

The overall goal of the lesson suggestions that follow is to acquaint students with some of the many types of Chinese and Japanese music and to have them study these types in terms of the elements of music: melody, rhythm, texture, timbre, and form.

Several songs are included and are given in the native language as well as in English. Children should be encouraged to use the native languages, since by doing so they will more closely identify with the people. It is also suggested that the songs will be learned most quickly by rote.

For the listening selections, children should have a chance to see and discuss the instruments before listening to them. Listening guides are given with each selection to help students follow the musical events. These may be duplicated for each student or may be placed on a transparency for the entire class to see.

Chinese Music

"Colorful Boats"

Grades: 4–6

Colorful Boats

Starting pitch: A
Meter: 2/4

Melody Collected by William Anderson

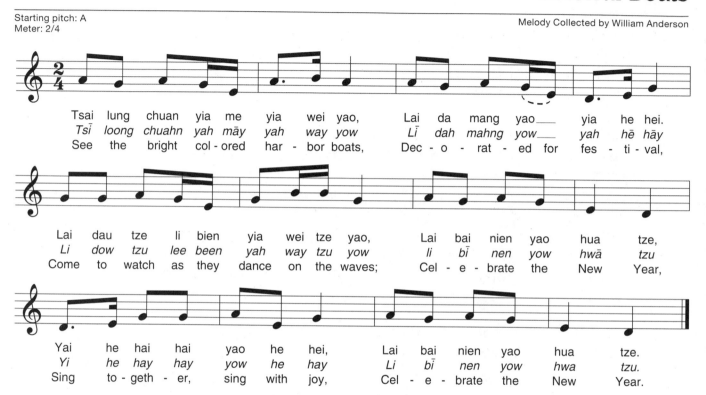

Tsai lung chuan yia me yia wei yao,   Lai da mang yao___ yia he hei.
Tsī loong chuahn yah māy yah way yow   Lī dah mahng yow___ yah hē hāy
See the bright col-ored har-bor boats,   Dec-o-rat-ed for fes-ti-val,

Lai dau tze li bien yia wei tze yao,   Lai bai nien yao hua tze,
Li dow tzu lee been yah way tzu yow   li bī nen yow hwā tzu
Come to watch as they dance on the waves;   Cel-e-brate the New Year,

Yai he hai hai yao he hei,   Lai bai nien yao hua tze.
Yi he hay hay yow he hay   Li bī nen yow hwa tzu.
Sing to-geth-er, sing with joy,   Cel-e-brate the New Year.

English words by Carol Kerr, in Silver Burdett Music, Book 4, © 1981. Reprinted by permission.

OBJECTIVES

Students will

1. Be introduced to China, its geography, and its culture.
2. Sing the song "Colorful Boats," and identify the following characteristics in the song: pentatonic melody, duple meter, monophonic texture.
3. Listen to the instrumental selection "Winter Ravens Flying over the Water," played on the zheng and xiao, identify the instruments by sight, identify the instruments by sound, classify the instruments (stringed or wind), describe the meter (duple), and describe the programmatic effects in the music.

Chinese zheng

Chinese xiao

MATERIALS

- Globe or map of the world
- Pictures of the instruments (zheng, xiao)
- Melody bells or xylophone
- Recording of "Winter Ravens Flying over the Water" (*China's Instrumental Heritage*, Lyrichord, LLCT 792).

PROCEDURES

1. Have the students locate China on the globe or map. Compare its size to that of the United States (approximates the size of the United States and Mexico). Then compare China's population to that of the United States (1.1 billion versus 255 million). Ask students to locate some of the main cities (Beijing, Shanghai, Canton).

2. Make a "Characteristics of Chinese Music" chart on the chalkboard or bulletin board. As each piece of music is studied, list the important musical characteristics learned.

3. Sing the Chinese song "Colorful Boats" about colorfully decorated boats at a New Year's celebration. Lead a discussion about Chinese New Year. The date for Chinese New Year varies each year, occurring between January 21 and February 19. The exact date is determined according to the lunar calendar, falling on the second new moon after the winter solstice. Each new year is designated by one of the animals of the Chinese zodiac: rat, ox, tiger, hare, dragon, serpent, horse, sheep, monkey, rooster, dog, and boar. (Children may wish to draw the animal of the particular New Year.) The Chinese New Year is a time of great celebration, often involving fireworks and paper dragons being carried through the streets.*

   a. Have students sing the song in both Chinese and English.

   b. As students sing, have them keep track of the rhythm by clapping hands together on beat 1 and waving hands outward on beat 2. They should be able to feel and see the *duple* meter.

Encyclopedia Americana, 1992, Vol. 6, p. 597

c. Write in scalewise fashion the pitches used in the song:

d. As students sing the song, note that there is only *one* line of music (even though many people are singing it). This music is described as monophonic (mono = one, phonic = sound).

4. Play a recording of the piece "Winter Ravens Flying over the Water," played on the *zheng* (also spelled *cheng*, and pronounced "zhung") and *xiao* (also spelled *hsiao*, and pronounced "she-ao").

a. Show pictures and describe the zheng and xiao. The zheng is a plucked stringed instrument. It normally has sixteen strings, which are tuned to a pentatonic scale. Note how the performer plucks the strings with his or her right-hand thumb and fingers and how the left-hand fingers glide along the strings to produce different pitches. The xiao is a wind instrument made from bamboo. Point out the notch at the upper end of the instrument, across which the performer blows air to produce the sound. Point out that there are no keys on the instrument.

b. Have students listen to the tone qualities of each instrument (clear, plucked string sound of zheng and breathy, wind sound of xiao).

c. Have the students keep track of the beat and follow the duple meter by clapping lightly on beat 1 and waving on beat 2.

d. Call attention to the "nature theme" in the title of the composition. This is programmatic music. Discuss how the music reflects this theme (sweeping melodic lines played on the zheng symbolize birds flying over water).

"Old Monk Sweeping the Buddhist Temple" and "The Heroes Defeated"

Grades: 4–6

OBJECTIVES

Students will

1. Explore tone color and texture in Chinese music by listening to the sheng composition "Old Monk Sweeping the Buddhist Temple."

2. Identify the sheng by sight and sound and classify the sheng as a wind instrument.

3. Compare the free reed structure of the sheng and the Western harmonica (its distant relative) and identify the distinctive harmonic texture produced on the instrument.

4. Listen to "The Heroes Defeated" played on the pipa and identify the pipa by sight and sound.

5. Classify the pipa as a stringed instrument.

6. Dramatize the programmatic ideas of of "The Heroes Defeated."

MATERIALS
- Pictures of instruments (sheng and pipa)
- Recordings of "Old Monk Sweeping the Buddhist Temple" (*China's Instrumental Heritage*, Lyrichord, LLCT 792) and "The Heroes Defeated"(*Chinese Classical Masterpieces*, Lyrichord LLST-7182, side 2, band 5)
- Harmonica

PROCEDURES
1. Have students listen to the recording of "Old Monk Sweeping the Buddhist Temple" played on the sheng (pronounced shung).
   a. Show a picture of the sheng and describe how the instrument is constructed. The sheng consists of a bowl-shaped base into which are inserted bamboo reed pipes, each designed to produce a different pitch. Within each pipe is a small reed, which vibrates to produce the sound as air moves through the pipe.
   b. Bring a harmonica to class. Show the reeds in the instrument. (They may be seen by looking carefully into the instrument; it may be possible to remove the upper or lower sections of the instrument to see the reeds clearly.)
   c. Play the harmonica. Notice that sound can be produced both by exhaling air into the instrument and by inhaling air from the instrument. Thus, one can produce *continuous* sound on the harmonica. The same is true for the sheng. Also, point out that one can produce several pitches at the same time on the harmonica, thus creating harmony. This is also true for the sheng.
   d. Have students listen to the distinctive tone color produced by the sheng.
   e. Point out the distinctive harmonic sounds that are often produced on the sheng.
2. Have students listen to the recording of "The Heroes Defeated" played on the pipa (pronounced pee-pah).
   a. Show a picture of the pipa and describe how it is constructed and played. (The pipa is a plucked stringed instrument somewhat similar in shape to the Western guitar. Point out the characteristic manner in which it is held upright as it is played. The strings are plucked with the fingernails of the right hand. Among the most characteristic sounds of the instrument are rapidly repeated notes in the melody executed by the quickly moving fingers of the right hand.)
   b. This piece is programmatic, depicting a battle between the kingdoms of Han and Chu. Have students listen to the manner in which the music depicts soldiers marching back and forth and the battle sounds of clashing swords.
   c. Plan dramatic movement to accompany the music.
3. Summarize by having the students add characteristics learned in the music of this lesson to the "Characteristics of Chinese Music" list on the bulletin board:
   - Instruments: Sheng—wind instrument with reeds activated by air; pipa—stringed instrument
   - Texture: Distinctive harmonic texture produced on sheng
   - Melody: Rapidly repeating notes produced by the pipa
   - Form: Programmatic ideas of the music

Chinese sheng

Chinese pipa

Japanese Music

"Sakura"

Grades: 3–4

Sakura

Starting pitch: A
Meter: 2/4, begins on 1

Trans. Joy E. Lawrence

SA - KU - RA SA - KU - RA YA - YO - I - NO SO - RA___ WA, MI - WA -
Sah - koo - rah sah - koo - rah yah - yoh - i - noh so - rah - wah mee wah
Sa - ku - ra Sa - ku - ra cher - ry blooms are eve - ry - where. Clouds of

TA - SU KA - GI___ RI, KA - SU - MI KA KU - MO___ KA NI - O - I ZO
Tah - soo kah - gee - ree kah - soo - mi kah koo - moh___ kah ni - o - i - zoh
glo - ry fill the___ air. Mist of beau - ty in the___ sky Love - ly col - ors

I - ZU___ RU. I - ZA - YA, I - ZA - YA ME NI YU - KA - N.
i - zoo - roo i - zah - yah i - zah - yah me ni yoo - kah n.
float - ing___ by, Sa - ku - ra, Sa - ku - ra Let us come___ and sing.

OBJECTIVES

Students will

1. Be introduced to the geography and some cultural characteristics of Japan.
2. Sing the song "Sakura" ("Cherry Blooms") in both Japanese and English, and identify the pentatonic scale and the duple meter.
3. Listen to "Variations on Sakura" played on the koto, identify the koto by sight and sound, and explain how the koto is constructed and played.
4. Identify the theme-and-variations form.

MATERIALS

- Globe or map of the world
- Piano or Autoharp
- Picture of koto
- Melody bells
- Japanese "props," such as kimono, fan, parasol
- Recording of "Variations on Sakura" (*Art of the Koto: The Music of Japan*, Elektra Records, CD 70234; also available on records accompanying Holt, Rinehart and Winston's *Exploring Music*, Book 4)

PROCEDURES

1. Using a globe, have the students locate Japan. Compare its size to that of the United States. (Japan's total land area is approximately equal to that of the states of Iowa and Minnesota combined, yet it has approximately half the population of the United States.) Japan is an island country; have the students find the four main islands: Hokkaido, Honshu, Shikoku, and Kyushu. Also have the class locate some of the main cities: Tokyo, Yokohama, Nagoya, Kyoto, and Osaka.
2. Have students sing the song "Sakura," one of the most popular folk songs in Japan. The song celebrates the national flower of Japan, which in springtime provides a profusion of pink and white blossoms throughout the countryside. Have them sing in both Japanese and English. The song should be performed unaccompanied, although you may wish to assist the students by playing the melody on a piano or plucking strings on an Autoharp.

Japanese koto

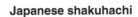

Japanese shakuhachi

3. Call attention to the theme of nature. Ask the students to identify the words (English) that refer to nature (cherry blooms, clouds, air, mist, sky).
4. Have the students write out, from low to high, the different pitches in the song.

Since there are five notes, this is a *pentatonic* scale. Play the scale on melody bells, then sing it on the syllable "loo." Notice the particular sound quality of the pentatonic scale.

5. Dramatize "Sakura" by creating stylized movements that express ideas in the song and by adding a kimono, Japanese parasol, fan, and so on.
6. Show the students a picture of the koto. The koto is one of the most important Japanese stringed instruments; it has a position in Japanese homes comparable to the piano in our own country. The instrument is approximately 6 feet long, 13 inches wide, and 2 inches thick. It has thirteen strings, which extend the length of the body and are tuned to the pentatonic scale by movable bridges inserted between the body of the instrument and the strings. The instrument is played with plectrums, which are attached to the right-hand thumb, index, and middle fingers. A variety of pitches and subtly executed ornamentation can be produced by the left hand pressing and pulling strings.
7. Play the recording of "Variations on Sakura" played on the koto. Have the students follow the outline of this form on the board.
   • Theme: "Sakura"
   • Variation 1: "Sakura" theme played with added melodic figures; *fast tempo*
   • Variation 2: "Sakura" theme played at a *slow tempo*
   • Variation 3: "Sakura" theme played with many "running figures"; *fast tempo*
   Plan dramatic movement to portray the changes in tempo.
8. Summarize the lesson by having the students make a list of "Characteristics of Japanese Music" on the chalkboard or bulletin board: pentatonic melody, duple meter, monophonic texture, theme-and-variation form, "nature theme."

"Deer Calling to Each Other in the Distance"

Grades: 5–6

OBJECTIVES

Students will

1. Listen to the composition "Deer Calling to Each Other in the Distance" played on the shakuhachi and identify (a) the shakuhachi by sight and sound; (b) the programmatic theme of nature, in which two shakuhachi players imitate deer calling to each other; and (c) how the sense of understatement is created through the slow tempo, soft dynamic level, and monophonic texture.
2. Show sections devoted to the koto and shakuhachi in the videotape or film *Discov-*

ering the Music of Japan. Note the following characteristics of Japanese traditional music: pentatonic scales, duple meter, tendency toward soft dynamic levels, programmatic nature of pieces, sense of understatement—creation of maximum effect from minimal materials.

MATERIALS

- Picture of shakuhachi
- Recording of "Deer Calling to Each Other in the Distance" (*UNESCO Collection: A Musical Anthology of the Orient—Japan III*, Barenreiter-Musicaphon BM 30 L 2014, side 2, band 2)
- Film *Discovering the Music of Japan* (BFA Educational Media, 2211 Michigan Avenue, Santa Monica, CA 90404; also available on videotape from West Music Company, P.O. Box 5521, Coralville, Iowa 52241)

PROCEDURES

1. Play the composition "Deer Calling to Each Other in the Distance" ("Shika no Tone") as performed on the shakuhachi.
2. Show a picture of the shakuhachi. This instrument is made from bamboo and is approximately 18 inches in length. Sound is produced by blowing across a small notch at the upper end of the instrument.
3. Call attention to the "nature theme" in the title of the composition. Listen to the manner in which the two shakuhachi players imitate deer calling to each other.
4. Place the following statements on a chart or the chalkboard. As they listen to the composition, have the students circle the appropriate items:

Music is loud	or	(Music is soft)
(One line of music)	or	Many lines of music
Strong beat in music	or	(Weak beat in music)
(Tempo is slow)	or	Tempo is fast

After the students have completed this task, call attention to the manner in which understatement is created by each of the items.

5. Show the videotape or film *Discovering the Music of Japan*. Three traditional musical instruments are played: the koto (plucked stringed instrument), the shakuhachi (wind instrument), and the shamisen (plucked stringed instrument). A short Japanese dance is also performed. While you may wish to use the entire film, the first two segments on the koto and shakuhachi, respectively, are suggested here. Before showing the videotape or film, review with the class some of the principal characteristics of Japanese music: pentatonic scales, duple meter, tendency toward soft dynamic levels, programmatic nature of pieces, sense of understatement— creation of maximum effect from minimal materials.

6. Call attention to the cultural setting of the music on the film: Beautiful color photography of a home and garden and a Japanese painting combine to create the proper setting (particularly the emphasis on nature) for the music.

7. Conclude the lesson by having the students summarize some of the general characteristics of Japanese music as they appear on the chalkboard or bulletin board.

MUSIC OF EUROPEAN PEOPLES

BACKGROUND INFORMATION FOR THE CLASS

The European continent extends from the Mediterranean Sea in the south to the Arctic Ocean in the north, and from the Atlantic Ocean in the west to the Ural Mountains in Russia (see Figure 10.3). In total land area, Europe is actually the second smallest continent (Australia is the smallest), having about one-fifteenth of the world's land area. However, its 500 million people make up about 10 percent of the world's population.

A great variety of cultural backgrounds and languages are present on the European continent. Some indication of the great ethnic diversity is clearly evidenced in the thirty-four countries into which the continent is divided and the nearly fifty languages spoken.

SOME GENERAL CHARACTERISTICS OF EUROPEAN MUSIC

Because of the large number of cultural groups present in Europe, there is considerable variety in the styles of music. Following is a list of general characteristics of European music. It should be understood, however, that not all of these characteristics will be present in music from every region. The attempt here has been to provide general guidelines for presenting European music in the classroom.

1. Melody is characterized by balanced phrases, particularly in western Europe; phrases of unequal length are sometimes present, particularly in eastern European music. Scales include major, minor, modal, pentatonic, and whole tone. Melodies from western Europe are not generally heavily ornamented; ornamentation is found in some music, however, particularly in eastern Europe.

2. Rhythm is characterized by a moderately strong beat, with tempo even and constant. Meter is mostly duple or triple; unequally divided meter (5/4, 7/8, etc.) is found in eastern Europe.

3. Homophonic and polyphonic textures are common, along with much use of chordal harmony. "Drone" harmony is present in many areas.

4. Timbre is characterized by a variety of vocal and instrumental tone colors. Open, relaxed singing quality predominates. Stringed and wind instrument tone qualities are most frequently found.

5. There is much use of form in which a musical idea is stated, followed by contrasting material, which is in turn followed by a return to the first musical idea (ABA).

Figure 10.3. Europe

TEACHING EUROPEAN MUSIC: SUGGESTIONS FOR LESSONS

Following are some suggestions for lessons on European music, designed to introduce students to some of the traditional music of Europe in terms of the elements of melody, rhythm, texture, timbre, and form.

Russian Music

"Song of the Volga Boatmen"

Grades: 4–6

Song of the Volga Boatmen

Key: A
Starting pitch: A
Meter: 4/4, begins on 1

Russia

Āy___ ŭh-nyēm   Āy___ ŭh-nyēm   yĕhs-chăh rāy-zik   yĕhs-chăh dăh răs
Yo,___ heave ho,   Yo,___ heave ho,   Pull to-geth-er,   Yo,___ heave ho.

Rah-zahv yōm___ mē___ bĭr-yō-zū   rah-zahv yōm___ mē dăh kud-ryah-voo
Yon-der birch-es___ on the shore,   We must reach___ them,___ Pull men more

ī-dă-dă ī dă   ī dă dă ī dă   rah-zahv yom-me dah   Kued___ ryah-voo
                                    Pull to-geth-er   yo,___ heave ho.

Āy___ ŭh-nyēm   Āy___ ŭh-nyēm   yehs-chăh ray-zik   yehs-chăh dah răs___
Yo,___ heave ho,   Yo,___ heave ho,   Pull to-geth-er,   Yo,___ heave ho___

OBJECTIVES

Students will

1. Be introduced to the geography and cultures of Europe with special attention to Russia.

2. Sing "Song of the Volga Boatmen," and identify the phrygian scale (F♯, G, A, B, C♯, D, E), duple meter, and AABCA form.

3. Listen to a Russian folk orchestra featuring the balalaika and correctly identify musical events.

MATERIALS

• Globe or world map

• Recording of Russian folk orchestra (*Virtuosi of the Accordian, Balalaika, and Domra*, Monitor Records, MFS-515E, side 2, band 2; last 2 minutes)

Russian balalaika

PROCEDURES

1. Using a globe or map, have the students find the European continent, individual countries, and some of the largest cities. Discuss with the class how closely many families in the United States are related to peoples from European countries. Undoubtedly some students in the class will be from families that originally came from Europe.

2. Have the class sing "Song of the Volga Boatmen" in both Russian and English. Point out that this song is about the Volga River, one of the great waterways of Russia and the longest river in Europe. Have the students find the Volga River on the map.

3. While singing, have some students conduct the 4/4 meter. Point out the four-measure balanced phrases.

4. Write the phrygian scale (F♯, G, A, B, C♯, D, E) on the board and have the students sing it or play it on instruments:

5. Diagram the form of the song:

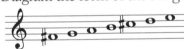

6. Play a recording of a Russian folk orchestra featuring the balalaika. The orchestra features a variety of folk instruments, including the balalaika (a triangular-shaped, string instrument), the domra (a long-necked plucked lute), and the Bayan (an accordian-like instrument). While listening to the music, ask students to circle the appropriate musical events below:

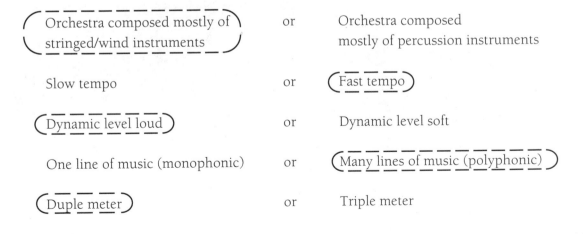

Orchestra composed mostly of stringed/wind instruments	or	Orchestra composed mostly of percussion instruments
Slow tempo	or	Fast tempo
Dynamic level loud	or	Dynamic level soft
One line of music (monophonic)	or	Many lines of music (polyphonic)
Duple meter	or	Triple meter

Greek Music

Kalamatianos

Grades: 4–6

OBJECTIVES

1. Listen to a Greek composition played on the santouri and guitar and identify the uneven quality of the 7/8 meter.
2. Perform movement to santouri and guitar music.

MATERIALS

- Recorded Greek music (*The Music of Greece*, National Geographic Society, 7th and M Streets NW, Washington, DC 20036, Record 2875, side 1, band 3)
- Picture of santouri

PROCEDURES

1. Show a picture of the santouri, a zither played by striking the strings with small hammers held in each hand of the performer.
2. Listen to Greek music in 7/8 meter performed on the santouri and guitar.
3. Have the students practice following the 7/8 meter:
   a. Without the music, count from 1 to 7 clapping on 1, 4, and 6. Repeat.
   b. Add the music, and count from 1 to 7 clapping on 1, 4, and 6. Repeat.
   c. Again, without the music, count from 1 to 7, emphasizing 1, 4, and 6 by lightly stamping your feet on the floor. Repeat.

Greek santouri

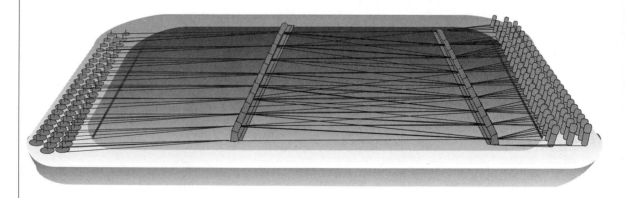

1	2	3	4	5	6	7
Right foot			Left foot		Right foot	
			and			

1	2	3	4	5	6	7
Left foot			Right foot		Left foot	

4. Repeat the foot movements in 3c, but this time with musical accompaniment.

5. Teach the dance Kalamatianos, which is done in 7/8 meter.

   a. Have students form an open circle, facing inward.

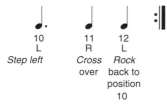

   b. Circle to the right:

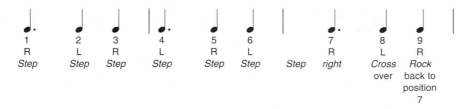

1	2	3	4	5	6	7	8	9
R	L	R	L	R	L	R	L	R
Step	Step	Step	Step	Step	Step	Step right	Cross over	Rock back to position 7

   c. Circle to the left:

10	11	12
L	R	L
Step left	Cross over	Rock back to position 10

1–6	Walk to the right starting with the right foot
7	Step to the right with the right foot
8	Cross left foot over right foot to the right
9	Rock right foot back to position 7
10	Step to the left with the left foot
11	Cross right foot over left foot to the left
12	Rock left foot back to position 10
Repeat.	

d. Teaching suggestions:

- Say the phrase "strawberry orange apple"
- Clap the first syllable of each word while speaking:
- Speak and bounce in place (feel this pattern with body):
- Speak and walk the pattern freely in the room starting with the right foot.
- Do the same with the music (all the above steps).
- Practice the "cross-rock" part without the music first, then with the music.
- Put the two parts together.
- At the beginning it helps to speak the phrase "strawberry orange apple" while dancing.
- The walking should be bouncy. You actually walk mainly on tiptoes.

Spanish Music

"There's a Fiesta"

Grades: 4–6

There's a Fiesta

Key: G

Starting pitch: G or B

Meter: 3/4, begins on 1

Spain

There's a fi - es - ta to - day, tra la la la,____ Gui - tars are be - gin - ning to play, tra la la la,____ Sweet - ly their mu - sic rings out, tra la la la,____ As ev - 'ry - one gath - ers a - bout, tra la la la____ Cas - ta - nets start keep - ing the beat, Danc - ers be - gin mov - ing their feet, Whirl - ing a - way while ev - 'ry - one cries out "O - lé!"

OBJECTIVES

Students will

1. Sing the Spanish song "There's a Fiesta," perform the composition in harmony, and identify the triple meter and the AAB form.

2. Listen to an example of flamenco singing in a type of musical composition known as a *sevillana* (performed by two female singers accompanied by two guitars and castanets), and identify the following characteristics: strong beat, duple meter, and minor quality.

MATERIALS

- Paper with letters A and B or two different geometric shapes

- Castanets, tambourines

- Recording of a *sevillana* (*The Music of Spain, Vol. 1*, National Geographic Society, 7th and M Streets NW, Washington, DC 20036, Record 740, side 2, band 1).

PROCEDURES

1. Have the students sing "There's a Fiesta." Ask the class what they think the Spanish term *fiesta* means (a celebration or festival).

2. Call attention to the Spanish instruments mentioned in the song (guitars, castanets). Also call attention to the word *dancers*; music often accompanies dance in Spain.

3. Have the class sing the song: first just the top melodic line until the words and tune are learned well; then with the singing divided by having the higher voices sing the top line and the lower voices the lower line.

4. As the students sing have them clap the triple meter.

5. Using letters or paper of different colors and geometrical shapes, have the students outline the form of the piece (AAB).

6. Add castanets or tambourines on the triplets (𝄽) to create a Spanish effect.

7. Play a recording of *sevillana*. This is music of the gypsies, a group of people who migrated from India across eastern Europe, finally coming to Spain around 1450. The gypsies have been known for their intensely emotional personalities, which are clearly reflected in their music and dance known as *flamenco*. The flamenco music of the gypsies may be sung alone, or played on instruments such as the guitar. Often it is sung with guitar and castanet accompaniment. The castanets are particularly important in accentuating the rhythm of the dance.

8. Place the following listening guide on the board, and have the students circle the appropriate musical events.

singing only	or	singing and instruments
guitars and castanets	or	brass and wind instruments
rhythm: weak beat	or	rhythm. strong beat
fast tempo	or	slow tempo
duple meter	or	triple meter
major quality to sound	or	minor quality to sound

British Isles Music

Bagpipe Songs
Grades: 4–6

OBJECTIVES
Students will
1. Sing the Irish song "Galway Piper" (see p. 226), and identify the following musical characteristics: balanced four-measure phrases, strong beat, duple meter, and AB form.
2. Listen to a medley of pieces played by a Scottish bagpipe band, and identify the following musical characteristics: ornamental melody, drone harmony, loud dynamic level, strong beat, and duple meter.
3. Listen to the Irish bagpipe composition "Rakish Paddy," and identify the following musical characteristics: ornamental melody, duple meter, fast tempo, and drone and chordal harmony.

MATERIALS
- Red and blue paper
- Recorded bagpipe music (*The Music of Scotland*, National Geographic Society, 7th and M Streets NW, Washington, DC 20036, Record 707, side 1, band 1, or *The Irish Piper of Finbar Furey*, Nonesuch H-72048, side 1, band 1)

PROCEDURES
1. Sing the song "Galway Piper." Point out that the song is about a bagpipe player, Piping Tim of Galway.
2. Using two pitches (D and A), have students sing a drone on the sound Raā, making it very nasal. Half the class can be bagpipes while the other half sings.
3. Call attention to the repetition in the melodic line (measures 1 and 4 nearly alike; measure 2 like measure 1 except down one step; measures 5 and 6 nearly alike; measures 5 and 7 exactly alike).

Bagpipe of Scotland

4. Have the students keep the beat and the duple meter in the song by clapping on the strong beats (1 and 3) and waving outward on beats 2 and 4.

5. Ask the students to diagram the overall form of the piece with letters and colored paper:

6. Listen to a medley of Scottish bagpipe pieces, with drum accompaniment.

7. Show a picture of the Scottish bagpipe. Explain that the bagpipe is one of the oldest and most widespread instruments in Europe. The instrument consists of several distinct parts: (1) a *pipe* through which the player blows air into (2) the *bag*, a device that acts as a storage reservoir for the air, which makes possible the continuous sound produced on the instrument; (3) the *chanter*, a pipe with fingerholes on which the performer plays melodies; and (4) *drone pipes*, which, like the chanter, are activated by air from the bag, but unlike the chanter normally produce only a single pitch.

8. Give students copies of the following listening guide, and as they listen to the music, have them circle the appropriate musical events:

brass and stringed instruments	or	*wind and percussion instruments*
one line of music	or	*several lines of music*
loud	or	soft
melody is plain	or	*melody is ornamented*
rhythm: strongly felt beat	or	rhythm: weakly felt beat
triple meter	or	*duple meter*

9. Play a recording of the Irish bagpipe composition "Rakish Paddy."

10. Show a picture of the Irish bagpipe to the class. Have the students look for differences between this bagpipe and Scottish bagpipes. (Instead of blowing air through a pipe into the bag, a *bellows*, which is attached under the right elbow of the performer, is pumped to fill the bag with air. In addition, the Irish bagpipes have keys on both the chanter and drones. Through these, the performer can produce simple chords.)

11. Place the following items on the board or on a handout. As they listen to the music, have the students circle the appropriate musical events:

wind instrument	or	stringed instrument
one line of music	or	*many lines of music*
the melody is plain	or	*the melody is highly ornamented*
fast tempo	or	slow tempo
duple meter	or	triple meter

12. Summarize the lessons by asking the class to list on the board some of the general characteristics of music they have studied.

AMERICAN MUSIC

BACKGROUND INFORMATION FOR THE CLASS

America is a huge continental land mass extending almost 9,500 miles from north to south and about 3,000 miles at its widest east-west expanse (see Figure 10.4). The continent is generally divided into two principal areas, North and South America, with the narrow intervening strip referred to as Central America.

With over twenty-five countries present on the American continent, there is considerable ethnic variety both among different countries and within countries. Much of the ethnic diversity of the United States results from numerous peoples who immigrated from other parts of the world. Some of the earliest inhabitants, those peoples commonly referred to today as American Indians, are thought to have come across the Bering Strait from Asia beginning as early as 50,000 years ago. In more recent times (beginning around A.D. 1000) people from a number of European countries traveled to the Americas. Shortly thereafter, numerous Africans were brought to both North and South America. In the past several hundred years, Asian peoples from a variety of countries have also immigrated to the Americas. It is clear that today many cultural groups now make up the United States and each has its distinctive music.

Figure 10.4. The Americas

TEACHING AMERICAN MUSIC: SUGGESTIONS FOR LESSONS

Because of the enormous ethnic diversity created by migrations of peoples from all over the globe to the Americas, it is impossible to describe a "typical" American music. The following sections outline suggestions for lessons on some representative American musics.

American Indian Music*

Mos', Mos'!

Key: C
Starting pitch: G
Meter: 2/4, begins on 1

Collected by David McAllester

Mos', mos', nai - ti - la, mos', mos', nai - ti - la,

Ka - nel - per - kye nai - ti - la, Ka - nel - per - kye nai - ti - la,

Mo - sa! Mo - sa! nya, ya, ya, ya, ya, etc.

"Mos', Mos'!"

Grades: 1–3

OBJECTIVES

Students will

1. Learn a Hopi song and the actions that go with it. They will also discuss the background of the song and text to broaden their understanding of the place of music in Native American life and some of the valuable perspectives in the various Native American views of the world.

2. View the film *Discovering American Indian Music* (BFA Educational Media, 2201 Michigan Avenue, Santa Monica, CA 90404), identifying types of Indian musical compositions and instruments.

*Lessons derived from Edwin Schupman (ORBIS Associates, Washington, D.C.) and David P. McAllester, "Teaching the Music of the American Indian," in William M. Anderson, *Teaching Music with a Multicultural Approach* (Reston, VA: MENC, 1991), pp. 39–43.

MATERIALS

• Map of the United States

• Videotape of David McAllester teaching the song "Mos', Mos'!" at the MENC Symposium on Multicultural Approaches to Music Education (*Teaching the Music of the American Indian*, Music Educators National Conference, 1991; available from MENC, 1806 Robert Fulton Drive, Reston, VA 22091, 800-336-3768)

• Film *Discovering American Indian Music* (Bernard Wilets/BFA, 1971, 24 minutes, color)

PROCEDURES

1. Look for pictures and make a bulletin board on American Indians. An excellent introduction, with maps and pictures, to American Indians appears in *The World Book Encyclopedia* (Chicago: World Book, Inc., 1991, Vol. 10, pp. 136–184). Invite a Native American to visit your class.

2. Locate the home of the Hopi tribe of Arizona on the United States map. (It can be found on several mesas extending east from Tuba City in western Arizona, east of the Grand Canyon.)

3. Have students learn the song "Mos', Mos'!" by singing along with the videotape.

4. Have the children "sit like a cat," holding up their hands like a cat's paws. they move their paws up and down on each beat, and where the cat says "nya, ya" they accelerate the tempo and pretend to scratch each other.

5. Discuss the role of animals in American Indian life. Native Americans feel a close relationship to the animal world. They believe that animals are creatures that think, feel, and even teach. Animals are our relatives who share this planet with us and with whom we should learn to live in harmony. (This is very different from the common Anglo/American attitude that animals exist for the benefit of humans.)

6. Discuss some of the basic features of the song: paired phrases and three-tone scale.

7. Show the film *Discovering American Indian Music*. This film includes songs, instruments, and dances of various North American Indian groups. Also included is a composition by American Indian composer Louis Ballard. Specific sections of the film are

   • Navajo (Plains) Corn Grinding Song

   • Seneca (New York) Farewell Song

   • Ute (Colorado) flute solo and Bear Dance accompanied by a serrated stick scraper

   • Kiowo (Oklahoma) Plains War Dance

   • Sioux (Plains) Love Song

   • Pueblo (New Mexico) Eagle Dance

   • Taos (New Mexico) Hoop Dance

   • Pueblo (New Mexico) Bow and Arrow Dance

   • Creek (Southeastern United States) Stomp Dance

- Tlinget (Northwest Coast) Chant (singing in harmony)
- Apache (Plains) Dance to Spirits of Mountain (bull roarer)
- Composition by American Indian composer Louis Ballard

Summarize with a short class discussion on the characteristics of Indian music studied in the lesson.

Round Dance

Grades: 3–5

OBJECTIVES

Students will

1. Put Southern Plains music in cultural and geographic perspective.
2. Recognize and be able to perform the distinctive long-short, dotted-eighth/sixteenth rhythm of a Southern Plains round dance.
3. Recognize and be able to perform the accented and unaccented beats of the round-dance dotted rhythm.
4. Understand basic concepts about the importance and significance of being a drummer, singer, or dancer in the American Indian world.
5. Identify both men's and women's voices on the recordings.
6. Perform the Southern Plains–style round dance.
7. Understand the basic significance and symbolism of the circle to American Indians, as represented in the shape of the round dance.

MATERIALS

- Several hand drums or one bass drum
- Recording: *Kiowa Round Dance Songs* (Indian Sounds Records IS 2501, side B, band 1) or *Powwow Songs: Music of the Plains Indians* (New World Records NW 343, side A, band 4)
- Map of the United States

PROCEDURES

1. Prepare students by informing them that they are going to listen to a recording of an American Indian song and dance style that comes from the tribes who originally inhabited large regions of the Southern Plains. Point out states such as Kansas, Missouri, Oklahoma, Texas, New Mexico, and Arizona. Before Oklahoma was a state it was known as Indian Territory: it is where most of these tribes now live after being placed there by the U.S. government in the nineteenth century. Some of the names of Southern Plains tribes are Kiowa, Commanche, Pawnee, Otoe, and Ponca.
2. Listen to a recording of a Southern Plains–style round dance. Have the students clap with the drum rhythm and say, "round dance, round dance." Note the long/short pattern.

3. Listen to a portion of the recording again. By yourself this time, clap along with the drum placing a little more emphasis, or clapping a little louder on the first of the two beats (*round* dance, *round* dance, *round* dance). Ask the students, "Is one of my claps louder or stronger?" "Which one?" "Is that the way the drummers are doing it, too?" Explain to them that this is known as an *accent*. Have the class clap and say the words again, this time accenting the first beat.

4. Have students play the round-dance drum rhythm on drums. Lay a bass drum flat on the floor. Have students sit around the drum in a circle, each one playing the drum with a single beater. This is similar to Plains Indian–style drumming. Students can play the rhythm on hand drums if no bass drum is available, but students should be told this is not contextually accurate.

5. Tell students that American Indians consider their drums and music to be very important to the well-being of the tribe. They treat their drums, their music, and their musicians with respect at all times.

6. Teach students the round dance. Although a social/nonreligious dance, the round dance is important to Indian people. The circle symbolizes the cycles of life, the shape of the earth, unity, and equality, no one person within the circle being distinguished above the others. It is considered a dance of friendship. Visitors to powwows—Indians and non-Indians alike—are frequently invited to join in the round dance as an expression of goodwill.

   a. If done in a more formal setting, the round dance is led by the head man and head woman dancers of the powwow, or sometimes by an armed forces veteran. All dancers face inward and dance sideways. The line of dancers forms a circle, or a spiral if there are many participants, which moves in a clockwise direction.

   Basic rhythm
   (drum beat):
   Foot movement: L   R   L   R   L   R   L   R

   b. Basic step: Begin with feet parallel, slightly spread facing inward. Lead with left foot, right foot follows. Left foot—lift knee slightly, take comfortable step sideways to left. Right foot—with less knee lift, bring foot to parallel position as at beginning. Continue around in a clockwise circle.

   HM = Head Man dancer
   HW = Head Woman dancer
   X = Other dancers

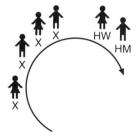

Folk and Country Music

"Old Joe Clark"
Grades: 3–6

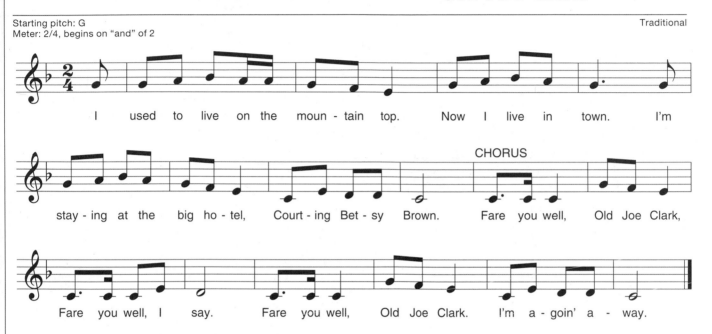

Old Joe Clark

Starting pitch: G
Meter: 2/4, begins on "and" of 2

Traditional

Jean Ritchie, *The Dulcimer Book* (New York: Oak Publications, 1974), p. 39.

OBJECTIVES
Students will
1. Sing the song "Old Joe Clark" and identify and perform the mixolydian scale (C, D, E, F, G, A, B♭).
2. Accompany the song with a mountain dulcimer.
3. Listen to "Old Joe Clark" being accompanied by the mountain dulcimer.

MATERIALS
- Mountain dulcimer
- Recording of "Old Joe Clark" (*Dulcimer Songs and Solos*, Folkways Records, FG 3571, side 1, band 2)

PROCEDURES
1. Sing "Old Joe Clark."
2. Place the mixolydian scale on the board and have the students sing and/or play it:

3. Accompany "Old Joe Clark" on the mountain dulcimer. Mountain dulcimers are

Mountain dulcimer

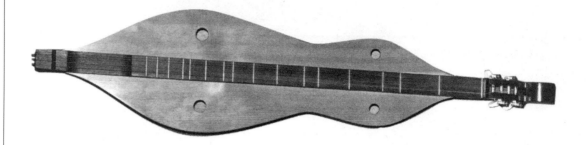

sold throughout the United States (one source is The House of Musical Traditions, 7040 Carroll Avenue, Takoma Park, MD 20912). The mountain dulcimer has four strings, two placed close together on which the melody is played and a third and fourth designed to produce a drone sound. The strings are "stroked" with a plectrum held in the right hand. Different pitches are produced by a small piece of wood, which is held in the left hand and slid along the strings.

4. Practice playing the mixolydian mode. The rest of the class should quietly "hum" along. Notice the "drone harmony" produced by the instrument.
5. Slowly sing "Old Joe Clark" accompanying on the dulcimer. Gradually increase the tempo as you develop facility.
6. Play a recording of "Old Joe Clark" being sung and accompanied on the mountain dulcimer.

Bluegrass Songs

Grades: 4–6

OBJECTIVES

Students will
1. Perform a square dance to "The Arkansas Traveler" played on fiddle, banjo, and guitar.
2. Listen to "Foggy Mountain Breakdown" and "Orange Blossom Special" played by a bluegrass ensemble and follow the musical and programmatic events.

MATERIALS

• Recordings of "The Arkansas Traveler" (*Music of the Ozarks*, National Geographic Society, 7th and M Streets NW, Washington, DC 20036,703, side 2, band 8), "Foggy Mountain Breakdown," and "Orange Blossom Special" (*The World of Flatt and Scruggs*, Columbia CGT 31964, side 1, band 1 and side 4, band 3)

• Pictures of various kinds of trains

PROCEDURES

1. Have the students square dance to a recording of "The Arkansas Traveler," performed by a country stringed group including fiddle, banjo, and guitar.

a. Form a square of four couples, with the boys on the left side of the girls.

   Students clap beat when not dancing.

b. Listen for 4 counts.

c. Introduction: All clap 16 beats (2 times).

d. Couples 1 and 3 make 4 steps to center, bow and return.

e. Couples 2 and 4 make 4 steps to center, bow and return.

f. Repeat steps d and e.

g. Each couple swings partner right (8 counts), then left (8 counts).

h. Repeat g.

i. Each couple passes shoulders with partner right (8 counts), then left (8 counts).

j. Repeat i.

k. Couples promenade counterclockwise and take new positions in square: Couple 1 is now located in couple 2 position, couple 2 is now in couple 3 position, etc.

l. Repeat steps c–k as often as needed.

2. Have students listen to "Orange Blossom Special" and "Foggy Mountain Breakdown" played by a bluegrass ensemble. Tell the class they are going to hear bluegrass music. The name *bluegrass* came from a performing group organized in the 1940s by Bill Monroe in Kentucky, the Bluegrass state. The bluegrass ensemble consists of guitar, fiddle, banjo, mandolin, string bass, and sometimes other instruments.

3. "Orange Blossom Special" is a programmatic composition about a train. Discuss the sounds and movement of various kinds of trains. Show pictures or have children bring in miniature trains. Listen to the manner in which this music imitates the sounds and movement of a train. You will hear a call to board the train, the train whistle, and the "chugging," pulsating motion of the engine. The piece is characterized by virtuoso fiddle playing.

4. The words *Foggy Mountain* in the title "Foggy Mountain Breakdown" allude to the often "misty" mountains of the Appalachian region. *Breakdown* refers to a piece that breaks down into a number of sections, each featuring a solo instrument. Follow the theme-and-variations form of the piece:

  I. Theme played by banjo with string bass accompaniment

 II. Theme played by fiddle with banjo, guitar, and string bass accompaniment

III. Theme played by banjo with guitar accompaniment

IV. Theme played by guitar with banjo and string bass accompaniment

 V. Theme played by harmonica with guitar, banjo, and string bass accompaniment

VI. Theme played by banjo with guitar, banjo, and string bass accompaniment

(You may wish to make a listening chart for "Foggy Mountain Breakdown" using line drawings of instruments.)

Mexican (Spanish-American) Music

"Cielito Lindo" and "La Raspa"

Grades: 2–5

La Raspa

Mexico

Key: G
Starting pitch: D
Meter: 4/4, begins on "and" of 4

OBJECTIVES

Students will

1. Sing "Cielito Lindo" in Spanish and in English.
2. Perform the Mexican song "La Raspa" and add a dance.

MATERIALS

- Castanets
- Tambourines
- Maracas

PROCEDURES

1. Sing "Cielito Lindo" (see p. 366), first in Spanish, then in English. On the chorus, have children follow the triple meter by tapping against their legs on beat 1, clapping on beat 2, and waving outward on beat 3.
2. Have students sing the song "La Raspa."
3. Add the designated instrumental accompaniment with castanets, tambourines, and maracas.
4. Once students have learned the song well, add the following dance:
   a. Form a circle alternating boys and girls.

   b. Have the students place their hands on their hips.
   c. Students execute the following movement four times:
      • Hop on left foot and at same time extend right foot forward with heel down and toe up (beat 1)
      • Hop on right foot and at same time extend left foot forward with heel down and toe up (beat 2)
      • Feet pause (beat 3); clap (beat 4)

African American Music

Jazz—Improvisation

Grades: 4–6

OBJECTIVES

Students will

1. Listen to several selections of jazz and identify characteristic features.
2. Listen to "Hotter Than That" and identify the Dixieland ensemble, "scat" singing, and improvisatory form.
3. Listen to "Summertime" and identify improvisation in jazz performance.

MATERIALS

• Recordings of "Hotter Than That" (*The Smithsonian Collection of Classic Jazz*, Washington, DC, compact disc I, band 16), Gershwin's "Summertime" from *Porgy and Bess* (Phillips CD 115158 or Angel Records CD 263729), and "Summertime" performed by Miles Davis with the Gil Evans Orchestra (*The Smithsonian Collection of Classic Jazz*, Washington, DC, compact disc IV, band 12)

PROCEDURES

1. Play a recording of "Hotter Than That" performed by Louis Armstrong and His Hot Five.
2. Point out that Dixieland is the earliest form of jazz. As its name implies, Dixieland began as a musical style of the southern United States. However, it spread from the South throughout the United States and the world. The Dixieland ensemble in this selection features cornet, trombone, clarinet, piano, banjo, and guitar. The cornet player here is the famous Louis Armstrong, who also improvises with vocal syllables in a style called "scat" singing. One of the distinctive features of the Dixieland style is the emphasis on improvisation.
3. Place this outline on the board for the students to follow:
   a. Introduction: cornet and trombone
   b. Cornet improvising: flat-four accompaniment (strongly felt 4-beat measures):

   c. Clarinet improvising: flat-four accompaniment
   d. "Scat" vocal improvisation
   e. Vocal and guitar interlude; flexible rhythm
   f. Trombone improvising: flat-four accompaniment
   g. Cornet and guitar improvising
4. Play a recording of the song "Summertime" from George Gershwin's opera *Porgy and Bess*, having the students follow the words and listen to the melody. Then play Miles Davis's jazz version of "Summertime" with the Gil Evans Orchestra.

5. Provide the following background information: One of the most important characteristics of jazz is its emphasis on improvisation. Jazz artists develop extraordinary ability to improvise on given melodies. In the jazz version of "Summertime," the trumpeter, Miles Davis, first plays the theme and then improvises using melodic fragments from the theme along with newly created melodic and harmonic ideas. Listen carefully for the familiar segments of the melody and then the newly improvised phrases.

6. Ask the class to search for other jazz recordings (in their home, school, or public libraries) and identify improvisation in selections. Have them bring their favorite jazz recordings to share with other members of the class.

Blues

Grades: 4–6

OBJECTIVES
Students will
1. Listen to "Boll Weevil Blues" sung by Leadbelly and identify the twelve-bar blues form.
2. Listen to "Lost Your Head Blues" sung by Bessie Smith and identify the AAB form.

MATERIALS
• Recordings of "Boll Weevil Blues" (*Negro Folk Songs for Young People*, Folkways Records FC7533, band A3) and "Lost Your Head Blues" (*The Smithsonian Collection of Classic Jazz*, compact disc I, band 4)

PROCEDURES
1. Listen to "Boll Weevil Blues" sung by Leadbelly. In this recording, Huddie Ledbetter (better known as Leadbelly), one of the most famous singer/songwriters, accompanies himself on the guitar. This piece represents a type of African American music known as the *blues*. As implied in the name, the blues were initially pieces in which black people could talk about things that gave them melancholy, "blue" feelings. (Listen to the explanation given by Leadbelly at the beginning of this selection.) In this piece Leadbelly sings of the destruction caused by the boll weevil, an insect that destroys cotton products.
2. Blues are cast in twelve-bar (or measure) segments. Students can follow this twelve-bar form by quietly counting

```
1 2 3 4    2 2 3 4    3 2 3 4    4 2 3 4
5 2 3 4    6 2 3 4    7 2 3 4    8 2 3 4
9 2 3 4   10 2 3 4   11 2 3 4   12 2 3 4
```

3. Play Bessie Smith's "Lost Your Head Blues." Blues are most often cast in AAB form. For example, "Lost Your Head Blues" begins with a short instrumental introduction, which leads to:

   • A Section: "I was with you baby when you did not have a dime."

   • A Section repeats: "I was with you baby when you did not have a dime."

   • B Section: "Now since you got plenty . . . money, you have 'throwed' your good gal down."

   AAB form continues with new segments of text.

4. Particularly note the characteristic features of blues melodies: "scoops" and "slides" between notes and descending melodic contours.

5. Have the students look for other recordings of the blues (home, library, record store) and bring them to class.

Call-and-Response Music

Grades: 2–5

Swing Low, Sweet Chariot

Key: F
Starting pitch: A
Meter: 2/4, begins on 1

Spiritual

OBJECTIVES

Students will

1. Perform the spiritual "Swing Low, Sweet Chariot" and identify the solo/chorus (call-and-response) style of performance and the pentatonic melody.
2. Listen to the jazz composition "Jumpin' at the Woodside" and identify the families of instruments (brass, woodwinds, percussion), harmonic texture, pulsating driving beat, ostinato, and short phrases passed among instruments in call-and-response form.
3. Sing the African composition "Kye, Kye Kule," particularly noticing the short phrases and call-and-response form, and compare it to "Swing Low, Sweet Chariot" and "Jumpin' at the Woodside."

MATERIALS

• Recording of "Jumpin' at the Woodside" by Count Basie.

PROCEDURES

1. Have students sing the spiritual "Swing Low, Sweet Chariot." Spirituals are a very old form of black music sung in the United States, although they actually contain aspects of both black and white musical styles. Spirituals should be sung in a flexible rhythmic style that permits the full emotional impact to be obtained from the song. Pay particular attention to the alternating solo-chorus (call-and-response) style of performance, a very common African method of musical performance. Also notice the pentatonic (five-tone) organization of the melody.

2. Listen to "Jumpin' at the Woodside" performed by Count Basie. This type of jazz, known as *swing,* differs from Dixieland in its use of a larger ensemble consisting of families of instruments. Thus, instead of just one of each instrument, there are multiple trumpets, trombones, saxophones, and percussion instruments. With the larger ensemble, it became necessary to have written arrangements in swing jazz. Swing often contains an interesting mixture of European and African traits. Large numbers of instruments playing together with written arrangements and a strongly harmonic musical style are European traits. Some prominent "African traits" in the music include the pulsating driving beat, the use of ostinato, and the short phrases passed among instruments in call-and-response form.
3. As students listen to the music, have them follow the outline:
   a. Piano plays "up and down" scale figures; repeats 4 times; strong, pulsating beat
   b. Full orchestra—short melodic figures passed among instruments in call-and-response form
   c. Saxophone solo with orchestral accompaniment
   d. Full orchestra—short melodic figures passed among instruments in call-and-response form
   e. Piano solo

    f. Full orchestra—short melodic figures passed among instruments in call-and-response form

    g. Trumpet solo with orchestral accompaniment

    h. Saxophone solo with orchestral accompaniment

    i. Clarinet and muted trumpet pass short melodic figures back and forth

    j. Clarinet and saxophone improvise and pass melodic figures back and forth

4. Have students sing the African song "Kye, Kye Kule" (p. 405) and compare the short phrases passed back and forth in call-and-response form in this selection to the same characteristic found in "Jumpin' at the Woodside."

Pulsating Beat, Ostinato, Syncopation

Grades: 2–5

OBJECTIVES

Students will

1. Sing the African song "Twa-Mu-Sanga" (p. 406), following the steady, pulsating beat and the repeated melodic/rhythmic phrases (ostinato).

2. Listen to a steel drum ensemble from Trinidad and identify both African and Euro-American traits in the music (African—strong, pulsating beat and short, repetitive phrases [ostinato]; Euro-American—orchestra made up of families of soprano, alto, tenor, and bass instruments).

3. Listen to the jazz composition "Take Five" and follow the steady, pulsating beat, the repeated melodic/rhythmic phrases (ostinato), and the 5/4 meter, and identify the use of syncopation.

MATERIALS

Recordings of "High Life" (*Steel Band/Trinidad: The Sound of the Sun*, Elektra/Nonesuch, 72016) and Dave Brubeck's "Take Five" (Columbia compact disc CK 40585, band 3)

PROCEDURES

1. Have students sing the African song "Twa-Mu-Sanga." They should clap the steady, pulsating beat as they sing. They can follow the repeated melodic/rhythmic phrases (ostinato) by moving their arms back and forth in the air.

2. Play the steel drum selection "High Life." Steel drums are fashioned from oil drums. Dents are made in the tops of the drums to produce different notes. Today steel drums are designed in a great variety of sizes that are arranged, like a Western orchestra, with soprano instruments ("Ping Pong"), alto instruments ("Guitar Pan"), tenor instruments ("Cello Pan"), and bass instruments ("Boom"). Ensembles can also include other instruments such as rattles (gourds filled with seeds). The title of this selection is derived from African popular music with the same name. Review the following "African characteristics" in this music:

a. Strong pulsating beat; have the students follow the beat by clapping their hands or tapping the top of their desks with pencils.

b. Use of ostinato:

   Have the students clap this rhythm over and over, first without the music, then as they listen to the music. Call attention to the short, repetitive phrases.

3. Play "Take Five" performed by the Dave Brubeck Quartet.

4. Identify the instruments in the quartet (piano, saxophone, string bass, and drums).

5. Follow the strong, pulsating beat by counting the 5/4 meter and clapping on beats 1 and 4:

6. Clap the repeating ostinato figure. Particularly notice the use of syncopation:

7. Ask students how the saxophone improvises over the repeating ostinato figure. (For example, "scoops" and "slides" in the melody.)

8. Ask the class to make a list on the board of some characteristics of African American music.

QUESTIONS FOR REVIEW

1. Why is it important to teach music from a multicultural, global perspective?

2. What are some sources in the school and community that you can draw on for planning units of study (including music) on various cultures?

3. How would you go about planning a bulletin board around the theme of studying other cultures?

4. How might you as the classroom teacher collaborate with the art teacher, the music teacher, and the physical education teacher to study other cultures?

5. Give some examples of how you might combine music with social studies and language arts units in studying other cultures.

6. Discuss some characteristics, with actual musical examples, of African, Asian, European, and American musics that you could teach to children in Grades K–2, 3–4, and 5–6.

7. How would you go about planning a multicultural or international festival for your school?

EXPERIENCES WITH MUSIC AND OTHER ARTS

This chapter is devoted to exploring ways of combining the study of music with that of other art forms. It is clear that the visual, literary, and musical arts each provide distinct ways for achieving aesthetic experiences. For example, in the visual arts of architecture, sculpture, and painting, ideas and feelings are expressed through elements such as color, line, texture, volume, perspective, and form. It is the skill with which artists manipulate these elements within their choice of media (such as marble, wood, steel, plate glass, in architecture and sculpture; water color, oils, fresco, mosaic, egg tempera, in painting) that determines the expressiveness and meaning in a work of art. In the literary arts, writers express ideas and feelings by using words, both for their meaning and for their sound. They use such elements of literature as grammar, figures of speech, rhyme, rhythm, and form. In music, composers express ideas and feelings by organizing sounds in terms of melody, rhythm, texture, tone color, and form. In all of these arts, it is clear that a perception of basic elements is essential to understanding any single art medium.

While it is evident that arts such as music, painting, sculpture, and poetry are separate and discrete, it is also possible to go beyond the perception of elements unique to a single art form and draw relationships among various art forms through understanding characteristics they share. For example, all art forms share the principles of enlargement through repetition, contrast, unity, and balance. Further, thematic, historical, and cultural ideas often inspire similar expressions in different art forms.

As a classroom teacher, you are in a unique position to help students interrelate their experiences in music with other areas of the school curriculum. Teachers can often enhance an experience with a particular musical artwork by showing students how some of its elements are shared by other art forms. Further, classroom teachers can help students understand how the arts are often closely allied with many other subject areas, like history. In all experiences, the ultimate goal is to assist students in perceiving relationships among different modes of aesthetic experience and increasing their understanding of how and why the arts are so closely intertwined with people's lives.

There are many ways to organize a study of music and the arts. The sample lessons that follow center on four basic approaches: (1) an analogous-concepts approach; (2) a thematic approachs; (3) a historical approach; and (4) a cross-cultural approach. The lessons are designed as a general guide and may need to be modified for use in various settings and with different interests and grade levels. Further, teachers are encouraged to develop other lessons based on the ideas presented here.

USING ANALOGOUS CONCEPTS TO RELATE MUSIC AND THE ARTS

The analogous-concepts approach is based on studying concepts held in common among different art forms. These include such fundamental relationships as repetition/enlargement, contrast, sense of unity, and balance.

Suggestions for Lessons

Repetition and Enlargement

Grades: 1–3

OBJECTIVES

Students will

1. Create a visual picture that can be enlarged through repetition.
2. Examine poems that feature repetition and create a poem that shows enlargement through repetition.
3. Lengthen a song by repeating or adding verses or rhythm patterns.
4. Identify repetition as a means of enlargement in music, visual, and literary arts.

MATERIALS

- Construction paper strips
- Reproduction of Andy Warhol's *Campbell Soup Cans* painting
- Rhythm instruments
- Poems: "I Saw a Fish Pond" and "There Was a Crooked Man"

PROCEDURES

1. Create a paper chain by cutting out small strips of paper, forming loops, and linking and stapling them together. Students can make bracelets, necklaces, or even jumpropes by adding loops. Call attention to the use of repetition to enlarge or expand the chain.

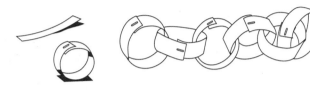

2. Bring a "slinky" to class and ask students to make a large shape by expanding the slinky. (Be sure not to stretch it too much or it will not return to its original shape.) Ask the students what is repeated to make the large shape (metal circles).
3. Select one student to be a leader. Have other students line up one at a time behind the leader. Notice how the line becomes longer (expands, enlarges).
4. Ask students to bring in soup cans and build a picture or shape based on repetition of these cans.

Andy Warhol's *Campbell Soup Cans*

5. Show students a picture of Andy Warhol's *Campbell Soup Cans*. Discuss how one can "build" by repeating an idea.

6. Read the poem "I Saw a Fish Pond." Call attention to the repetition of the phrase *I saw*.

I Saw a Fish Pond

I saw a fishpond all on fire
I saw a house bow to a squire
I saw a parson twelve feet high
I saw a cottage near the sky
I saw a balloon made of lead
I saw a coffin drop down dead
I saw two sparrows run a race
I saw two horses making lace
I saw a girl just like a cat
I saw a kitten wear a hat
I saw a man who saw these too
And said though strange they all were true.

7. Read the following nursery rhyme and identify the words that are repeated.

There Was a Crooked Man

There was a crooked man, and he went a crooked mile;
He found a crooked sixpence against a crooked stile;
He bought a crooked cat, which caught a crooked mouse,
And all lived together in a little crooked house.

8. Perform "If You're Happy" (p. 135). Notice that the song is lengthened by adding verses.

9. Play a simple ostinato pattern on a percussion instrument as students sing "If You're Happy." Note the repetition of the rhythm pattern. You can use this rhythm as an introduction and ending (or coda).

10. Play "Tue, Tue" (p. 408), an African folk song. Identify the words that are repeated and count the number of times.

CLOSURE AND EVALUATION

1. Ask students to identify ways an artist repeats ideas in music, visual art, and poetry.

2. Ask students how repetition can make a work of art larger (or longer).

The Roman Colosseum

More Repetition and Enlargement

Grades: 4–6

OBJECTIVES
Students will
1. Identify repetition as a means of enlargement in music, visual art, and poetry.
2. Create a music composition, a visual artwork, and a poem that show enlargement through repetition.
3. Identify repetition in music, visual art, and poetry as a technique in creating a mood or expressing feelings.

MATERIALS
- Pictures: Vasarely's *Vonal Ksz* (H. H. Arnason, *History of Modern Art*, New York: Harry N. Abrams); Roman Colosseum; Pisa Cathedral
- Poems: "Money" by Richard Armour and "Slowly" by James Reeves
- Recording: Ravel's *Bolero*

PROCEDURES
1. Show the picture *Vonal Ksz* by Vasarely. Discuss the various optical illusions created by the repeated rectangles—for example, curved line, looking into a tunnel, looking down into a well.
2. Show the students a side view of the Roman Colosseum or the Pisa Cathedral. Ask them to look for repeated lines or shapes (rounded arch, Greek columns). Also ask them to point out how the building is made larger by such repetition.
3. Have the students create their own pictures by making use of enlargement through repeating lines, shapes, colors, and so on.
4. Read the following poems and identify the poets' use of repetition. What is its effect?

*Money**

Workers earn it,
Spendthrifts burn it,
Bankers lend it,
Women spend it,
Forgers fake it,
Taxes take it,
Dying leave it,
Heirs receive it,
Thrifty save it,
Misers crave it,
Robbers seize it,
Rich increase it,
Gamblers lose it . . .
I could use it.

Slowly†

Slowly the tide creeps up the sand,
Slowly the shadows cross the land,
Slowly the cart-horse pulls his miles,
Slowly the old man mounts the stile.

Slowly the hands move round the clock,
Slowly the dew dries on the dock.
Slow is the snail—but the slowest of all
The green moss spreads on the old brick wall.

5. Have the students make up poems based on enlargement-expansion through repetition.

6. Have the students sing "Row, Row, Row Your Boat" as a round, first as a two-part, then as three-part, and finally as four-part.

   a. Put the following diagram on the board illustrating the beginning of the singing of the four-part round:

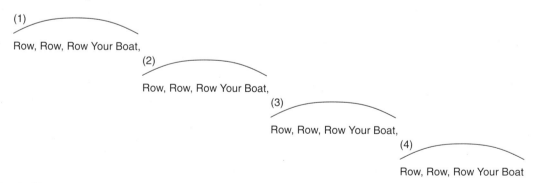

   b. Call attention to the organizational principle of enlargement-expansion through repetition.

7. Play a recording of Ravel's *Bolero*. During the first two minutes of the piece have students softly play the following triple-meter pattern:

$\frac{3}{4}$ 1   2   3
       Drum   Tambourine   Tambourine
               shake   shake

Have the rest of the class clap the underlying rhythmic motif that repeats throughout the piece:

CLOSURE AND EVALUATION

Ask students how moods or feelings can be created through the use of repetition.

Contrast

Grades: 1–3

OBJECTIVES

Students will

1. Identify characteristics of contrast in music, visual art, and poetry.
2. Create a sound composition in ABA form for each of the following: dynamics (loud/soft), and tempo (fast/slow).

MATERIALS

- Pictures: *Orion MC by* Victor Vasarely, *Broadway Boogie Woogie* by Piet Mondrian, photographs of stained glass windows at Chartres Cathedral
- Poem: "This Happy Day" by Harry Behn
- Percussion instruments, word cards, colored letters, chalkboard
- Recording: Saint-Saëns, *The Carnival of Animals*

PROCEDURES

1. Place the word *contrast* in different colors on a flannel board. Emphasize that the word *contrast* refers to things that are different. Have letters cut in different colors, sizes, and shapes. Ask the students to create various arrangements of the word on the chalkboard.
2. Explore contrast by having the students print their names in at least six different ways (using different sizes, shapes, colors, and so on).
3. Inflate several balloons of varying sizes and colors and arrange them in highly contrasting ways.
4. Ask the students to look for contrast in paintings such as Victor Vasarely's *Orion MC*, Mondrian's *Broadway Boogie Woogie*, or stained glass windows from the Cathedral of Notre Dame at Chartres, France. (They should find contrast in colors, sizes, and shapes.)

Victor Vasarely, *Orion MC*

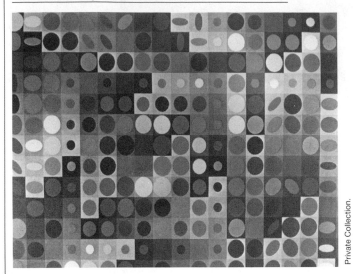

Private Collection.

5. Encourage students to create their own pictures, making use of contrast in colors, shapes, lines, sizes, and so on.

6. Read the poem "This Happy Day" by Harry Behn, and discuss how the poet uses contrast to express his idea of morning and night. What is repeated, and what is different?

This Happy Day*

Every morning when the sun
Comes smiling up on everyone,
It's lots of fun
To say good morning to the sun.
   Good morning, Sun!

Every evening after play
When the sunshine goes away,
It's nice to say,
Thank you for this happy day,
   This happy day!

7. Perform the song "Tinga Layo" (p. 98). Use metal percussion instruments to accompany the verse and wooden percussion instruments to accompany the chorus. Discuss how these are "contrasting" sections.

8. Play selections from *The Carnival of Animals* and use cards with words to describe the sounds or expressiveness of various animals (for example, elephant—slow; birds—high and fast).

---

*From *The Little Hill*, Poems and Pictures by Harry Behn. Copyright 1949 by Harry Behn. Copyright renewed 1977 by Alice L. Behn. Reprinted by permission of Marian Reiner.

CLOSURE AND EVALUATION

1. Ask students how contrast was used to add interest to selected examples.
2. Create a short rhythm composition in ABA form (twelve measures), in which the B section is different (contrasting).
3. Using your composition, experiment with contrasting instruments, contrasting dynamics, and so on.

More Contrast

Grades: 4–6

OBJECTIVES

Students will

1. Identify characteristics of contrast in music, visual art, and poetry.
2. Create a sound composition in ABA form for each of the following: (a) dynamics (loud, soft), (b) tempo (fast/slow), (c) tessitura (high/low), and (d) texture (thick/thin)

MATERIALS

- Different kinds of balls
- The word *contrast* in different sizes, shapes, and colors
- Rhythm instruments
- Poem: "Trucks"
- Pictures: Vasarely's *Orion MC* or Mondrian's *Broadway Boogie Woogie*
- Recording: Ravel's *Bolero*

PROCEDURES

1. Ask half the class to shout "School's out!" and the other half to whisper "School's out." Discuss the difference (include not only loud and soft but also the vocal mechanisms involved, such as shouting and whispering).
2. Show various kinds of balls, such as a football, basketball, tennis ball, Ping-Pong ball. Discuss how they are different.
3. Place the word *contrast* in many shapes and colors on a chalkboard.
4. Play the following rhythm and ask individual students to respond with a contrasting rhythm in the same meter signature:

Create several different rhythms that contrast with one another. Play these rhythms on contrasting rhythm instruments or sing them at different pitch levels.

5. Ask students to look for contrast in paintings such as Vasarely's *Orion MC* or Mondrian's *Broadway Boogie Woogie*. Ask them to identify contrast in clothing, comic books, textbooks, and magazines.

6. Ask students to look for ways in which contrast is achieved in Tippett's poem "Trucks" (such as contrast in rhyme scheme—ABCB—and in word sounds: *big, rumbling, heavily, little, turning, rushing*).

*Trucks**

Big trucks for steel beams
Big trucks for coal,
Rumbling down the broad streets,
Heavily they roll.

Little trucks for groceries
Little trucks for bread,
Turning into every street,
Rushing on ahead.

Big trucks, little trucks,
In never ending lines,
Rumble on and rush ahead
While I read their signs.

7. Play selections from Ravel's *Bolero* and discuss how the composer creates interest through contrast, while at the same time repeating the melody and rhythm.

CLOSURE AND EVALUATION

1. Ask students to identify the ways/techniques a composer may use contrast in a musical composition to express an idea, mood, or feeling.

2. Create an ABA musical composition using bells, xylophone, or percussion instruments.

Unity

Unity refers to the process of "tying" an artwork together through systematically repeating certain elements.

Grades: 5–6

OBJECTIVES

Students will

1. Identify how unity is created in music and in the visual and literary arts.
2. Create artworks that illustrate the concept of unity.

MATERIALS

• Pictures: Roman Colosseum, Pisa Cathedral; Mondrian's *Broadway Boogie Woogie*, Vasarely's *Orion MC*

*Edna Johnson et al., *Anthology of Children's Literature*, 5th ed. © 1977. By permission of Houghton Mifflin Co.

• Recordings: "Spring" from Vivaldi's *The Seasons,* Rondo from Mozart's *Eine Kleine Nachtmusik*

PROCEDURES

1. Reread the poem "Money" (p. 456).
2. Ask students how the word *it* ties the poem together.
3. Call attention to the use of the same number of syllables in the second word of each line (*earn, burn, lend, spend, take, fake*).
4. Ask students which words rhyme, and what effect this technique has on the poem.
5. Have the class create a short poem in which a word or words are repeated to tie the work together and provide a sense of unity.
6. Show pictures of the Roman Colosseum, the Pisa Cathedral, Mondrian's *Broadway Boogie Woogie,* and Vasarely's *Orion MC.* Discuss how items are repeated to provide a sense of unity in these structures and artworks.
7. Have the students create their own examples of visual art using repetition of items (shapes, colors, textures, and so on) to provide unity.
8. Listen to "Spring" from Vivaldi's *The Seasons.* This musical work is tied together by repeating the opening section throughout the composition. Follow the chart:

Listening Guide for Vivaldi's *The Seasons*

A Section:	Vigorous, joyful melody—spring has arrived
B Section:	Twittering of birds suggested by high trills in violins
A Section:	Return of a portion of the melody from beginning of piece
C Section:	Gentle breezes and lazy streams of water portrayed by soft, lyrical music
A Section:	Return of a portion of the melody from beginning of piece
D Section:	The sky begins to turn black, and thunder and lightning signal an approaching storm; vividly portrayed by low quivering string sounds followed by passages that sweep upward
A Section:	Return of a portion of the melody from beginning of piece
E Section:	Storm is now over and birds begin to sing, again portrayed by trills and embellishments on violins
A Section:	Return of melody from beginning of piece

9. Ask students to create a listening guide by using red strips of construction paper to indicate the main theme in the Rondo from Mozart's *Eine Kleine Nachtmusik* (see p. 280 for more information on listening guides). Discuss how the repetition of the main theme provides unity to the composition.

CLOSURE AND EVALUATION

1. Have students look at various artworks and identify unifying principles.
2. Ask students to identify techniques used by composers to unify their works.
3. Read poems of your choice and discuss how the poet unifies his or her work.

Balance

Grades: 5–6

OBJECTIVES

Students will

1. Identify balance in music and in the visual and literary arts.
2. Create artworks that illustrate the concept of balance.

MATERIALS

- Geometric figures (square, circle)
- Red construction paper
- Rhythm pattern chart ()
- Nursery rhyme: "The Goblin"
- Pictures: Taj Mahal, da Vinci's *The Last Supper*
- Recording of the Rondo from Mozart's *Eine Kleine Nachtmusik*

PROCEDURES

1. Have the students balance on one foot, as an ice skater might do, with arms extended in a "swan" position.
2. Have students cut out geometrical figures (square and circle, for example) and place them on a flannel board so that the square represents a fulcrum and the two circles represent equal weights on each end:

3. Place the following rhythmic pattern on the board. Clap the pattern with the class. Ask the students to discover balance in the rhythmic pattern. (What is the song?)

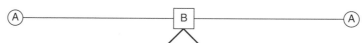

4. Have the students read the nursery rhyme "The Goblin" and discover balance (opening words are repeated at end to make an ABA design); compare this structure to the ABA rhythm pattern.

Taj Mahal, Agra, India

The Goblin*

A goblin lives in *our* house, in *our* house, in *our* house,
A goblin lives in *our* house all the year round.
He bumps
And he jumps
And he thumps
And he stumps.
He knocks
And he rocks
And he rattles at the locks.
A goblin lives in *our* house, in *our* house, in *our* house,
A goblin lives in *our* house all the year round.

5. Show the students pictures of the Taj Mahal (Agra, India) and *The Last Supper* by Leonardo da Vinci; ask them to identify how balance is achieved in these artworks.
   a. da Vinci: *The Last Supper*
      • Christ is the center, with six apostles on either side
      • Large window behind Christ has two small windows, one on each side
      • Wall area behind apostles has equal sides of wall on left and right
      • Table in front of apostles has a center area with equally proportioned sections on either side
   b. Taj Mahal, Agra, India
      • Dome area in center has equal portions of building on either side
      • Two minarets are on either side of the building
      • Large, ogive-shaped door and window opening in center with smaller ogive-shaped window openings on either side

*Adapted from *Sugar and Spice*. Edited by Rose Ryleman. Reprinted by permission of Western Publishing Company, Inc.

6. Sing "We Wish You a Merry Christmas" (p. 76). Ask students if they hear the same melody in several places in the song (first eight measures and last eight measures). Cut out different geometrical shapes in several colors of construction paper. Place an A on two pieces of paper with the same shape and color, and a B on a contrasting color and shape. Have the students place the construction paper diagrams on a chalkboard to indicate the form of the piece.

CLOSURE AND EVALUATION

1. Ask students to identify techniques used by poets, visual artists, and composers to "balance" their works of art. Find other songs that show balance.
2. Create a musical composition, poem, or work of visual art that shows balance.

USING A THEMATIC APPROACH IN RELATING MUSIC AND THE ARTS

One of the most frequently used approaches to relating music and other arts is through a common theme. Visual artists, writers, and musicians use a large number of themes in their works, including religion, love, war, freedom, people, machines, nature, stillness, and activity. In organizing units of study in a thematic approach, the intent is to discover how musicians, painters, and poets have been able to express a particular theme using materials that are unique to their art (e.g., sounds in music, words in poetry, and paint in visual art).

In this section suggestions for lessons provide opportunities to explore: (1) the portrayal of nature, (2) the portrayal of stillness, and (3) the portrayal of activity.

Suggestions for Lessons

The Portrayal of Nature

Grades: 4–6

OBJECTIVES

Students will

1. Identify phenomena of nature, such as storms, flowers, sunrise, sunset, waterfalls.
2. Identify how nature themes are portrayed in selected examples of music, poetry, and visual arts.
3. Create original works of music, visual art, and poetry that focus on themes of nature.

MATERIALS

- Pictures: Durand, *Scene from Thanatopsis*; Hicks, *The Peaceable Kingdom*
- Poems: Wordsworth, "I Wandered Lonely as a Cloud"; Keats, "On the Grasshopper and Cricket"; Japanese Haiku, "Snow Fell Until Dawn"

Edward Hicks, *The Peaceable Kingdom*

New York State Historical Association, Cooperstown

- Rhythm instruments
- Recordings: Beethoven, "The Storm," *Symphony No. 6* (fourth movement); Smetana, *The Moldau*; Britten, "In Freezing Winter Night" from *Ceremony of Carols*

PROCEDURES

(May need to be over several days)

1. Lead a short discussion on ways we experience nature each day (walk past trees on way to school, see and hear birds, watch fish swim in a pond, and so on).
2. Make a bulletin board titled "Nature." Look for good pictures of landscapes, trees, birds, and animals.
3. Show the students pictures of Asher Durand's *Scene from Thanatopsis* and Edward Hicks's *The Peaceable Kingdom* and ask them to find evidences of nature in the paintings (river, hills, trees, animals, and so on). Ask students to look for other examples of paintings that have a nature theme.
4. Have students create pictures on themes of nature, such as sunrise, sunset, waterfall.

Asher B. Durand, *Scene from Thanatopsis* (formerly known as *Imaginary Landscape*)

The Metropolitan Museum of Art, Gift of J. Pierpont Morgan, 1911

5. Read the following poems. Discuss how the writers portray nature (descriptive words).

a. "I Wandered Lonely As a Cloud," by William Wordsworth. (References to nature: Cloud that floats; vales and hills; a crowd; a host of golden daffodils; lake; trees; breeze; stars that shine and twinkle on the milky way; bay; waves beside them danced; sparkling waves.)

I Wandered Lonely as a Cloud

I wandered lonely as a cloud
    That floats on high o'er vales and hills,
When all at once I saw a crowd,
    A host, of golden daffodils.
Beside the lake, beneath the trees,
    Fluttering and dancing in the breeze.

Continuous as the stars that shine
    And twinkle on the milky way,
They stretched in never-ending line
    Along the margin of a bay:
Ten thousand saw I at a glance,
    Tossing their heads in sprightly dance.

The waves beside them danced, but they
    Outdid the sparkling waves in glee:
A poet could not but be gay,
    In such a jocund company.
I gazed—and gazed—but little thought
    What wealth the show to me had brought:

For oft, when on my couch I lie
    In vacant or in pensive mood,
They flash upon that inward eye
    Which is the bliss of solitude;
And then my heart with pleasure fills,
    And dances with the daffodils.

b. "On the Grasshopper and Cricket," by John Keats. (References to nature: birds, hot sun, cooling trees, hedge, mead, grasshopper, weed, frost, cricket, grassy hills.)

On the Grasshopper and Cricket

The poetry of earth is never dead:
When all the birds are faint with the hot sun,
And hide in cooling trees, a voice will run
From hedge to hedge about the new-mown mead;
That is the Grasshopper's—he takes the lead
In summer luxury—he has never done
With his delights; for when tired out with fun
He rests at ease beneath some pleasant weed.

The poetry of earth is ceasing never:
On a lone winter evening, when the frost
Has wrought a silence, from the stove there shrills
The Cricket's song, in warmth increasing ever,
And seems to one in drowsiness half lost,
The Grasshopper's among some grassy hills.

c. "Snow Fell Until Dawn," Japanese Haiku.* (References to nature: Snow, twig, grove, sunlight.)

Snow fell until dawn
now every twig in the grove
glitters in sunlight

6. Have the students compose their own poetry (no more than four lines) based on themes of nature.

7. Have the students create some of their own examples of music focusing on a theme or themes of nature. For example, using rhythm instruments, they might create a score that expresses the approach, arrival, and departure of a storm.

8. Have students listen to the following musical compositions portraying themes of nature and identify what the composer does.

a. Beethoven, *Symphony No. 6,* movement 4, "The Storm." (1) As the piece begins the low stringed instruments depict the rumbling of thunder in the distance. (2) The music gets louder and louder, leading to explosive fortissimo sounds portraying thunder and lightning, which are now close. (3) Timpani and brass instruments add to the musical depiction of the fury of the storm. (4) As the movement ends, the storm subsides and the music becomes soft and tranquil.

b. Smetana, *The Moldau.* This composition is a symphonic poem that tells the story of a famous river, the Moldau, which runs through the country of Bohemia (now Czechoslovakia). Follow the "musical trip" of the river: (1) In the shade of the Bohemian forest two springs bubble, their waves rippling over rocks to form a brook. Active, rippling passages in the woodwinds depict the movement of the water. (2) As the brook winds through the Bohemian coun-

*From *Cricket Songs: Japanese Haiku,* translated by Harry Behn. © 1964 by Harry Behn. © renewed 1992 Prescott Behn, Pamela Behn Adam, and Peter Behn. Reprinted by permission of Marian Reiner.

tryside, it gradually grows into a mighty river, the Moldau. A long, smooth melody played by the stringed instruments portrays the Moldau. (3) The Moldau flows through dense forests in which the sounds of hunting horns, aptly portrayed by brass instruments, are heard. (4) The river flows through a meadow where a peasant wedding is being celebrated with jubilant dancing. The orchestra plays dance music in 3/4 meter. (5) As night falls, the river flows quietly in mysterious stillness as the moonlight sweeps over its surface. Fortresses and castles, projecting skyward on the surrounding slopes, remain as mute witnesses of the bygone glories and splendors of knighthood. This section is portrayed by slow, soft, lyrical music. (6) Daybreak comes and the Moldau, again depicted by the long flowing melody in the stringed instruments, flows onward through a valley. (7) The river now passes through a rough, rocky area, depicted by loud, turbulent sounds in the orchestra. (8) As the rocky area is passed, the river again flows in majestic peace (portrayed by flowing, lyrical melody) toward Prague (the capital of Czechoslovakia), where it passes another ancient fortress, afterward disappearing beyond the poet's sight.

c. "In Freezing Winter Night," from *Ceremony of Carols* by Benjamin Britten. Notice the dissonance and repetition of both harp accompaniment and melodies.

CLOSURE AND EVALUATION

1. Ask students to identify techniques used by artists to portray events in nature (storm, river, winter).
2. Create a musical composition, poem, or work of visual art that focuses on some aspect of nature.

Stillness

Stillness is a state of quietness and calm. The word has many synonyms: subdued, hushed, peaceful, silent, tranquil, serene. In artworks a sense of stillness can be achieved in a number of ways: muted colors, horizontal lines, descriptive words (whisper, sleep), soft dynamic levels, slow tempos, and so on.

Grades: 2–3

OBJECTIVES

Students will

1. Identify how stillness is achieved in selected examples of music, visual art, and literature.
2. Create their own artworks portraying stillness.

MATERIALS

- Pictures: Miro's, *Blue III*; Tohaku's, *Pine Grove Screen*
- Poems: Livingston, "Whispers"; Sandburg, "Fog"; de la Mare, "Silver"
- Handout: Listening guide for "Ave Maria"
- Recordings: "Ave Maria" (*Understanding of Music, Enrichment Album*, Columbia, C5-10268, record 1, side 2, band 3; available from Wadsworth Publishing Co., 10 Davis Dr., Belmont, CA 94002); "Deer Calling to Each Other in the Distance" (*UNESCO Collection: A Musical Anthology of the Orient, Japan III*, Barenreiter Musicaphon, BM 30 L 2014, side 2, band 2); Ives, "Serenity" (*Charles Ives Songs*, Folkways Records, FM3345, side 2, band 5)
- Classroom instruments

PROCEDURES

(May need to be over several days)

1. Have the students sit perfectly still for 1 minute and then describe how they feel. Ask for ideas about what causes stillness and quietness.
2. Find pictures of things that are still. Find words that describe things that are still, such as *sleep, quiet, slow, mist,* and *darkness.*
3. Read the following poems with the class, focusing on how the writer has achieved a sense of stillness.
   a. "Whispers," by Myra Cohn Livingston. Call attention to the word *whispers,* which is repeated several times.

      Whispers*

      Whispers
         tickle through your ear
         telling things you like to hear.
      Whispers
         are as soft as skin
         letting little words curl in.
      Whispers
         come so they can blow
         secrets others never know.

   b. "Fog" by Carl Sandburg.

      Fog†

      The fog comes
      on little cat feet.
      It sits looking
      over harbor and city
      on silent haunches
      and then moves on.

---

*From *Whispers and Other Poems* by Myra Cohn Livingston. © 1958 by Myra Cohn Livingston. Reprinted by permission of Marian Reiner for the author.

†Excerpt from *Chicago Poems* by Carl Sandburg. Reprinted by permission of Harcourt Brace & Company, Inc.

c. "Silver," by Walter de la Mare. Call attention to the use of the words *slowly, silently, sleeps,* and *moveless;* notice the use of alliteration with many words beginning with *S,* a sound that conveys tranquillity.

Silver*

Slowly, silently, now the moon
Walks the night in her silver shoon;
This way, and that, she peers, and sees
Silver fruit upon silver trees'
One by one the casements catch
Her beams beneath the silvery thatch;
Couched in his kennel, like a log;
With paws of silver sleeps the dog;
From their shadowy cote the white breasts peep
Of doves in a silver-feathered sleep;
A harvest mouse goes scampering by,
With silver claws, and silver eye;
And moveless fish in the water gleam,
By silver reeds in a silver stream.

4. Have the students write their own poems or phrases using words that create a sense of stillness.

5. Have the class draw pictures that convey a sense of stillness. Explore not only stillness as a theme for a picture but also ways for achieving the feeling of stillness or calmness (use of colors such as blue and green, which are more subdued than the active colors of red and orange; use of horizontal lines, and so on).

6. Show pictures of paintings that portray stillness and tranquillity.

   a. *Blue III* by Joan Miro (Gaston Diehl, *Miro* [New York: Crown Publishers, 1979], p.72). Ask the class how the elements of line, shape, and color are used in the painting to create a sense of stillness, quietness, and inactivity (open, unobstructed space; color of blue; long, curvilinear line; round shapes).

   b. *Pine Grove Screen* by Tohaku (*Art and Man: Japan,* vol. 2, no. 2 [Englewood Cliffs, N.J.: Scholastic Magazines, 1971]). Ask students to point out how the sense of stillness is created through delicate lines depicting the "mistiness" of the scene, by the areas left "open" in the painting, and by the use of soft, pastel colors.

7. Listen to several selections of music that portray stillness and tranquillity.

   a. "Ave Maria, ' Gregorian chant. Have students circle the elements on the listening guide below that help create the sense of stillness/calmness in the music:

(smooth, stepwise melody;)	or	jagged melody with large skips
strong beat	or	(weak beat)
(slow tempo)	or	fast tempo
loud dynamic level	or	(soft dynamic level)

Discuss the "setting" of the music and why it needs to convey a sense of calm-

---

*Edna Johnson, et al., Anthology of Children's Literature, 5th ed. (Boston: Houghton Mifflin, 1977). By permission of The Literary Trustees of Walter de la Mare and The Society of Authors as their representative.

ness (performed as part of a religious service; quiet, serene atmosphere of a cathedral).

    b. "Serenity," by Charles Ives. Notice how the sense of stillness and calmness is created in the music to express the text "the silence of eternity" (soft dynamic level, weak feeling for the beat, slow tempo).

    c. "Deer Calling to Each Other in the Distance," as performed on the Japanese shakuhachi (wind instrument). Discuss how the soft dynamic level, the flexible rhythm, the slow tempo, the weak feeling for the beat, and the monophonic texture contribute to the sense of stillness, inactivity, and calmness in the music.

8. Have the class improvise with classroom instruments or their voices to convey a sense of stillness. Discuss how slow tempo, soft dynamic levels, smooth stepwise melodies, flexible rhythm, weak feeling for the beat, and so on help to create a sense of stillness or calmness.

9. Ask the students to make up movements that express the stillness of the music.

CLOSURE AND EVALUATION

1. Ask students to identify techniques used by artists to express stillness in works of art.

2. Ask students to create a musical composition, poem, or work of visual art that shows stillness.

Activity

Activity involves the state or condition of being energetic, lively, and vigorous.
Grades: 5–6

OBJECTIVES

Students will

1. Describe how artists, poets, and musicians create a sense of activity in their works.

2. Create their own artworks that convey a sense of activity.

MATERIALS

- Picture: Kandinsky's *Sketch I for Composition VII*
- Poem: Morrison, "The Sprinters"
- Recordings: Stravinsky, "Dance of the Adolescents" from *The Rite of Spring;* Beethoven, "The Storm" from *Symphony No. 6* (fourth movement)
- Handout: Listening guide for "Dance of the Adolescents"
- Classroom instruments

PROCEDURES

(May need to be over several days)

1. Lead a class discussion of ways in which students see activity in everyday life.

2. Make a list on the board of words that convey a sense of action.

3. Read the poem "The Sprinter" by Lillian Morrison. Note the sense of action in words such as *explodes, pummeling, pistoning, fly, smash, outpace, runs, streaks, faster, shout, pound,* and *grace-driven stride.*

*The Sprinters**

The gun explodes them.
Pummeling, pistoning they fly
In time's face.
A go at the limit
A terrible try
To smash the ticking glass,
Outpace the beat
That runs, that streaks away
Tireless, and faster than they.

Beside ourselves
(It is for us they run!)
We shout and pound the stands
For one to win
Loving him whose hard
Grace-driven stride
Most mocks the clock
And almost breaks the bands
Which lock us in.

4. Have the students compose their own poems or phrases using "action" themes and words.

5. Ask students to draw pictures that convey a sense of action. Explore not only action themes (running, playing ball, skating) but also ways for achieving the feeling of action in a painting (sharp, jagged lines; use of active colors, such as red; juxtaposition of strongly contrasting colors).

6. Look for ways in which the sense of action is created in Kandinsky's *Sketch I for Composition VII* (H. W. Janson, *History of Art*, 4th ed. [New York: Harry N. Abrams, 1991], p. 715). Ask the students to discover what qualities in the painting create the feeling of vigor or activity (warm, active colors of red and orange; contrasts of colors; twisting, swirling lines; diagonal lines).

7. Play "Dance of the Adolescents" from Stravinsky's *Rite of Spring.*
   a. Ask students to listen for ways in which activity is created in the music by circling the correct items:

weak beat	or	(strong, pulsating beat)
(strong accents)	or	no accents
(loud dynamic level)	or	soft dynamic level
smooth, lyrical sounds	or	(short, staccato sounds)
(jagged, skipping melody)	or	smooth, stepwise melody

   b. Ask the students to make up a set of movements that express the activity of "Dance of the Adolescents."

*From *The Ghosts of Jersey City*, T. Y. Crowell Co. Copyright © 1967 by Lillian Morrison.

8. Play "The Storm" from Beethoven's *Symphony No. 6*. Identify how activity is created by very loud dynamic levels, dramatic contrasts between loud and soft dynamic levels, and moderately fast tempo.

9. Have the students improvise with classroom instruments or voices to convey a sense of activity. Discuss how loud dynamic levels, fast tempo, strong accentuation, syncopation, melodies with large skips, and so on help create a sense of action in sound.

CLOSURE AND EVALUATION

1. Ask students to identify techniques used by artists to express activity in works of art.

2. Ask students to create a musical composition, poem, or work of visual art that shows activity.

STUDYING MUSIC AND THE ARTS AS PART OF UNDERSTANDING OUR PAST

An interesting approach to integrated learning experiences in the classroom involves art experiences that contribute to understanding our past. For example, students discover that events in a particular historical period, such as the American Revolution, are often reflected in sculpture, painting, and music. Through studying the arts as part of a particular historical period, students not only learn about aesthetic aspects of the arts but also develop a broader perspective on the people and events in an era.

In addition, dominant philosophical ideas in a period sometimes lead to similar "events" in different art forms. This is aptly reflected in the lesson on the Age of the Knights (medieval period) that follow.

Classroom teachers will find that interaction with examples of architecture, sculpture, painting, literature, and music greatly enhances students' understanding of their past. In effect, multiart presentations help students go beyond the memorization of facts about peoples and places in a particular time period and experience an era through actual examples of its finest artistic products.

The following two lessons are given as sample presentations only; you can use them as models for designing lessons on other historical periods.

Suggestions for Lessons

The Age of the Knights

The age of the knights occurred during the medieval period, which spanned the years from approximately A.D. 500 to 1400. In this period the Catholic church was one of the most important institutions in Europe, greatly influencing all aspects of life. Many great cathedrals were built throughout Europe. In the latter part of the medieval period many huge castles were also built where kings lived along with their knights. These men often dressed in metal armor to protect themselves in battle.

Grades: 5–6

OBJECTIVES

Students will

1. Identify characteristics of music and visual and literary arts of the medieval period.
2. Identify how the visual and literary arts and music were closely allied with beliefs of Christianity during the medieval period.

MATERIALS

- Pictures: Medieval cathedrals, such as Notre Dame in Paris, Notre Dame in Chartres, and Canterbury in England; stained glass windows; diagram of cathedral floor plan; medieval castles; suits of armor; tapestries; map of England

- Stories: Anthony Mockler, *King Arthur and His Knights* (New York: Oxford University Press, 1984); *King Arthur and His Knights Sound Recording*, as told by Jim Weiss (Benicia, CA: Greathall Productions, 1990); Chaucer, "The Friar," *Canterbury Tales*

- Recordings: Gregorian chant, "Ave Maria" (*Understanding of Music, Enrichment Album*, Columbia, C5-10268, record 1, side 1, band 3; available from Wadsworth Publishing Co., 10 Davis Dr., Belmont, CA 94002); motet "Ave Gloriosa Mater—Ave Virgo—Domino" (*A Treasury of Early Music*, Vol. 1: Music of the Middle Ages, The Haydn Society (P.O. Box 2338, Hartford, CT); "Kalenda Maya" (*Medieval Music and Songs of the Troubadors*, Everest 3270, side A, band 1)

- Handout: Listening guide for "Ave Maria"

- Film or video: *Discovering the Music of the Middle Ages* (BFA Educational Media, 2211 Michigan Avenue, Santa Monica, CA 90404)

PROCEDURES

(May need to be over several days)

1. Show the students pictures of some of the cathedrals built during the medieval period: Notre Dame (Paris, France), Notre Dame (Chartres, France), and Canterbury (England).
   a. Call attention to the tall spires of the Chartres Cathedral. Ask the students why people living during this period might have built such tall spires (to draw attention upward toward "heaven").
   b. Show a diagram of the cross on which Jesus died. Call attention to the three upper points of the cross, representing the Trinity ("three") of the church: God as (1) Father, (2) Son, and (3) Holy Ghost. Look at a diagram of the floor plans of the cathedrals, noticing that they are laid out in the form of a cross.
   c. Look at the windows and doorways in the Chartres Cathedral, noticing that they were also built in threes.
   d. Show pictures of the stained glass windows that were placed in the very tall walls of the cathedrals. Note that these pictures are about religious subjects: people from the Bible; rose window with its groups of twelves representing the twelve disciples.

2. In conjunction with showing pictures of the Canterbury Cathedral, have the class plan a "hypothetical trip" from London to Canterbury. Put a map of England on

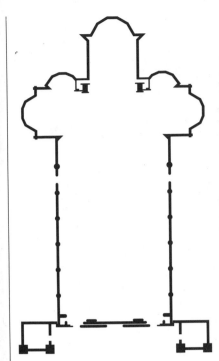

the bulletin board and highlight the travel route. Discuss that during the medieval period a group of people traveled by foot to the town of Canterbury to see the cathedral and the archbishop. To pass the time on such a long trip, travelers often told stories. Read with the class several selections from the *Canterbury Tales* (such as "The Friar," about a man who enjoyed having a good time!) by Geoffrey Chaucer, one of the most famous writers of the period.

3. Play recordings of some of the music performed in the church (Gregorian chant, "Ave Maria").

   a. Take the students on a "hypothetical trip" to a religious service in a great cathedral during medieval times. Discuss what the mood is as one enters the great building (calmness, quietness, peacefulness, tranquillity). As you listen to the Gregorian chant, which was sung as part of the religious service, how does this music reflect the setting? Have the students circle the appropriate items on the listening guide handout as they listen to the music.

(melody is smooth, stepwise)	or	melody has many large skips
strongly accented beat	or	(weak feeling for the beat)
(one line of music)	or	many lines of music
women singing	or	(men singing)
(dynamics soft)	or	dynamics loud

   b. Play the motet "Ave Gloriosa Mater—Ave Virgo—Domino." Note that there are three lines of music, two sung and one played on instruments:

   • Top line: Text, "Hail, Royal Virgin, Mother of Mercy . . ."

   • Middle line: "Hail, Glorious Mother of the Savior . . ."

   • Bottom line: Played on recorder (wind instrument) and viola da gamba (bowed stringed instrument)

Clap the meter of the piece, noting that it is grouped in threes (triple), symbolizing the Trinity of the church.

4. Show students pictures of some of the great castles built during the medieval period. Discuss how these buildings were fortified to help protect their inhabitants against attack. Show pictures of the armored suits worn by men to protect themselves in battle. Also show pictures of some of the large, multicolored tapestries that were hung on the walls of the castle. Have the students make a bulletin board titled "Life in a Castle."

5. Read with the class stories about King Arthur and the Knights of the Roundtable.

6. Play a popular piece of music from this period, "Kalenda Maya" ("The Month of May"). This is dance music featuring a woman singing (text centers on the joyous feelings experienced during the springtime month of May) accompanied by recorder (wind instrument), rebec (bowed stringed instrument), drum, and nakers (small kettle drums). Particularly note the distinctive nasalized tone color of the singer's voice and the triple meter.

7. Show the film or videotape *Discovering the Music of the Middle Ages*. This film contains selections of vocal and instrumental music. Included are wind instruments such as the krummhorn, recorder, sackbut, the portative organ, and the vielle, a stringed instrument.

8. Discuss contributions that artists of the medieval period have made to our world today. In your community look for examples of medieval-style architecture in churches and stained glass windows.

The Age of the American Revolution

The age of the American Revolution occurred more than 200 years ago. At that time the American colonies were seeking their freedom from British control. Growing frustration with the British eventually led to the writing of the Declaration of Independence (1776), which in turn set the stage for the Revolutionary War. In this conflict the thirteen colonies were pitted against the forces of the British Empire. Freedom became a major theme of the period.

During the eighteenth century the people and arts of ancient Greece and Rome became sources of inspiration for the revolutionary spirit that was under way not only in the American colonies but also in Europe. Leaders such as Napoleon Bonaparte looked to the past for models and found them in such men as Alexander the Great and Julius Caesar. Napoleon, for example, used the eagles of the Roman legions for insignia in the French army and ultimately was crowned with the laurel wreath, an ancient symbol of fame. In the visual arts Greek and Roman architectural and sculptural ideals greatly influenced innumerable artworks produced in the period.

Grades: 2–5

OBJECTIVES

Students will

1. Design a bulletin board that will include examples of the arts and personalities of the eighteenth century.
2. Identify examples of visual arts from the eighteenth and early nineteenth century and demonstrate an understanding of how they reflect the period.
3. Sing songs that center around themes and personalities related to freedom and independence.
4. Identify the "classical" qualities of music of eighteenth-century composers.

MATERIALS

- Pictures: George Washington, Thomas Jefferson, Benjamin Franklin, Wolfgang Amadeus Mozart, Franz Joseph Haydn; colonial Williamsburg; the British flag; Monticello; John Trumbull, *The Declaration of Independence*; Horatio Greenough's sculpture, *George Washington*; Houdon's sculptures of Franklin and Jefferson; Wedgewood pottery

- Recordings: Mozart, "Ah vous dirai-je, Maman," K. 265 (Deutsche-Grammophone, CD-429808); Michael Haydn, *Toy Symphony,* first movement (Angel 35638)

- Handout: Listening guide for "Ah vous dirai-je, Maman" (Grades 4–5—words; Grades 1–3—pictures)

- Melody bells

PROCEDURES

(May need to be over several days)

1. Make a bulletin board; include pictures of some of the most outstanding personalities of the eighteenth century: George Washington (Peale), Thomas Jefferson (Peale), Benjamin Franklin, Wolfgang Amadeus Mozart, Franz Joseph Haydn.

2. Show several pictures or slides of colonial Williamsburg, asking the students to describe how the buildings are different from those built today. Ask if anyone has seen buildings like these. Where? Are there any similar ones in your community? Show a picture of the British flag, which hung (and still hangs) over the capitol building, and ask the students why this flag would be flying in Williamsburg (Britain ruled the American colonies in the eighteenth century).

Gilbert Stuart, *George Washington*

John Trumbull, *The Declaration of Independence*

3. Draw the students into a brief discussion about events that happened in this country around the year 1775 (Declaration of Independence, Revolutionary War).

4. Look at the painting *The Declaration of Independence*, by John Trumbull. Do the students recognize any of the figures? (Benjamin Franklin, Thomas Jefferson, John Hancock)

5. Read the first two paragraphs of the Declaration of Independence and identify the theme of the document (emphasis on freedom).

6. The call for freedom in the Declaration of Independence rallied Americans in the thirteen colonies to go to war against the mighty British Empire. Have students sing the following song from the period to the tune of "America":

> God save the thirteen states,
> Long rule the United States
> God save our states,
> Make us victorious, happy and glorious,
> No tyrants over us
> God save our states.

7. Have students sing "Yankee Doodle," one of the most famous melodies of the period. Notice the reference to Washington, who would become commander of the Continental armies.

8. Show the class pictures of Monticello, Thomas Jefferson's home near Charlottesville, Virginia. Ask students to identify the influences of ancient Greek and Roman architecture: Greek columns (doric), Roman dome over center of building, emphasis on symmetry and balance. Have the students look for pictures of Greek and Roman architecture and place them on the bulletin board beside examples of Monticello.

Yankee Doodle

United States

Key: G
Starting pitch: D
Meter: 2/4, begins on "and" of 2

1. O, fath-'r and I went down to camp a - long with Cap - tain Good' - in, And
2. And there we saw a thou - sand men as rich as Squire___ Da - vid, And
3. And there was Cap - tain Wash - ing - ton up - on a slap - ping stal - lion, A -

there we saw the men and boys as thick as hast - y pud - ding!
what they wast - ed ev - 'ry day, I wish it could be sav - ed.
giv - ing or - ders to his men; I guess there were a mil - lion.

Yan - kee Doo - dle, keep it up, Yan - kee Doo - dle Dan - dy.

Mind the mu - sic and the step, and with the girls be hand - y.

Monticello

9. Show the students a picture of Horatio Greenough's sculpture of George Washington. Note that Greenough's Washington is patterned after an ancient Roman figure holding a toga, a one-piece cloth worn by Roman citizens in public. In addition, put on the bulletin board pictures of Houdon's sculptures of Franklin and Jefferson and of Wedgewood pottery, much of which was modeled after Greek artifacts (urns, for example).

10. Show a picture of Wolfgang Amadeus Mozart, the famous European musician who lived from 1756 to 1791. Explain that Mozart was considered a child prodigy and that at a very early age he played both the piano and violin. Compare the dress of Americans with that of Mozart. Note that the white powdered wigs, buckles on shoes, and long dress were in style both in Europe and America. Discuss reasons for this (Americans had come from Europe seeking freedom here and had brought their culture and traditions with them).

11. Listen to a recording of Mozart's piano composition "Ah vous dirai-je, Maman," K. 265, better known as "Variations on Twinkle, Twinkle, Little Star."
    a. Sing and play on melody bells the tune "Twinkle, Twinkle, Little Star."

Horatio Greenough, *George Washington*

The National Museum of American Art. Transfer from U.S. Capitol.

Twinkle, Twinkle, Little Star

Nursery Rhyme

Key: D
Starting pitch: C
Meter: 2/4, begins on 1

First-grade children dramatizing life during the eighteenth century

b. Hand out copies of the following outline to each student (Grades 4–5). Play the recording and have the students follow the variations and circle each variation number. In each variation encourage the students to listen first for the tune and then for ways in which the tune is varied. If time permits, discuss how repeating the "Twinkle, Twinkle" melody ties together or unifies the musical composition and how the variations provide contrast so that the piece will be more interesting. For Grades 1–3 have the students make up movements for each variation.

Variation 1: Melody heard with running melodic line in the right hand

Variation 2: Melody in right hand, running melodic line in left hand

Variation 3: Melody heard in triplet (3's) figure

Variation 4: Melody in right hand, triplets in left hand

Variation 5: Melody with off-beat patterns

Variation 6: Melody in right hand, running melodic line in left hand

Variation 7: Melody heard in running scale patterns in right hand

Variation 8: Melody heard in minor; use of imitation

Variation 9: Melody presented in clear, staccato fashion

Variation 10: Melody in right hand with accompaniment in left hand

Variation 11: Melody in slow, lyrical presentation

Variation 12: Melody in right hand with decoration

Variation 13: Melody with many fast running notes.

12. Play a recording of the first movement of the *Toy Symphony* by Michael Haydn. This is a three-movement work (Allegro, Minuet, Finale [Allegro]) featuring toy instruments, such as one-note trumpet, rattle, triangle, and drum. Call attention to the lighthearted quality of the music and the different bird calls executed by the instruments (twittering of the nightingale and the descending minor third [G, E] of the cuckoo).

13. Ask the students to summarize by making a list of some of the things they have learned in this lesson. Put the items on a bulletin board under a general topic heading such as "18th Century." Group the items into categories (political events, people, dress, music, and so on).

STUDYING MUSIC AND THE ARTS AS PART OF UNDERSTANDING OTHER PEOPLES

In the elementary school curriculum students learn about other people of the world. They study their geography, history, customs, and beliefs. One significant way to help students better understand other people is through an examination of their arts. Often very basic tenets of a cultural tradition are clearly reflected in the visual, literary, and aural arts.

Following is a suggested lesson on the arts of Japan. The intent of this lesson is to illustrate some fundamental ideas that help students better understand Japanese peoples. The lesson focuses on (1) an interest in placing people in harmony with nature, and (2) an interest in understating and achieving maximum effect with minimal materials.

Arts of Japan

Grades: 4–6

OBJECTIVES

Students will

1. Identify how the Japanese interest in their surrounding "natural world" is reflected in visual art, literature, and music.
2. Identify how the Japanese interest in understating and achieving maximum effect with minimal materials is reflected in visual art, literature, and music.

MATERIALS

• Pictures: Japanese countryside, buildings (particularly the Phoenix Hall of the Byodoin Temple in Uji [*National Geographic*, September 1967, p. 320]), and gardens

• Paintings: Motonobu's *Landscape with Waterfall and Crane* (p. 119), Goshun's *Landscape in the Rain* (p. 187), and Okyo's *Pine Tree in Snow* (p. 186) from Akiyama Terukazu, *Japanese Painting* (New York: Rizzoli, 1977)

• Recordings: "Isumi" (*Art of the Koto: The Music of Japan*, Electra Records, CD70234); "Deer Calling to Each Other in the Distance" (*UNESCO Collection: A Musical Anthology of the Orient—Japan III*, Barenreiter—Musicaphon BM 30 L 2014, side 2, band 2)

• Film or videotape: *Discovering the Music of Japan* (film from BFA Educational Media, 2211 Michigan Avenue, Santa Monica, CA 90404; videotape from West Music Co., P.O. Box 5521, Coralville, IA 52241)

PROCEDURES

(May need to be over several days)

1. Have the students make a bulletin board on Japan, highlighting the scenic natural beauty of the countryside. Discuss how such surroundings might affect the lives of people, particularly the products turned out by painters, writers, and musicians.

2. Show students pictures of Japanese buildings, calling attention to the emphasis on a natural setting. Look at a picture of the Phoenix Hall of the Byodoin Temple in Uji, noting the placement near the building of ponds filled with water lilies. The outside surroundings of buildings are often developed into immaculately tailored gardens, which are artistically arranged with rocks, trees, flowers, and ponds to create a kind of microcosm of nature. Japanese buildings themselves often strongly reflect themes of nature. Many are constructed of wood with the "natural look" preserved through large numbers of unpainted surfaces. Within the buildings, many rooms have a *tokonoma*, a recessed area in the wall containing a print or scroll of a nature scene with a flower arrangement placed in front of it.

3. Show the class examples of Japanese paintings: Motonobu's *Landscape with Water-fall and Crane*, Goshun's *Landscape in the Rain*, and Okyo's *Pine Tree in Snow*. Ask the students to identify the references to nature in each painting (birds, pine tree, waterfall, rain, snow).

4. Read the class the following Haiku poems.* Ask the students to identify references to nature (mountain, skylark, snow, twig, grove, sunlight):

High on a Mountain
we heard a skylark singing
 faintly, far below.
            Basho

Snow fell until dawn
Now every twig in the grove
 glitters in sunlight
            Rokwa

5. Sing the song "Sakura" (p. 420). Call attention to the references to nature in the words of the song: cherry blooms, flowering, wind, mist, clouds, air, cherry trees.

6. Listen to "Isumi" ("A Spring"), a composition played on the koto, a popular Japanese stringed instrument. Listen to the "running" lines of music, which attempt to depict a stream of water gushing from a mountainside.

7. Show the paintings again, calling attention to the manner in which Japanese artists seem to place emphasis on *understatement* and achievement of maximum effect with minimal materials. Note the emphasis on simplicity and detail. The pictures are composed of a number of delicately drawn lines, which are subtly manipulated to indicate depth and volume. Colors in the pictures seem to complement the delicacy, with their penchant toward pastel shades. Further, a large number of open-space areas contribute to a sense of understatement and simplicity.

8. Show some pictures of Japanese building interiors, noting how they seem to be directed toward simplicity. Much of the house's interior is left open and unclut-

*From *Cricket Songs: Japanese Haiku*, translated by Harry Behn. © 1964 by Harry Behn. © renewed 1992 Prescott Behn, Pamela Behn Adam, and Peter Behn. Reprinted by permission of Marian Reiner.

tered by a lot of furniture. The feeling of openness is enhanced by doors that slide back to expose large areas of the house. The walls of rooms are often constructed of simple, unpainted surfaces that are tastefully accented with paintings.

9. Read the haiku poetry again with the students. Call attention to the sense of simplicity and directness. The poems are very short, being composed of just three short lines arranged in groups of five, seven, and five syllables.

10. Play the recording of "Deer Calling to Each Other in the Distance" played by two Japanese shakuhachi players. Notice how the sense of understatement is created by monophonic texture (just one line of music), slow tempo, flexible rhythm, and subtly executed ornaments.

11. Show the first two segments on koto and shakuhachi from the film or videotape *Discovering the Music of Japan*. Direct particular attention to the emphasis on nature and the sense of simplicity and understatement.

PLANNING AND PRESENTING A PROGRAM

PURPOSE

Planning and presenting a program that integrates many different classroom activities such as music, visual art, language arts, history, geography, and physical education is a common expectation of the classroom teacher. Of course cognitive learning takes place in the preparation of such a program, but social learning also occurs. For example, students develop responsibility, exercise creativity, exert leadership, and work together. Careful planning by both teacher and students is essential. A primary purpose of such an activity is to share what students have learned with parents, relatives, and friends in the community.

PLANNING

The entire class should be involved in the selection of the overall theme so that many activities and ideas can be related to it in meaningful ways. After the class has selected a theme, they should begin gathering resource materials for the program. These should include songs, pictures, poems, essays, ideas for dramatic presentation, and so on. As with all such activities, the opening number of the program should be performed especially well and enthusiastically; each subsequent event must be selected with emphasis on variety and interest; and the conclusion should be an upbeat activity that leaves the audience excited about the program and what the students are learning. The accompanying boxes present three sample programs for a fifth grade, with resources included for each.

REHEARSALS

Rehearsals must occur with enough care and frequency that *nothing* is left to chance. For a 30-minute program, fifth-grade students would need a minimum of six weeks' preparation (twice a week), with a few more props and special effects added each week. Since this is an integrated program, all students should be involved in the planning and performance, with each student contributing his or her best musical talent and skill.

PROGRAM I: A MUSICAL HORN OF PLENTY (THANKSGIVING)

"America the Beautiful"

Introduction: Words of Welcome

Thanksgiving Poem:

Now Thank We All Our God
Now thank we all our God
With hearts and hands and voices,
Who wondrous things has done,
In whom his world rejoices
Who, from our mothers' arms
Has blest us on our way
With countless gifts of love,
And still is ours today.

O may this bounteous God
Through all our life be near us,
With ever joyful hearts
And blessed peace to cheer us,
And keep us in his grace,
And guide us when perplexed,
And free us from all harm
In this world and the next.

(Rinkhart, tr. Winkworth)

Introduction to Rondo

Trumpet Concerto in E Flat Major, Rondo........................W. A. Mozart
(movement interpretation: ABACA)

Introduction to Theme and Variation

"Simple Gifts" from *Appalachian Spring*.....................Aaron Copland
(puppet interpretation)

"Tinga Layo"
(p. 98; ostinato accompaniment: claves, bongo drums, maracas)

"Magic Penny"
(p. 29; accompaniment: chords on resonator bells)

"Praise and Thanksgiving"
(p. 129; three-part round)

Thanksgiving Poem: Psalm 150

Praise Ye the Lord
Praise ye the Lord.

Praise God in his sanctuary;
Praise him in the firmament of his power.

Praise him for his mighty acts;
Praise him according to his excellent greatness.

Praise him with the sound of the trumpets;
Praise him with the psaltery and harp.

Praise him with the timbrel and dance;
Praise him with stringed instruments and organs.

Praise him upon the loud cymbals;
Praise him upon the high sounding cymbals.

Let every thing that hath breath
Praise the Lord.

Praise ye the Lord.

"Oh, Be Joyful"
(p. 124; descant: vocal; harmony: vocal and xylophone; instrumental interludes and accompaniment: piano, guitar, xylophone, glockenspiel)

Closure: Words of thanks and appreciation

PROGRAM II: LIBERTY

"The Yankee Doodle Boy"

Introduction: Words of Welcome

The Meaning of Freedom (short essay)

How can we define liberty? What is freedom? For the people of East Berlin, 1989 was a time of freedom, when the Wall separating East and West Berlin crumbled and people were allowed to move freely between the two sections of the divided city. It was a time when people of eastern Europe began to experience freedom of choice for the first time. People throughout history have known the value of freedom and paid a price. Who were these people? What price did they pay? What were their rewards? The United States of America was founded on the concept of liberty. Ralph Waldo Emerson, an American poet, expressed the spirit of freedom when he wrote the *Concord Hymn*, first sung at the completion of the Battle Monument at Concord, Massachusetts, on July 4, 1837. This is what he wrote:

Concord Hymn
By the rude bridge that arched the flood,
    Their flag to April's breeze unfurled,
Here once the embattled farmers stood
    And fired the shot heard round the world.

The foe long since in silence slept;
    Alike the conqueror silent sleeps;
And Time the ruined bridge has swept
    Down the dark stream which seaward creeps.

On this green bank, by this soft stream,
    We set to-day a votive stone;
That memory may their deed redeem,
    When, like our sires, our sons are gone.

Spirit, that made those heroes dare
    To die, and leave their children free,
Bid Time and Nature gently spare
    The shaft we raise to them and thee.

(Ralph Waldo Emerson)

Yankee Doodle Boy

Words and Music by George M. Cohan

Key: G
Starting pitch: B
Meter: 2/4, begins on 1

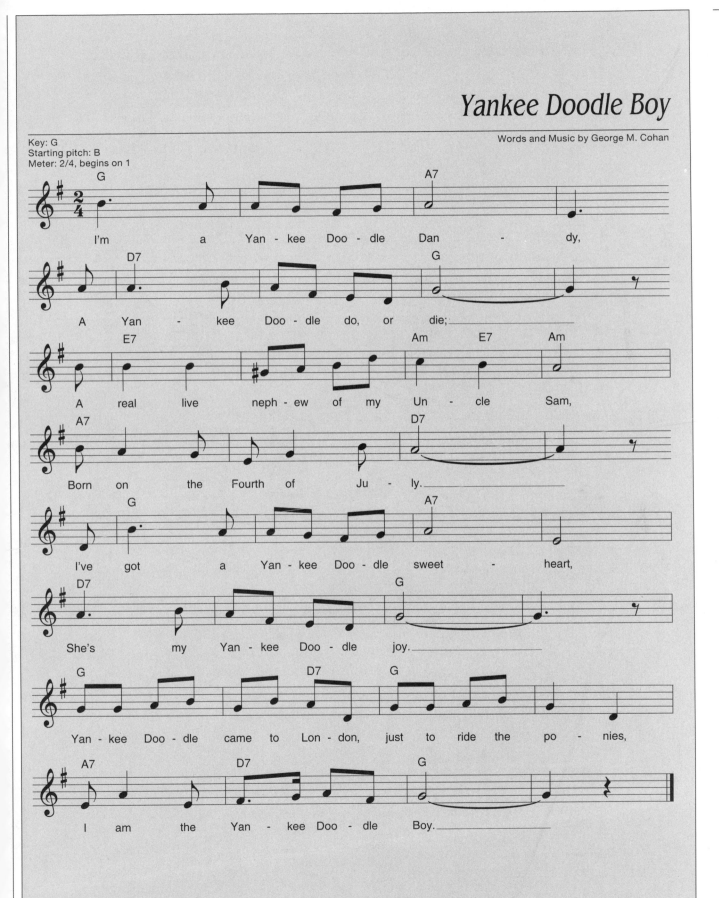

Introduction to "There Are Many Flags in Many Lands"
The United States was founded on freedom from oppression—a nation composed of people from all cultures and religious beliefs, come together as Americans.

"There Are Many Flags"
(Tableau: four or five students with flags of several nations)

There Are Many Flags

Key: A♭
Starting pitch: A♭
Meter: 4/4, begins on 3

Traditional
Words by Mary H. Howliston

There are man-y flags in man-y lands,

There are flags of ev-'ry hue;

But there is no flag, how-ev-er grand,

Like our own Red, White, and Blue.

REFRAIN

Then hur-rah for the flag, our coun-try's flag,

Its stripes and its white stars, too,

For there is no flag in an-y land

Like our own Red, White, and Blue.

Introduction to Revolutionary America
"Yankee Doodle"
(p. 479; ostinato accompaniment: guitar, drums, rhythm sticks; tableau: three minutemen)

Introduction to War of 1812
"The Star Spangled Banner"
(p. 41; tableau: Francis Scott Key writing song)

Introduction to Civil War
"Dixie"
(accompaniment: harmonica, guitar)
Theme and Variations: "American Salute," Morton Gould
(CD RCA Gold Seal 6806-2RG; movement interpretation)

Introduction to World War I
"Over There"
(*America in Song* 90-3700 Book of the Month Club, side 4, band 5; accompaniment: snare drum, bass drum; movement interpretation)

Introduction to World War II
"Marine's Hymn"
(*America in Song* 90-3700 Book of the Month Club, side 1, band 4; accompaniment: snare drum, bass drum; tableau: raising of flag at Iwo Jima)

Introduction to a Fanfare
"Fanfare for the Common Man," Aaron Copland
(CBS MY-37257 [record]; MYK-37257 [CD]; listening guide of tone colors—emphasis on brass and percussion)

Introduction to Gettysburg Address
Lincoln Portrait (III), Aaron Copland
(CBS MK-42431 [CD]; tableau: Lincoln giving speech at Gettysburg; people listening)
"Battle Hymn of the Republic"
(p. 179; audience is invited to join in singing the chorus)

Finale: "You're a Grand Old Flag"

Introduction

There are many symbols of a country; ours is the American flag. It stands for everything that is special about being an American. The "Star Spangled Banner" is played and the American flag is raised whenever an American wins a gold, silver, or bronze medal in the Olympics.

The American flag is composed of red and white strips representing the original thirteen states, while the stars on the field of blue represent the fifty states that make up our country. The American flag is presented to American families when a loved one is killed in battle, and we show our respect for the flag by taking off our hat or facing the flag when it goes by in a parade. In the United States we honor the American flag on June 14, known as Flag Day.

(entire class sings song and joins in choreographed march)

Closure: Words of appreciation and thanks

You're a Grand Old Flag

Key: F
Starting pitch: C
Meter: 2/4, begins on 2

Words and music by George M. Cohan

PROGRAM III: A MUSICAL FIESTA: SOUTH OF THE BORDER

Introduction: Words of Welcome

The Meaning of a Fiesta (short essay)

The song "The First of January" is a folk song from Mexico. It features counting from one to seven in Spanish: uno, dos, tres, cuatro, cinco, seis, siete. On the seventh of July, people of Spanish origin sing this song, which celebrates the fiesta in honor of the Spanish Saint Fermin. We will sing it in Spanish and then in English. Handclaps, tambourines, and triangles as well as chording instruments (Autoharp, guitar, or Omnichord) provide the accompaniment.

Handclaps: 6/8

Tambourines: 6/8

Triangle: 6/8

The First of January (Uno de enero)

Folk Song from Mexico

Key: C
Starting pitch: G
Meter: 6/8, begins on 4

"La Raspa"
(p. 235; song and dance)
Dramatics
(a short play with hand puppets or stick puppets featuring an aspect of Mexican life)
"De Colores"

De Colores

Key: C
Starting pitch: G
Meter: 3/4, begins on "and" of 1

Traditional
English Words by Alice Pirgau

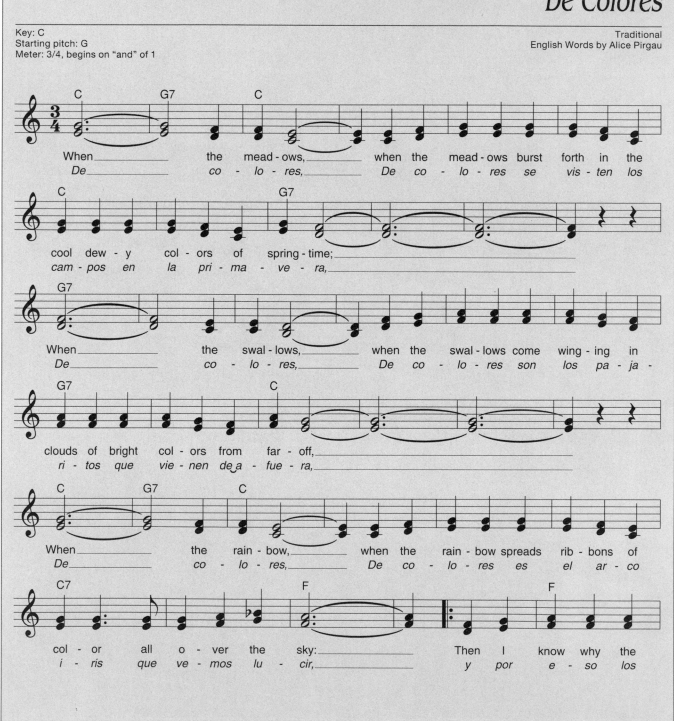

When _____ the mead - ows, when the mead - ows burst forth in the
De _____ co - lo - res, De co - lo - res se vis - ten los

cool dew - y col - ors of spring - time; _____
cam - pos en la pri - ma - ve - ra, _____

When _____ the swal - lows, _____ when the swal - lows come wing - ing in
De _____ co - lo - res, _____ De co - lo - res son los pa - ja -

clouds of bright col - ors from far - off, _____
ri - tos que vie - nen de a - fue - ra, _____

When _____ the rain - bow, _____ when the rain - bow spreads rib - bons of
De _____ co - lo - res, _____ De co - lo - res es el ar - co

col - or all o - ver the sky: _____ Then I know why the
i - ris que ve - mos lu - cir, _____ y por e - so los

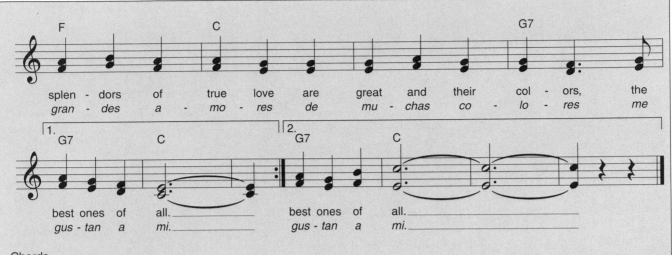

splen - dors of true love are great and their col - ors, the
gran - des a - mo - res de mu - chas co - lo - res me

1.
G7   C
best ones of all.
gus - tan a mi.

2.
G7   C
best ones of all.
gus - tan a mi.

Chords

C   C7   G7   F

Each person is assigned a note; thus, three people play the C chord and four play the C₇ chord (on Autoharp, guitar, or Omnichord and bells or xylophone)

"La Cucaracha"
(p. 361)

A song that is often sung in Mexico is "La Cucaracha." We will sing it today both in Spanish and English accompanied by maracas, claves, and chording instruments. The claves and chording instruments will keep a steady beat while the maracas improvise an appropriate rhythm.

"Cielito Lindo"
(p. 366)
(recording: World of Music CD-4:2, 1991, book 4, p. 63)

A Mariachi band or ensemble is composed of street musicians playing guitars, violins, and trumpets who stroll into restaurants or open-air cafes during the long lunch hour. Sometimes the mariachi ensemble is hired to play for an entire evening. Raise your hands when you hear trumpets, violins, or guitars.

Piñata Ceremony

The piñata is a papier-mâché object filled with candy or nuts and made to look like an animal. The breaking of the piñata is accomplished at the close of the nine days of Christmas celebrations in Mexico. Each child is blindfolded and has a turn with a stick in hopes of breaking the piñata. After it is broken, children gather up their treats. First we will sing "Piñata Song" in Spanish and then in English.

Piñata Song (Al Quebrar la Piñata)

Key: C
Starting pitch: G
Meter: 3/4, begins on 2

Christmas Song from Mexico
English Words by Verne Muñoz

In the hap - py days of Christ - mas,
En las no - ches de po - sa - das,

Sounds of glad - ness fill the air;
La pi - ña - ta es lo me - jor;

When it's time for the pi - ña - ta,
La ni - ña más re - mil - ga - da

There's ex - cite - ment ev - 'ry - where.
Se al - bo - ro - ta con ar - dor.

1. Take a stick and whack it, Be the one to crack it;
2. *Da - le, da - le, da - le, no pier - das el ti - no,*

Win pi - ña - ta's trea - sure, Can - dies for your plea - sure.
Que de la dis - tan - cia se pier - de el ca - mi - no.

Closing: Thank you for coming and we hope that you will join us for refreshments.

COMMITTEES

Students should organize the following committees in the classroom:

1. Program committee
   a. Songs and accompaniments
   b. Instruments needed
   c. Welcome, poems, essays, "connecting" statements, closure
   d. Dramatics
   e. Order of events
2. Classroom decorations
   a. Put up decorations
   b. Take down decorations
3. Refreshments
4. Table decorations
5. Costumes
6. Audio recording
7. Video recording

QUESTIONS FOR REVIEW

1. What is an analogous concept approach to studying the arts?
2. What is a thematic approach to studying the arts?
3. How is studying the arts important to understanding our past?
4. How does studying the arts through cultural diversity contribute to an understanding of other people?
5. How can relating various art forms such as poetry and music, or visual art, poetry and music, enhance the learning in your classroom?
6. What are some objectives for a lesson on repetition?
7. What are some objectives for a lesson on contrast?
8. Why do children in Grades 1–3 have some difficulty with the concepts of balance and unity, while older children do not?
9. What are some nature themes popular with children?
10. What are some advantages to your class in planning a program based on a mutually agreed upon theme?
11. What are some other themes relevant to your class that you could select for programs?

EPILOGUE THE CONTINUING PLACE OF MUSIC IN THE LIVES OF CHILDREN

This book has focused on integrating music into the elementary school classroom. You, the classroom teacher, have been given detailed descriptions of ways to assist students in learning to sing, play instruments, listen to music, move to music, and create music. You have been encouraged to integrate music with other areas of the arts and with a study of people and places in the world. There is little doubt that if you carry out the suggestions of this book, your students will receive an excellent introduction to music as a significant phenomenon of human experience.

One of the principal outcomes of music instruction in elementary schools is that children come to value music as an important part of their lives. Since learning experiences in school encompass only a small portion of one's life, it is hoped that students will develop the necessary skills and understanding to want and be able to continue musical study beyond the school itself. It is clear, however, that if teachers wish to foster a continuing place for music in the lives of their students, they will indeed need to set the foundation for such endeavors in the school music program itself

A TRIP TO BUY A RECORDING

Students should be encouraged to begin to build their own libraries of recorded music, including classical, folk, and popular genres. Such a library might begin by teachers suggesting that students ask for recordings as gifts at birthdays, Christmas, and so on.

Teachers should assist students in making lists of their favorite pieces and performers. It is hoped that many of these selections will be those actually studied in school. In addition, however, students will undoubtedly include a number of pieces heard outside the school either on radio or television or in live performance.

School librarians should have copies of the Schwann Record and Tape Catalogue for reference. This catalogue lists currently available commercial recordings of musical selections by composer or country. You can help students by suggesting recordings by some of the major orchestras, such as those in Boston, Chicago, Cleveland, New York, Philadelphia, and San Francisco, and well-known artists such as Pavarotti, Perlman, Wild, and so on. Music teachers in your school or in the community can help you decide which are the best performing groups, artists, and recordings.

Below are some general directions to help students in purchasing and organizing a recording collection:

1. Is the recording by a well-respected performing ensemble, conductor, or solo performer?
2. Is the recording well crafted and engineered?
3. Is the recording a good bargain— that is, does it fit within my budget?

Invite students to bring recordings from home. These may be organized according to composer, country, or recording company, and displays can be made of the cassette or compact disc packages. The class may wish to make a list on the bulletin board of the best-known conductors and performing artists. If available, you might invite the owner/manager of a record store to visit the class. He or she may speak on a variety of topics, such as how recordings are made (especially the digital process), how owners decide which recordings to stock in the store, and which composers' works seem most popular today. If a record store is near your school, the class may wish to take a trip to the store itself, where they can see how recordings are arranged by type of music (classical, jazz, rock, country, folk, and so on), some of the important recording companies, and different price ranges of cassettes and compact discs.

ATTENDING CONCERTS

One of the principal goals of music instruction in schools is to instill in students a desire to attend live performances of music—classical, jazz, folk, and so on. There is little substitute for being present as a creative musical performance takes place. The excitement of actually hearing and seeing ensembles and conductors, the virtuoso technical achievements of professional musicians, the distinctive tone colors of voices or instruments, and the special acoustical qualities created by the distinctive architecture of a great concert hall all combine to provide truly memorable experiences.

Teachers can do a number of things to help students learn to enjoy and want to attend concerts. Students should carefully study and listen to pieces to be performed. Outlines of pieces to be heard, in terms of the major musical events, are especially important. Students should listen to recorded pieces following these outlines until they have at least a fundamental grasp of the compositions, thus acquiring some sense of what to listen for in the live performance they will be attending.

Study of musical compositions should also include information about when and where composers lived, types of music they composed, and some of the principal characteristics of each composer's music. Whenever possible, musical information should be placed in a larger framework through comparisons with other events and people of the same period. But while such information is quite valuable, it should always be secondary to the listening experience itself

Students should also know something about the performers they will be hearing. This might include information about conductors, featured soloists, and outstanding members of the orchestra. Students will be interested to know of performers who have overcome major handicaps (such as Itzhak Perlman, crippled by polio, and Stevie Wonder, George Shearing, or Ray Charles, blind pianists) to become distinguished performing artists.

Basic understanding of the structure of ensembles should include the number, type, and arrangement of instruments. Diagrams are especially helpful for assisting students in quickly understanding how, for example, an orchestra is seated.

Another important nonmusical item to be considered is proper concert behavior. Students need to be instructed to sit quietly and not to talk or whisper as the music is being performed, not to chew gum or eat candy during a performance, to clap at the end of entire pieces and not between individual sections, and at all times to be courteous with each other.

A number of free children's concerts are offered by major professional orchestras and college or university orchestras throughout the country. Materials for preparing students to attend such concerts are often provided by the educational departments of the orchestras. In some communities volunteers visit schools and assist the classroom teacher in such musical preparation.

PERFORMING WITH FRIENDS

Another principal goal of a school music program is for students to learn to value singing, playing, and creating music, so that such experiences can be carried beyond the school itself. Boys and girls should be encouraged to perform either alone or in small groups, with members of their family, in schools, and in the community. Churches and civic organizations are particularly interested in having groups of students perform for various occasions. A number of communities throughout the country have choruses, bands, and orchestras composed of interested citizens from the community. Often there are groups for beginning students that provide opportunities for younger performers and act as feeder organizations to adult groups. Many such groups provide scholarships for serious music study by talented students. Teachers can encourage student participation in a variety of community ensembles by inviting such groups to perform at the school or by inviting the conductors of various organizations to come to the school and speak with classes.

In addition to participating in formal musical performing groups in the school or the community, children should be encouraged to form their own ensembles and perform together for enjoyment and recreation. Students who play brass instruments, for example, may wish to form an ensemble to play compositions from a number of easy ensemble books currently available commercially. (Easy ensemble materials for woodwind and stringed instruments are also available.) Your school instrumental music teacher will be able to offer suggestions.

Students greatly enjoy playing for get-togethers such as parties and birthdays, PTA meetings, and meetings of service clubs such as Kiwanis and Rotary. They can have great fun in organizing a "neighborhood circus" in the summertime and providing their own music for various segments of the show, or having a talent show within their class. You should encourage students to think of the many ways they can perform music for all types of occasions, both at the school itself and in the surrounding community.

In summary, the ultimate goal of this book is to provide classroom teachers with the knowledge, skill, and confidence for teaching music to children so that they will seek out and participate in musical activities at every opportunity. Such an interest in music is often born in the early years of a child's life, and if musical experiences of significant breadth and depth are provided in the elementary schools, there is good likelihood that music will continue to hold a special place in the lives of children, not only during their subsequent school years but as they grow into men and women who value music as an indispensable part of their lives.

APPENDIX A SOPRANO RECORDER FINGERINGS
(BAROQUE SYSTEM)

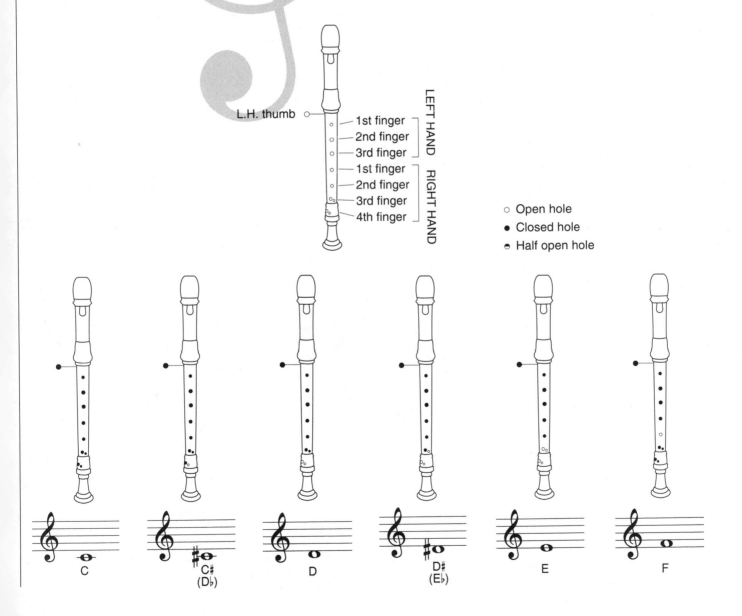

○ Open hole
● Closed hole
◖ Half open hole

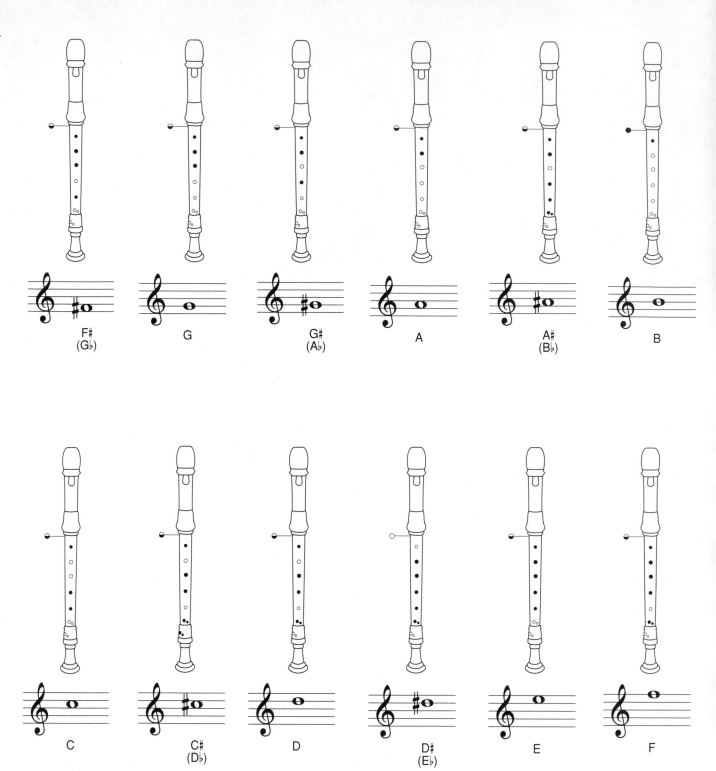

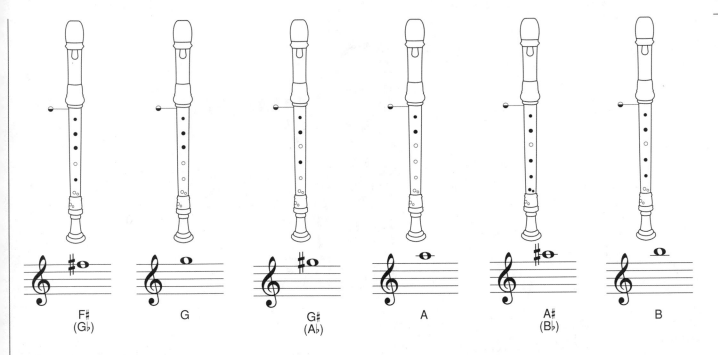

F#
(G♭)

G

G#
(A♭)

A

A#
(B♭)

B

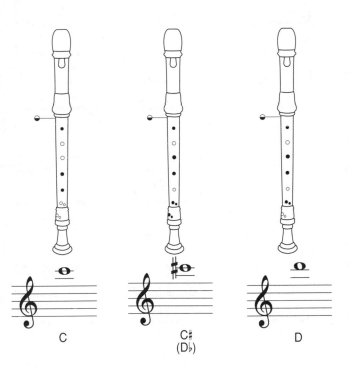

C

C#
(D♭)

D

APPENDIX B Common Chord Fingerings for the Guitar

Symbols:

X = String not played

0 = Open string

1 = Left index finger

2 = Left middle finger

3 = Left ring finger

4 = Left little finger

R = Root of chord

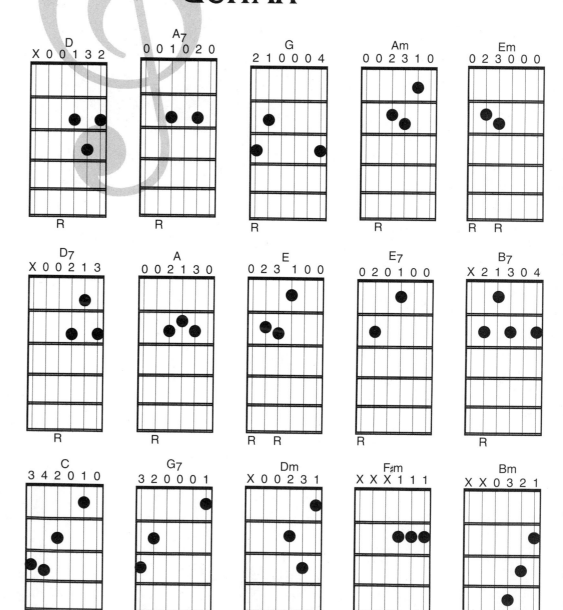

GLOSSARY

A cappella. Without instrumental accompaniment. The phrase is Italian for "in chapel style"—that is, in the style of a small place of worship.

Accelerando, accel. Gradually become faster.

Accent. Greater emphasis on note or chord. Often indicated by ^ or > placed above the note or chord.

Accidental. A sharp (♯), flat (♭), or natural (♮) that appears in the musical score but is not part of the key signature.

Adagio. Moderately slow tempo.

Ad lib, ad libitum. A direction indicating that the performer may vary the tempo in a musical composition.

Affective. Having to do with feeling.

Agogo bells. An African percussion instrument consisting of conical metal bells, each having a different pitch.

Allargando, allarg. Slowing of tempo.

Alto. The lowest female voice.

Analogous concept. A concept used in the same way across the arts, such as repetition, contrast.

Aria. An accompanied song for solo voice.

Articulation. The way in which musical tones are attacked. It is related to the clarity in vocal or instrumental performance. Legato and staccato are types of articulation.

A tempo. A return to the previous tempo.

Atonality. The lack of a tonal center.

Augmentation. Presentation of a melody in longer notes.

Autoharp. An American stringed instrument that can be plucked or strummed and is often used to accompany songs.

Balalaika. A triangular-shaped Russian stringed instrument.

Ballad. A narrative song.

Bar line. A vertical line drawn on the staff to divide music into measures.

Baroque music. European music from the period between 1600 and 1750.

Bass. The lowest male voice.

Behavioral objective. A statement that contains specific skills or behaviors that learners are expected to acquire.

Binary form. Music composed of two contrasting sections, A and B.

Bongo drums. Two connected drums of different pitches. The player holds them between the knees and strikes them with his or her hands.

Cabasa. A rhythm instrument with metal beads encircling a large wooden spool.

Cadence. A melodic or harmonic formula that indicates the end of a section or piece.

Canon. A strict form of imitation in which a melody is stated in one part and is repeated in one or more other "voices."

Cantata. A sacred or secular choral composition of several movements.

Changing meter. Frequent changes of meter in a musical composition.

Chant. A single, unaccompanied melody.

Chord. Three or more tones sounding simultaneously.

Chorus. A large group of singers. The term is also used to denote a refrain or a choral segment of an oratorio.

Chromatic scale. A scale entirely composed of half steps.

Classical music. European music from the period between 1750 and 1825.

Clef. A sign placed at the beginning of the staff to designate the names of pitches.

Coda. A composed ending for a composition.

Cognitive. The process of mental learning.

Concept. A general term, often applied to a set of ideas that are the same, such as repetition, contrast, rhythmic pattern.

Concerto. A composition for solo instrument and orchestra.

Concerto grosso. A composition that contrasts more than one solo instrument with the orchestra.

Conjunct. A term used to describe melodies that move by stepwise intervals.

Contour. The shape of a melody.

Countermelody. A melody that is added above or below the main melody.

Crescendo. Gradually becoming louder.

Cut time. Dividing the meter by two, for example, 4/4 = 2/2 or ¢.

Da capo (D.C.). Go back and repeat from the beginning.

Dal segno al Fine (D.S. al Fine). Repeat from the sign, and perform until the word *Fine*, which means "end."

Descant. A countermelody that is always above the main melody.

Diminution. The presentation of a melody in shorter note values.

Disjunct. A melody in which the intervals are larger than a major second.

Dominant. The fifth degree of a scale.

Double bar. Two vertical lines that signify the end of a composition.

Downbeat. The first beat of a measure.

Dulcimer. A name given to several types of American traditional stringed instruments, including the plucked dulcimer and hammered dulcimer.

Duple meter. Meter based on two beats or multiples of two.

Dynamics. Term indicating degree of loudness or softness in a musical composition.

Enharmonic. Descriptive of notes that have the same sound but different names, for example, F# = G♭.

Fermata. To hold or pause.

Fine. The end.

Flat (♭). A musical symbol that lowers the pitch half a step when placed before a note.

Form. How a work is designed, its structure.

Forte. Loud.

Fortissimo. Very loud.

Fugue. A musical composition based on imitation. It consists of an exposition, episodes, and reappearance of the subject in different "voices."

Grand staff. The G and F clefs joined together.

Half step. The interval from one pitch to the next adjacent pitch, ascending or descending.

Harmony. The performing of two or more pitches simultaneously.

Harpsichord. A stringed keyboard instrument shaped like a modern grand piano but whose strings are plucked rather than hammered to make the sound when the keys are depressed.

Homophonic. A musical texture in which a prominent melodic line is supported with an accompaniment.

Interval. The distance between two pitches.

Key signature. The sharps or flats placed at the beginning of a musical composition to affect the entire composition.

Koto. A Japanese stringed instrument that has thirteen strings and movable bridges.

Legato. Connecting pitches smoothly.

Listening guide. A chart that uses graphics or words to depict various events as they occur in the music.

Major scale. A seven-tone scale comprised of W-W-H-W-W-W-H steps.

Mbira (also called kalimba). An African instrument consisting of metal or wooden strips of different sizes attached to a resonator (gourd) and played with the thumbs.

Measure. A group of beats between the bar lines on the staff.

Melismatic. A melodic passage in which one syllable is sung on several different consecutive pitches.

Melodic rhythm. Rhythm in which words and music notation are the same.

Melody. An organized succession of pitches.

Meter signature. The numbers placed at the beginning of a composition. The upper number indicates the number of beats per measure, while the lower number tells what kind of a note will receive one beat.

Metronome. An instrument used to indicate a steady tempo.

Minor scale. A seven-tone scale commprised of W-H-W-W-H-W-W steps.

Minuet. A French country dance in triple meter.

Mixed voices. A combination of male and female voices.

Mode. Scalar arrangements of pitches with dis-tinctive intervals. Common in Medieval, Renaissance, and folk music.

Modulation. Changing from one key to another within a composition.

Notation. A system for writing music that indicates pitch and duration.

Note. A musical symbol that may indicate both pitch and duration.

Obbligato. A second melodic line that accompanies the main melody.

Octave. The interval of an eighth between the lowest pitch and the highest.

Opera. A musical drama in which all or most of the dialogue is sung.

Operetta. A musical drama in which the dialogue is generally spoken.

Ostinato. A repeated melodic or rhythmic pattern that recurs throughout a composition.

Pentatonic scale. A five-note scale.

Phrase. A division of a musical line, comparable to a line or sentence in poetry or prose.

Pipa. A pear-shaped Chinese stringed instrument that is held upright and plucked by the fingers of the right hand.

Pitch. The highness or lowness of a tone.

Polyphonic. Music in which there are two or more independent melodies.

Polyrhythm. Two or more contrasting rhythms sounding at the same time.

Presto. Very fast.

Psychomotor learning. Learning through movement.

Recitative. A declamatory style of singing.

Recorder. A small vertical, flutelike instrument. The pitch is determined by covering and uncovering holes with the fingers.

Refrain. A relatively short section that is repeated at the end of each verse of a song.

Relative major and minor. The major and minor scales that have identical key signatures; for example, C major = A minor.

Renaissance. The European historical period extending from approximately 1400 to 1600.

Repeat sign. Sign indicating that the section should be performed again.

Rhythm. The organization of the duration of sound.

Romantic period. The European historical period from approximately 1825 to 1900.

Rondo. A musical form diagrammed ABACA.

Rote. The process of learning a song by imitation.

Rote-note. The process of learning a song by imitation and notation.

Round. A song in which two or more groups perform the same melody but start at different times.

Rubato. Flexibility of tempo.

Santouri. A Greek stringed instrument that is played with small hammers.

Scale. A succession of ascending and descending tones.

Sequence. A melodic pattern that is repeated beginning on another pitch.

Shakuhachi. A notched, end-blown Japanese wind instrument.

Sharp (♯). A musical symbol that raises the pitch of a note half a step.

Sheng. A Chinese wind instrument made of bamboo reed pipes placed into a bowl-shaped base.

Slur. A curved line above or below two or more notes, indicating that they should be performed legato.

Solfège. A system for identifying the pitches of the Western scale: *do, re, mi, fa, sol, la, ti, do.*

Sonata form. A European musical form that consists of thematic exposition, development, and recapitulation.

Soprano. The highest mature female voice.

Spiral learning. An approach in which an idea or concept reappears at intervals with increasing sophistication and complexity.

Staccato. Short, detached tones.

Staff. A graph of five horizontal lines on which musical notes are placed.

Stem. The vertical line attached to a note head.

Stepwise. A melodic progression of pitches ascending or descending without skips.

Syllabic. Music in which each syllable is sung on one note (pitch).

Symphony. An orchestral composition in four movements: fast, slow, moderately fast, and fast.

Syncopation. Emphasis on a normally weak beat.

Synthesizer. A contemporary instrument that produces sounds electronically.

Tempo. The speed of a musical composition.

Tenor. The highest mature male voice.

Ternary form. A musical form in three sections (ABA).

Terraced dynamics. Sudden contrasting dynamic levels.

Text painting. Music that describes or enhances the words in the song.

Texture. Description of the number of lines of music and the relationships among the lines.

Timbre (tone color). The unique quality of a sound.

Tonal center. The key center or home key of a piece.

Tonality. How melodic and harmonic elements are organized around a tonal center.

Treble. Another name for the G clef.

Triad. A chord of three pitches, arranged in thirds.

Triple meter. Meter in threes.

Upbeat. One or more notes that occur before the first measure of a musical composition.

Verse. A stanza of a poem or song.

Vocal techniques. Ways of teaching children to sing.

Whole step. An interval formed by two half steps.

Xiao. A Chinese wind instrument made from bamboo.

Zheng. A plucked stringed instrument from China. The traditional form has sixteen strings; modern versions may have twenty-one strings.

GENERAL INDEX

INDEX OF LISTENING EXAMPLES

INDEX OF LITERATURE

INDEX OF VISUAL ARTS

INDEX OF NATIONALITY SONGS